EVERYDAY KLANSFOLK

EVERYDAY KLANSFOLK

White Protestant Life and the KKK in 1920s Michigan

Craig Fox

Michigan State University Press
East Lansing

Copyright © 2011 by Craig Fox

∞ The paper used in this publication meets the minimum requirements of ANSI/NISO
Z39.48-1992 (R 1997) (Permanence of Paper).

   Michigan State University Press
East Lansing, Michigan 48823-5245

Printed and bound in the United States of America.

17 16 15 14 13 12 11   1 2 3 4 5 6 7 8 9 10

LIBRARY OF CONGRESS CATALOGING-IN-PUBLICATION DATA

Fox, Craig.
    Everyday klansfolk : white protestant life and the KKK in 1920s Michigan / Craig Fox.
    p. cm.
    Includes bibliographical references and index.
    ISBN 978-0-87013-995-6 (pbk. : alk. paper) 1. Ku Klux Klan (1915–)—Michigan—
Newaygo County—History. 2. Middle class—Michigan—Newaygo County—History.
3. Protestants—Michigan—Newaygo County—History. 4. Social conflict—Michigan—
Newaygo County—History. 5. United States—Social conditions—1918–1932. I. Title.

HS2330.K63F64 2011
322.4'20977458—dc22   2010051930

Cover art demonstrates mainstream commercial sponsorship for the Klan at Jackson, 1924.
Source: Michigan State University Special Collections.

Cover design by David Drummond, Salamander Design, Inc.

Book design by Scribe, Inc. (www.scribenet.com)

green press INITIATIVE   Michigan State University Press is a member of the Green Press Initiative and
is committed to developing and encouraging ecologically responsible publishing
practices. For more information about the Green Press Initiative and the use of recycled
paper in book publishing, please visit www.greenpressinitiative.org.

Visit Michigan State University Press at:
www.msupress.msu.edu

To my family, and to the memory
of my brother

DAVID FOX
(1978–2003)

Contents

Figures

Tables

Acknowledgments

My sincere thanks must first go to the Arts and Humanities Research Council in England, for the generous support that made the groundwork for this book possible. Also to Julie Loehr and the staff at MSU Press, for doing their best to make a first-time author's journey run smooth.

I am most grateful, too, to Richard Bessel and to Claudia Haake, whose advice, support, patience, and unflinching good humor helped to shape what the project eventually became. Also to the many friends, colleagues, and teachers who have helpfully commented, guided, or otherwise encouraged along the way, particularly Jon Adams, Cassie Hague, Simon Titley-Bayes, Louise Wannell, Alan Forrest, Alex Goodall, and Tony Badger.

I would like also to thank the army of librarians and archivists at the many Michigan institutions at which I spent countless hours and days, all of whom, without exception, were both helpful and courteous. Much gratitude, particularly, to the staff at the Bentley Historical Library and the Labadie Special Collections unit in Ann Arbor, as well as to Randall Scott and Peter Berg at Michigan State University's Special Collections library in East Lansing. The Clarke Historical Library at Central Michigan University in Mount Pleasant, meanwhile, became like a second home for the better part of a year, and my heartfelt thanks go to everyone there at the time, including Jeff Hancks, Marian Matyn, Jennifer Wood, Julie Paveglio, Grace Gorton, and Mary Graham, not just for their practical help with, and interest in the project, but also for the welcome, and the friendship. The KKK manuscript material, stretched over many collections at the Clarke, is at the very heart of my work, and without those collections this book would not exist. In particular I am indebted to Dr. Frank Boles, who played a key role in rescuing the Newaygo County membership cards from the auction room intact. I am also grateful for the endeavor of the late Dr. Calvin Enders, whose driving interest in the Michigan Klan is apparent from his papers, as well as to his surviving family for donating those papers to the Clarke, where they have proved, and will continue to prove, an invaluable resource.

I owe most of all to my partner, Kate, whose serenity, encouragement, and sacrifice has gone a long way to seeing this work complete. Living these years amidst the relics of the "Invisible Empire," she has put up with much and asked very little. Her faith in me has far outshone my own. There are no words.

Introduction

The prevailing idea of the Ku Klux Klan in today's popular discourse overwhelmingly involves a sinister and violently terroristic secret brotherhood, operating at society's marginal, criminal, and racist extremes. Brought to mind, even just by mention of the initials KKK, are ghoulish images of menacing figures prowling the night, garbed in trademark white hoods and robes, plotting—or even carrying out—unspeakable acts of racial hatred by the light of an ominous fiery cross. Such striking scenes, perpetuated by countless cultural depictions of anti-black vigilante violence in both the Reconstruction and Civil Rights eras of American history, are by no means unreasonable in their portrayal of the Klan in either period. Despite almost a century of separation, the distinct Klan movements emerging in and around the 1860s and the 1960s shared many common characteristics, with a small but fanatical membership, a firm focus upon racial violence, and a concentration largely confined to the Southern states. At the same time, however, these scenes fall short of providing an entirely accurate and full account of the American experience with the hooded organization.

Sandwiched chronologically between its Civil War–era predecessor and its Civil Rights–era successor was a very different Klan, surfacing all over the United States in the early 1920s. Unusual for its wide-ranging popular appeals to Protestant morality, prohibition, and law enforcement, rather than an overt reliance upon vigilantism, this "second" Klan achieved staggering membership figures that dwarfed all other Klan movements in America before or since. With recruits numbering well into the millions by mid-decade, the 1920s Klan transcended the borders of the old South to attain widespread national prominence, and was able to successfully present itself, for a brief period, as a positive force in American life before finally fading into obscurity even before the onset of the Great Depression. Though ultimately short-lived, it is apparent that the 1920s version of the Ku Klux Klan exercised a peculiarly compelling allure, its pull reflected in its sheer numerical popularity in towns and cities nationwide. Unlike its historical namesakes, the organization involved largely ordinary citizens, from all walks of life. In this sense, it is the mainstream rather than the extreme period of Klan history upon which this book concentrates.

CHANGING INTERPRETATIONS OF THE 1920s KLAN: A SELECTED HISTORIOGRAPHY

"The Ku Klux Klan," wrote *Outlook* journalist Stanley Frost in 1924, "has become the most vigorous, active and effective organization in American life, outside business." Controlling whole towns, counties, and states, he continued, "it is growing with tremendous speed. Its members are already beyond four millions and are increasing at the rate of a hundred thousand a week." In its brief blaze of glory—from its reemergence in 1915 as a men's secret fraternal order to its steep decline by 1926—the second Ku Klux Klan's "Invisible Empire" would eventually gain up to six million members nationwide and score political victories of varying enormities all across the United States. Its national leaders, in Frost's unlikely sounding words, were ultimately "reaching for the Presidency," with a growing political presence beginning to exercise an influence in virtually every area of the country.[1] Commanding such a broad base of popular support, it is difficult to imagine that the Klan's appeal was based purely upon the vicious and bigoted doctrines with which it is most often associated. This, however, is exactly the assumption that has been made by Klan scholars up until relatively recently, and the first writers to commentate upon the 1920s KKK described it in similar fashion to its historical Reconstruction namesake. For them, this was a deeply racist, excessively violent movement, and a vehicle by which economically backward and socially conservative residents of rural, primarily Southern, backwaters of the United States could express a fundamentalist rage against the onset of big-city cosmopolitanism.

The most influential work in this vein was sociologist John Moffat Mecklin's *The Ku Klux Klan: A Study of the American Mind*, written at the very peak of the Klan's popularity in 1924. Mecklin's thesis held that the typical Klansman dwelt rurally, suffered from the "petty impotence of the small-town mind," and carried around with him an unsophisticated "provincial fear of all things foreign." Preyed upon by a cynical and calculated hate movement, he was "the most dangerous weakness in a democracy . . . the uninformed and unthinking average man." In this and similar interpretations, the Klansman represented the "loser" in a booming economic age.[2] Unable to adjust psychologically or economically to the forces of modernity that confronted him, he came to resent the symbols of modern success and vibrancy—the culture of wealth, automobiles, jazz music, and consumer goods epitomized by the modern city. As a reaction, he blamed the un-American and corrupting influences of the foreign immigrant for his status insecurity. The Klan's appeal, by this argument, was reserved primarily for "the unwashed residents of America's hinterlands, those who felt threatened by urban-industrial society and wanted to lash back at ethnic minorities and the wicked ways of the city."[3] Drawing its particular venom from a considerable strain of residual postwar nativism, the Klan, for Mecklin, also offered a preposterous line in ritualistic hogwash that would allow the "mediocre" man a welcome reprieve—however temporary—from the rustic drudgery that otherwise defined his existence.

Journalists of the Klan era readily took up Mecklin's themes, while also offering fresh perspectives regarding the rapid rise of the movement. Commentators such as Stanley Frost and, in particular, Robert L. Duffus began very early on, for instance, to write about the KKK's growing power and influence in non-Southern states, most notably in the Pacific Northwest and Midwest.[4] In most respects, Duffus's analysis was almost entirely in congruence with Mecklin's model, depicting a movement of middling men with nativist tendencies. Succumbing to an opportunistic recruitment campaign, they had enthusiastically accepted the Klan's reasoning, adopting the figure of the immigrant "alien" as an easy scapegoat for the frustrations of small-town life.

This view of the 1920s Klan, writes Leonard Moore, "has been set in concrete for many years"—so much so that it has "become doctrine among American historians," most of whom "remain content with the idea that there is little new that can be learned about the Ku Klux Klan."[5] Indeed, historians continued into the 1950s and 1960s to repeat variations upon the standard theme outlined by Mecklin. Among them, William Randel, Richard Hofstadter, and Arnold Rice all portrayed a vigilante movement at the disaffected fringes of society. For Hofstadter, Klan radicalism found its greatest support among the status-anxious in this prosperous new age of social fluidity: it occurred "in the small towns, where gullible nativists gathered," and sought to cultivate and channel their collective resentments in the direction of that most wicked and feared of all incarnations of corrupt modernity—the city-dwelling immigrant. In chronicling the interwar Klan's considerable political impact, Rice, too, concluded ultimately that the order was comprised of the socially maladjusted, attracting little more than the "dregs" and the "lovers of horseplay." Similarly, Randel's book points to an inherently violent movement that sought to exploit and profit from an easily fooled public.[6] Largely concurring with this view was David Chalmers's *Hooded Americanism* (1965), a meticulous state-by-state history that documented the various Klan movements from the 1860s until the 1960s. While on one hand continuing to emphasize the traditional view of the Klan as a violent, white-supremacist secret terrorist society, Chalmers also succeeded in pointing out something new—that KKK influence extended throughout the whole nation during the 1920s, thriving not simply within the rural context, but in many urban areas as well.[7]

At around this time, other historians began to question and challenge some of the more stereotypical and longstanding assumptions about the 1920s Klan, and both Charles Alexander and Kenneth T. Jackson wrote pioneering Klan studies in the mid-1960s.[8] Alexander's *The Ku Klux Klan in the Southwest* (1965) examined the movement in Texas, Arkansas, Oklahoma, and Louisiana. While admitting that isolated episodes of vigilante violence could be linked to the Klan in these regions, he found also that the movement's main concern seemed not to be race, but rather the defense of "law and order" and traditional codes of morality. The targets of Klan aggression, for Alexander, were not necessarily immigrants, Catholics, Jews, African Americans, or Mexicans, but much more specifically those who crossed the boundaries of conventional morality—typically gamblers, bootleggers, or abusive husbands, many of whom were both white and Protestant. In spite of occasional controversies, the Klan here appeared to devote itself to civic, social, and religious activities, and in doing so succeeded in gaining a certain mainstream acceptance.

Jackson's *The Ku Klux Klan in the City*, while again reaffirming many established notions of Klan scholarship, also broke startling new ground, indicating a movement of more complexity than had been seen before. His study located the power of the organization not in the rural Southern and Midwestern hinterlands, but in the nation's great cities, North and South. The Klansman's motivation, for Jackson, was still one born of displacement, though in a vastly different setting. Living in close proximity to, and competing residentially with, ever-expanding populations of immigrants and African Americans, his battle was a "battle for control of urban neighborhoods," and his Klan membership a measured response to real social problems, rather than the fanciful product of imaginary fears. He was "no yahoo or yokel, but rather a disturbed American looking for solutions to problems that threatened to engulf him." Neither situated at the racist extremes, nor especially inclined to violence, he was the decent, if still slightly pathetic and undistinguished advocate of a movement that provided a "salve for his wounded pride" and "enabled him to fight rather than face the future." While previous studies had tended to overexaggerate and generalize about racist Klan violence throughout the movement, both Alexander and Jackson looked to explain Klan activity within given localities, often finding not extremism, but diverse motives linked to real social conditions, involving essentially ordinary citizens.

The traditional (Mecklin-style) interpretation, however, was far from dead within KKK scholarship. Indeed, as Leonard Moore wrote in 1990, "from the late 1960s to the present, most historians have continued to adhere to the traditional interpretation of the 1920s Klan," only occasionally incorporating elements from outside of this view. Robert Moats Miller, for example, criticized the more recent perspectives on the Klan, arguing that "one is almost lulled into concluding that [it] was harmless." He retained a traditional standpoint, stating in a 1968 essay that the Klan of the 1920s was "first and foremost" a movement "to keep the black man in his place." While many thousands of ordinary citizens had been attracted to its moralism, he argued, its true purpose was still racism, anti-Semitism and anti-Catholicism. The many normal Americans who had joined had done so in ignorance, wrote Miller, and merely "failed to discern the Klan's true nature." In 1970 Seymour Lipset and Earl Raab similarly reprised older themes, depicting a Klan made up of low-status individuals, fundamentalists, and the "less educated." This Klan struck out in anger at the political, religious, and ethnic others in its midst, seeking a halt to the advance of the urban, cosmopolitan world that they had come to represent.[9]

It is only with the most recent work on the 1920s Klan that the prevailing interpretation appears to be changing. Specifically, a group of scholars who, according to Glenn Feldman, called themselves the "Populist-Civic School" emerged in and around the 1980s and early 1990s. Providing an array of local examples from diverse corners of the nation, they stressed the complex, nuanced, and often regionally specific nature of the order and demonstrated "that the second Klan was far more ensconced in American life than many of us would like to admit."[10] Collectively, the case studies produced by this group—which included Christopher Cocoltchos (California), Larry Gerlach (Utah), Robert Goldberg (Colorado), David Horowitz (Oregon), William Jenkins (Ohio), Shawn Lay (Texas and Buffalo, New York), and Leonard Moore (Indiana)—depicted the KKK not as a strongly nativist movement, but variously as a "populist organization," a civic-minded response to local issues, and "one of the largest and most influential grass-roots social movements in American history."[11] Working, according to Moore, "as a kind of interest group for the average white Protestant," the Klan found its enemies more often among self-serving local business elites than ethnic minorities. Rather than being a backward movement of the bigoted extremes, its major popular appeal lay in its usefulness as an instrument of reform, and it took an active, progressive role in civic and municipal issues such as crime prevention, prohibition enforcement, clean local government, and public school–building.

These studies, taken together, says Moore, "make it nearly impossible to interpret the 1920s Klan as an aberrant fringe group motivated primarily by its overwhelming hatred of ethnic minorities." According to the Populist-Civic school of thought, the Klan in this era is seen as working towards an empowering community cohesion rather than employing an aggressive vigilante approach to social problems. The incidence of violence in the movement has been greatly downplayed in this viewpoint, with extralegal activities—where they existed at all—perpetrated only by an unrepresentative fringe in virtually every local context in which the Klan was studied. Its bigotry, though readily apparent in KKK ideology, was also partly dismissed as a product of the age, part of a wider 1920s white Protestant society "awash with defensive ethnocentric concerns" in which, for Moore, "the Klan's ideology stood as a particularly important example of white Protestant attitudes, not a deviant exception to mainstream thinking." Taking up this point, Lay concluded that Klansmen, "although assuredly racist and bigoted, were average citizens in the context of the times." Also argued was a general absence of any serious ethnic conflict, with the Klan most clearly successful in areas of virtually unthreatened white Protestant hegemony, and choosing to "all but ignore small communities of Catholics, Jews, and blacks" when they did exist in close proximity. Rejected, too, were claims of widespread religious fundamentalism in the rank-and-file Klan membership, the order in reality drawing upon "average citizens representing nearly all parts of America's white Protestant society."[12]

Other more recent studies have also aimed to explore new and fresh perspectives on the Klan of the 1920s. Nancy MacLean's *Behind the Mask of Chivalry* (1994), for example, looks to interpret the nature of the KKK through "a sustained examination of Klan ideology," innovatively reading Klan rhetoric from a class- and gender-driven perspective. Describing the rise of the KKK as "reactionary populism," a middle-class backlash against economic threats from both above and below, she even goes so far as to draw parallels between the ascent of the Klan in America and the ominous rise of European Fascism. Also unambiguous is a conscious parting from "the trend in recent historical writing about the Klan to de-emphasize the racial hatred of its politics and the violence of its practice." For MacLean, the Invisible Empire of the twenties was based upon an inherently aggressive and intolerant vigilantism, with hostile Klan ideology logically translating into extralegal action. "Vigilante violence," she writes, "was the concentrated expression of that culture, and the brutal determination to maintain hierarchies of race, class and gender that Klansmen sought to control with a mask of chivalry."[13]

Kathleen Blee's 1991 study *Women of the Klan*, meanwhile, examined the (heretofore largely overlooked) role of white Protestant females in the movement, discovering in the women's order an appeal beyond mere racism in "its purported quest for women's rights and in its offer of collective support, friendship, and sociability among like-minded women." This study was based largely upon the author's personal interviews with former members in Indiana, and Blee's informants offered remarkably open and often telling commentary—describing, for instance, a white community life in which "everyone was in the Klan," and where the hooded order provided "just a celebration" or "a way to get together and enjoy." Strikingly, past lives of Klan membership seemed to conjure up little need for regret on the part of interviewees, but instead "simply needed no explanation. What needed to be explained was the reputation that the 1920s Klan later acquired, the peculiarly negative way in which it was recorded in history." Even so, the Klan's racial politics "percolated easily, unremarkably, through this world," and though the majority of informants turned out not to be "the caricatured bigots" of the author's first expectations, this fact, according to Blee, cannot "diminish the destructive power" of the movement.[14]

FROM THE GROUND UP: THE CASE STUDY APPROACH AND THE KKK IN NEWAYGO COUNTY, MICHIGAN

Most recent work on the 1920s Klan has seen scholars emphasize the importance of studying the local grass-roots unit at close quarters. By way of suggestions to researchers following in their footsteps, in fact, many have advocated, as the most useful way forward, a methodology focused squarely upon examining the local scene rather than the monolithic national organization. In the conclusion to *The Invisible Empire in the West*, for instance, Shawn Lay and his associates look forward to a future national profile of the 1920s Klan experience constructed entirely from "a sufficient number of case studies from a variety of regions." Going back much further, too, Norman Weaver's 1954 work on the KKK in four U.S. states came to the realization that "in some senses . . . it is possible to maintain that there was no 'Klan movement' at all, just many local Klans." Often operating virtually autonomously of higher organizational echelons at the national and state levels, the local unit was in essence "the heart of the whole Klan movement . . . the part of the whole that touched the lives of individuals both within and outside the Klan." Weaver went on to propose that further research building upon his own might include "a series of community studies" that, in order to foster greater understanding of the organization's membership, would require "concentration . . . to be on the individuals who joined the Klan."[15]

The clandestine nature of the KKK, however, has often made in-depth study of the order a problematic prospect. The possibility for developing regional case studies has always depended entirely upon the fortunate and infrequent discovery of surviving organizational records, which are notoriously rare, and of wildly varying quality. Often, official documentation was simply destroyed routinely by the organization itself in a protective move designed to preserve the secrecy of its members. In other cases, Klan documents have survived only to be subsequently destroyed upon discovery by offended parties or descendants of members, who viewed them as somehow objectionable or shameful relics of a best-forgotten past.[16] A more recent trend, too, has seen the Klan's controversial public image put to work for financial gain, with the highly lucrative sale of such artifacts, often as macabre keepsakes, to the highest bidder at public auction. Sold off individually, records discovered together become separated and scattered beyond recovery, making the task of accurate historical reconstruction significantly more difficult, and in some cases almost impossible.

The accidental uncovering of a startling collection of Klan membership records in rural Newaygo County, Michigan, then, presented an outstanding opportunity to study the KKK in a locality where its presence had never before been documented. In October 1992, auctioneers preparing to sell the Anderson family farm in Fremont happened upon three trunks hidden away in a boarded-up attic area. Having gone untouched for almost seven decades, the trunks were found to contain a wealth of papers, ledgers, and paraphernalia relating to the 1920s Klan in the area. The remarkable cache had apparently been held in storage by local bookkeeper Ledford Anderson, who—though by now deceased—as a young man had served loyally as treasurer of the Fremont-based Klavern throughout its existence. In the words of a relative, after disbanding, the Klan in question "didn't have a place to store their stuff, so they dumped it all" upon Anderson, who then evidently did his best to keep it safely hidden. Providing comprehensive membership records for the local KKK chapter as well as its auxiliaries, these unique documents detailed the life of the organization known as "Newaygo County Klan No. 29" from its inception as a small provisional unit in summer 1923, right the way through its 1925 peak, official chartering, and subsequent decline as the twenties wore on.

Regrettably, the Newaygo County Klan collection was all but decimated by the irresistible lure of market forces just a few days after its discovery had been reported. Amid huge regional press interest, the attic find was split into individual lots and systematically sold off at a packed public auction. Lost to the drop of the hammer, and to history, were countless items of correspondence, bookkeeping, meeting minutes, and photographs that, kept together, could have revealed perhaps more than ever before about the lives of the members of a local unit, their relationships with one another and with the world outside their Klavern.[17] Mercifully, the unit's full membership rolls, bought by a local university library, at least remain intact and available for academic study. Though representing only a fraction of the original Fremont find, these records are still without doubt the most vital of the Newaygo County Klan's organizational relics, and—having previously gone unutilized—provide the basis for the local case-study element of this project.[18]

THE INVISIBLE EMPIRE IN 1920s MICHIGAN: A STORY LARGELY UNTOLD

As well as examining the as-yet undocumented Newaygo County KKK in some depth, this book also argues that as a local unit, it represented only a small and fairly typical part of a much wider, vital, and thriving regional KKK scene. Operating alongside it, often in cooperation, were countless comparable units named for towns, cities, and counties right across the state—or, in Klan terms, the "Realm"—of Michigan. The idea of a Klan movement in Michigan that was both populous and popular, as well as being geographically widespread, has not been particularly well supported in the past. While the activities of the secret order have been amply documented in many other states, the presence of the Ku Klux Klan in 1920s Michigan has received very little academic attention by comparison. Even the few exceptions—most notably work by Norman Weaver and Kenneth T. Jackson—have touched, but certainly not concentrated upon the Wolverine State. They have also tended to focus the bulk of their analysis around the inner workings of the organization in the city of Detroit, where the Klan was most conspicuous and politically visible. In doing so, certainly, they have uncovered key details about the order in this locality: explaining the relatively late "Kluxing" of Michigan in 1923; documenting Klan attempts to elect candidates to various Detroit and state political offices; and highlighting a flawed and unstable state leadership structure plagued by political and financial infighting.[19]

What these works have not done, however, is reveal much of real substance about the organization outside of Michigan's most populous urban center, or its propagation throughout the rest of the state. Weaver's emphasis, in particular, upon the Motor City reflects his stated conviction that the Klan was almost irrelevant beyond its metropolitan bounds. "The investigator working in Michigan," he writes of his research, "comes to feel that the Klan must have been relatively small and unimportant in the state outside of Detroit, for records of Klan activity are extremely thin."[20] Jackson is slightly more expansive, and while he maintains that Detroit accounted for approximately half of Michigan's Klan population, he names nine other major cities—Grand Rapids, Flint, Bay City, Jackson, Lansing, Kalamazoo, Saginaw, Pontiac, and Muskegon—in which the secret order "had active chapters."[21] Even this, though, does not go nearly far enough in terms of illustrating the spread of the Klan across the state at this time. A close inspection of rare official correspondence of the Michigan Realm KKK headquarters in fact indicates the presence of a far more pervasive Klan population, with at the very least 150 active Klan units in Michigan. Local press accounts, too, report no less than 215 units operating in all parts of the state, before taking into account the many related but separate auxiliary divisions for women, children, and the foreign-born.[22]

The figure most commonly quoted in reference to maximum Klan strength in the state of Michigan is around 80,000 members, an estimate put forward by Weaver in 1954, and since cited in the work of both Jackson and David Chalmers.[23] There are, however, a number of other possibilities. Some of the very first Klan organizers arriving in Michigan towns outside of Detroit claimed that "80,000 belong in Michigan" as early as July 1923, well before the Klan's major growth spurt there.[24] Of course, with an organization so famously keen to make a public impression, there is every chance of exaggeration in these claims. Other sources, though, continue to point to larger numbers. D. C. Stephenson, Grand Dragon of neighboring Indiana, claimed that Michigan's Klan was "about the same size" as his own at around 315,000, while Henry C. Warner, in a 1928 court case against the Klan, estimated Michigan's numbers at 265,000.[25] Perhaps most incredibly, the *Washington Post* placed Michigan Klan membership for 1925 at 875,130, a "totally absurd" figure according to Jackson. The *Post* described a national movement of almost nine million members during its "halcyon days of 1925," labeling it "the world's most high-powered 'racket' . . . one of the biggest money makers of all time, a shining example of big business in a big way." At the height of the Klan boom, the article claimed, "Michigan held a dominating membership," leading every other state in total number of members admitted up to 1927. Whether or not the outlandish numbers can be believed, the *Post*'s article certainly makes clear that Michigan was an important rather than a marginal Klan state, or at least was perceived as being one.[26] Michigan's U.S. Representative Earl C. Michener was certainly aware of the organization's presence and spread within his constituency. "The Ku Klux Klan," he wrote in a February 1924 letter, "is very active in Michigan. The city of Jackson alone has over 5,000 members. Adrian had over 800 members and I was reading . . . that a new crowd of 500 had been initiated . . . and what is true of Adrian and Jackson is true of every other town in the district."[27]

In addition, Weaver's method of identifying areas of particular Klan strength in Michigan is primarily based upon political factors and voting patterns, measured by "votes cast for avowed Klan candidates running on state-wide tickets." While a useful analysis, this is not a perfect gauge, with Klan units clearly having a strong and visible presence in many areas in which they did not prove to be especially influential politically. In one instance, Weaver singles out the "Holland Dutch" as a particular influence and source of political Klan strength in the western counties of Michigan, claiming that as a group they "took to the Klan and joined in large numbers" there. Since that time, however, in a short statistical study of one such western Michigan Klan, Calvin Enders has directly disputed this assertion, finding that the Dutch in fact "comprised only a small percentage" of the Holland area's Klan, and in fact "did not flock to the Invisible Order."[28] This suggests that the basis of Klan membership and growth—here and probably elsewhere—was likely to have been determined not only by conventional politics but also by countless other factors and appeals operating quite beyond the realms of the purely political.

It is this theme—the idea that the Klan's attraction was wide-ranging, popular, and not always necessarily political—with which the first two chapters of this book are broadly concerned. Chapter 1 argues that the advance of the 1920s Klan across the Michigan landscape was part of a wider nationwide marketing drive, carefully planned and lucratively executed by a calculating KKK recruitment machine. Propped up by its own advance publicity depicting a world of thrilling intrigue and exclusive membership, the Klan typically came to town under a shroud of veiled secrecy, announcing itself with the dramatic burning of a cross or a mysterious declaration in the local press. The excited gossip, packed meeting houses, and surprise street parades that invariably followed fueled a wave of enthusiasm not only for the secret order itself but also for the many and varied lines of Klan-themed merchandise that surrounded it at every turn. Characterized almost everywhere by a faddish consumer culture, the Klan's popular period saw the manufacture and sale by opportunistic individuals of everything from Klan records and adventure novels to Klannish fireworks, jewelry, household ornaments, toys, and other assorted novelties. Alongside the mass production of regulation robes and regalia, this ensured that, even if only as part of a short-lived merchandizing craze, representations of the Invisible Empire would enter the everyday lives and homes of white Protestant Americans in some of the most banal and insidious respects imaginable.

Chapter 2 looks more closely at some of these representations and images, charting the ways in which the Klan attempted to propel positive depictions of itself (and perhaps more strikingly, negative depictions of its alleged enemies) into the realms of popular culture. As the movement exploded onto the scene in the early 1920s, so did a supporting array of pamphlets, periodicals, and public speakers discussing its societal significance. Often operating, too, through already popular, accessible, and entertaining cultural mediums, the Klan took a literary route, looking to reinforce its demonological imagery through movies, plays, and even the pages of romance novels. In Michigan, the Catholic Church bore the brunt of the Klan attack, via, among other things, a plethora of colorful anti-papal conspiracy fantasies and a series of crowd-drawing lectures on sexual immorality, salaciously relayed by "escaped" nuns and priests. Among whispered tales of a grasping, power-hungry Pope and Catholic corruption in local and national government, the Klan continued to add fuel to the fire by implicating its demonic and caricatured foe in almost every matter of genuine public concern. Exploiting common anxieties—over prohibition violation, rising crime levels, declining public morality, burgeoning European immigration, and a long-running political debate over the legitimacy of parochial schools in Michigan—"un-American" religious doctrines were made the scapegoat for all ills. Against this backdrop, the Klan was very self-consciously "100% American," self-cast as the country's noble defender in an ideological war against the forces of evil—the righteous protector of community, morality, womanhood, and, crucially, Protestantism.

Chapters 3 and 4 move away from the ethereal realm of Klan imagery and towards a more practical examination of the organization's mechanics. Taking a local unit in Michigan as a basis for analysis, the aim is to reconstruct, as far as possible, the Klan in Newaygo County and the lives of the individuals who became its members. Providing an insight into the nature of the Klan's spectacular arrival and gestation in this and many other localities much like it, patterns shown in the Newaygo records bear out the notion of a brief, if intense fascination for the KKK brand and all that came with it. Once recruitment began in earnest in August 1923—the Klan having announced its presence with a number of very public cross burnings—membership in the area soared. Reaching a peak in the latter months of 1924, the Newaygo County Klan could count citizens of a great variety of ages, occupations, and socioeconomic standings among its multitude of converts. Newaygo's Klan, in line with local Klans everywhere, also began to widen its criteria for entry, reflecting the mood of the organization at the national level. Despite the second Invisible Empire's beginnings as a narrowly exclusive, male-only concern, then, it responded to increased demand by opening its doors to women, children, and even foreign-born white Protestants, with the only genuine remaining barrier to membership being an inability to pay the required fee. Also examined here are the routes by which ordinary citizens of Newaygo County ultimately became members of their local Klan organization. Coming to the fore in this respect are local patterns of sociability that consisted primarily of acquaintances made through family, work, and fraternal associations. As well as utilizing such organic social recruitment channels, through which members helped bolster the ranks by recommending others, the Klan also appears to have made very conscious and definite advances toward attaining members well-placed in specific positions of local sway. Targeting, in particular, the community's establishment figures—including holders of local political office, newspapermen, and citizens active in church and school administration—the order was intent upon demonstrating its capability to attract members who were prominent, influential, and above all, respectable.

Taking up the themes of respectability and community involvement, chapter 5 explores the roles played by the Michigan Klan—visible and invisible, as it were—at the center of local life. Detailed first is a notably high incidence of civically active, demonstrably community-minded citizens who, in addition to sincere efforts in their civilian lives at improving local conditions, were also very much present within the ranks of the Newaygo County Klan. The example of these so-called "best citizens" not only acted as an inducement for others to sign up, but also gave a certain local credence (especially given that the KKK in Michigan was not masked) to the Klan's insistence upon its own basic respectability. Similarly, when prominent local ministers began publicly to endorse the hooded order, and even to visibly conduct religious ceremonies under the organization's auspices, they did much to normalize its presence and acceptability in community life. Such public appearances also served to perpetuate a remarkable popular interest in the spectacular KKK brand of pageantry. All across Michigan, in fact, the Klan's lively parades, picnics, and mass celebrations became a source of popular, family-friendly entertainment, incorporating under the Klannish banner a range of otherwise very mainstream and commonplace activities and leisure pursuits. These gatherings also served a greater, if less tangible, function, providing as they did an accessible space in which members of scattered regional Klans from across the state regularly came together in open celebration of their common culture and affiliation. Helping to foster a sense of solidarity and group belonging, such events enabled the disparate parts of Michigan's Invisible Empire to find community cohesion amid the everyday trappings of an ordinary white Protestant world.

Very much in line with the recent Populist-Civic school of thought on the 1920s Klan, this project aims, at base, to present the case of the hooded order in the state of Michigan not as a fanatical fringe group inhabited by violent and ill-educated vigilantes, but as an accepted mainstream presence, largely populated by "average" or "ordinary" citizens. In doing so, it makes use of the unique and relatively recently discovered membership records of the Newaygo County Klan, examining the specifics of this entirely undocumented local unit within its context as part of a wider regional Klan movement. Evident across the length and breadth of the state, the network of local Klaverns that constituted the KKK Realm of Michigan has itself been largely neglected by historians, and has therefore remained little understood. This book attempts to contribute in some small way to a richer nationwide picture of the 1920s Klan experience by plugging a regional gap in our knowledge of the organization. The fact that the Newaygo records, or anything resembling them, were simply unavailable to previous scholars of Michigan history is a significant one. What they reveal, in conjunction with corroborating accounts of Klan activity from other Michigan locations, is what perhaps had once appeared unlikely—that the KKK thrived in the Wolverine State, and that its influence certainly extended well beyond Detroit, and even into some of the most provincial of outposts. By rendering itself unremarkable within the context of white Protestant culture, the Klan was at its most effective when operating at the level of the commonplace, even the banal, and it was here that it touched the lives of the majority of its members. Its multifaceted and yet everyday appeal was the key to phenomenal Klan success in this, the short-lived "popular" phase of its history.

Marketing, Membership, and Merchandise
The Klan Brand Comes to Town

THE KU KLUX KLAN, AS A FRATERNAL MEMBERSHIP ORGANIZATION, enjoyed phenomenal success throughout the United States during the early to mid-1920s. Its support, measured in the millions, was both geographically widespread and culturally mainstream. At least part of the reason for the Klan's great success can be found in the very systematic and business-minded methods by which the organization recruited members. Exported nationwide from Atlanta, the hooded order arrived locally as a ready-made "product," and traded willfully upon an image that combined an appealing aura of exclusive mystery, thrilling visual drama, and contemporary, contentious edge. Less spontaneous than perhaps it would have liked to appear, every piece of official literature, ritual, and regalia was strictly copyrighted, and the organization's full official title—"The Knights of the Ku Klux Klan, Incorporated"—gives a clue as to its essentially commercial intentions.

As it had done elsewhere, the Klan swept across Michigan like wildfire, an extended recruitment drive seeing the hooded order arrive in villages, towns, and cities throughout the state during the summer months of 1923. Everywhere, its method was the same—its enigmatic presence and conspicuously shrouded movements designed to incite local gossip and an excited anticipation of the exclusive world of fraternal mysteries that lay hidden inside. In many locations, and particularly in the small-town rural districts such as Newaygo County, the arrival of the Klan provided the most exciting spectacle in town—the best, perhaps only, source of a vicarious thrill, to which seemingly "everyone" had begun to subscribe. Making this palatable, politically speaking, was the Klan's avowed devotion to the values and concerns of white Protestant Michigan's respectable mainstream. Calling for "law and order," for prohibition enforcement, for public morality, for clean politics, and for limited European immigration, the Klan's outward pleas for a straightforward Protestant, patriotic pro-Americanism echoed many themes already commonplace within the dominant social milieu. Also playing an important role in popularizing the Invisible Empire, meanwhile, was an innovative and responsive entrepreneurial element operating around the movement's fringes. Opportunistically offering a wide variety of affordable and eye-catching Klan-related wares, it appealed strongly to the sensibilities of what was an emergent, enthusiastic consumer culture, and continued to find novel ways in which to make the KKK appear both attractive and conventional.

MICHIGAN ABLAZE: THE KLAN ARRIVES IN NEWAYGO COUNTY

In a tone oscillating somewhere between cautious trepidation and excited gossip-mongering, the *Newaygo Republican* of 6 September 1923, detailed the first tangible signal that the "Invisible Empire" was present on its very own doorstep. Just a few nights earlier, a crowd of perplexed residents of this rural mid-Michigan county, "no doubt . . . unaware as to just what was going on," had found themselves standing by in anxious wonderment as "a large, fiery cross was burned on Bunker Hill." Announcing that this was apparently a symbol of the Ku Klux Klan, the *Republican*'s on-scene reporter had been informed personally that the blazing cross was in fact loaded with meaning, that its sudden appearance against the night sky "designated a membership of the first five hundred in the county." Hard facts concerning the mysterious order were, of course, typically and deliberately evasive—the reporter's information coming courtesy of a conspicuously anonymous "travelling man."[1] Indeed, the promoters of the Klan in Michigan, as elsewhere, traded heavily upon a combination of visual drama and the vicarious interest generated through the cultivation of rumor and hearsay. The Michigan edition of the Klan news organ the *Fiery Cross* made a point of noting the Newaygo community's obvious surprise at this first startling show of flames, as well as the tantalizing implications as the cross "threw its light skyward, informing the inhabitants here that the Ku Klux Klan was among them."[2]

Having left the community to speculate wildly for precisely a week, the next issue of the *Republican* contained a large public notice, placed by parties unnamed. Spanning two columns of the page, the announcement on one level promised to provide clarification, while at the same time it set about perpetuating the growing sense of mystery surrounding the organization. "There will be a public meeting somewhere in the city of Newaygo Wednesday night," it read, where "a national speaker will expose the true facts about the Ku Klux Klan"—adding that "everybody [is] invited." In order to take up their invitations to a meeting without either time or venue, however, the public were urged that they would need to keep their eyes open and "look out for the hand dodgers."[3] In reality, nobody would have to look far at all, as "representatives of the mysterious and much discussed Ku Klux Klan" soon bombarded the entire county with handbills promoting the upcoming event, which was to feature an official KKK lecturer publicly outlining the principals of the organization. Taking place at the Park Theatre movie house in Newaygo, immediately after the regular film showing, the meeting drew a crowd of five hundred, pulling in visitors from surrounding towns and villages, and even travelers from neighboring counties. Addressing an arena packed to capacity, the Klan orator, whose identity would remain "unannounced and unknown" throughout, was reportedly "received with marked enthusiasm." Clearly impressed with a performance "beyond the expectations of many who gathered," the local press, while giving scant detail, went on to praise him as "a brilliant speaker [who] commanded the strictest attention of his audience," and said "nothing . . . of a nature that would offend." Portraying an otherwise morally bankrupt and unnervingly cosmopolitan modern world, the Klan orator hailed the hooded order as a reliable rock of uncomplicated patriotism. His speech proved a roaring success, described by the *Republican* in terms that had become synonymous with the KKK across the United States by this time: "just a plain talk on one hundred percent Americanism."[4]

In the weeks following the meeting, the sight of bold Klan imagery continued to decorate Newaygo County's night skies on a regular basis. On September 22, another huge wooden cross blazed atop Newaygo's Schoolhouse Hill, to be followed by similar incidents in the town of White Cloud (the county seat, some ten miles to the north) on the nights of September 28 and October 2.[5] Two weeks later, the *White Cloud Eagle* noted in a front-page headline that someone or something was "Still Burning Crosses Here," citing the latest examples of October 12 and 16, where on both occasions fiery crosses accompanied by fireworks displays had appeared on the school grounds and upon Chalfant Hill, respectively. The same article also detailed a large and recent Klan gathering just over the county line in the nearby city of Big Rapids. Here, "in the lurid glow of a huge fire," curious citizens had been lectured on the nature of the organization by a Protestant minister and KKK organizer from the sizzling Klan hotbed that was the state of Indiana,

Michigan's southerly neighbor. While declaring the Klan to be "an organization of white Protestants," excluding all other groups from membership on religious and racial grounds, the minister depicted it primarily as a force for law and order, "the arch enemy of the corrupt politician, the major vices, the bootlegger, the moonshiner, the radical agitator and the alien." At the close of his address, copies of the Klan's own publication, the *Fiery Cross*, were distributed widely among the crowd, along with small cards on which the personal details of interested individuals were taken, "a preliminary step towards making it possible for citizens to join the Klan."[6]

Highly visible demonstrations of Klan presence, designed to intrigue and enthrall the public at large, continued in Newaygo County throughout the latter part of 1923 and well into 1924. The hills and open spaces of the towns of Newaygo and White Cloud, in particular, saw repeated appearances of the now infamous fiery cross, most often accompanied by one or more attention-grabbing fireworks "bombs."[7] It was in the county's most populous city, Fremont, however, that the Klan seemed to concentrate most of its early promotional efforts. Here, at the Ideal Theatre, D. W. Griffith's sprawling big-screen epic *The Birth of a Nation*—a noted KKK recruitment tool used throughout the 1920s—appeared in early February 1924. Famously glorifying the original Klan of the Reconstruction era, and celebrating that organization as the binding force that united a nation torn asunder by civil war, the extravagant picture was lauded by the *Fremont Times-Indicator* as "epoch-making" and a "masterpiece." Such was the lingering power of the movie's reputation since its original release in 1915 that its promotional ads could claim "no explanation necessary for this picture," asking only that "it should be shown to everybody in and near Fremont."[8]

A public meeting in April 1924 saw the community building in Fremont filled to capacity as more than one thousand people, representing every town in the county and a few from beyond, assembled to receive the lecture of a visiting Klan official. Once more, the speaker chose to remain unidentified, yet proved to be a most "forceful and eloquent" orator, who followed an opening prayer with a lively address, "punctuated with frequent applause" from the excited crowd. Again, the organization he represented was painted as an army of impossibly heroic supercitizens, the sworn enemies of "the crooked, grafting politician," and active enforcers of the prohibition laws in a murky world where immorality and vice held sway. Vowing to destroy America's underworld and "make the bootlegging business impossible," the speaker also "paid a beautiful tribute to pure womanhood," adding that all members of the secret order were sworn by solemn oath to act as gallant "protectors of women." While making it abundantly clear that such lofty responsibilities could only be entrusted to white Protestant Americans, he was careful to point out that the Klan bore no malice toward parties ineligible for membership, going so far as to declare his organization a "friend of the Negro and the alien."[9]

Most public or informational meetings held by KKK organizers tended to follow a similar formula, with the Klan employing charismatic speakers to stoke the fires of interest in the organization, continually emphasizing its propensity for useful and patriotic public service. Almost always, these speakers were Protestant ministers brought in from areas where the Klan had already flourished. The fact that these individuals were often unknown in town meant that they could frequently play along with the secret order's penchant for intrigue by withholding their identities, while still maintaining an air of authenticity bestowed by their status as men of God. In some cases, however, traveling Klan speakers had become so strongly identified with the organization that their names were not concealed, and even served as a definite crowd-puller for the Klan cause. One such speaker was Rev. Fred Ross of Battle Creek, Michigan, who gave "a rousing address on the principles of the Ku Klux Klan" at the Fremont community building in July 1924.[10] Invitations had been sent out some time beforehand to those eligible who might be interested in the organization, and around eight hundred men from across Newaygo County were present, their curiosity roused by an event billed, on this occasion, as suitable for male ears only. Seizing the opportunity to publicly venerate the organization, Rev. Ross explained to those assembled that the Klan "is not a political party . . . but a movement and a crusade for better Americanism . . . built on the principles of the Christian religion . . . [and] working for real democracy in this country." Keen to dazzle as well as to persuade, he went on to outline the strength of the movement nationwide, and in doing so exhibited one of the Klan promotional machine's trademark characteristics—a shameless flair for gross exaggeration of its own might. While the Klan was indeed enjoying its numerical pinnacle during this period, the projections voiced by Rev. Ross for future expansion were, at best, startlingly overoptimistic, if incredibly impressive-sounding to a receptive audience. The organization, which had become a nationwide phenomenon since its incorporation in 1915, was now, he claimed, "growing by 75,000 new members a week . . . and expected to have a membership of 30,000,000 within a year."[11]

The Klan's trumpeted arrival in Newaygo County was an entirely typical scene within Michigan during the organization's relentless recruitment drive of summer 1923, and local Klan units or "Klaverns" sprang up in very similar circumstances in towns and cities throughout the state. "Michigan," declared the August issue of the *Fiery Cross*, "is engulfed in a Klan wave" and is "coming into her own as enthusiasm sweeps north" from the more established KKK strongholds of Indiana and Ohio. With a stream of "glowing reports" arriving from all over the Wolverine State, the Indiana-based Klan organ even announced the imminent launch of a Michigan-specific edition of its paper, as well as describing with admiration the impact of the Invisible Empire in the state:

> Applications for membership are increasing at a rapid rate . . . Today is high tide in Klandom! Today Michigan is calling for Klan speakers; fiery crosses dot the hillsides and each and every night classes from twenty-five to classes numbering in the late thousands are being initiated. Inquiries from the most remote spots in this big state are being received by state officials, in which citizens make known their desire to become affiliated with this great Protestant movement. Communities that have as yet had no speakers are clamoring for information. Those places that have been favored with addresses concerning the Klan are asking for more.[12]

Though this portrait of a vibrant and enthusiastic KKK presence in Michigan comes from an obvious pro-Klan source, its assertions of impressive organizational growth and spread during this period are well-founded. Even a cursory survey of the regional press for the summer months of 1923 (which still constitute only the very early stages of Klan recruitment in Michigan) reveals KKK activity in at least—and probably a great deal more than—a hundred named towns and cities, including appearances in some of the more secluded hinterlands of the state's Upper Peninsula.[13] Official Klan documents listing local Klaverns by name and number also support such a scenario. The regular news bulletin produced by Michigan Grand Dragon George E. Carr, in fact, makes specific reference to individual units numbering at least up to 150.[14] Of these 150, it has been possible to positively identify the whereabouts of 109 Klaverns, the results pointing to a spread that spanned huge portions of the state.

Incomplete an indicator as this may be, it nonetheless makes a striking point, demonstrating that no less than sixty-four of Michigan's eighty-three counties were home to branches of the Klan. In some counties, such as Newaygo, one Klavern covered the whole county. Other counties, especially around major cities, supported multiple units. The KKK, though, was certainly no urban phenomenon, and with many of the most remote

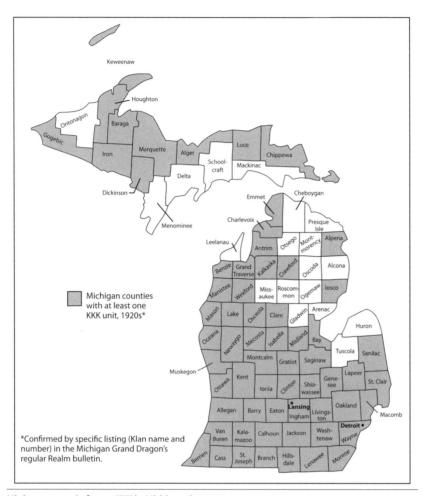

Minimum spread of 1920s KKK in Michigan, by county

and rural parts of the state already covered here, it seems highly likely that the remaining forty-one units that are known to have existed (though as yet are geographically unaccounted for) would have seen the organization represented in virtually every county in the state. Meanwhile, other sources go on to indicate an even stronger Klan presence—the *Owosso Argus Press*, for instance, specifically reporting in October 1926 that there were no less than 215 Klan units operating within Michigan at that time.[15] In addition, scattered references to the all-female auxiliary Women of the Ku Klux Klan in its Michigan organ *Wolverine Women* detail a statewide network of at least

74 chapters, numbered separately from the men. Also chartered in various Michigan locations were Klan auxiliaries for foreign-born Protestants, as well as junior orders for both boys and girls, though no detailed organizational records of these survive.[16]

As in Newaygo County, the materialization of the iconic fiery cross was usually the first—and without doubt the most recognizable—indication of Klan activity in any given neighborhood. Towering at heights of at least eight feet (and sometimes much more), giant wooden crosses bound in gasoline-soaked burlap cast roaring flames into the night skies, becoming, as summer wore on, an increasingly frequent and fearsome fixture upon some of the most conspicuous vantage points statewide.[17] Wherever the mysterious Klan declared its presence, a swirl of rumor, excitement, and intrigue, no doubt provoked intentionally, followed. Having recently witnessed the blaze of a fiery cross and seen the Klan's news organs hit its streets, the city of Holland, for example, was typical of many locations up and down the state in "getting no small degree of thrill out of the idea of the Ku Klux Klan coming." In the capital city of Lansing, the public expressed much curiosity over the veiled secrecy of the Klan's local operations, while its appearance in Grand Haven "has set the town talking, to put it mildly." Indeed, according to the *Grand Haven Daily Tribune*, "at club meetings and on the streets, in the factories and in the stores, the topic of conversation has turned . . . to the white hooded and robed fraternity." While some in the community instinctively responded to news of the imminent Klan invasion with opposition, the great majority of citizens "confess that they know nothing of the Klan, pro or con . . . no real information seems available." Meanwhile, over in the city of Owosso, Klannish rumor was rampant, with excited talk of visits by regional organizers, large gatherings of masked men in the woods outside of town, and fiery crosses "30 feet high and 20 feet across," with one story even claiming that "thirty two such crosses were burned in one night."[18]

In Clare, as in countless Michigan locations, the news of a Klan organizer's presence in town was met with "excitement and considerable conjecture," though the man in question remained a shady figure whose exact identity could never quite be pinned down by the local populace. Midland was similarly stirred by the arrival of an organizer or "Kleagle," described as "a stranger in the city who states that 'all of Michigan is being invaded by the order.'"[19] The town of St. Johns, too, looked on curiously as a certain young man based himself at a local hotel while going about his day job as a roving Klan promoter. His presence and intent here had by one means or another become common knowledge, not to mention the subject of much idle gossip, and yet typically no one seemed to be able to tell the organizer's name. While there were those "outspoken in their belief that effort should be made to have him 'move on,'" many others were interested to find out just exactly what he had arrived in town to say. Having milked his enigmatic-stranger status for over a week, the publicity-savvy Kleagle then readily agreed to a personal, if not completely frank, interview with a local reporter. "We could not learn his name," wrote the *Clinton County Republican*, the organizer having explained that the sacred oaths of his order stipulated absolute and inflexible secrecy in such matters. In other ways, however, he was more than happy to have himself and his viewpoints exposed to the public, especially as his relative openness and approachability would tend to show him in a sympathetic light as someone not unlike the average reader and potential convert. Cast in the role of a sincere and hardworking purveyor of uncomplicated traditional values, he revealed just enough of himself to convey a definite common-touch appeal while at the same time retaining much of the mystique surrounding the image of his employers. Bringing the much-touted Klan to the level of the people, then, was a "young man of possibly 30 years [who] wore a light colored suit, was well posted on his subject and claimed that he was in the work mainly because he thoroughly believed in it." He was careful to point out his own modest status as an average married man and father of two, claiming also that his work left him far from well paid. As for the Klan in Michigan, according to this Kleagle and many more like him, its chief concerns were in harmony with those of most ordinary, law-abiding "good citizens," namely the cleaning up of all forms of vice, and the practical assistance of the recognized authorities in enforcing prohibition laws.[20]

With the organization beginning to make initial inroads into communities across the state, its promoters, though always keen to court the opinion of the local press wherever possible, sought an audience first and foremost with ordinary members of the public. Advertisements in the local newspapers in both Saginaw and Mount Pleasant, for example, carried advance notice of open informational lectures at which the inquisitive general public "will be given an opportunity to hear the truth from the lips of an authorized speaker." Confident of mustering up sufficient levels of popular appeal for its own cause, the Klan asked in return only "the courtesy of a fair and open-minded hearing."[21] Always incredibly popular events, the open meetings provided promoters with opportunities to cast a positive light on the KKK for the benefit of local audiences. While claiming to be in no sense a political organization, the Klan's "constructive patriotic program" invariably included plans to fight corruption and crime, amid vaguely worded tributes to the honor of flag and country, declarations of loyalty to the Constitution of the United States, and eulogies to Protestantism, "pure womanhood," citizenship, and "100% Americanism." Furthermore, the Klan constantly took pains to point out that "We are not an 'anti' organization. We are a 'pro' body. We believe in the Christian religion." At the same time, it openly rallied for national immigration restriction and the outlawing of parochial schools in Michigan, and maintained an avowed belief in the basic superiority of the white race.[22] The organization was well aware, of course, of the controversy that it courted, and its general disdain for Catholicism proved a particularly effective draw in what were largely homogenous white Protestant areas. In September 1923, the Mount Pleasant City Commission vocally refused the Klan permission to hold its planned public meeting on city-owned land at Island Park, for fear of complaints from Catholic residents. "Even though the claim may be made that the Ku Klux Klan is not anti-Catholic," explained Mayor Webster H. Pearce, "it is so Protestant as to amount to the same thing." Buoyed by the fuss surrounding the affair, the meeting went ahead regardless at a local dance hall, where an inflated crowd was treated to the sight of an outraged Catholic priest seizing the rostrum from the Klan speaker, before being brought under control by local police.[23] Similarly, at an open Klan meeting in Saugatuck in the same week, the presence of opposition did nothing to detract from the popularity of the event, and if anything added a certain thrill to the proceedings. The crowd was, according to the *Commercial Record*, "enormous . . . pretty nearly everyone in town was on hand." The Klan speaker was no less impressive. "As an orator he is one of the best ever heard here, and held his audience, friends and foes alike—for both were there—with his mastery of the art of oratory."[24]

Around Michigan, the growing Klan had done much to promote its own image as a flamboyantly mysterious fraternity. The organization strove for a very conspicuous appearance of exclusivity, and teased the public's curiosity by allowing occasional limited, and very deliberate, voyeuristic glimpses of its inner workings. Commentary from a *Royal Oak Tribune* reporter upon an early outdoor KKK initiation meeting near Clawson, Michigan, demonstrates the predicament of the nonmember. Physically banished from experiencing events on the inside, he is nevertheless drawn toward them sensuously, irresistibly attracted by the remarkable sights and sounds that emanate from within:

> "Henry Ford for President!" shouted a stentorian voice. "Hurrah!" from the throats of a thousand or more . . . white clad members, like ghosts in the twilight, were on guard entirely round the woods . . . from the roadway (as close

as your correspondent could get) the hooded forms, moving about among the trees, presented a unique spectacle. Speeches, fireworks and refreshments followed the initiation, and the revelry was kept up into the early hours of the morning . . . Some of the speakers, blessed with powerful voices, could be heard . . . more than a mile away. The reflection of the fiery cross also could be seen for miles, and attracted many to the vicinity, where they enjoyed a splendid display of fireworks.[25]

Erecting fiery crosses in the most striking of locations, on the highest of peaks and the darkest of nights, the Klan advertised itself to all, but admitted—or at least wanted to appear to admit—only the select and chosen few. Describing another "weird meeting" lit dramatically by the moon and an electric fiery cross, this time in Northrup's Woods near Hartford, a local paper told how "guards met all comers seeking admission," which was strictly by invitation, and "only the friends of the Klan or those vouched for by them were passed into the weird group." In Flint, the local Klan broadcast its presence, and its intention to hold mass initiation rites, by virtue of a thirty-foot-high flaming cross. At the same time, Klansmen decided to make their meeting a little more exclusive by "facing their automobiles toward the road with headlights turned on, thus making it harder to see the ceremonies."[26]

Unsurprisingly, the Klan's own newspapers perpetuated stories of public clamor for the organization throughout Michigan. The huge "scramble to get in" among Saginaw citizens, or the "rush to sign up" in Manistique were typical descriptions of popular demand. Also typical was the stress upon the supposed high quality of successful recruits—one Detroit chapter, for instance, populated only by the "best people," while in Ionia, "as usual the better class of citizens are found among the ranks."[27] More telling, perhaps, is the support for such notions of popularity and respectability in the mainstream provincial press. The *Adrian Daily Telegram* in July 1923 reported that on the organization's first arrival in town, a group of about thirty men "listened for more than three hours to an elucidation of the principles of the Klan as outlined by a state and national organizer." At the end of that time, "all but two" of the men signed membership application cards, one of the two exceptions being the reporter himself, who had been present in a purely professional capacity. A reporter in Dowagiac relayed tales of "weird Klan initiation scenes" during which a sizable number of local people were inducted into the mysteries of the Invisible Empire. Of those admitted, many were well-known to the newspaperman, who described them as "eminently respectable people who stand well in this community," though he had promised "on his oath . . . not to reveal their names." The *Barryton*

Press, meanwhile, in the aftermath of the Klan's first meeting in that town, betrayed a certain charmed absorption with the organization that allowed it to enjoy the benefit of the not inconsiderable doubt that surrounded it. "From what we hear," read the editorial, "there are several members in this vicinity and they are all good citizens, so the Klan does not appear to be so bad as some would call it. At present it is sort of a mystery to most of the people around here, but there must be lots of good to it or there would not be so many members joining it every week."[28] Keen to demonstrate its discerning exclusivity and the respectability of its membership, the Klan attempted to reach out ever higher, even toward the intellectual elite, apparently with some success. "Several professors and students from the University of Michigan," declared a July 1923 issue of *Dawn*, "were naturalized into the Knights of the Ku Klux Klan at a recent ceremonial." This, though, was nothing new, as reports claimed that "all Big Ten universities are thought to have strong, well organized chapters," alongside already well-established Klaverns at both Harvard and Princeton.[29]

THE BUSINESS OF BELONGING: THE KKK AS A CENTRALIZED FRATERNAL INDUSTRY

As Mary Ann Clawson has noted, by the early twentieth century, most of America's many fraternal organizations, in an increasingly competitive market, had ceased to rely upon the lodge-building efforts of enthusiasts, whose gentle recruitment activities tended to draw only limited local attendance. Instead they began to utilize systematic promotion techniques, employing insistent agents whose energies were devoted solely to the task of soliciting memberships. Many lodges were increasingly becoming "entrepreneurial organizations that operated so as to maximize membership growth and financial profit," and specialist fraternal agents organized lodges "for a living, paid on commission, like traveling salesmen, to sell the product of lodge membership."[30] The Klan's nationwide success in the early 1920s was a particularly forthright example of the rewards to be gained from such a direct and business-minded approach. Widespread growth of Klan organizations around Michigan, and simultaneously across the United States, was due in no small part to a well-established and aggressive recruitment strategy, orchestrated on a national scale from the Imperial Palace in Atlanta, Georgia.

In 1915 William J. Simmons, a failed Alabaman minister-turned-salesman and self-described fraternalist, had brought the second Ku Klux

Klan into existence as "a purely patriotic fraternal organization designed to memorialize the Klan of the Reconstruction period." In an elaborate service conducted atop Georgia's Stone Mountain on a cold Thanksgiving evening, he ceremoniously installed himself as the new organization's first Imperial Wizard. While undoubtedly crediting him with the creative impetus behind the secret order, to say nothing of his conception of all its convoluted ritual and regalia, Klan histories unanimously agree that Simmons was all but incompetent as an organizer, describing him invariably as "impractical" or "a dreamer."[31] This, it seems, was not an uncommon quality among the types of men who founded ritualistic fraternal orders in America, as the work of Mark Carnes attests. Many such founding fathers, ultimately proving ineffective as organizers and leaders, were more commonly labeled "'idealists,' or 'visionaries' whose special skill was one of perception . . . marginal men [who] retreated from the routine patterns of work and family and immersed themselves in romantic literature, history, or mystical religions . . . channelling widely-shared anxieties and then discharging them harmlessly through the medium of liminal ritual."[32] True to this form, Simmons's order, though rich in ceremony and mythical hocus-pocus, endured its first five years in abject obscurity and financial struggle under his sole direction, confined to the Southern states and floundering around for memberships.[33] Only in 1920, when Simmons finally conceded his lack of organizational talent and hired a professional advertising company to bring the Klan to an unsuspecting public, did the fortunes of the order take a dramatic turn for the better.

The Atlanta-based Southern Publicity Association, consisting of promotional agents Edward Young Clarke and Mrs. Elizabeth Tyler, was drafted by Simmons to manage the membership drives of his struggling order. Efficient and money-minded, Clarke and Tyler quickly set about completely reorganizing the Klan's finances and implementing a sophisticated marketing system. Their small publicity agency was transformed into the Klan's official Propagation Department, deploying a paid army of over a thousand full-time recruiters, or Kleagles, to communities across America.[34] These nonstop "Kluxing" drives saw recruiters tirelessly beating the drum of patriotic "100% Americanism"; the defense of traditional standards of law, order, and social morality; and (cross-denominational Protestant) church attendance. Having endeavored to paint the Klan as a benevolent society of American morality, and to glorify the virtues of its secret fraternal mystery, Kleagles also frequently traded upon exaggerated postwar fears that the country was gravely threatened by organized "enemies within," chiefly in the forms of the immigrant Catholic and the "international Jew." Memberships were sold en masse, region by region, with success peaking around

1924 at anything between three and six million members nationwide.[35] Typically, a Kleagle would initially target the prominent and influential citizens in any given locality, sending exclusive-looking invitations to members of Masonic lodges, fraternal orders, and patriotic societies. The recruitment of a town's foremost businessmen, politicians, or public officials would then act as a prestige-enhancing signal to the average citizen considering joining the Klan, with aspiring members safely assured of elite company in the claim that "all the best people" were in. Often among the very first to be approached were Protestant ministers, many of whom were offered free membership and office-holding positions as "Kludds" (chaplains) in newly established Klaverns, as well as complimentary subscriptions to the leading Klan periodicals. In return, countless local pastors agreed to exercise their not inconsiderable influence in convincing large portions of their congregations to follow suit and join the militantly Protestant lodge that claimed Christ himself as "our criterion of character."[36]

It had become apparent very quickly to the Propagation Department that the KKK had huge potential for growth, and, more importantly, a huge potential for generating lucrative business. Kleagles were sent into the field on a commission basis, almost indistinguishable from traveling salesmen, for a set percentage of each "Klecktoken" (membership fee) that they managed to solicit. With the signature of each new convert secured, the Klan chain of command operated as a channel to suck profits back to national headquarters in Atlanta. Of the $10 initiation fee paid by each individual recruit, $4 was kept by the Kleagle who signed him up. The remaining $6 was remitted to a King Kleagle (state-level sales manager), who kept $1, sending $5 to the Grand Goblin (district sales manager) of the geographical "Domain" to which he was attached. The Grand Goblin retained $.50, sending $4.50 to the Imperial Kleagle (Edward Young Clarke, the national sales manager) in Atlanta, who in turn kept $2.50 of this, paying the final $2 into the coffers of the Imperial Wizard himself.[37] With everyone in the Klan sales hierarchy standing to gain financially, the emphasis of Kleagles in the field fell unmistakably upon volume of memberships sold, rather than any thin pretense of principle. Predictably, corruption was rife, and with Imperial headquarters unable to exercise complete control over their agents, dishonest Kleagles filed reports detailing fewer recruits than they had actually signed up, allowing them to pocket the difference in initiation fees. Frequently, too, recruitment was conducted indiscriminately, and far from exercising the exclusivity and selectivity it so boasted of in its literature, the Klan opened its doors to almost anyone who could pay the required $10 membership fee.[38]

By the time the Klan came around to systematic recruiting in Michigan in the summer of 1923, both Simmons and Edward Young Clarke had been wrested from their positions of power in the secret order. Each man had been disposed of by a new and ambitious Imperial Wizard, Texan dentist Hiram W. Evans, who had vowed to reform the organization's financial excesses, and place Kleagles on salaries rather than commission.[39] Kleagles, nonetheless, continued to be accused of opportunism, gearing their sales pitch toward particular local conditions rather than an overarching national policy, meaning that they might oppose or support a particular group within one town, and indiscriminately do the opposite in the next town, so long as this led to the maximum possible membership applications. In a series of *World's Work* articles, journalist Robert Duffus famously labeled traveling Kleagles as "salesmen of hate," lamenting the fact that recruiters had been peddling "the Klan's concentrated hate pill with such success at $10 a package." The movement, he charged, effectively provided "all things to all men," amalgamating the fears of diverse groups of recruits and converting their "vague ideas about woman, home, God, Americanism, and Anglo-Saxon supremacy . . . into magniloquent phrases." The Klan, to its opponents, was a "cumbersome monster of an organization, ill-planned in every way except as a means of raising money to line the pockets of Kleagles, Goblins and Wizards."[40]

Trading upon a surface appeal to fraternal, communal, and traditional American values, the Klan of the 1920s was in reality clearly geared toward much more monetary and expansionist goals, with the rank and file financially exploited for the benefit of those higher up the chain of command.[41] As well as finding a source of advancement in terms of rank and prestige, Klan leaders also found in the movement a great many opportunities for material benefit. Before departing from the order, founder William Simmons and chief promoter Edward Young Clarke, in particular, had done much to capitalize upon its runaway success. Among the most visible of spoils was a burgeoning portfolio of Klan-owned property in Atlanta, all bought and managed by the Clarke Realty Company, which had been set up for the purpose. Klan "gifts" to the organization's highest office holders included the premises of the national headquarters or Imperial Palace, a lavish $65,000 Southern mansion on Atlanta's famous Peachtree Street; a nearby ten-acre lot upon which a meeting hall seating 5,000 was erected; Simmons's palatial $45,000 "Klancrest" home (which had apparently arrived in his possession along with complimentary sedan); and a $25,000 apartment for Clarke.[42]

Footing the bill for such extravagances was the ordinary Klansman, who, in addition to initiation fees and the cost of purchasing a robe, was also expected to pay quarterly taxes to the Imperial (national) and Realm (state) coffers. All of this was over and above the regular cash dues demanded of each member by his local Klavern, the collection and reporting of which were carefully monitored, with failure to remain "in good standing" being punished by immediate suspension from the order. Local Klan chapters were not financially supported by either the state or national administrations, and should funds run low in a local Klavern treasury, the monetary burden fell squarely at the feet of its members. Through "voluntary," though seemingly obligatory contributions, it was common for local members to cover miscellaneous running costs such as Klavern building, maintenance or rent, travel expenses for officials or visiting speakers, accountancy fees, equipment and regalia purchase, charity funds, church donations, and subscriptions to Klan publications.[43] In common with many other fraternal orders, the national headquarters of the Klan also made attempts to introduce a lucrative life-insurance scheme. Various early incarnations finally culminated in the establishment in early 1924 of the Empire Mutual Life Insurance Company, controlled by the Insurance Department of the Imperial Palace, and strongly recommended to all loyal Klansmen.[44]

Perhaps the most profitable enterprises associated with the Klan—namely, the manufacture of robes and associated regalia, and the production of all official KKK printed matter—were operated as a vast monopoly, under complete control of the Imperial Palace, and protected by legal copyright. In early 1922, Wizard Simmons formed the Atlanta-based Searchlight Publishing Company for the purpose of producing the first official KKK organ, *The Searchlight*. By mid-1923, however, Simmons and *The Searchlight* had been replaced by Hiram Evans, second Imperial Wizard, and his newly established Ku Klux Klan press. The official press churned out the national Klan newsletter the *Imperial Night-Hawk*, as well as every other item of Klan-endorsed literature to be disseminated to units around the nation.[45] Making its debut appearance in March 1923, the first edition of the Klan weekly stated in no uncertain terms its intention to act as a channel of solidarity and communication for all disparate corners of the national KKK network:

> This publication . . . aims to carry a weekly message from the Imperial Palace to every Klansman in America . . . the name NIGHT HAWK, courier to the Exalted Cyclops and messenger to the Klans, indicates the mission of this magazine . . . to keep Klansmen informed of activities at the Imperial Palace in their behalf and of the progress and advancement of the Knights of the Ku Klux Klan throughout the nation. The magazine will be published once each week and will be made available to every Klansman at his Klavern.[46]

This and subsequent official organs, notably the *Kourier* magazine, guaranteed the Klan revenue through prepaid subscriptions taken up either by local Klaverns or by individuals. They also helped spread the Klan's message far and wide throughout the nation, allowing even the smallest, most isolated provincial Klavern to experience a sense of connection to a much larger social network. The morale of small units around Michigan, for instance, would be greatly boosted by a mention in the local news section of one of the larger nationally circulated Klan organs, and such recognition served only to reconfirm the relevance of their own activities and relationship with a wider, like-minded Klan world.[47] Establishing the place of the local Klavern in the context of the whole movement, national organs provided a site of interaction between the Klans of the nation, allowing them to measure their progress against one another, swap ideas and opinions, share news, and indulge in friendly competition. As the Klan grew in popularity, they also began to carry countless advertisements for a growing market in affiliated literature and Klan-themed lines of merchandise.

The manufacture of Klan robes was always a booming business, and grew ever more lucrative with the expansion of the movement itself. From the beginning, the Klan had sold robes to its members for $6.50, initially contracting the work out to a local garment maker in Atlanta. Each robe cost around $4 to produce, leaving the Klan with a profit of $2.50 per member. In 1921, Wizard Simmons decided to take this business in-house, and oversaw the establishment of the Gates City Manufacturing Company, a factory concern purpose-built for the manufacture of Klan robes and paraphernalia. Operating as a Klan-controlled monopoly, it slashed production costs to just $2 per robe, meaning a clear profit of $4.50 on each $6.50 robe sold. Within a year of opening its doors for business, the Gates City Manufacturing Company was given a credit rating of $350,000 by Atlanta bankers.[48] In September 1923, Hiram Evans, having seized the reins from Simmons and promised to improve the financial efficiency of the order, brought the regalia factory and printing plant together as one operation. Trading out of Buckhead, Georgia, near to the Imperial Palace, a new regalia factory and printing plant mass-produced both robes and literature under the same roof. During its first month of operation, it was reported that "one shift in the plant is putting out approximately 3,000 robes each week . . . [and] it is hoped to speed up production . . . to the number of 10,000 a week." At that time, "40 skilled workers" were employed, with plans in place that "this force will be greatly increased."

Such was the demand from the thousands regularly joining the Klan that in mid-1924 the Buckhead plant had to be expanded, with a new three-story factory and office building being erected. Reportedly taking the words "twenty-four hour service" as its motto, the factory operated both night and day, maintaining a surplus of 20,000 robes at all times. Evans, keen to avoid the wasteful and indulgent image of his predecessor, took great pains to emphasize through the Klan press that "the savings made since the robe factory and printing plant were established . . . have paid for every piece of machinery now in operation," as well as the buildings in which the machinery stood. Perhaps conscious, too, of avoiding the image of exploitative boss, he also took every opportunity to trumpet the good morale of his factory workforce, who were "all Klansmen," publicizing a number of happy, family-oriented social occasions at the plant, in which he had played a full part.[49] The new Imperial Wizard insisted that he was sweeping away the greed and individual graft that had gone before him, abolishing "useless departments . . . cutting needless expenses" in order to save expenditure on the part of the ordinary Klansman. His modern production plant had meant that "printing costs were cut almost in two" and that robes "will be given to Klans at actual cost. All profit is eliminated." As testament to this, the Klan made a grand gesture, slashing the selling price of robes from $6.50 to $5 amid promises that "better and more substantial material will be used . . . [and] delivery of robes will also be expedited."[50]

Bringing together the work of the two big Klan enterprises was the *Catalogue of Official Robes and Banners*, an extravagantly illustrated 32-page brochure, printed in impressive full color by the Ku Klux Klan Press. Released in 1925 with the intention that "Klansmen of the nation should be better posted" as to the range of products available for purchase from the national office, it presented a flamboyant variety of visual options. Though the basic Klan robe had indeed been reduced in price to $5, to order one of these was to own the most workaday and basic of Klan apparel, whereas in the catalog there were no less than sixteen different variations of robes, featured in eye-catching greens, oranges, reds, blues, and whites, with elaborate silk accessories and assorted trimmings. Ranging in mail-order cost according to officer rank and to grandiosity, robe prices went as high as $40, with, in some cases, the option of an upgrade from cotton to satin at an extra $10. Also featured were a range of elaborately stitched Klan banners for use at public gatherings. Embroidered in silk on a satin background and varying in color and style, each featured popular KKK slogans and symbols and retailed at a cool $40, even without the supporting pole. Not to miss any opportunity, the catalog also carried an ad for a $1 waterproof robe-carrying bag, complete with separate compartments for robe and helmet, as well as urging local Klaverns to send all their printing and binding work in the direction of the national printing press.[51]

THE KU KLUX KRAZE: REGIONAL KLAN
COMMERCE AND HOODED CONSUMERISM

Perhaps viewing the commercial successes of the Klan national office with covetous eyes, Michigan's official Klan administration made its own attempts at cashing in, with chaotic results. In a series of lawsuits filed against the Michigan Klan after its demise, various former KKK employees testified to having had knowledge of underhand financial scheming, revealing that "in many respects the Michigan Klan had become only a means by which individual members . . . could put over deals that would bring them profits." Among a number of much-vaunted commercial projects for which the state Klan solicited funds from Michigan members were the formation of a Klan music recording company, purchase of a Klan airplane, construction of a grand new KKK temple in Detroit, sale of land lots on a planned all-Klan resort at Schwartz Lake in Oakland County, and a $225,000 stock issue for the purchase by the Invisible Empire of the *Saginaw Star.* Characteristically of a state administration that would become notorious for petty wrangling and embezzlement, not a single one of these projects ever materialized, nor were any funds returned to those Klansmen who had invested or donated.[52]

Even as the Michigan Klan's own business ventures imploded, the wider KKK industry (much of it unofficial, profiting from the organization's popularity without being owned by it) performed a good deal more buoyantly. Pro-Klan newspapers were both a key part of the industry and, through advertising, the means by which the industry grew. Though later controlled by the Klan's central bureau of publications in Washington, DC, the *Fiery Cross* newspaper first operated out of Indianapolis, and began producing a Michigan State edition in 1923 in response to demand from Klansmen in the Wolverine State. The *Fiery Cross*, a weekly broadsheet publication, retailed at five cents, and offered yearly and five-yearly subscriptions at $2 and $10 respectively. Boasting some 200,000 paid-up subscribers by September 1923, the paper regularly pointed to evidence of its own burgeoning popularity. Its pages continued to cite ever-rising circulation figures, as well as claiming that newsboys' ample stocks, hawked at Klan events all around Michigan, were consistently exhausted amid flurries of great excitement within moments of going on sale.[53] While the publishers of the newspapers themselves no doubt turned a handsome profit, it was the space devoted to commercial advertising within their pages that afforded the real opportunities for serious profiteering. As news stories and features brought the realities of the Klan movement to the attention of Michiganians, a plethora of eye-catching ads running alongside them brought its distinctive representations, symbols, and watchwords—disarmed and reduced to the level of novelty by their application to even the most everyday of products—into their very homes.

The Klan's fondness for visual expression was abundantly catered to, with ads for patriotic flags, banners, and decorations appearing in multitudes. Countless competing merchants pushed their own variations, offering a mind-boggling assortment of designs, colors, and sizes, including the standard Stars and Stripes of "Old Glory," various "Christian Flags," pennants, bunting, drapery, decorative canes, balloons, and hat bands typically adorned with either "KKK," "100% American," or "The Flag I Love." Meanwhile, for the discreet traveling Klansman, the "Klan Kit Kompany" offered a specially designed carrier "for your paraphernalia and a wardrobe on your trips." Also very widely advertised in the pages of the Michigan Klan papers were an elaborate array of patriotic fireworks. The E. S. Wolfe Fireworks Company promised the "biggest and best shooters of Klan fireworks in America," delivered by a corps of experts, all of whom were assuredly "One Hundred Percent." The company also offered pre-manufactured fiery crosses and illuminated KKK signs, "in any size up to six feet."

E. S. Wolfe Fireworks Co.

326-328 Juliana St.   Parkersburg, W. Va.

LEADERS IN

Fireworks Displays

A Corps of Expert Men Always at Your Service
All One Hundred Per Cent

Programs Submitted on Any Amount by Return Mail

Fiery Cross, K. K. K. in Any Size Up to Six Feet

The Motto: One Country, One School, One Flag

E. S. Wolfe   Parkersburg, W. Va.

Ad for patriotic Klan fireworks and fiery cross
Source: *Fiery Cross (Michigan State Edition)*, 28 September 1923, 10

Similarly, the M&S Fireworks Company of Tippecanoe City, Ohio, in addition to regular ads in the *Fiery Cross*, produced an annual catalog detailing its wares. Boldly claiming to be "first in Klandom," this color brochure outlined thirty-four pages worth of visually spectacular products "manufactured expressly for the use of the Knights of the Ku Klux Klan." Among set-piece fireworks for sale were relatively simple illuminated crosses, "100%" and "KKK" signs, alongside more complex combustible creations detailing the American flag, the "Little Red Schoolhouse," and even a fiery bust of President George Washington. Priced according to size and sophistication, they were shipped to Klans "ready to fire." Huge stage-managed displays, ranging from a basic fireworks show at $100 to a $750 "Klan Revue" extravaganza, promised a "combination of aerial wonders and ground devices that display in real patriotic splendor, the principles of the Knights of the Ku Klux Klan." Indeed, these were "specially adapted for entertaining large crowds at Konklaves . . . no more beautiful pyrotechnics can be obtained for the money." The final pages of the catalog comprised a large directory of "satisfied customers," listing 337 Klan units across the country that had purchased and enjoyed spectacular fireworks displays. Out of seventeen Michigan locations that received a mention, the Klans in the Newaygo County towns of Fremont and Newaygo, as well as nearby Hart and Muskegon, all featured.[54]

Forms of popular entertainment also began to receive the Klan branding treatment, with the production and sale of KKK-themed literature, drama, and film. Ad pages in the Klan press teemed with patriotic texts supplied by numerous independent publishing companies, and included such titles as *Americanism Plus*, the *Hundred Percent Magazine*, and *The Flag-Draped Skeleton*. In fiction, swashbuckling adventure novels such as *Harold the Klansman* and *Knight Vale of the KKK* featured dashing, clean-cut Klan heroes fighting against the forces of evil, and could be obtained for as little as $1.25 per copy. The National Emblem Company, a typical player in the Klan novelty market, proudly announced the release of its "Anti-Convent set," a series of six books detailing "the Pope's slave pens in America." The concerned reader could sample the joys of *Maria Monk*, *Confessions of a Nun*, *Thirty Years in Hell*, *Convent Life Unveiled*, *America's Menace*, and *Slaves of the God* for 75 cents apiece, and even save a dollar by going for the whole set at once. Should all of that prove a little heavy, there was always the possibility of relief in *Komic Kracs*, a "pioneer fun magazine" featuring "ART! HUMOR! SATIRE!" and put out every month for 25 cents a copy by the Patriotic American Publishing Company. Klan-themed stage plays also surfaced, sometimes in the form of copyrighted scripts sold to

Klaverns for amateur-dramatic interpretation by their members, other times as professionally produced shows for which tickets were sold. Klan plays *The Invisible Empire* (according to an ad in *Dawn* "the most talked about play in America") and *The Awakening*, for example, toured a number of American cities entertaining theater audiences.[55] Distribution agents for Klan-themed films, too, advertised directly to local Klavern heads, urging them to "have the first 100 percent motion picture sponsored by the KKK run in your city." As a result, new Klan films such as *The Toll of Justice* took in money at the box offices of cinemas across many parts of the United States, often alongside ever-popular reruns of *The Birth of a Nation*. Indeed, during 1924, the Newaygo County towns of White Cloud, Fremont, and Newaygo each enjoyed screenings of one or both Klan-promoted films.[56]

Likewise, KKK music was heavily advertised in the Klan press, in Michigan as elsewhere, as specialist performers and composers sprang up all over the country. As well as the numerous bands, vocalists, and quartets involved in Michigan's Klan, independent companies of songwriters appeared around the state, including in the cities of Alma, Flint, Hillsdale, Kalamazoo, and Lansing. Churning out Klan songs for commercial sale and performance, the product of their efforts could either be bought direct, or purchased through wholesale merchants specializing in the "best" of Klan music nationwide. One such merchant, the Lutz music company, was typical in offering "American music for the American home" from a mail-order catalog of over sixty titles available in a variety of formats. Phonograph records sold for $1 each (plus postage), as did player-piano rolls complete with lyrics, while sheet music went for 35 cents, and musical scores for use by bands, orchestras, and quartets cost 50 cents. Compilations of lyrics could also be purchased in the form of Klan song books. Though there were many solemn-sounding odes such as *The Honor of a Klansman, Onward Valiant Klansmen,* and *The March of the Klansmen,* the bulk of these songs tended to sport more playful and light-hearted monikers, such as *Ku Klux Steppin' Blues, That Dear Old Fiery Cross, The Happy Klansman, The Klucker and the Rain,* and *We're All Loyal Kluxers.* In many cases, they featured cartoon-like covers, and often they verged on self-deprecation, with titles like *Wake up America and Kluck, Kluck, Kluck; The Stuttering Klansman;* and even *Daddy Swiped the Last Clean Sheet (and joined the Ku Klux Klan).*[57]

Manufacturers of Klan jewelry and emblems frequently put out, in addition to myriad newspaper ads, detailed and stylish mail-order catalogs, very much resembling in appearance and layout those of contemporary home-shopping giants like *Sears, Roebuck and Co.* KKK paraphernalia bore close comparison in style and design to the popular trinkets of other fraternal

An example of KKK sheet music for commercial sale
Source: Library of Congress (Performing Arts)

brotherhoods, and was very often sold by the same dealers who supplied similar items to devotees of Masonry and Odd Fellowship. Fraternal prestige was clearly a selling point, and one dealer, in presenting "the latest additions to our exclusive line of KKK jewelry" boasted that "our emblems are worn and highly recommended by many high officials, influential members and thousands of Hundred-Percenters." Included in this seller's range were various decorative charms, buttons, scarf pins, fobs, cuff links, and belt buckles, all adorned with a patented triangular "triple K" symbol, a Christian cross, or a combination of the two. Depending upon the customer's preference for bronze, silver, and varying purities of gold, prices ranged from $1 to $8. Smartly presented pocket coins featured Klan mottoes "Non Silba Sed

Anthar" and "One Country, One Flag, One Language," and sold as "an introduction to any Klansman" for 50 cents each. Also on offer was a range of "specials for the ladies," with brooch pins and elegant rings in solid gold, Klannish symbol at the center, apparently "designed to meet the demands of the fastidious."[58]

Particularly common were items fashioned around the fiery cross symbol, including lockets, rings, and neck chains in gold and encrusted with red jewels, once again in a range of designs to suit all budgets, or made to specific order. Should a Klansman wish to "surprise [his] wife, daughter or sweetheart," he might even be persuaded to bring home a pair of fiery cross earrings or an elegant fiery cross brooch for $2.95. Competition between manufacturers ensured that fresh and ever more elaborate designs continued to be produced and sold. The National Emblem Company of Omaha, Nebraska, for instance, assured potential customers of its own place at the forefront of Klan fashion by showcasing the "very newest Klan ring made." As well as a range of rings for both sexes, its stock included brooches, scarf pins, lapel badges, charms, presentation medals, lockets, pendants, and pocket pieces. Designed to appear exclusive and mysterious, most rings featured either a triple-K symbol or the coded Klan message "AKIA" (A Klansman I Am), and were fashioned from solid gold, with options for diamonds, onyx, and rubies available. Despite the appeal to exclusivity, however, wholesalers were very anxious to move their products in bulk, and the sales focus was always unquestionably directed toward volume transactions. The National Emblem Company's price list advised Klansmen not to buy single charms, trinkets, and emblems, but to "SAVE MONEY: BUY IN SOLID DOZEN LOTS," offering discounted rates for bulk purchases. Similarly, in an ad for its most popular "AKIA" ring, the company encouraged individual Klansmen, rather than buying a single ring for the retail price of $5, to purchase three rings at a discount rate and then reap the benefits of their own business acumen. "Send your order for three rings at $10" the ad urged, and then "sell two of them to your friends at $5 each, and have one left for yourself, FREE."[59]

Having proved a ready market for merchandise produced largely outside of the state, by 1924 Michigan was also beginning to manufacture Klan-themed products of its own. One ad in the *Michigan Kourier* touted "a beautiful oil painting of Klansman on horse, painted by a noted artist" of Owosso, Michigan, printed in any size to order, and "sold to Klansmen only." Also on offer was the La Java 100% Cigar, "made by 100% work-men in a 100% factory for 100% men" in Jackson, Michigan. A Bay City company, too, produced the "Klansman's Life pocket coin," proudly "made by Klansmen for Klansmen . . . the only pocket coin with complete Klan creed," while a number of Detroit firms hawked "secret watch charms and all kinds of Klan goods."[60] Providing the context in which all of these products could be successfully promoted was a much wider national Klan novelty market, the range of which seemed almost boundless. The more diverse the assortment of products, and the more banal the items themselves that bore popular KKK imagery and slogans, the more commonplace and unremarkable the presence of such Klan imagery became. Alongside the decorative (KKK hats, balloons, and flags; fiery cross radiator caps for the family car; "patriotic pictures" for the living room), Klan imagery colonized the useful. Any Klansman, for example, might wish to obtain the "Kluxer Knifty Knife," a "two-bladed knife for two-fisted Americans," crafted, of course, from "best American steel" and available at just $1.25. Should health be a concern, then "100% water"—the mineral qualities of which had apparently proven beneficial in treating all manner of maladies including gastric disorders, diabetes, even alcoholism—provided a ready solution.

Aimed toward children, meanwhile, were products such as "U-Kno candies" and educational Klannish brainteaser games that promised that "when the puzzle has been worked the great question before America today has been stamped on the mind indelibly." Perhaps most absurd was the "Klean Kut Kid," sold alternatively as the "rubber Klan baby," an inflatable doll available in various sizes, each representing the figure of a fully garbed, masked, and decorated, if somewhat infantilized, Klansman. Prospective buyers were urged that, more than any other item, "this novelty sells on sight," due to the notion that "you can have a world of fun with the Klean Kut Kid . . . every hundred percenter wants one." Only by writing in with a small fee of 25 cents could samples and price lists be obtained, along with other specialty catalogs "covering a general line of good snappy money-making novelties."[61]

Bringing together the Klan world and the domestic world were products such as "Klan-Lite, the wonder lamp for American homes." Depicting the figure of a lone Klansman bearing a fiery torch, this item claimed not just practical uses, but also a wealth of lofty meaning, "symbolizing the beliefs and aims of a great American conception." Apparently a "beautiful work of art" in its own right, it also represented the "beacon of American ideals," and to purchase it was to actively demonstrate one's patriotic loyalty. To cater for rural dwellers devoid of electricity, the ivory-finished piece with "crimson flame shaped bulb" could be easily substituted for a wax candle. Either way, "IF YOU LOVE AMERICA," urged the ad, then "BURN A KLAN-LITE IN YOUR HOME." Meanwhile, the Klansman fond of correspondence was similarly prompted to "show your colors" by buying "handsome stationery

Typical ads for popular KKK novelties

Source: *Dawn*, 15 December 1923, 15

with [a] bright fiery cross on," while yet another nearby ad assured him that a set of bronze-finished bookends featuring Klansmen on horseback might prove the perfect addition to the furniture in his home library or study. Such items, merging the Invisible Empire's bizarre symbolism with elements of the everyday, the commercial, and the functional, played a part in the normalization, even domestication, of the Klan image. In this context, the supposedly secret order could be profitably brought out into the open, and even put on display, in the dues-paying American home.[62]

The faddish explosion of consumerism surrounding the Klan was symptomatic of a U.S. advertising industry that, while substantial before, had spectacularly mushroomed in the 1920s. During the course of this decade, the United States had emerged as an economically booming consumer-oriented society, with members driven by the pursuit of a heretofore unattainable level of prosperity, pleasure, and possibility. Advertisers and salesmen "assaulted the older virtues of thrift and prudence," and it was "consumption, not hard work and self-restraint [which] became the path to

"Klan-Lite, the wonder lamp for American homes"
Source: *Dawn*, 8 December 1923, 24

fortune and personal happiness." Not simply selling products, "but qualities like social prestige, which the possession of the products would allegedly secure," the insistent efforts of advertising men ensured that "conspicuous consumption had become a national mania" throughout this period.[63] As the idea of personal debt began to lose the stigma of shame it had once carried around, a huge rise in installment buying was encouraged by advertisers' calls to "buy now, pay later." Prospective customers were bombarded with desirable imagery, with slogans, with promises of efficiency, of low cost, of status-enhancing qualities. Commercials increasingly colonized not just the pages of town and city newspapers, but highway billboards, radio airtime, movie intermissions, and the glossy lifestyle magazines that had found their way into American homes. Suddenly, the art of capturing the public's attention and convincing it of the virtues of all manner of products and services, in every conceivable variation, became big business. In this golden commercial era, it must have seemed that nothing was impossible. As Zelda Fitzgerald, wife of great Jazz Age novelist F. Scott Fitzgerald, once noted, "We grew up founding our dreams on the infinite promises of American advertising . . . I still believe that one can learn to play the piano by mail and that mud will give you a perfect complexion."[64]

These were heady days for the fast-growing occupation of professional salesman, which "rose to new levels as a career [and] . . . was widely proclaimed as one of the easiest ways to make money in a decade when the earning of money seemed the highest goal."[65] Magazines and newspapers featured articles on the art of salesmanship, and a new generation of career salesmen came into their own, with an increasing number of American colleges beginning to run courses specifically geared toward sales techniques. Modern methods of selling were unapologetically aggressive, placing much emphasis upon personal psychology and upon skillful manipulation of the "prospect." In a heavily result-oriented business, that of creating a market for an ever-burgeoning line of commercial products, the idea was not to serve the customer, but to make the most of opportunities, to thoroughly convince, and above all, to sell. Assertive and confident, the successful salesman was a revered figure, a symbol of optimism and prosperity. As a national image, he came to represent all that was vital and charismatic about self-assured masculine Americanism. In the words of Sinclair Lewis's *Babbitt*, this new and impressive American salesman was "the real He-man, the fellow with Zip and Bang," quite typical of a modern breed of "fellows with hair on their chests and smiles in their eyes and adding machines in their offices."[66]

A thriving market for Klan-themed commercial products offered one way into this world of apparent opportunity, prestige, and moneymaking. Ads in Klan organs frequently carried the postscript "Agents wanted," soliciting men—and not necessarily Klansmen—to put themselves forward as regional salesmen for whichever line of KKK trinkets happened to be in vogue at the time. One such ad promised agents "100 per cent profit selling the Flaming Fiery Cross scarf pin," while another urged its readers to "make money selling the *Fiery Cross* . . . agents wanted in every town and city . . . to increase circulation of America's greatest patriotic newspaper." The Empire Publishing Company in Detroit similarly beseeched prospective regional sellers of the *Klan Kourier* to "help the Klan and make money." A December 1923 notice in *Dawn* even went so far as to advertise for "Klan organizers," stipulating that such men "must be of exceptionally high character, unusual ability," and willing to provide both "complete details of personal and business life . . . [and] references from men of unquestioned standing." Those able to prove their acceptability "will be given a real opportunity in northern Illinois."[67]

All manner of non-Klan businesses, too, advertised for sales representatives in the pages of Klan organs. Typically, recruitment material featured appealing, if unlikely, rags-to-riches success stories:

> Only a short time ago I was practically broke . . . I worked in a factory. I was not the owner, not the superintendent, not the boss. I was a wage-earner . . . a slave to my job—no real money, no real future . . . Today I am a successful businessman. I have a large income, money, investments. I have hundreds and hundreds of friends. I get a lot of pleasure out of life. I have no boss. I work just four hours a day and only five days a week . . . I have succeeded beyond any dreams I may have had a few years ago. And please remember I consider myself only an average man. There is no secret to my success . . . I am the local representative for the Comer Manufacturing Company.

The particular company in question actually specialized in the production and sale of nothing more glamorous than "all-weather raincoats." Its ads, however, outlined the multiple testimonies of successful company salesmen who had gone before, invariably weaving magical yarns of new and exciting lives, of adventurous men quitting the drudgery of their old jobs in favor of seemingly effortless existences packed with wealth and accomplishment. Only too happy to ply its trade in the Michigan KKK press, this company showcased a "special offer to Klansmen," pledging in a brash quarter-page commercial to "offer you $200 a week," and setting up any willing Knight in business for himself within a matter of days. Not only this, but "in addition to your big earnings we offer you a Buick touring car, without a cent of cost, that you can use to help you in developing this great business." Far from unusual, other similarly themed ads appeared regularly in the regional Klan papers, with the B. E. Taylor Company of Detroit, for instance, offering a proposition to "100% salesmen wishing to learn [the] real estate business."[68]

From examples such as these, it seems clear that up-and-coming Klan entrepreneurs, while offered many commercial opportunities in Klan-related industries, were sometimes explicitly recruited, via direct appeal to their KKK connections, to work in fields not necessarily associated with the order. Indeed, a large number of the advertisers in Michigan Klan organs, though seemingly unconnected with the order in any way, were nevertheless eager to adopt the distinctive triple-K moniker. Dozens of Klannish slogans littered the pages of the Michigan *Fiery Cross*, peddling everything from food and drink ("Kwality Koffee Kounts," "Kones-Kream-Kandy") to clothing ("Kaufman's Kampus Klothes," "Klassy Kut Kaps") to fuel ("Kind Kareful Kurteous coal," "Klean Klinkerless Koal for Kranky Kustomers") to motoring ("Krippled Kars Kured," "Korrect Kar Kleaner Kleans Kars Kwick Keeps Kars Klean") and even laundry services ("Kromer Klean Klothes," "Klean Klansman's Klothes," "Kareful Klothes Kleaners"). Sensing an opportunity to curry favor among Klansmen, opportunistic business owners simply jumped, quite overtly, on the commercial Klan bandwagon. Many others did the same thing in a slightly more subtle way, with a host of unremarkable businesses including hardware stores, barber shops, undertakers, chiropractors, restaurants, poultry dealers, grocery stores, and electrical contractors, to mention but a few, very commonly tipping a hat to the Klan cause by promising "100% service."

Incredibly, this was not the first time that the Klan's peculiar image had exerted such a fashionable influence. As Philip Dray has pointed out, even back in the Reconstruction-era South, where the original KKK emerged, there were instances of a similar sort of cultural and commercial absorption with the organization. "Despite, or rather because of [Nathan Bedford] Forrest's notoriety," he writes, "interest in the Klan soared. In Nashville, a children's baseball team took 'Ku Klux Klan' as its name, as did a circus and purveyors of a range of useful products, from knives to tobacco and even a kind of paint . . . the carryings-on of a mysterious masked brotherhood of avenging horsemen held strong appeal."[69] The spectacular rebirth of the Klan in the 1920s, however, saw public fascination with the Invisible Empire, not to mention the commercial opportunities afforded by such fascination, reach unprecedented heights. In addition to Klan-related merchandise, official and otherwise, the philosophical argument over the fast-expanding organization's place within society provided a ready market for pamphleteers. Self-appointed authorities on the Klan emerged from every corner, each offering their own book-length, apparently impartial debate pieces for public sale, with titles such as *Faults and Virtues of the KKK; Catholic, Jew, KKK: What They Believe, Where They Conflict;* and *Is the KKK Constructive or Destructive?* So long as interest could be maintained, and the Klan issue upheld as a hot, sensationalist topic, then there was always profit to be had in perpetuating the debate, with mass production of tabloid-like printed matter both for and against.

Even those who claimed staunch opposition to the Klan stood to gain financially from vast popular interest in the movement, a fact typified by the appearance of countless muckraking exposés. The titles of Lem Dever's *Masks Off!: Confessions of an Imperial Klansman,* and Marion Monteval's *The Klan Inside Out,* to name two prominent examples, are suitably self-explanatory. Penned by alleged ex-officers or undercover infiltrators, they offered, for a price, to lift the lid on the order's sinister secrets (in much the same way, in fact, that the Klan itself was doing with its anti-Catholic "ex-nun" stories). One of the KKK's most vocal and visible critics was Aldrich Blake of Oklahoma City, whose energetic denunciations of the order saw him packing lecture halls across the nation as well as releasing his lecture notes for sale in published form. The title of Blake's famous anti-Klan speech, *The Ku Klux Kraze,* summed up brilliantly and succinctly the money-making, mystery-shrouded phenomenon that had come to grip the nation. "There is no reason in it . . . it is purely psychological," argued Blake. "The Ku Klux Klan is a craze—as much so as the one-piece bathing suit, Ma Jongg, and bobbed hair. When a man joins the Ku Klux Klan a sensation seems to come over him as definite as falling in love. He simply drops out of society and enters a new world."[70] Though overtly scornful of the Klan's shallow enthrallment of the public, it was a "Kraze" from which Blake benefited directly, and which, through the popularity of his lectures, he was partly responsible for maintaining. Indeed, for the many who had something to say, or more to the point, to sell on the subject—the novelty of which would begin to fade and disappear as the decade passed its mid-point—the time was ripe to exploit a curious, and paying, audience in whose imaginations the ambiguous figure of the Klansman had been planted.

Systematically sold and evidently meeting with interest in virtually every part of the state, the Ku Klux Klan clearly developed a real presence in 1920s Michigan, the magnitude of which has never really been fully recognized. In one sense, the fact that Michiganians (and Americans in general) were so taken with the Klan in this period can be seen as a function of the emergent consumer culture of which they were a part, a world in which the salesman was king, and the KKK had become the latest in fashionable novelty. Driven often by slick advertising, the real life and energy of the Klan "Kraze" emerged not so much in the order's solemn principals, but in the opportunistic merchandizing fad that surrounded its distinctive image: the elaborate robes donned at cloak-and-dagger Klannish meetings; the colorful parades, banners, and flags; the novels, song sheets, fireworks, jewelry, toys, or even table lamps that came as part and parcel of association with the order. It was in this arena, certainly, that the fun was to be had; here where otherwise sleepy small towns, normally starved of excitement, temporarily became parade grounds of the mysterious Invisible Empire; here that the coffee shops and laundry services adopted the triple-K moniker to boost popularity; and here that Klan iconography ultimately became run-of-the-mill, acquiring a status so commonplace and banal as to be able to enter America's consciousness and homes with relatively little fuss. In another sense, it was the organization's stated principles, rather than its outward trappings, that had allowed it to prosper. The conservative, moralistic, and patriotic ideals to which the KKK clung, after all, were not distinctively its own, but largely those of the much wider white Protestant culture so abundant within Michigan. With this in mind, it should be no surprise that the Klan found such easy coexistence, and some degree of social approval, in such a setting. Though the novelty element of the KKK would inevitably wear thin before long, the culture and the values that had underpinned it, had found expression and even celebration through it, would endure well beyond the days of white sheets and fiery crosses. If nothing else, the Klan was, in its own much-repeated words, a "one hundred percent American" organization.

The Knights in Image and Idea

Popular Klannish Fantasy, Self-Portrayal, and Political Demonology

THE 1920S VERSION OF THE KU KLUX KLAN WAS HIGHLY CONSCIOUS of its place in the popular imagination, seeking above all else to convince the American public of its good intentions, and in doing so gain the wider social acceptance that would allow it to thrive. Klan promoters took particular care to create positive associations for the order, which, in essence, meant a public alignment with the traditional values of conservative white America, and an emphasis upon wholesome morality, pious Protestantism, and dutiful patriotic service. As a background to this, the phenomenal popularity of D. W. Griffith's epic 1915 movie *The Birth of a Nation* had already done much to crystallize the popular image of the Invisible Empire as a force for good, or at least for "Americanism." Not only did it depict the historical Klansmen of the Reconstruction days as heroes, but as the very saviors of a threatened white American nation. The influential film, by all accounts "the most widely seen single cultural document of the industrial age," was well received by millions nationwide.[1] Often credited as the direct inspiration for the formation of the new Klan, *Birth* certainly became a staple of KKK recruitment drives, and its heroic Klansmen a template for the modern organization's self-projections.

The modern Klan movement, too, would find other ways of engaging mass popular audiences, producing its own movies, plays, and romance novels, as well as participating forcefully in the forum of public debate. All of these avenues provided accessible, and in many respects entertaining, vehicles by which the Klan could promote not only its heroic notions of self but also its corresponding portrayals of sinister and demonic "enemies." In

1920s Michigan, as in much of the northern United States at this time, the hooded order's agenda was religious rather than racial in focus, and its ire directed much more politically than physically. Reveling in its self-appointed position as "defender of Americanism" (or, at least, its own conception of Americanism), the Klan took mainstream and legitimate concerns and populated them with worrisome, if caricatured, specters of foreign villainy. Propelling its fantasies of ungodly international conspiracy into the public domain, the Klan unleashed its sinister and, crucially, "un-American" creations to wreak havoc in the political shadows of a nation already wrestling anxiously with the notion of the "melting pot."

GUARDIANS OF LIBERTY:
POPULAR IMAGES OF A HEROIC KLAN

In January 1924, a front-page headline in Newaygo County's *Fremont Times-Indicator* heralded the imminent arrival of an "epoch-making spectacle" at the town's Ideal Theatre. Describing "D. W. Griffith's Masterpiece, *The Birth of a Nation*," the writer added rather grandly that there was "no explanation necessary for this picture," and insisted that it should be shown to everybody in and near Fremont. Griffith's film, read the Fremont weekly, though now a decade old, "has excited keener curiosity than any other offering" in cinema, and arrived in Newaygo County on the crest of an enthusiastic nationwide revival, the highlight of which had seen 150,000 people attend showings during a recent two-week "record-breaking return to New York." Depicting the traumatic Reconstruction days that had followed the American Civil War, the movie not only claimed a thorough historical accuracy, but also credited the KKK with a key role in the nation's reunification. As the *Times-Indicator* noted, the crowning glory of the script revolved around lavish scenes detailing a heroic "uprising of the Ku Klux Klan and the overthrow of the carpetbagger regime." Compounding this rosy portrayal, meanwhile, was a love interest, featuring "Ben Cameron, the gallant Clansman . . . in the role of romantic hero"—the Southerner's affection for a northern maiden eventually overcoming regional conflict, uniting feuding families on either side of the Mason-Dixon Line, and symbolically restoring national harmony.[2]

It was certainly no coincidence that such a positive representation of Klan heroism should be put on public display in Fremont at this time. The 1920s version of the Invisible Empire had made its entrance into Newaygo County less than six months before, and had very recently begun to recruit heavily in Fremont itself. In such an atmosphere, the local response to *The Birth of a Nation*'s return to the silver screen was evidently an enthusiastic one, and the proprietor of the Ideal Theatre—himself a Klansman—would be compelled to bring the film back for yet another run just a few months later. Perhaps mindful of the number of Klan converts in the vicinity, the *Fremont Times-Indicator* promoted the film's latest run, and pointed to its patriotic significance, in words reminiscent of any contemporary KKK pamphlet:

> Its continued popularity lends color to the claim that the men who conceived and executed it built into it something that is expressive of the vital American spirit of the land, something true to the hearts and minds of all Americans . . . the great picture, now ten years old seems to have well proved by its recent runs in all parts of the country that it has lost nothing of its power to grip and hold the audiences that see it . . . no effort has been made to do other than present a true story of the times, and each scene is historically correct and painstakingly accurate . . . *The Birth of a Nation.* "An American film for Americans."[3]

In other Newaygo County towns, too, the very real rise of the new Klan organization was accompanied by the movie glorifying a "historic," romanticized vision of its Reconstruction forebear. During June 1924, for instance, the *Newaygo Republican* reported that "a large crowd gathered in White Cloud Thursday night to see the free picture show." This, though, was no ordinary movie screening—coinciding with the heaviest month of Klan recruitment that the town of White Cloud would ever see, and distinctively marked by the fact that "a cross was burned just as the show was out."[4] The town of Newaygo, similarly, had hosted multiple showings of *The Birth of a Nation* as the Klan grew there, with the *Republican* never missing an opportunity to sing the movie's praises both as a spectacle and a work of real social importance. As well as being "a picture with a thousand thrills," it was "the picture that millions have seen again and again, that more millions will see, that you MUST see; that you are sure you want to see again even if you have already seen it once, or even twice before." Despite its age, declared the *Republican*, this was still "the greatest and most enduring motion picture ever produced . . . it shows how this country fought inhumanity, treachery, political stupidity, and WON!" Bringing together the heroic celluloid Klan with its modern material equivalent was Newaygo's Park Theatre, whose proprietor, just like his counterpart in Fremont, was a dues-paying member of the local Klavern. Not only did his theater host all of the town's screenings of *Birth*, it also served as a welcoming public venue for official Klan speakers visiting town in search of a sympathetic audience.[5]

The cultural impact of *The Birth of a Nation* is difficult to overstate—its 1915 release, according to a multitude of sources, marking the beginning of modern cinema itself. With a script based upon the hugely popular, though deeply white-supremacist novels of Thomas Dixon (most notably *The Clansman: An Historical Romance of the Ku Klux Klan*),[6] Griffith created a technically unprecedented cinematic experience. At a time when most films were merely nickelodeon novelties, lasting perhaps just thirty minutes over three or four reels, Griffith used twelve reels, bringing Dixon's bigoted themes to the public in a romantic tale running almost three hours long. With prodigious talent and "a skill that was to shape the creative techniques of the industry," Griffith invented and employed methods that "changed movies forever." Before *Birth*, "even the most highly regarded films were little more than a series of long shots and static tableaux, featuring stage acting and a camera that remained in one location." Griffith, however, "moved the camera along different planes, cut scenes short, dissolved from tearful close-up to panoramic battle scene—in essence, took control of the narrative film medium in a way no one had before."[7] Most memorable and enduring of his visual effects was the triumphant ride of the chivalrous Klan, cast in the role of crusading heroes, protectors of white womanhood, and saviors of the American nation. In the words of journalist Walter Lippmann in 1922, "No one who has seen the film will ever hear the name [Ku Klux Klan] again without seeing those white horsemen."[8] Griffith himself, when questioned on the title of his movie, made no secret of the historical credit he had given to the Invisible Empire. "The birth of a nation began," he replied, "with the Ku Klux Klans, and we have shown that."[9]

Despite its controversial racial content, plaudits had immediately rolled in for the picture, *Vanity Fair* hailing "a remarkable film" that "must undoubtedly command a certain admiration." Popular journalist Dorothy Dix, meanwhile, called it "history vitalized" and urged others to "go see it, for it will make a better American of you."[10] Opponents of the movie, notably members of the National Association for the Advancement of Colored People (NAACP), mounted protests that were spirited, but ultimately doomed to failure in the face of popular enthusiasm for a product touted as "the eighth wonder of the world" and "the most wonderful movie ever made." The President of the United States himself, Virginia-born Woodrow Wilson, received a private showing of *Birth* in the White House in February 1915. Watching "spellbound," surrounded by his family, his cabinet, Dixon, and Griffith, he was thrilled by the conjured images of renegade ex-slaves and conquering Klan horsemen. His response was rapturous—"It is like writing history with lightning," he enthused, "and my only regret is that it is all so terribly true." *Birth* was later voted "the greatest motion picture in the first fifty years of the industry" by a *Variety* poll of two hundred film critics. Even at a hefty $2 admission fee, the crowds turned out in sellout droves, breaking theater attendance records in city after city across the nation. By 1927, over 50 million Americans had paid to see the film, "millions more people than had ever seen any other movie, more than would see any other movie for half a century."[11]

As Philip Dray has pointed out, at the time of *The Birth of a Nation*'s release, "no-one yet felt comfortable saying how significant or powerful a societal force film really was . . . it was not clear how and to what extent viewers related what they saw on screen to real life."[12] Almost a decade later, as Newaygo County was preparing to receive Griffith's film for anything but the first time, the discussion continued. Making his point in the *White Cloud Eagle*, a local pastor warned of the potential dangers. "Many serious minded people have become not a little concerned," he wrote, "over the fact that the motion picture has gained such a hold on the public mind . . . especially upon the minds of the youth."[13] Reformer and NAACP board member Jane Addams, after witnessing raucous crowds "roused to the point of clapping enthusiastically . . . whenever the Ku Klux Klan appeared," publicly judged *Birth* in particular to be "full of danger,"[14] and the palpable fear of this kind of viewpoint was that the film would somehow arouse a literal return to the Klan's night-riding mythical past.

In a certain sense, that fear found realization when William Simmons of Atlanta, Georgia, founded the second Invisible Empire within a short time of the movie's initial release. Very definitely inspired by the Klan epic's popular appeal, Simmons placed ads for his fledgling order beside those for showings of the film, and "feeding on the excitement, Klan recruiters worked the theater lobbies."[15] That the growth of the 1920s Klan was influenced by a popular culture that generally regarded the Klan in a positive light seems plain. Tellingly, the one symbol that came more than any other to epitomize the KKK did not come from the original, historical organization at all. The infamous fiery cross, instead, "emerged from the fertile imagination of Thomas Dixon,"[16] and represented a sure sign of his inspiration to the modern order. That a ten-year-old Klan blockbuster continued to prosper in Newaygo County while local citizens signed up by the hundreds, too, tells its own story. As William Randel has noted, "Without the novels glorifying the Klan, and without the film that one of them became, it may well be doubted whether the modern Klan would have been born."[17]

Accompanying the arrival of the 1920s version of the Ku Klux Klan was a glut of laudatory literature designed to promote the order and build up its positive public image. The Invisible Empire portrayed here was both righteous and self-sacrificing, a band of proud Protestant crusader-Knights dedicated to the defense of the American realm and its noble ideals of freedom and democracy. The Klansman himself was a picture of rugged masculinity—a chivalrous, decisive hero figure to whom the protection of family, home, and "pure American womanhood" was all-important. Declaring an unconditional love of the U.S. flag and Constitution, as well as the Christian Bible, his associations were entirely wholesome. Crucially, his concerns were very much in line with the traditional conservative values of white Protestant America, paying lip service to law and order, to free public schools, to regular church attendance, to patriotic duty, and to old-time morality.

Typical of the genre were the publications of crusading evangelist Bishop Alma White, founder of the Pillar of Fire Church, which had branches spanning the nation as well as a number of overseas mission establishments. In addition to editing the rabidly anti-Catholic periodical *The Good Citizen*, White published lengthy tracts including *Heroes of the Fiery Cross* and *Klansmen: Guardians of Liberty*, which honored the KKK and credited the men in white with far-fetched acts of nation-saving heroism.[18] Appearing alongside icons of Americanism such as Uncle Sam, Paul Revere, and George Washington, and often accompanied by an open Bible or Star-Spangled Banner, the Klan tackled modern issues including corrupt "Roman" influence in politics and the enforcement of prohibition.

Placing the Klan directly in league with the Christian God, too, White's *The Ku Klux Klan in Prophecy* drew direct links between the Klan and the Bible, using passages from Scripture that purportedly supported and justified the Invisible Empire and denounced its "pagan," "primitive," and "superstitious" Catholic adversaries. Her language and imagery warned explicitly of looming apocalyptic religious warfare, and according to the book's introduction, White had "long been considered one of the foremost warriors in the battle between light and darkness," and aimed here to "bring out vividly the titanic struggle now taking place."[19]

Imperial Wizard Hiram Evans was similarly keen to stress his Klan's biblical inspiration. "The apostle Paul, in his epistle to the Romans," he reasoned, "carries the ideal of Klannishness to its highest levels, and in the twelfth chapter of that great exposition . . . he sets up a standard of character and of conduct by which every true Klansman must measure his life." The ideal Klansman, in Evans's words, would lead an existence driven by "dedication of life to a service of sacrifice," and possess a character in which "egotism dies, and esteem and considerateness of others become dominant."[20] KKK literature held up the Son of God as an exemplary template,

UNCLE SAM: "WE DON'T NEED YOU IN THE U. S."

An illustration from *Klansmen: Guardians of Liberty*
Source: Michigan State University Special Collections

and the much-repeated phrase "Christ is a Klansman's Criterion of Character" was used often and widely in pro-Klan tracts.[21]

Significantly, Wizard Evans's version of Christ was a rugged, masculine one. This Christ "was fit," he was "a robust, toil-marked young man who had conserved both his physical and mental strength," a proud example of the standard of manhood required for the Klan's mission.[22] Furthermore, it was only such fine and worthy specimens who were truly able to heed the pioneering call of the Klan's militant American Protestantism. In the words of Imperial Klazik Brown Harwood, "the spirit of Klankraft is bringing untold thousands of big, manly men into the fellowship of Klankraft and filling the pews of Protestant churches throughout America . . . The rich, red blood of American patriots and Mourned Martyrs runs through your veins." Only the weak and the corrupt, the "degenerate sons of illustrious sires" would betray their heritage and fail to rise to the task of defending Protestant America.[23]

In the Klan's own hazy and sentimental portrayals, the Invisible Empire's myth of origin saw it indelibly identified with the spirit of those who had founded the American nation. The essence of Klankraft was entwined with U.S. history at all points, evidenced in its most poignant moments and visible in the actions of its most influential and inspiring figures. The gathering of masked participants for the Boston Tea Party, for example, was hailed in official literature as "the first Ku Klux Klan meeting on record." The spirit of such men was apparently "a thing of rugged steel," a psychic relic of the pioneer experience, "tempered and forged in the terrific stress of the task of wresting a continent from savages and from the wilderness . . . It is welded of convictions, independence, self-reliance, freedom, justice, achievement, courage, acceptance of responsibility, and the guidance of his own conscience by each man personally." This enduring "traditional American spirit, the Americanism of the pioneers," declared Evans in a 1925 *Forum* interview, "has been bound up from the first with the spirit of Protestantism . . . [which] is a vital part of all Americanism, of all successful democracy." Customarily employing such broad platitudes, Evans had earlier stated, through an article in *Kourier* magazine, a bold belief that "the Klan has become the leader and trustee of Americanism" and that "defeat for the Klan means defeat for Americanism."[24] By neatly equating Protestantism with Americanism, and Americanism with the Klan, champions of the Invisible Empire left the order's detractors, and indeed all non-Protestants, wide open to accusations of disloyalty to the nation at a time when xenophobic paranoia was rife, and questions of patriotism and allegiance paramount.

Inspired by the earlier literary successes of Thomas Dixon and *The Birth of a Nation*, the modern-day knights set about bringing their own sympathetic vision of the KKK to the broadest audience possible. Hoping to popularize and integrate this vision into the cultural mainstream, they utilized fashionable mass entertainment forms as a vehicle. Particularly common was Klan literature that adopted the conventions of the romance novel, typically employing a Klansman in the role of clean-cut, physically impressive, and chivalrous hero; his sweetheart as an example of virtuous, chaste, and vulnerable American womanhood; and the wholesome love between the two threatened by a corrupt and cunning enemy whose chief evil lay in his sinister un-Americanism. *Knight Vale of the KKK* was exactly such a novel, billed as "a fiction story of love, patriotism, intrigue and adventure" and cast in the exciting cloak-and-dagger Klan world of the twenties, amid illegal bootleggers, scheming immigrant politicians, and libelous, crooked newspapermen. Throughout the novel, wider debates over "alien" elements in society—namely, the "Roman hierarchy" and the "international Jew"—were played out in speculative conversation between main characters. The cast of villains, meanwhile—including debauched priests, unscrupulous vote-controlling Catholic city officials, petty criminals directed to pose as Klansmen, and businessmen bought by the Roman Church—amply demonstrated the depravity and corruption that the Klan claimed was rife in non-Protestant faiths.

Initially skeptical, protagonist Fairfax Vale is won over to the Klan only when confronted with undeniable, first-hand proof of the horrible and bloodthirsty Catholic plot to destroy America. Striking close to his own heart, the Roman menace forces him into action when his sweetheart is duped, kidnapped, and imprisoned in a convent, never to return to the free world outside. Unperturbed, Fairfax (abbreviated to "Fair," reflecting the Klan's idea of itself) is exhilarated at the opportunity to perform his duty, which "has always seemed to me to be rescuing some fair maiden from the hands of villains and assassins who would rob her of her most priceless treasures." Needless to say, with the help of his brother Klansmen, Vale soon stages a daring rescue, snatching back his helpless love from the clutches of the seemingly impenetrable convent. Having saved her, in more than one sense, he lovingly wraps her shivering, naked form in his Klan robe, setting up a final few lines that strive, like the Klan of its time, to somehow intermingle Protestant righteousness, romantic sentimentality, and an all-conquering American patriotism:

> As he approached the unmounted horse at the head of the parade he was heard to shout "The Star Spangled banner, Say—does she still wave?" And as he mounted his waiting steed with his burden in his arms the first noise from the long mounted line broke onto the stillness—a great, a rousing cheer. "Yes. Yes, knight Vale—She still waves!" and with the words the gorgeous folds of Old Glory were unfurled over the knight and the rescued maiden . . . with wet eyes pressed against a woman's cheek he was thanking God.[25]

Here, as in similar prominent titles such as *The Final Awakening*, *A Klansman's Loyalty*, and *Harold the Klansman*, the romantic literary Klansman found himself portrayed as noble Knight and protector.[26] In that sense, he was reasserting a symbolic claim to a position that he was in real danger of losing in the real, rapidly modernizing, morally ambivalent world—that of lord and master, defender, protector, even controller of "pure American womanhood." The Invisible Empire's clear-cut projections also very plainly delineated good and bad, light and dark, Protestant honor and Catholic corruption, and provided an unambiguous, simplified, and accessible image of the "enemy" for wider public consumption. The enormity and clearly demonstrated evil of the alien threat gave the literary Klansman free license to dispense of his own, and by association America's, despicable foes by whatever means necessary.

Having broadened its appeal through the medium of romantic fantasy, fictionalizing both itself and its enemies in the process, there was also a sense in which the Klan sought to ground its material in authentic, everyday life—to reel its cartoon imagery back in and relate it in a meaningful sense to its audiences' experience. *Harold the Klansman*, according to its sales publicity, "is a wholesome love story—fascinating in interest"; but as well as merely entertaining, the novel also aimed at "making plain the real purpose and practices of the Ku Klux Klan." Readers were assured, too, that "you will enjoy an acquaintance with the characters in this story, they are types of men and women who are found in every village and city." Taking the idea of social authenticity to its extremes, one reviewer even claimed that "*Harold the Klansman* is a great social novel destined to make its impress on the thought of America, and in years to come it will be one of the great historical novels of this generation."[27]

In the Chicago theater scene, too, the Central Amusement Company claimed to be staging "the most talked about play in America" with their extravagant production *The Invisible Empire*. Tapping into the popularity of earlier stage and screen triumphs, it was billed as "a sequel to *The Clansman* . . . a modern American mystery play presented by a RECOGNIZED BROADWAY CAST and a scenic production of unusual beauty." Running initially for a three-week season, "*The Invisible Empire* is to the speaking stage what *The Birth of a Nation* has been to the screen." Not only this, but the play also came with a social agenda, given its bootlegger- and speakeasy-ridden surroundings. This show, wrote a *Dawn* reviewer, "should be seen by every man and woman in Chicago." Its plot, in which "the evil influence [has] the upper hand and the strong arm of the law [is] not in [a] position to give protection . . . is very adaptable to the present situation in Chicago."[28]

In the summer of 1923, the *Imperial Night-Hawk* reported on an ambitious project that aimed to raise the Klan's cultural profile to new heights. "*Armageddon*, a motion picture which will depict the patriotic work of the knights of the Ku Klux Klan," read the report, "will be a stupendous spectacle dealing with the modern-day Klan. In some of the scenes several thousand Klansmen will participate." Not only this, but "D. W. Griffith will be asked to direct it and motion picture stars of international fame will take the leading roles."[29] Whether the project ever materialized is unclear, but it turned out to be just one of many similar offerings, with Klan movies *The Toll of Justice* and *The Traitor Within* translating the themes of Klan romance novels to the silver screen, and bringing the Klansman-hero to large crowds in towns all over Michigan and Indiana.

In Michigan's rural Newaygo County, *The Toll of Justice* made much-publicized appearances in both Fremont and Newaygo at a time when the local Klan unit was operating at the peak of its numerical strength. The Newaygo screening took place at the Klan-run Park Theatre, which would also host open KKK meetings and reruns of *The Birth of a Nation*. Noting an entertaining feature "full of laughs, thrills and heart throbs," the *Newaygo Republican* was also generous in its praise of the film's more serious message, describing

> a lesson in Patriotism, which arouses in the bosom of the sturdy youth a love for his native flag and causes the blood of the old to flow with new zest. It carries you through the various periods of militant American history and grips you from the outset as one of the very cleanest pieces of American fiction ever produced. This production is sponsored by the Ku Klux Klan and designed to acquaint the uninformed public with the true principles of the organization and counteract the poisonous propaganda circulated by alien enemies who have declared their determination to wipe out the Klan.[30]

Over in Fremont, meanwhile, anticipation of the "Big Klan picture" was such that the film was shown not in the movie theater, but in the much more public surroundings of the community building. "Depicting the work of the Ku Klux Klan," enthused the *Fremont Times-Indicator*, "it is said to be the greatest American photo-play since *The Birth of a Nation*." Not only this, but it featured an "all star cast" and "is filled with love, mystery, intrigue and thrills of many degrees." The plot itself was a predictable one, revolving around "the love affair of a manufacturer's daughter" caught between two suitors. Instinctively, "she prefers the upright manly qualities of Thomas Grant," a chivalrous member of the Invisible Empire, but is instead taken in by the charms of the villainous "Haskell, who poses as a stock broker." With "Americanism" triumphing by the story's end, the scoundrel's corruption becomes clear in the heinous revelation that "in reality he is king of a gang of drug addicted bootleggers."[31]

The resemblance between Klan creations and fashionable literature of the age is often a striking one, and Sean McCann has pointed out that Klan material and the emerging American genre of "hard-boiled" crime fiction, in particular, "developed in close proximity." Such fiction, whose pioneers included Dashiell Hammett and Carroll John Daly, appeared regularly in the pages of magazines that were also busily debating the moral rights and wrongs of the Klan. The concerns of the two were also linked by a common, moralistic theme:

> Like the jaundiced private detective, [the Klan] spotted the signs of corruption in urban vice and moral decline. And, like the hard-boiled heroes, Klansmen imagined that the only effective response to social ills was a form of vigilante justice that imposed order on the confusions of an urbanizing society . . . in both . . . the American city was riven by illicit sexuality, corruption and crime—closely linked forms of social disarray that demanded the control of vigilant men.

While the Klan and hard-boiled crime fiction eventually "developed different answers" to their common concerns, the huge subsequent success of the peculiarly American detective story, with which the Klan had "competed on the same ground during the twenties," does imply the presence of a broad popular appeal and enthusiastic mainstream audience.[32]

ENEMY AT THE GATES: THE INVISIBLE EMPIRE BATTLES IMMIGRATION AND IMMORALITY

The popular image of the Klansman in the mid-1920s, though eliciting nothing like the universally negative response that it would justifiably receive in later decades, was still a controversial one. The sheer and sudden popularity of the movement at its brief peak—with millions flocking to join—made it an issue of huge public interest, and from the outset, the Klan had many fierce opponents who charged its members with ignorance and religious bigotry. Counteracting these were its many allies and members, drawn in by talk of moral reform, law and order, and prohibition enforcement, whose presence makes it difficult to dismiss the 1920s organization (unlike every Klan group since that time) as marginal or inherently extremist. During this period, the KKK became the hot debate topic of the times. National newspapers hostile to the movement denounced it and frequently ran exposés on alleged masked violence in some Southern states. The Klan replied with claims that it was victim to a barrage of abuses and inventions on the part of an unfairly biased Catholic- and Jewish-controlled press.

An official congressional investigation of the Klan's affairs, brought about by pressure from an antagonistic press, and in particular the *New York World*, failed to uncover anything concrete with which to charge the organization, and instead served only to provide the secret order with priceless nationwide publicity.[33] Popular magazines devoted generous space to the Klan issue, giving free rein to the arguments on either side of the debate. Just a few illustrative examples include *Current History*, which ran the Imperial Wizard's article "The Catholic Question As Viewed by the KKK," while *Literary Digest* gave the case "For and Against the KKK," and the *Forum* asked, "Is the KKK Un-American?" Book-length pieces such as *Does the USA need the K.K.K?* quickly found their way into the public domain, as did *Is the KKK Constructive or Destructive?*—a printed debate between prominent Jewish intellectual Israel Zangwill (who, incidentally, coined the term "the melting pot") and the Klan's Imperial Wizard.[34] The battleground was national, and opinions were polarized. Was the KKK right or wrong? Good or bad? Did it serve the best interests of America or undermine the fundamental values of the republic? The fact that these and similar questions were considered so widely and taken so seriously says one thing above all others—that the Klan during its remarkable "popular" phase could be attacked, but it could not be ignored.[35]

The appearance of the mysterious organization in towns and cities across Michigan stirred both heady excitement and intense speculation.[36] Reporting colorfully upon the "Klan question" as viewed from the streets of Detroit was Kenneth Blass, a young Michigan Klansman who worked for the U.S. Postal Service in the growing metropolis during this period. A self-confessed and proud "small-town product," Blass had grown up around five miles outside of Newaygo County (in the rural outpost of Baldwin, Michigan) and retained social connections there. His parents were well-known in the county, having been married in White Cloud, and had also operated the Atlantic hotel in the town. Kenneth's uncle and cousin, too, were hoteliers in the town of Newaygo. Both were also members of the Newaygo County Klan. Having moved to Detroit for work, Blass himself experienced Klan membership from a more distinctly urban perspective than his Newaygo counterparts, and relayed his thoughts on the matter through an almost daily correspondence with his fiancée Marie back in the provinces.[37]

As a mail carrier working the city streets, Blass felt particularly closely connected to the ebb and flow of popular opinion, and was more than happy to take part in the often fractious business of debate. "In my daily life on the street and in the office," he writes, "I hear nothing that does not have some bearing on the present political situation . . . the main subject of discussion here is 'Klan' . . . from the newspapers and every chance acquaintance." The growth of the Invisible Empire, in Kenneth's words, "is the biggest question in the United States today, outside of law enforcement, and the two are connected more or less." Furthermore, "if a person is eligible . . . he's accused of belonging." On one occasion, Kenneth describes being witness to a skirmish on Woodward Avenue in downtown Detroit, in which a police riot squad "arrived and broke up a crowd of about 200 persons listening to a speech by a man denouncing the KKK"[38]

Lively discussion of the Klan was fueled by the easy availability of the organization's own news organs, including the *Michigan Kourier*, which Blass often, apparently, picks up on the way home.[39] Speaking from the podium and very often the pulpit, too, self-proclaimed experts of national reputation on both sides of the debate came to the city and invariably played to packed and excitable houses. In September of 1924, for instance, Blass looks forward with great anticipation as he and a group of friends make a social event of "going to St. Mark's Cathedral [to] hear Dr. Stidger talk about the KKK." Such is the huge popularity of the occasion, though, that his party is denied entry by a fire marshal's ruling, with both seating and standing room filled beyond safety capacity. Determined to "get in anyway, [even] if we can't get a seat," the excited young group sneak around to a side door and eventually manage to find a cramped spot from which to take in Dr. Stidger's speech, which does not disappoint their lofty expectations. Casting himself as an impartial observer, the eminent pastor "said there were some things . . . that he didn't think right about the Klan," although "he did laud the moral, intellectual and fighting qualities of Klan members." "Wish you could have heard him," enthuses Blass to his fiancée in that particular evening's letter; "people say they do not like to hear politics in church, but he sure does get the crowds."[40]

Klan-themed public events were scheduled with some regularity in Detroit. Within a few weeks of Stidger's speech, for example, Blass mentions a sensational exposé of the KKK by "Soap Box" Jack O'Brien (editor of the leading anti-Klan magazine *Tolerance*), as well as a visit to Detroit's Arena Gardens for the highly acclaimed lecture tour of top Klan opponent Aldrich Blake. Blake's speeches, based on condemnations of Klan violence in Oklahoma, were vastly popular and covered many U.S. cities where the Klan had a presence. Described authoritatively in promotional flyers as an "ORATOR, STUDENT, THINKER," Blake, in his 1924 election-season tour of the Wolverine State, visited Michigan cities including Eaton Rapids, Dewitt, and St. Ignace as well as Lansing and Detroit, and his standard speech was published and widely circulated as *The Ku Klux Kraze*.[41]

At the Detroit event, Blake's publicity and reputation saw another bumper crowd assembling, and Kenneth found himself among the six thousand unlucky stragglers who, failing to make it into the lecture hall, were left outside. According to the *Detroit Free Press* report the following day, this body of people was actually an aggressive pro-Klan crowd, deliberately assembled in protest of Blake's lecture, the presence of which they had taken as a "personal challenge" to their beliefs. Supposedly intent upon disturbance, the crowd had "exploded bombs that gave off nauseating smells," as well as blocking Woodward Avenue with their vehicles, filling the air with "the disquieting din of a thousand automobile horns." The police, "drawn in on a riot call from every precinct in the city," had apparently found it necessary "to draw their guns and wield their clubs in addition to making liberal use of tear gas before order was restored."[42] In sharp contrast to such accounts, Blass maintains that "there was not a hand raised in the whole affair against anyone and the crowd was just like a happy New Years, or any holiday crowd." Taking a view typical of Klansmen of his era wherever local media was hostile to or dismissive of the order, he points toward a sinister press conspiracy against the Invisible Empire. "The *Free Press*," he charges, "deliberately lies about the affair in several ways and the *Times* exaggerates considerably." The Klan's side of the story, according to Blass, "is altogether different from the daily papers . . . which really are most all controlled by Jews or Catholics."[43]

As this last comment hints, Klan aggression in 1920s Michigan was overwhelmingly directed against the Roman Catholic (and to a much lesser extent, Jewish) faith. Klan propagandists in Michigan shrewdly exploited a powerful underlying enmity toward Rome that had long been a feature in the state's history. At the root of this were the residual effects of the fiercely anti-Catholic "American Protective Association" of the 1890s, which had claimed the Midwest, and the city of Detroit in particular, as its stronghold. The Motor City had not only been home to the organization's national president and national secretary, but was also the publishing place of the "papal conspiracy" sheet *The Patriotic American*, the themes of which the Klan took up anew.[44] Though the KKK did not abandon completely the familiar ground of the "race problem," African Americans received relatively little attention in this period as (particularly outside of Detroit) they were perceived to pose very little imminent threat to white Protestant homogeneity. Citing the (at this time prevalent) theories of Ivy League–educated eugenicists Lothrop Stoddard and Madison Grant, Klan literature added an air of pseudoscientific legitimacy to its argument, declaring that the idea of a fundamental equality across the races had "been abandoned by all thoughtful men," so much so that it was hardly necessary to argue the point any further.[45] Instead, the Klan focused upon a much more pressing and actively malevolent foe, namely the non-Protestant immigrant, who would have his "otherness" defined primarily in religious rather than racial terms.[46]

It was the Klan's acrid anti-foreign rhetoric and openly virulent opposition to immigration that characterized its politics in the 1920s, and in no uncertain terms, it sought to curb a supposed tidal wave of immigration by non-Protestant "hordes" from the darker reaches of the globe. Particularly dangerous, it was claimed, were alien ideas and religious doctrines imported from Catholic Europe, which not only threatened the very basis of American cultural identity but also could be identified as the root cause of almost all of the great social and moral problems of the day.[47]

The city of Detroit, whose factories had attracted a large, recent influx of immigrant labor, and whose border with Canada had made it an important center for the bootlegging industry, was predictably fertile territory for the Klan's message.[48] In the thick of that very environment, Kenneth Blass had certainly absorbed the Klan line, claiming of Catholics that "people who owe allegiance to any foreign power are not as good citizens as those who look up to their own country next to God." Of Jews, similarly, he writes that "as a class [of] immigrants [they] are not good American citizens," urging his fiancée Marie that she "should read Henry Ford's little books on the Jews."[49] Explaining that "one of the principles of the Klan [is] to Americanize the immigrant," Kenneth goes on to lament the current situation in Detroit, and the harm done to the nation by the refusal of recent arrivals to assimilate to American ways:

> Look at the bunch of bums that have been brought or sent . . . over here the last ten to fifteen years . . . [I] don't think they are on the right track to finding the place, or holding it, that America and the United States should have in the world . . . Take a walk through the colored district, Corktown, Hamtramck, Chinatown . . . See if you think they are the type who made what the U.S. is today . . . they keep to their own kind continuously except when they can get some money or favors from the American suckers.

The KKK did, however, make certain distinctions. On the one hand were the unskilled, unwashed, irreligious labor agitators and anarchists, the morally and intellectually inferior undesirables, and "the refuse population of other lands." Coming as they did to "suck from [America's] Bosom" while deserving native-born sons were "pushed into the background," their great menace was to be found in their reluctance to assimilate into American society and religious practice. On the other hand were what the Klan saw as the more acceptable face of immigration, namely its own likely ancestors. Comparing "good" with "bad" immigrants, Blass asks, "How many Germantowns, Scotchtowns, Englishtowns, [or] Swedetowns did you ever hear of in Detroit or any other city? . . . The first generation born here was immediately absorbed . . . mainly because they were human tolerant, white, Protestant, gentile people."[50]

Far from representing an extreme viewpoint, the Klan line on immigration tapped into a very mainstream cultural vein in American life, and one that had been present long before the Invisible Empire came to town. Newaygo County's newspapers, for example, had long called for "immigration prohibition," the *Fremont Times-Indicator* back in 1920 claiming that "America is being made the dumping ground for the wrecks of the war and the hordes of radicals." It added, too, that "we cannot make a good American out of a foreigner" unless he understands that "American ideals and traditions must become a part of his life." On another occasion, the *Times-Indicator* had outlined "the kind of immigration we want," declaring that "we should take every precaution to see that none of the undesirable sort gets into this country." Similar articles in the *Newaygo Republican* warned of the dangers of Americans being "out-bred," and advised "closing the doors of immigration to foreign agitators." A Fremont Ford agency, meanwhile, which would shortly be owned and run by members of the Newaygo County Klan, proudly advertised itself as an outlet for Henry Ford's notoriously anti-Semitic *The Dearborn Independent*, which had made the "international Jew" a pet subject of discussion. "Henry Ford's ideas are sound. They work for him and they will work for you," the ad claimed. "*The Dearborn Independent* prints facts which other publications hesitate to publish. It is the chronicler of the neglected truth."[51]

Other prominent voices had also paved the way for the Klan's stance toward "Americanization." One of them was Woodrow Wilson, whose presidential voice had lent such legitimacy to *The Birth of a Nation* back in 1915. In wartime speeches, he had publicly attacked "citizens of the United States . . . born under other flags . . . who have poured the poison of disloyalty into the very arteries of our national life." Of particular concern was the "hyphenated American." According to Wilson, the hyphen was "the most un-American thing in the world." Taken as evidence of an immigrant's loyalty to his foreign home and doctrines over the institutions of America, the hyphen "looked to us like a snake . . . any man who carries a hyphen about with him carries a dagger that he is ready to plunge into the vitals of the republic."[52]

Likewise, the Klan's preferential treatment of certain nationalities over others merely echoed attitudes already apparent at the highest echelons of U.S. federal immigration policy. In his first message to Congress, President Calvin Coolidge had declared that "America must be kept American." In 1924 he signed the National Origins Act on immigration reform, which established a draconian nation-specific quota system, severely limiting the total annual number of new arrivals to the United States. As well as being in accordance with a general spirit of postwar superpatriotism, this discriminatory legislation was also credited as having a "scientific" basis, again given authenticity by the widespread popularity of eugenics theory.[53] Supposedly protecting the interests of the genetically endangered "founding" Nordic races, the act specifically reduced the influx of southern and eastern Europeans, whose number had been increasing steadily since the 1890s, and prohibited immigration from Asia completely. Meanwhile, the vast majority of the new 165,000 annual immigration quota was allocated to the British Isles, Germany, and other Northern European countries.

In the mushrooming cities, in particular, the KKK perceived a rampant corruption and a disquieting sense of moral crisis, with bootlegging, smut, and petty crime supposedly raging unchecked. In this dangerous atmosphere, an apprehensive white Protestant America looked on as Victorian moral values and traditional family roles decayed, to be replaced by the threatening sexual freedom of a younger generation liberated by the automobile and "corrupted" by the movies. The blame for cosmopolitan squalor, vice, and illegal alcohol trafficking could be laid firmly at the feet, the Klan claimed, of the morally "inferior" foreign doctrines imported with recent Catholic and Jewish immigrants.

Always, these grubby images of immorality, corruption, and crime were set against romantic notions of a more innocent and heroic American small-town life. Blass, for instance, expresses genuine disgust at the shameless criminality he sees around him in Detroit, the "wide-open saloons . . . [with a] steady stream going and coming" making him long for the relative innocence of his rural Michigan roots. "I am a small town product," he writes, "and believe myself to be about as broadminded as they make them, but I can't stand the underhanded crookedness that I see around me on all hands every day without saying something about it." The small town, he claims, is "the only place where real life manifests itself in the daily good will toward men."[54] Such sentimental idealizations of small-town life, however, were exactly that, and in reality, rural regions were experiencing on a smaller scale many of the problems that the Klan associated with city life. Newaygo County, certainly, was far from immune to rising levels of petty

A Klan organ links city immorality and Catholicism
Source: Dawn Publishing Co., Chicago

crime in the mid-twenties, and this may, in fact, have provided a legitimate motivation to join an organization that actively aligned itself with morality and crime prevention. On every occasion that Klan speakers had held public meetings in the county, they had declared the KKK to be a "law and order" organization, working hard "to get every bootlegger," or simply "active in law enforcement."[55] Little surprise, then, that (in addition to a number of Newaygo County lawmen who also belonged) at least seven individuals who had recently suffered major thefts, holdups, or had cars stolen should join the Invisible Empire in the towns of White Cloud, Fremont, and Newaygo.[56]

The Newaygo County press, too, had made much of the questionable moral codes that it associated in particular with the automobile culture of the nation's youth. As well as regularly denouncing the dangerous, the drunken, and the underage driver, who between them "have been permitted to drive cars . . . almost without restriction,"[57] the papers also pointed to more worrying sexual misdemeanors. The *Fremont Times-Indicator*, edited by soon-to-be-Klansman Don VanderWerp, warned in June 1922 of "the abominable practice" of "accosting girls and young women," in which "a number of young men of Fremont and vicinity" had lately been engaging. "These fresh young fellows have taken the liberty . . . especially at night, inviting and urging them to take automobile rides in the country." This "reprehensible practice," through which "many a young woman has come to grief by innocently accepting such invitations," had seen chief of police Amos Bacon (another future Klansman) promise to come down hard with fines and possible jail sentences for "any young man convicted of this offense." The same paper later expressed concerns over the late closing of the area's dance halls, causing "delinquency amongst the young

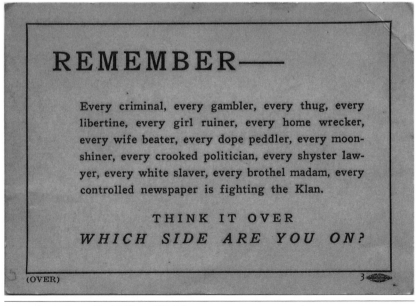

Law, order, and morality, Michigan KKK style
Source: State Archives of Michigan

folks." Specifically, the problem concerned young girls who "accepted rides from various people to their homes . . . quite frequently reports were made that young girls had left the dance halls with young men and had failed to return to their homes that night."

Klan-era newspapers in Newaygo County seemed particularly preoccupied with condemning promiscuity, especially where this involved young, sexually assertive females. On the subject of "the flapper," one editor noted that "she does not have the elusive charm of a former generation, when the shrinking violet type was idealized by women." But all was not yet lost, he added, and "if these flappers will listen to wise advice from their mothers, and not pursue the male animal too aggressively, they should . . . accomplish much in life." The *White Cloud Eagle*, meanwhile, reported the case of a young woman who had "had illicit relations with men and boys in the community . . . [and] had been a contributing factor to other delinquencies in the district." Apart from disclosing the unsavory detail that "several of her acquaintances were probably diseased," the paper urged that "everyone who comes in contact with the youth of the state from ages of 14 to 21 . . . can perform a needed service by calling attention to the fact that immoral conduct is punishable by imprisonment." Immorality imported from the cities could lead not merely to prison, but also to premature death, according to the *Times-Indicator.* While "every town has its girl problem since the advent of the modern scheme of things," it said, "what originates in the cities radiates through the country . . . [and] if smoking becomes respectable for city women . . . country women of the more daring make-up will take it up." The article included a grieving father's account of his daughter's recent tragic suicide, claiming that "the whirl of social life and cigarette smoking finally resulted in a nervous breakdown, which I attribute as the cause of Margaret's death. I warned her repeatedly, but was unable to change her ways."[58]

That the Klan's traditional white, Protestant, conservative constituency in the 1920s was strait-laced to the point of sexual repression seems readily apparent not only from its preoccupations with regulating public morality, but also from the nature of the material it produced to attack its enemies. Central to KKK assault upon Catholicism were voyeuristic diatribes charging a widespread sexual immorality, depravity, and masochism—both physical and mental—within the Roman hierarchy. This accusation was by no means a new one, having been popularized throughout the period between 1910 and 1920, notably in the pages of *The Jeffersonian* magazine, whose Georgian editor Tom Watson had also produced titles as suggestive as *The Inevitable Crimes of Celibacy*, and *What Goes On in Nunneries.*[59] The Klan, recognizing the power and popular appeal of such sensationalist tittle-tattle, seized and elaborated upon the theme. Its caricatured priests and nuns were frequently painted as sexual deviants, their unnatural abstention from marriage and thus "normal" marital relations lying at the very root of their perversion, forcing their animal desires to take other, more sinister directions.

A staple of the priest's religious training, for instance, allegedly included intensive study of "a book on fleshy subjects titled *de Sexto*," a book "so corrupt from top to bottom, and from center to sides" that it "may not be lawfully published in America in the English language." Having finally completed his training, "this holy man and his saintly confreres" was then able to display a "most wonderful amount of knowledge . . . on bestiality, sodomy and kissing."[60] Almost always, the Catholic Church was implicated from within, via the dubious tales of "ex-nuns" and "ex-Romanists," "those who have renounced this religion, and by those who have escaped from its prison-like institutions." Having borne witness to countless "heinous crimes against morality . . . committed by supposedly religious impeccables," they told tales of routine debauchery and behind-closed-doors torture, as well as revealing details of cunning Roman plots to overthrow the Protestant nation from within. Young Catholics, it was said, were encouraged to marry outside the fold of the Church in order to boost its numerical strength through converted spouses and the resultant offspring. Furthermore, Roman leaders supposedly advocated active displays of premarital sexual availability as a means by which to tempt, trap, and forcibly convert unthinking but otherwise good American Protestants. "Ask any close observer," came the Klan challenge, "how often he has seen innocent girls and unsuspecting boys lured into indiscretion and forced into alien wedlock, in order to cover their shame."[61]

The scheming priest, meanwhile, sought to undermine and usurp American manhood and assert control over the nation's womenfolk, through the apparatus of the confessional box. Becoming, during confession, "the confidante of another man's wife," the priest would use guilt as leverage and lecherously pump for intimate information, laying bare a woman's "inmost secrets . . . all that is sacred between her husband and herself." His unholy interest, of course, would be piqued by the finer details of "sexual procedures and techniques with her husband, extra-marital activities, masturbation, homosexuality, and unnatural fornication." Ever mindful of such popish degeneracy, the Klan produced numerous righteous exposés, including *The Devil's Prayer Book, or an Exposure of Auricular Confession*. Abundantly clear from the book's telling subtitle was the patriarchal, sexually anxious nature of its anti-Catholic concerns: *An Eye-Opener for Husbands, Fathers and Brothers*.[62]

The author of this particular tract, one William Lloyd Clark, was as prolific as anyone in the Klan's literature war against the Roman church. He advertised regularly in KKK organ the *Dawn*, promoting subscriptions to his own publication *The Rail Splitter*, proclaiming it to be "the greatest anti-Catholic monthly paper on the American continent." Also on offer from *The Rail Splitter's* press, and demonstrating the buoyancy of its market, were an "assortment of tracts, 10 cents; 1 dozen red hot anti-Catholic post cards, all different, 10 cents; 100 for 80 cents; 1000 for $4.00." Indeed, demand for such inflammatory material was more than keen enough to support lucrative public lectures in addition to the plethora of pamphlets. "HEAR! HEAR! HEAR!" cried an ad in the *Dawn*, offering up the "famous editor of *The Rail Splitter* in an address on the menace of Romanism . . . Protestants invited."[63]

Others, too, were far from reticent in their exploitation of public fascination with anti-Catholic imagery. Celebrated "ex-Romanist" L. J. King was a veteran campaigner, having published an annual compendium of all things anti-papal since 1911. His *Converted Catholic and Protestant Missionary* continued production well into the 1920s, embracing and actively championing the reemergent Klan, as well as advertising hundreds of other anti-Catholic tracts and authors. Featuring heavily in the substantial annual were countless tales of enduring Roman debauchery, of unnatural desires and the perversions of celibacy, of enslavement and ritual torture of innocent young girls, of incarceration behind barred windows, bolted doors, and unassailable prison walls.

Perhaps King's most prominent and successful associate was notorious "ex-nun" Helen Jackson. Her hugely popular autobiography, *Convent Cruelties; or My Life in the Convent* held particular resonance for audiences in the state of Michigan, as it told the sorry tale of her supposed torture and abuse during a lengthy stint in "captivity" at the House of Good Shepherd convent in Detroit. Denied outside contact by heartless nuns who intercepted her mail, she was put to work under horrendous conditions, and made to suffer constant humiliation at the hands of her sadistic captors. Among the catalog of inhuman and merciless tortures forced upon Jackson were "ducking" in baths of cold water, followed by a vicious "whipping . . . into insensibility" while clothed in only a wet nightgown; "burning hands with a red-hot poker," being held down and "forced to drink dirty soup," as well as being bound and compelled to "lick tea like a dog." The greatest source of her outrage, however, is that these shocking papal injustices were taking place not in Rome, but within the borders of the American nation, denying the inmates their "God-given rights to live and enjoy freedom as guaranteed by the American Constitution." Having eventually staged a daring escape, Jackson laments the ordeals of all good Protestant girls abducted into servitude, and makes it her mission to see them released. "I have helped many other girls since then," she writes, "and with God's help, I shall continue in the work."[64]

Teaming up as a crowd-drawing double bill, Jackson and L. J. King took their anti-Catholic peepshow on the road, promoting the interests of the KKK with high-profile public lectures all over the Midwest. Whereas in her preface to *Convent Cruelties*, Jackson had contended that "the material is fit for any child or lady to read, because the repulsive material is excluded," the lecture tour had no such moral restraint. Jackson and King regaled large and enthusiastic crowds with titillating, highly sexualized stories of Catholic perversion behind the bolted gates of an international network of convent prisons. In this world, fornication, mutilation, rape, abortion, and infanticide were commonplace, with priests and nuns conspiring to conduct lives

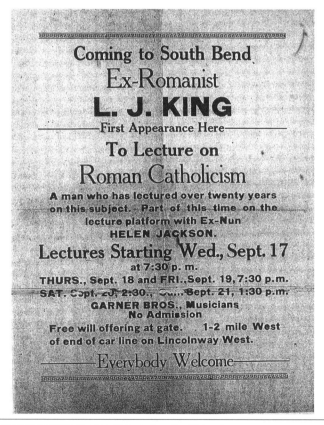

An "Ex-Romanist" and "Ex-Nun" combine to tour the Midwest
Source: Library of Congress

of illicit sadomasochistic pleasure in each other's grubby embrace. Depravity of every kind was rampant in these "slave dens," and the stories were many, varied, and colorful, including one of nuns being "confined in coffins filled with human excrement" for the gratification of the priests. To cover the worldly evidence of their moral abominations, the inevitable offspring of their unholy unions were without fail destroyed, either by cutting them out of the pregnant nun's stomach, or by brutal murder upon their birth. Jackson even went to the length of displaying small leather bags for her audience—apparently used to dispose of aborted fetuses and murdered newborns, all fathered by decadent, sex-hungry priests.[65]

Helen Jackson was only the best-known of a number of alleged escaped nuns and ex-Romanist traveling lecturers who appeared in Michigan. That such scandalous, sexualized, and often gory tales were widely known in Michigan, and—whether believed or not—were at least passed on, is evident from the letters home of Kenneth Blass. Expressing outrage at the existence of "these walled-in Catholic girls' institutions," he laments the plight of the "many girls who are subjected . . . that have been used and abused under the cloak of the Catholic religion and who are taught that priests can do no wrong." Full of the Klan's conspiracy theories alleging a Rome-controlled press, he contends that "we all know that the complaints have been numerous enough . . . I wish just one paper, in Detroit alone even, would take up the subject thoroughly and honestly."[66]

Jackson and others had been touring the state as early as 1921, employed by anti-parochial school campaigner James Hamilton to denounce the excesses, real and imagined, of the Catholic faith, and prepare the ground for KKK recruitment.[67] Their explosive "revelations" blended compelling oratory with scandalous content, and ensured notoriety, animated crowds, and a lasting impression upon audiences. As Kathleen Blee has found in interviews conducted in neighboring Indiana in the late 1980s, "memories of the sexual tales spread by the Klan" some sixty years on "are still fresh in the minds of former Klansmembers and contemporaries of the 1920s Klan movement."[68] Much of the impact undoubtedly came from the thrill of hearing licentious, semipornographic material aired in public. Outwardly, the Klan championed the rigid moral standards of the traditional American small town, arguing for Puritanism, purity of womanhood, chastity, and "clean living." In its graphic sexual demonization of the Catholic Church, however, it created a sanctioned outlet for the repressed passions of its constituents.

By airing such "filth" in the righteous denunciation of a common and recognized enemy, it provided a space in which to vicariously indulge hidden appetites—desires that, expressed almost anywhere else, would without question have met with social disapproval. Often, the experience took place with the added exhilaration of a clandestine, sex-segregated environment, with particular snippets of information deemed so corrupting as to be suitable only for certain ears. It should be no surprise, therefore, that the Klan's propaganda found a hungry audience among moralistic white Protestants, eager enough to combat the Catholic menace, but perhaps somewhat more eager to hear tales of its carnal dangers. Reporting on a lecture by Rev. Dr. Eli Forsythe in June 1924, which had been advertised as strictly "for women only," the *Michigan Catholic* took a predictably dim view of events. "The women enjoyed the tearing away of the veil of common decency and the uncouth words of the speaker," it objected, citing as evidence "the bursts of applause that greeted a most disgusting tirade . . . that poured from the lips of Dr Forsythe." Although "most of the talk . . . was unfit for publication," his concluding point was unmistakable, namely that it was the duty of all good Americans to do their bit to foil the Catholic peril, and "see that only Ku Kluxers are on guard!"[69]

BEWARE THE CATHOLIC "MENACE": THE POLITICS OF CONSPIRACY IN MICHIGAN

In the midst of the wider social and moral malaise that it alleged, the Klan claimed a particularly insidious encroachment of "Romanist" corruption in the state's political and administrative infrastructures. Even in the most mundane of circumstances, Klan advocates chose to see conspiracy. At his own place of work (Detroit's U.S. Mail depot), for instance, Kenneth Blass cannot help but view every petty conflict in terms of a battle between upstanding Americanism and shady Catholic menace. On a number of occasions, he furiously laments the discriminatory treatment that he believes is received by Klansmen on the basis of their membership in the order. "A fellow that works as a clerk at the main office," he writes, "was called before the Superintendent of mails last week and threatened with dismissal for being a propagandist and soliciting membership in the Klan." This, he insists, is due solely to the Roman Catholic connections of both the superintendent and the head of the route-inspection department, "two dirty pups," who by consensus of "general knowledge" between them "run the Post office, regardless of the Postmaster's wishes." This and similar incidents Blass sees as indicative of "the persecution of right thinking, clean-living, honest-to-God he-men and Americans," the aggressors being those "dirty, sneaking, grafting, petty politicians, looking to feather their own nests and gain power and prestige . . . for themselves and their political organization called a church."[70]

Municipal politics, too, Blass declares to be "interesting but too darned crooked," adding that "the leaders of the dirty political machines are, for the most part of [the Catholic] faith. That's why most men in public office and the majority of the laws of the country benefit those of the Catholic faith more than the rest." Repeating a line of argument that could have been plucked directly from any number of Klan pamphlets, he announces that "Catholicism runs counter to Americanism," attacking the "Roman hierarchy" as "a very profligate, greedy, political organization that gains its power through the church . . . a menace to the welfare of our country." Standing in the country's defense, then, is the Klan, which, according to Kenneth, stands for "the U.S. government as written; public schools; the Bible; the home; pure womanhood; separation of church and state . . . nothing more, in the main, than what you or any other good U.S. citizen believes." Working diligently to "drive the power of the Pope out of American politics," the instrument of reform is the ballot box. "The only means I know of," Blass writes, "is a secret organization of white, Protestant, American citizens who will unite in a common cause for the good of the whole country, as well as their own community." Indeed, "if the Klan is as good as its followers claim," he adds, "I hope they will be able to put honest men in office."[71]

Very real attempts were indeed being made, in Michigan, as in the rest of the nation, to install representatives of the KKK into political office. In the 1924 Detroit mayoral election, for instance, a Klan-friendly candidate, Charles Bowles, slipped into the running late and almost unnoticed, quickly becoming a serious contender on the back of strong support from the Invisible Empire. Entering the race as a political unknown, his candidacy came as a bolt from the blue, with support as abundant and vocal as it was unexpected. As reported by the *Detroit Times*:

> The big surprise of the campaign was the showing made by Charles Bowles, an attorney, whose name was filed in the Mayoralty contest only a few minutes before the closing of nominations . . . so far as the public was concerned Bowles dropped into the contest out of a clear sky. His name had not been heard before it was filed, and for several days, the question "who is Bowles?" was on almost everybody's lips, particularly those who were supposed to know all about politics . . . he made it plain that he had never been in public life before . . . [and] it was apparent during the closing days of the campaign that Bowles was the Klan choice . . . [though he] stated he was not a Klansman.

When election day came, though Bowles had gathered large numbers of votes and come very close to his experienced opponents, he was eventually defeated by a narrow margin, amid controversy over spoiled ballots that might well have seen him elected mayor. His campaign, however, was spirited enough to at least rudely awaken the political establishment in the city of Detroit. With a substantial backing for "the only Protestant among the three leading for mayor," the Klan announced itself as a force to be reckoned with in public life.[72]

The Detroit mayoral race aside, without doubt the key issue for the Klan at the 1924 Michigan election was a referendum on the proposed "parochial schools amendment," a bill that, if passed, would amend the state constitution so that "all children residing in the state of Michigan, between the ages of seven and sixteen years, shall attend a public school until they have graduated from the eighth grade."[73] Aimed squarely at outlawing all parochial or religious educational institutions, the impetus for this measure in Michigan preceded the arrival of the Klan by some way, demonstrating a more enduring anti-Catholic political tradition there. The campaign against parochial schools had long been the pet project of James A. Hamilton and his "Wayne County Civil League," and Hamilton had even made a run for the state governorship on the issue in the Republican primary election of 1920. Defeated on that occasion, Hamilton had come back for a second attempt, securing enough signatures to place the amendment back onto the ballot for the 1924 election, and this time running for governor as head of the "Public Schools Defense League."[74] The timely emergence, and likely support, of the anti-Catholic Klan in Michigan gave Hamilton cause for renewed optimism, as did the fact that a similar law had very recently been passed in the state of Oregon, another Klan stronghold.[75]

Recognizing an opportunity to instill political relevance into their anti-Catholic crusade, Klansmen lined up behind the campaign throughout Michigan.[76] In Newaygo County, a KKK speaker addressed a crowd of one thousand in the Fremont Community Building, insisting that "every American boy and girl should be compelled to attend the public school," which he called "the keystone of American liberties."[77] In the Newaygo County press, too, in letters to the editor as well as editorials, opinions ran strong on both sides. An advocate of the amendment, without giving away too much of the Klan line on Catholicism, advised his fellow Fremonters simply to "read the *Michigan Kourier*, a weekly paper . . . for sale at the local newsstand. It may open your eyes."

Meanwhile, in a letter to the *Times-Indicator*, seventy-two-year-old Fremont Klanswoman Florence M. Spooner was far less restrained. The only people who could possibly oppose the amendment, she said, were those "ignorant of the actions of the Roman Catholic Church in America." Recounting tales of Catholic mobs attacking "patriotic speakers," newspapers "controlled by threatened boycott . . . from printing anything detrimental to Roman Catholics," and acts of vandalism carried out upon Protestant property, she denounced "Roman Catholic bigotry and intolerance." The U.S. Constitution, Mrs. Spooner continued, "upholds free speech, free press and free assembly. The Roman church demonstrates its opposition to all three. There is scarcely a week that the daily papers do not record something of the kind." In parochial schools, she claimed, Catholic children were "taught to defy the law and nearly everything American." Not only this, she had also apparently heard rumors from Chicago and New York that "the Roman Catholic Priest goes into the public school to teach his church catechism and whatever else he pleases, because he has control of the school board."[78]

On the other side of the debate, one Fremont resident, speaking out against the amendment, claimed that its supporters were "trying to stir up religious hatred and intolerance" and called it "a bagful of bolshevism sealed and labeled 100% Americanism." Others warned of thoughtless "obeisance to the Pope or the KKK."[79] The *Times-Indicator*, in particular, carried opinion on the matter from outside of the county, notably from the state's educators, who seemed roundly to condemn the proposal. Detroit superintendent of schools Frank Cody called the measure "un-American in character," and his feelings were widely echoed by University of Michigan faculty members who labeled it a "violation of the fundamental principles of democracy," a "vicious piece of legislation," and "a fair specimen of the intolerance showing itself in all parts of the country." The dangerous sentiment behind the proposal, they argued, "has manifested itself crassly and brutally in the Oregon school law" and now threatened to do the same in Michigan.[80]

Opponents of the amendment need not have worried, as despite energetic campaigning, the proposal was defeated by a commanding margin across the state of 760,571 votes to 421,472. While this meant a crushing political blow for James Hamilton and his Klan backers as regards the passage of the law,[81] the results do throw up a few interesting points when compared to the vote on the same issue four years before.

The result across the state in 1924 remained virtually identical to that of the previous election, with the proposal to outlaw parochial schools defeated by a vote of roughly 64 percent to 36 percent on both occasions. Looking more closely at Newaygo County, however, it becomes clear that sentiment there was, if anything, swinging the other way. Not only did Newaygo vote *for* the amendment on both occasions, the margin by which it did

Votes for and against the Michigan "Parochial Schools Amendment," 1920 and 1924

1920	*For*	*Against*
Newaygo County	2,415 (52.1%)	2,220 (47.9%)
State of Michigan	353,817 (36.7%)	610,699 (63.3%)
Michigan Counties carried (of 83)	9	74
1924	*For*	*Against*
Newaygo County	3,161 (57.3%)	2,351 (42.7%)
State of Michigan	421,472 (35.7%)	760,571 (64.3%)
Michigan Counties carried (of 83)	20	63

Source: Figures from the *Fremont Times-Indicator*, 13 November 1924.

so increased the second time around, as did voter turnout (in what was, according to the census, a slightly declining population between 1920 and 1930). Newaygo was far from alone in this, and other counties echoed the same pattern. Though Michigan as a whole remained stable on the emotive subject, more than double the number of counties voted yes to outlawing parochial schools in the Klan era than had done so just four years previously, in the days before the Invisible Empire came to town.[82]

Quite how much of this inner shift can be seriously attributed to the influence of the Klan, and its anti-Catholic propaganda on the schools issue in particular, is a matter of conjecture. Perhaps the figures speak, at a more fundamental level, of a growing internal tension within the state (and indeed most states at the time), reflecting the wider anxieties of a declining rural population in the face of an ominous metropolitan and cosmopolitan encroachment. Certainly, though, the KKK and the presence of such anxieties tended to go together in this era. If not claiming direct responsibility for the growing religious intolerance evident in large parts of Michigan, the Invisible Empire did at the very least find there an atmosphere conducive to its own operation, and one in which it might exploit and fan the flames of prejudice in the service of its own ends.

Whereas the school debate provided a rare opportunity for Klan propaganda to interact with the real world, much of its most memorable political imagery belonged firmly in the realms of the fantastic. Drawing heavily upon the anti-papal creations of the nativist "American Party" (or "Know-Nothings") of the 1850s, monolithic conspiracy tales abound in Klan literature.[83] The overthrow of the American government and subjection of the country to despotic Roman rule was a specter that loomed large and imminent in cartoon-like accounts. "The enemy is at our very gate," bellowed a *Dawn* headline in 1922, while the *Kourier* magazine deplored "Roman treason against our HOMES" and asked, without prospect of a positive answer, "Can a loyal Catholic be a loyal American?" Of particular concern were Catholic candidates for office, who were invariably portrayed as enemy agents striving to infiltrate the higher echelons of American politics. With the White House itself thus within the grasp of the Pope, and a subversive army of minions already in place in the United States, the Romanist machine allegedly stood poised to strike at the nation's democratic foundations, and, in the words of the Imperial Wizard, "gain control of the free channels of government in America."[84]

That the rumors of an impending "Romanist" revolution percolated down to become the gossip of the towns and villages of Protestant Middle America is clear from the numerous accounts of those who lived through them.[85] Recalling the Klan days in the central Michigan town of Mount Pleasant, the following description is not untypical:

> The Ku Klux Klan created quite a stir in our area in the years between 1921 and 1925 . . . there were no Negroes in our area, but it isn't difficult to create a villain and the Pope and the Catholics became the rallying point for the Klan . . . The lure of the masses to the Klan was being told the Catholics were going to take over the country and the Pope would be installed as the King. The Ku Klux Klan was recruiting with fervor. Stupid people joining?? No, not at all. Two or three people can fuel the fires of hate if reason leaves the mind. It could happen again.[86]

At the heart of much of the Klan's Romanist conspiracy talk was the Catholic fraternal service organization, the Knights of Columbus, which it charged with being the Pope's very own "militia in the United States." Supposedly stockpiling weapons in the basements of Catholic churches everywhere in preparation for the great religious battle to come, the "K of C" had "trained and equipped an army of . . . more than five to each one of the United States army." In addition, said the Klan, come the moment of reckoning, every ordinary Roman Catholic now present in the nation would show his true colors, namely, that he "owes his allegiance first to the Church of Rome, its monarch and its hundred throned kings in America before his allegiance to the United States."[87] This, perhaps, helps explain why local Klans in Michigan, Newaygo County included, felt compelled to make both the number of Roman Catholics as well as the "membership of K of C" in their own vicinities a matter of organizational record.[88] As evidence of the foul plot, the KKK cited the alleged "Bloody Oath of the Knights of Columbus," a scurrilous document of which many versions had long circulated in Michigan, predating the Klan's arrival by up to a decade. Claiming to represent a strict pact signed by all recruits to the fraternal and military arm of the Roman Church, its many controversial passages included a promise that:

> I will, when opportunity presents, make and rage relentless war, secretly and openly against all heretics, Protestants and Masons . . . I will spare neither age, sex or condition, and that I will burn, hang, waste, boil, flay, strangle and bury alive these infamous heretics; rip up the stomachs and wombs of the women, and crush their infants' heads against the walls in order to annihilate their execrable race.[89]

Henry Peck Fry, a former Klan recruiter who later turned his back on the organization, denounced the oath as "bogus," an article that "among the ignorant classes of people . . . was accepted as genuine, and was the means of securing a large number of members for Ku Kluxism."[90] Closer to the point, perhaps, is that this was sensationalist Klan rumor-mongering at its most gruesome, graphic, and therefore most appealing best. Whether or not people genuinely believed its content, such fantasies were gripping, and the indulgence of entertaining them, however seriously, provided a certain enjoyable excitement.

For those who chose to believe in the prospect of sinister plots and anti-Protestant terrorism, the Klan's conspiracy theorists and gore-mongers always seemed to manage to find enough of a basis in the news from which to spin out their improbable scribblings. Perhaps the best example in Michigan came in May 1927, when a dramatic explosion all but destroyed the public school building in the town of Bath.[91] With Andrew Kehoe, a member of the school board, very quickly identified as the culprit by a unanimous press, the Klan was quick to point toward his faith.

"Roman Catholic Dynamites Bath Public Schools," read the pamphlets, charging Kehoe (who also perished in the blast) with "the greatest premeditated murder of children since the St. Bartholomew massacre." Not only this, but they dramatized their descriptions to include "little bodies of children" and "flesh, thumbs and limbs scattered upon the ground . . . these forty-five lives sacrificed to satisfy the lust of a shrewd mind poisoned by intolerant religious dogma."[92] Kenneth Blass, having attended a Klan meeting on the subject, takes the Klan's account of the Bath tragedy as moral vindication of his own forthright views. "I have no reason to doubt that all this and more could truthfully be said about the affair," he writes of the anti-Catholic version of events. "In fact, the Grand Dragon did say more . . . anyone acquainted with the facts, and [who] cares for the future of the public schools will at least vote to keep Catholics off the school boards and Catholic-school educated

ROMAN CATHOLIC DYNAMITES BATH PUBLIC SCHOOLS.

THE GREATEST PREMEDITATED MURDER OF CHILDREN SINCE THE ST. BARTHOLOMEW MASSACRE MURDERING 30,000 FRENCH PROTESTANTS

Newspapers Suppress Known Facts

THE KNIGHTS of the KU KLUX KLAN, DEFENDER OF THE PUBLIC SCHOOLS, PRODUCES THE FACTS

BATH, MICHIGAN, PUBLIC SCHOOL TRAGEDY

Andrew P. Kehoe, **Roman Catholic**, after much premeditation, evidenced through the preparation and explosion of huge amounts of dynamite, planned to take the lives of 250 pupils and teachers. This explosion occurred May 18, 1927. Immediately thereafter, search was made for bodies of the dead and injured and upon completion of the survey it was found that 45 adults and children had lost their lives and many others seriously wounded, with sufficient unexploded dynamite found in the structure to have wrecked the entire village had it responded.

Klan reaction to the Bath School Disaster, May 1927
Source: Michigan State University Special Collections

teachers out of public schools." In an instant, improbable bloodthirsty fantasy and harsh, tragic reality had come crashing rudely together, to the advantage of the Klan's public image. "This," insists Blass, "is no song of hate but what I consider protecting ourselves and our ideals."[93]

KLAN SELF-DEFINITION AND SYMBOLIC ENEMIES: SOME WIDER THEMES

In its denunciations of Romanism, KKK literature attacked overelaborate ceremony and dictatorial hierarchy; it attacked the subordination of the individual will to the group interest; it attacked a strict and immovable allegiance to ideology and intolerance of dissent; it attacked the "closed community" and religious "clannishness"; and it attacked the operation of political "machines." Yet all of these things, in one way or another, also characterized the Invisible Empire. In this sense, the organization best fitting the Klan's description of its mortal enemy was none other than the Klan itself.[94] Following the idea through to its superficial and fanciful extremes, the KKK even imitated the Roman Church to the point of replicating the Inquisition, in a modern setting. Conversely favoring the Protestant point of view, Klansmen, in support of America's established dominant religion, crusaded to expose the legions of heretics and dissenters wherever they existed within their midst. Not only this, but they carried out their mission sporting robes every inch as distinctive as (and some would argue strikingly similar to) those worn by their historic Catholic counterparts. Flippant an observation as this may appear, it does hint at the nature of the 1920s Klan's dilemma, and points, perhaps, to an important theme in its particular brand of antagonism. As Michael Rogin has noted in his work on American "countersubversive" movements, "the need to draw rigid boundaries between the alien and the self suggests fears of too dangerous an intimacy between them."

Klan anti-Catholic propaganda, then, becomes less a concern with reality than an exercise in self-definition, a ritual of full and final separation from the unwanted "other." Rogin goes on to state that "the alien comes to birth as the American's dark double, the imaginary twin who sustains his brother's identity. Taken inside, the subversive would obliterate the American; driven outside, the subversive becomes an alien who serves as repository for the disowned, negative American self."[95] The yardstick of self-definition in this era of social flux was a simple, yet unquantifiable measure: "Americanism." As served up by Klan literature, the immigrant, and more particularly the Catholic, became a sinister embodiment of the ultimate un-American, set in absolute opposition to the Klan's proud, self-declared community of "100% Americans." The perceived existence, however tenuous, of such an adversary served to more sharply define the Klansman's role, his claims to Americanism becoming legitimate precisely because of his possession of all attributes antithetical to his foreign foe. Having lined up in no uncertain terms with the cause of Americanism (or at least, the Klan conception of what was meant by Americanism), the KKK dealt in absolutes. The nation, it told the public, was in the midst of an apocalyptic battle between Good and Evil, with no middle ground. To declare against the Klan was to declare against America itself.

The monsters conjured up by the KKK, the degenerate legions of corrupt European immigrants seeking to overthrow freedom and democracy with foreign religious doctrines, were not actual, but symbolic enemies, to all intents and purposes. Certainly, there were very few, if any, actual battles. For all the Klan's posturing and all its anti-Catholic vitriol, in the state of Michigan, Norman Weaver has noted, "none of the meetings or parades produced anything violent . . . there was no violence at all connected with the wolverine Klan."[96] Instead, its images represented a demonized "other" in some far-flung place; they provided the dark and ever-threatening (though seldom, if ever, seen) shadow of evil against the Knights' supposed pristine white. As persuasive as the Klan's conspiracy theories might have sounded in the meeting hall or on the story page, they did not tend to interact well with everyday reality, particularly when that reality threatened to bring such images uncomfortably close to home.

Robert Coughlan, for instance, had watched the KKK descend upon his own community of Kokomo, Indiana, and in the process had heard the full gamut of tales—from debauched priests and nuns, to bludgeoned babies, to Catholic firearms stockpiling in the church basement, even the Pope's imminent arrival on the next train into town. Brought up as a Roman Catholic in "a neighborhood which was almost a hundred per cent Protestant and strongly pro-Klan," he nevertheless found that his religious affiliation gave him no cause for alarm at all, even at the Klan's highest peak. As taken as the local Protestants were with their anti-Roman stories, it soon became happily apparent that "not all Catholics were in on the plot: for example, the Catholics you knew." The Klan's demons, then, did not stand up as real, concrete enemies, but rather as imagined, overblown, and exaggerated ones, operating not in the realms of the actual, but the incredible. They were not designed for their own intrinsic worth, but rather constructed as symbols and scapegoats to service the needs of a contemporary American society that, beneath the tired veneer of old-time respectability, uneasily harbored an ambiguous anxiety, grasping all the while for definition and direction as it struggled to integrate the old and the new. As Coughlan ably elaborates:

> I know of no explanation for the lack of violence, for Kokomo was one of the most "Klannish" towns in the United States. Perhaps the answer lay in the dead level typicalness of the town: a population overwhelmingly white Protestant, with small, well-assimilated numbers of Catholics, Jews, foreigners and Negroes, and an economy nicely balanced between farming and industry. There were few genuine tensions in Kokomo in 1923, and hence little occasion for misdirected hate to flame into personal violence. It may be asked why, then, did the town take so whole-heartedly to the Klan, which made a program of misdirected hate? And the answer to that may be, paradoxically enough, that

the Klan supplied artificial tensions. Though artificial, and perhaps never quite really believed in, they were satisfying. They filled a need—a need for Kokomo and all the big and little towns that resembled it during the early 1920s.[97]

At the most superficial level, the Klan's stories were a colorful source of entertainment, utilizing the movie, the romance novel, and the public forum to popular effect in an era that predated the advent of the golden age of radio. Through *The Birth of a Nation*, in particular, it became possible to present the Invisible Empire to a large and receptive audience not just in a positive light, but in a heroic one—as an organization that pitted a strong, unified, and righteous Americanism against all comers. Growing out of the enthusiasm for such an image, the 1920s version of the Klan portrayed itself similarly as an upright, defensive, all-American moralistic movement, and framed the "plight" of modern Protestant America in mythical and apocalyptic terms.

The demonological fantasies conjured up by the 1920s Klan, while specific and contemporary in their condemnation of Catholicism and "alien" immigration, were also characteristic of a much broader and more enduring theme in American history. The "countersubversive tradition" in America, according to David Brion Davis and subsequently Michael Rogin, is a phenomenon that has been apparent throughout the life of the nation. Richard Hofstadter made a similar observation of what he famously labeled "the paranoid style in American politics." As explained by Rogin, "the creation of monsters" has occurred "as a continuing feature of American politics by the inflation, stigmatization, and dehumanization of political foes," and "American history"—while stopping short of claiming a national monopoly on the phenomenon—"has constituted itself in binary opposition to the subversive force that threatened it."[98]

This distinctive tendency or "willingness of American people to believe in monolithic conspiracies" has recurred at regular intervals over the course of American national life, in various different guises, with successive "anti" movements continuing to emerge in mobilization against a perceived seditious alien enemy. Students of the 1920s Klan alone invariably draw lines of direct descent from, at least, the "Know-Nothings" and the American Protective Association of decades before. The leaders of all such movements have invariably framed their conspirational fantasies in the rhetoric of good versus evil, without room for compromise of any kind. With an impending crisis of cosmic proportions afoot, the immensity of the supposed threat is as large as time is short, and nothing less than complete ideological victory will suffice. In this worldview, the issue of allegiance becomes crucial, with the enemy's particular danger derived from his traitorous loyalty to foreign doctrines rather than from any obvious distinguishing physical marks.

The key figure here is the symbolic renegade from the enemy cause—in the Klan's case the ex-nun and ex-priest—whose "inside" testimony confirms the scope of the enemy's depravity, and whose flight and reform can be held up as proof positive of the redemptive power of good over evil. As Davis has demonstrated with numerous movements, including anti-Masonic, anti-Catholic, and anti-Mormon groups in the mid-1800s, propaganda imagery associated with differing enemies tends very often to conform to one standard—that of sexual and moral degeneracy, focusing particularly upon taboo-breaking perversions, incest, and sadism. Hofstadter, too, noted that throughout American history, "anti-Catholicism has always been the pornography of the Puritan."[99] In this, as in other aspects, the twenties Klan conforms to the pattern: If the moralistic and austere supporters of the KKK can be called Puritan, then its Romanist propaganda can certainly be called pornography.

Historically, such movements, though decades or centuries apart, have tended to share common distinguishing attributes including, but not limited to, an obsession with the menace of a hostile foreign power; an equation of Protestant Americanism with freedom and morality; a battle to maintain public confidence in the face of an aggressive or questioning media; a fear of the corruption of the sacred American heritage won by the founding fathers; and an absolute belief in America's divine mission as the savior of mankind.[100] Without doubt, the Klan of the 1920s falls within the scope of this tradition, its defensive superpatriotism dressed as moral, divinely inspired righteousness, and its modes of operation conforming uncannily to the standards of movements that had gone before. In this sense, it can be clearly located as just one episode in a much broader terrain of American countersubversive history. That said, the KKK's nationwide scope, iconic cultural impact, and large following do make it a peculiarly distinctive episode. As Hofstadter notes, "It is the use of paranoid modes of expression by more or less normal people that makes the phenomenon significant."[101] There can be few better examples of exactly this point than the immense mainstream popularity of the interwar Ku Klux Klan.

An Everyman's Klan

Behind the Masks in Newaygo County

AROUND TWENTY MILES FROM THE WESTERN SHORE OF MICHIGAN'S Lower Peninsula, and about the same distance north of the city of Grand Rapids, lies the county of Newaygo. Predominantly rural, it is tucked away among picturesque inland lakes and woodland, with more than half of its land mass engulfed by the pastoral, leafy splendor of what is now the Manistee National Forest. The settlement of Newaygo County had been based, initially, around the booming nineteenth-century logging industry. A wilderness richly abundant in white pine, it had first attracted the attention of Chicago businessmen in the 1830s, with the county's first sawmill appearing shortly afterwards. The subsequent years were characterized by the springing up of small, busy pioneer communities, established on the county's major rivers, most notably the Muskegon, which became one of the most crucial pine-log transportation channels in the entire state of Michigan.

By the time the Klan came to Newaygo County in 1923, the picture had changed. While the logging industry had established the county and its principal towns and infrastructures, its fortunes had peaked during the 1880s and declined steeply thereafter. The focus of major activity on the Muskegon in the early years of the twentieth century had shifted away from pine and toward power, concentrating on the construction of a series of large hydroelectric dams. Though a small lumber industry remained, the county's livelihood by the twenties was centered much more around agriculture. According to the U.S. Bureau of the Census, a huge 84.8 percent of the county's total land area (462,018 of 544,640 acres) was taken up by farms in 1920. Principally fruit-growing establishments, they were supported by subsidiary industries including produce-canning plants and creameries, which, alongside a scattering of manufacturing concerns

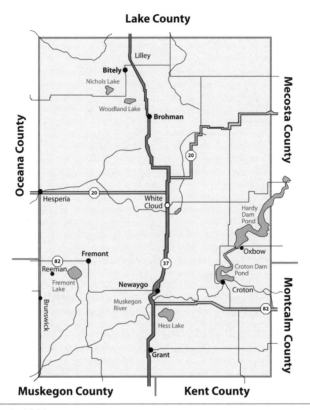

Lake County

Lilley

Bitely

Nichols Lake

Woodland Lake

Brohman

20

Hesperia

White
Cloud

Fremont

Reeman

82

Fremont
Lake

Newaygo

Muskegon
River

Brunswick

Hess Lake

Grant

37

Oxbow

Hardy
Dam
Pond

Croton Dam
Pond

Croton

82

Oceana County

Mecosta County

Montcalm County

Muskegon County

Kent County

Newaygo County, Michigan

(notably the county's cement production plant), provided much of the area's employment.

In addition to a number of small settlements and communities, Newaygo County was home to three distinct towns, namely, Newaygo, Fremont, and White Cloud (the administrative center and county seat), as well as the village of Grant, and part of the town of Hesperia, around half of which sat over the county line in neighboring Oceana County. Each of these established settlements had, by the 1920s, developed its own version of a budding small-town consumer economy, each sporting its own weekly newspaper as well as a variety of merchants, banks, physicians, craftsmen, and countless other small enterprises. Despite this, Newaygo County struggled to maintain its population levels, its relative lack of large industry forcing many to seek employment in the nearby cities of Muskegon and

Grand Rapids, and sometimes looking further, in Detroit or Chicago.[1] The county's largest settlement, the "city" of Fremont, boasted only just over 2,000 residents. In total, the population of Newaygo County in 1920 was 17,378, and would decline slightly over the next ten years to 17,029 by 1930. Newaygo's 1920 average of 204 people per square mile compared unfavorably with a Michigan average of 638, and a Wayne County (which included Detroit) average of 18,944 people per square mile. Both the Michigan and Wayne County averages would rise significantly by 1930, while Newaygo's figure would continue to recede slightly over the same period. Similar patterns in other Michigan counties would seem to demonstrate, almost without exception, one of the defining trends of the era—a general decline in the rural population, and a corresponding growth in numbers drawn to the burgeoning cities. What was happening to the population in Newaygo County was indicative of small-town populations everywhere— the most mobile, frequently younger, and often most promising residents lured away by the opportunities and possibilities, economic and social, of more "modern" urban environments.

The population that did remain in Newaygo County was a largely homogeneous one: overwhelmingly white, typically Protestant, and generally conservative in outlook. Of 17,378 county residents in 1920, the census listed a total of 17,347 (or 99.8 percent of the population) whose ethnicity was "White." The 15,452 who were both "White'" and "Native" to the United States made up 88.9 percent of the population, significantly above Michigan's state average of 78.4 percent. Just thirty-one Newaygo County residents were listed as "Negroes," and absolutely none were listed under "Indians, Chinese, Japanese and all other races."[2] According to the 1926 *Census of Religious Bodies*, various well-established Protestant churches accounted for at least 79 percent of Newaygo County's church membership. A further 12 percent, listed simply as "all other bodies," may have included a number of lesser-known Protestant establishments. Only 9 percent of Newaygo County's church members, in contrast, were practicing Roman Catholics, equating to just 2 percent of the county's total population. Jewish congregations were nonexistent, without a single member listed in the census.[3] To put this in context, Catholics in the state of Michigan as a whole accounted for 47.2 percent of total recorded church membership, and Jewish congregations 4.7 percent. In simplistic terms, then, in a relatively solid white Protestant state, rural, sparsely populated Newaygo County was both significantly "whiter" and more Protestant than the Michigan average. The county also retained a traditional political conservatism, and was represented in the state senate throughout the 1920s by prominent

Michigan Republican and Fremont resident Orville E. Atwood. Unlike many other areas of the state, notably the bigger, more cosmopolitan cities, Newaygo County was seemingly without any sort of liberal press. All four of the county's own weekly newspapers (namely the *Newaygo Republican*, the *Grant Herald and Independent*, the *Fremont Times-Indicator*, and the *White Cloud Eagle*) listed their political affiliation as pro-Republican in the 1920s, and any other viewpoint would have to be imported in the form of one of the larger dailies from the metropolis.[4]

THE KLAN IN NEWAYGO COUNTY: A NUMERICAL OVERVIEW

The very earliest membership list available for Newaygo County was probably compiled during the summer months of 1923, when the Klan began in earnest to make serious inroads into all parts of the state of Michigan. This list details the "Newaygo (Provisional)" organization, under the supervision of an enigmatic Kleagle, or officially appointed recruiter, of whom little is known beyond the name "E. E. Rorer."[5] In addition to Rorer himself, the list included forty-two men from across the county—ten from Newaygo, twenty-two from Fremont, three from White Cloud, and one from Grant. Also included under the Newaygo group's command were the names of provisional Klan members from towns actually outside of, but close to, Newaygo County—four men from Hart, and two from Kenneth Blass's home town of Baldwin, including a close friend of the Detroit Klansman.[6] Like Blass, two of the Newaygo provisional Klan worked as mail carriers. Even this early on, however, it was evident that this was not simply an organization of the laboring classes—its infant ranks including a school teacher, a chief of police, a highway commissioner, and two city superintendents, alongside a variety of merchants, manual workers, and farmers.

Having gained a valuable foothold in the area, the provisional Newaygo Klan organization was charged by the Michigan state KKK headquarters with raising "a quota of 1,075 members" in order for it to be awarded an official Klan charter of operation, and thus recognition as a bona fide participant in the national movement.[7] This must have appeared no mean numerical feat, considering that the general population here was in decline, that so few were concentrated together in large settlements, that many had moved away to seek work in the distant cities, and that the catchment area contained, even before adjusting downward to account for religious "ineligibles," a relatively slim total of 8,242 native-born white adults—the absolute maximum who might possibly qualify, let alone sign up. Nevertheless, the Newaygo County provisional Klan set about its task with some vigor, and it did indeed receive its charter from national headquarters, on 29 September 1925. At a specially organized meeting held at the White Cloud Baptist Church, a representative from Atlanta made the charter presentation, just over two years after the Invisible Empire's first appearance in the area.[8]

The wait, incidentally, for the provisional organization to become a chartered one was typically long. Monetarily speaking, a provisional Klan was permitted to take only a small fraction of each local recruit's "Klectoken," or $10 membership fee, with the rest finding its way into the treasuries of the state and national organizations. Once fully chartered, however, a local Klan unit had a greater degree of official power and was entitled to a larger cut. As such, it was in the financial interest of the national office to promote heavy recruitment prior to chartering, with quotas set high to prolong provisional status. This situation was very common in Michigan, and had even erupted into a much-publicized dispute between the national office and the Detroit Klan, who charged that its charter had been held back unjustly in order that the Klan administration could "milk" its members at will. In protest, Detroit Klansmen then formed their own independent version of the Invisible Empire, known as the SYMWA (Spend Your Money with Americans) Club, which remained in operation as a Klan in all but name until an official charter was eventually received.[9] As a result of such deliberate delaying tactics by the national office, by the time of actually receiving its charter, many a Michigan provisional unit had already recruited as many men as it was ever going to. In Newaygo County, certainly, only four new recruits appeared on the Klan rolls after the charter date, three of whom had transferred in from existing, neighboring Klans.

At the time of chartering, membership numbers were assigned to all fully paid-up recruits, who then became charter members of the newly christened Newaygo County Klan No. 29. With 682 such members belonging to the men's organization at this point, and 382 to the corresponding women's unit, Newaygo County was successfully taken above its quota of recruits by the presence of a further 21 members of the recently created "American Krusaders" auxiliary for foreign-born Klan advocates. These numbers, though impressive enough in themselves for a sparsely populated county, still do not quite illustrate the full extent of the Klan's numerical influence in Newaygo. Local Klan records and correspondence reveal at least a further 160 individuals affiliated with the chapter, who, for a variety of reasons, did not appear on the rolls as official, numbered charter members at its time of incorporation. Having moved out of the area entirely or, more frequently,

Klan Membership among Native-Born White Adults in Newaygo County

	Native-Born White Adults, Newaygo County (1920 census)	Affiliated with Newaygo County KKK (1923–1925)	
		Number	*Percent*
Men	4,292	816	19.0
Women	3,950	408	10.3
Total	8,242	1,224*	14.9

*By virtue of their non-U.S. birthplace, this total necessarily excludes the 21 male and female members of the American Krusaders auxiliary unit.

found themselves unable to keep up with dues payments, these names had nevertheless appeared on Newaygo's KKK records during its years as a provisional organization.[10] The inclusion of these individuals gives a grand total for the county of 1,245, representing a significant proportion of the eligible population.

Roughly speaking, then, around one in five eligible men and one in ten eligible women were involved with the Klan in Newaygo County. Even this robust estimate of total Klan strength can be considered conservative, as the census figures used here are based upon a definition of "native white" that encompasses all white individuals born on American soil, including those with foreign-born parents. As such, the total is likely to have included an unknown number of Catholics and other non-Protestants who, though American-born, retained an attachment to the religious practices of their recently immigrant families and nations of origin, which would have made them ineligible for Klan membership, thus shrinking the organization's pool of potential converts. Whatever the implications and inherent complications of the statistics, their main purpose is to provide a good general indication of the enormity of the Klan movement in the area. One particularly striking figure is the overall county membership of 1,245—which, when considered relative to the size of Newaygo's actual settlements, looms particularly large. According to census figures detailing the populations of the county's five largest "incorporated places," the villages of Hesperia (191 residents), Grant (473), White Cloud (618) and Newaygo (1,160) were all in themselves numerically inferior to the county Klan organization. Only Fremont city, with 2,180 residents, contained more inhabitants than the local branch of the Invisible Empire did.[11]

Of those who did actively affiliate themselves with the KKK, a survey of birthplaces reveals a predictably strong Midwest-reared core membership.

Of 1,064 individuals for whom such information is available, 67.3 percent were born and raised in Michigan. A further 23.6 percent originated in Indiana, Ohio, Illinois, and Wisconsin—the four closest states geographically, not to mention culturally, to Michigan. This left just 9.1 percent who were born outside of the immediate region, and despite the Klan's stereotypical identification with the South, only 1 percent of Newaygo County Klansmembers, or eleven individuals, were born in states that can be remotely described as Southern.[12] The relative cultural homogeneity of the Klansmembers is further demonstrated by using census data to trace their heritage. Of 1,021 individuals for whom this was possible, fully 73.5 percent were the children of two American-born parents, which is perhaps unsurprising given the Klan's trumpeting of "America for Americans." Some 13.5 percent, though, had one parent born in a foreign land, and a further 13 percent were the children of both an immigrant father and mother, meaning that, in all, around one quarter of Newaygo's Klan population were directly descended from recent immigrants, which might at first seem something of a contradiction. Looking at this a little more closely, however, it very quickly becomes clear that the overwhelming majority of such ties were to the least foreign, culturally speaking, of foreign lands, being mainly to English-speaking nations, or to European countries with predominantly Protestant religious traditions. Of foreign-born parents of Klan members, 30.2 percent came from Canada, 24.5 percent from Scandinavia, 16 percent from England and Scotland, 13 percent from Germany, and 9.8 percent from the Netherlands, with just a scattering from other places. Distinctly lacking in this category were immigrants from Catholic Poland, Italy, Ireland, or Mexico. In this respect, such immigrant ties were acceptable to the KKK and fitted in comfortably with the Klan's notion of "good" and "bad" immigration, a theme that would find its ultimate expression in the creation of the American Krusaders auxiliary unit.

Pre-Charter Klansfolk

As well as those officially listed by the Newaygo KKK as charter members in 1925, various other local individuals' names appeared on Klan records.[13] There were, for instance, thirty-five Newaygo County residents named who actively recommended others for Klan membership, and yet did not seem at first glance to belong themselves. Clearly advocates of the organization, sometimes recruiting multiple members to its ranks, and often with close family members who were "in," these were active, if technically unofficial players in the workings of the Newaygo County Klan organization. In most, if not all cases, they were Klan members who had joined in other locations previously, and so were registered elsewhere, notably in the nearby counties of Muskegon, Oceana, Mecosta, and Ionia, as well as the city of Detroit, having had family, work, or residential connections to these places at some point previously.

Also excluded from the list of charter members were around 120 individuals who had been members of the provisional chapter, most having joined throughout 1923 and 1924. These errant members, though, had seemingly failed in some way to keep up their obligations to the Invisible Empire sufficiently enough to remain in good standing by the September 1925 official chartering date. A good number of these had simply moved out of the county during this period, with many young men, in particular, leaving to work in nearby Muskegon, or seeking fortunes further afield in Detroit and Chicago, taking their Klan memberships with them to bolster other local units at their destinations. Similarly, two small groups of Klansmen, initially listed as part of the provisional Newaygo County Klan, had split off to establish new local units slightly closer to their own homes. Hailing originally from the towns of Baldwin and Hart, the growing popularity of the KKK in Michigan allowed these men to form the Lake County Klan and the Max E. Tyler Klan No. 50 respectively. The latter chapter was in fact named in honor of one of the Hart men originally appearing on Newaygo's rolls. At least three other men had even more compelling reasons to be absent from Newaygo's Klan rolls, having died in the period between signing up and the county charter being awarded. One of these, at least, received a flamboyant KKK sendoff, with a fully garbed procession of Klansmen bearing his coffin through the streets before conducting his funeral under Klan auspices.[14]

Overwhelmingly, though, provisional Newaygo Klansmembers failed to become charter members typically for one reason and one reason alone—financial inability to keep up with the Klan's monetary demands. In a letter dated 7 May 1925, Newaygo Exalted Cyclops Jim Keller cautioned provisional members that "our records show that you . . . have not as yet completed your obligation." By "obligation," Keller referred to the payment in full of the $10 initiation fee, and the bringing up to date of all membership dues payments before the official chartering of the organization. "We want to give you a square deal," he went on, impressing the fact that "this order may charter most any day now, and . . . you will be required to pay the regular fee." Above all, the extraction of dollars was paramount, with the exclusive allure of genuine nationwide Klan affiliation dangled as bait. "To be fair," wrote Keller, "we feel that if your obligation is completed within six weeks, you can become a charter member."

Of those provisional Klansmen and women who did not progress to the status of charter members, it seems no coincidence that the vast majority came from occupations—mostly farmers, manual laborers, and even high school students—in which disposable income was least likely to be abundant. While all had made down payments of at least $1 or $2 to secure their initial Klan membership, they had struggled to make further installments. A selection of the comments noted on their dues cards reflects a common predicament: "I promise to pay $10 . . . as soon as possible"; "Paid $2, balance in 30 days"; "$1—balance in 60 days"; "will pay as soon as I can"; "unable to pay"; "Not financially able"; or, simplest and most honest of all, "No Money." The tension between organizational loyalty and financial capability is clearly illustrated in the following note to Exalted Cyclops Keller from an undoubtedly enthusiastic but terminally insolvent young Klansman:

Dear Sir,

I'm sorry but I cannot come to the meeting at White Cloud because we are having our senior play by the High school. As I am going to school I cannot make the money to pay up but would like to. I hope the order can wait till I get to work and make the money. If it is not so you can wait, can I ever have another chance to come to this organization? I would hate so very much to have to be dropped and all my brothers go on with the great work.

Yours Truly,
Albert Golden,
Box 97, Hesperia, Michigan.[15]

For provisional Klansman Golden and many like him, those unable to muster up this final financial sacrifice, or as Keller put it, to "complete your work," there was an amicable-sounding, but ultimately rather hollow Klan message: "We hope to retain your friendship," it read, "and you can feel free to call on us at any time for assistance that we can give you. We wish to feel the same toward you. We would much rather know that you are to be one of the Charter members, but you alone must be the judge." For such poor relatives of an upward-striving Klan movement, there was no reproach, but equally, there was no assistance and no concession. The choice was a fairly straightforward one: pay up and enjoy the secret world of the organization proper, or be cast aside and miss out on all the excitement.

Despite such obvious loyalty and desire on the part of men like Golden to serve the Invisible Empire in its "great work," the Newaygo County Klan, as so many other Klans have been accused of doing, certainly seemed to take a view that favored financial clout over dedication to the cause. These sentiments were a far cry from the Klan's self-conscious public image, flying directly in the face of views expressed in some of the organization's most celebrated recruitment materials. Coming to mind in particular here is the staple Klan anthem *God Give Us Men*, a literal rallying cry for the active enlistment of all willing, principled, and loyal troops, and a lament against financial corruption and self-serving money lust of all kinds:

> God Give Us Men! The Invisible Empire demands strong
> Minds, great hearts, true faith and ready hands,
> Men whom lust of office does not kill;
> Men whom the spoils of office cannot buy;
> Men who possess opinions and a will;
> Men who have honor; Men who will not lie;
> Men who can stand before a demagogue
> and damn his treacherous flattering without winking!
> Tall men, sun crowned, who live above the fog
> In public duty and private thinking;
> For while the rabble, with their thumb-worn creeds,
> Their large professions and little deeds
> Mingle in selfish strife, Lo, freedom weeps,
> Wrong rules the land, and waiting justice sleeps,
> God give us men!
> Men who serve not for selfish booty,
> But real men, courageous, who flinch not at duty;
> Men of dependable character; men of sterling worth;
> Then wrongs will be redressed, and right will rule the earth.
> God give us men![16]

A Klan "propagation" (recruitment) speech delivered in Michigan was at least more honest about the criteria required of aspiring Klansmen. On the one hand, the speaker invoked a typical KKK call to arms, declaring that "in this great movement, there is a crying need for men, real men, men of conviction, men who dare to be right . . . you have an opportunity to join hands with millions of men representing the best type of citizens in our country." Amid all of the rhetoric that followed, however—all the talk of rugged patriotism, manliness, and duty to God and country—the crux of the message ultimately boiled down to the same familiar financial imperative. "There are only three reasons that should keep you from petitioning for membership in the Ku Klux Klan," declared the speaker: "First, you haven't the courage to be right; secondly, you promised your wife that you wouldn't join the Ku Klux Klan; and thirdly, you haven't the $10 donation which we ask of all applicants. Which is it?"[17]

Publicly, the Klan claimed to be morally discerning, accepting into its ranks only the finest and most upstanding of citizens. From the evidence available in Newaygo County, at least, there is very little to suggest that this was the case there, with the membership records throwing up the names of only two men who it deemed "not likely" to be suitable for chartered membership for anything other than a financial reason. According to notes on his provisional membership record, Willard Shutts of Newaygo failed to make the grade because of the perception that he "talks too much." His neighbor and coworker at the local cement plant, and a man that he himself endorsed for membership, Howard Siders, was also rejected on the grounds that his wife "is very much against [the Klan]." Even these two cases, the only on official Newaygo Klan record, look flimsy, and seem to suggest more a fear of bad publicity or the leaking of fraternal secrets than any genuine concern over morality. The fact that the two rejected men were so closely linked to one another as neighbors, colleagues, and friends could also suggest some sort of personal grudge or dislike on the part of the officer making the decisions.

That said, there is evidence in other regional case studies to suggest that the publicly moralistic Klan was often wont to exercise its high-flown principles in private. David Horowitz, for instance, in analyzing secret Klavern minutes of a unit based in La Grande, Oregon, notes that "Klavern leaders insisted upon standards of strict morality before accepting anyone. After endorsement by individual Klansmen, officers read aloud the names of applicants before they were turned over to the board of Klokans for investigation of religious background and character." Such men could face disqualification "because of alleged moral problems," questionable "character and affiliations" or simply a "bad reputation." Even if they successfully became members, they continued to face "surveillance of their demeanor, organizational loyalty, and behavior."[18] It is always possible of course, that Newaygo County's records are incomplete, that crucial documents detailing failed Klan applications were destroyed, and that many other names of Klansfolk and would-be Klansfolk have been lost along the way. Certainly, official Klan policy dictated as much, and Cyclops Keller informed provisional members in 1925 that if they did not wish "to advance in this work by time of chartering," then "we will be compelled to destroy your records." If this was indeed the case, then the numbers of people moved to seek membership in the Klan in Newaygo County are even more impressive than the totals already apparent from existing documents. It is difficult, however, given the well-publicized KKK penchant for covert surveillance and information-gathering, to take the organization's word on this score, and the fact that the records of 120 pre-charter Klansmen and women still exist today suggests that the order may not have made good on its promise.

Propagation and Spread across the Newaygo County Landscape

Leaving auxiliaries aside for the moment, and concentrating purely upon the activities of the main—that is to say the men's—Klan organization, it is possible to trace a clear chronological and geographical order in its recruitment assault upon Newaygo County.[19] Having concentrated its initial efforts upon the town of Newaygo, the Invisible Empire shifted the focus of its enlistment operations toward the larger town of Fremont, and later the county seat of White Cloud in its constant search for new pools of potential converts to its ranks.

The town of Newaygo, situated on the Muskegon River, was the first hotbed of recruitment in the whole of Newaygo County. Here, on 27 August 1923, Kleagle Cyril D. Waters, a member of Chicago's Thomas A. Watson Klan No. 16, signed up his first three recruits to the fledgling Newaygo County Klan. Forty-eight hours later, their number had risen to thirteen. The coming months, particularly the half year leading into 1924, were to be a whirlwind of activity for Waters and his converts in Newaygo, a period in which the town's brief infatuation with the Klan would eventually see 193 local men become involved. Only after consolidating its strength here did the organization seek a real foothold in the immediately surrounding area. Despite lying only just over five miles south of Newaygo, the village of Grant, for instance, did not gain its first Klan member until Newaygo had well over one hundred. Once aroused in October 1923, however, interest among the few residents of Grant was immediate, the order being at its busiest during the latter months of 1923, and continuing to make steady progress throughout 1924. In all, thirty-five Grant men joined the Klan cause.

The city of Fremont, some ten miles northwest of Newaygo, and the county's most populous settlement, was only systematically "kluxed" as 1923 turned into 1924. In the months before December 1923, while Newaygo-dwellers signed up in droves, Fremont had enrolled only six rather isolated Klan members in total. The turn of the year saw this pattern completely reverse, however, and while Newaygo's recruitment rate slowed considerably, the Klan enjoyed its halcyon period in Fremont, averaging thirty recruits per month between December 1923 and September 1924, and amassing 353 male members in total in the vicinity. The town of White Cloud, the county's administrative as well as its geographical center, followed this same pattern relative to Newaygo, albeit slightly later and on a slightly less grand scale than Fremont. Recruitment began in earnest here only in March 1924, and continued apace through October at a rate of around fifteen recruits per month before tailing off, having netted a total of 151 converts to the men's ranks.

During the same few months that White Cloud took to the Klan, the village of Hesperia, fifteen miles due west, followed suit. Hesperia was unique, however, in that it was bisected by the county line, with only the eastern half of the village belonging to Newaygo County, and its western half belonging to neighboring Oceana County. In the portion of the village falling under its jurisdiction, the Newaygo County Klan managed to raise a total of forty-six male members. This, clearly, was done with the active cooperation of already Klannish neighbors, and around 40 percent of Newaygo County's recruits here were brought into the organization by members of the Oceana County Klan. Aside from the KKK population located in Newaygo County's five main settlements, just over fifty more men signed up, their memberships being drawn from around a dozen tiny hamlets in all corners of the county. With the notable exceptions of Biteley (eleven members), Volney (six), and Woodville (six), these places typically harbored just one or two Klansmen each.

In looking for obvious patterns in all of this, it becomes apparent that the reason for the Klan's shifting its recruitment drive away from Newaygo and towards Fremont and White Cloud could be that, after five months of canvassing, it had simply exhausted its options in this small and uneventful town. Perhaps more likely, though, the move was an overtly tactical one, and one that demonstrates the effectiveness of the wider organization's system of information-gathering. On 7 December 1923, Michigan's state Klan headquarters in Grand Rapids had sent the Newaygo unit a document that it called "G-2 Michigan's Special Report, Covering Your County." This document, the state office continued, was "furnished to you for your guidance in conducting the work in your county" and would "no doubt give you a much better understanding of your county than you have ever had before." The report outlined the town of Newaygo in some detail, listing population figures (broken down by race and religion); the town's newspapers, post offices, and churches; as well as the names of elected officials and school-board members. For all of the individuals listed, it also attempted to establish their church and fraternal affiliations, marking a distinctive "100%" beside any that were already Klansmembers.[20]

Having operated almost exclusively in Newaygo during its five months since arriving in the county, the Klan by the time of this report had already made substantial inroads into the town's social and administrative infrastructure, with the pastor of the local Methodist church, three of the five listed members of the board of education, and six of the twelve listed elected city officials, including the chief of police, city clerk, and city treasurer, all marked as being "100%." Also attributed to the Klan here were the postmaster, the reporter for the town's only newspaper, and the newspaper (the *Newaygo Republican*) itself. In addition to the attention given to Newaygo town, the report contained a more general survey of the county as a whole, and listed in particular the names and affiliations of fifteen elected county officials. The county clerk and treasurer, the sheriff and his deputies, the probate judge, and various commissioners—undoubtedly the names listed here would have been some of the most influential and powerful around. It is perhaps telling that just one of these was based in Newaygo, and that the majority of the others resided in Fremont and, in particular, White Cloud. Faced with all of this information in black and white for the first time, it seems likely that the Newaygo County Klan came to two conclusions: firstly, that it had already done an effective job in Newaygo itself, and secondly, that there was more, much more, to be had in other, as yet untapped areas of the county. Little coincidence, then, that recruitment should tail off in Newaygo and suddenly snowball in Fremont (and subsequently White Cloud), beginning the very same month that this report arrived at the local Klavern.

The mysterious report itself, attributed to "G-2 Michigan" and accompanied by a note that it "must never fall into the hands of anyone else," was a product of a sophisticated national network of surveillance that had been put in place by the infamously ambitious Klan empire-builder D. C. Stephenson, Grand Dragon of Indiana. In a 1927 exposé of Stephenson's often underhanded methods, Edgar Allen Booth explains that "under Stephenson's system . . . [the department known as] 'G-2' meant investigation." This was "a system of spying . . . based on the Russian spy system . . . by this means he was kept informed of everything which went on within the Klan and many things that transpired outside the robed organization. This spy system was composed of men who carried guns and many times deputy sheriff badges."[21]

"GOD GIVE US MEN!": THE COUNTY'S MALE RECRUITS

Of the men recruited to the Newaygo County Klan between its first arrival in August 1923 and its official chartering in September 1925, data detailing age (at joining) and marital status are available for 768 individuals.[22] The oldest man to join the Klan here was eighty-four years of age, and the youngest eighteen. Between those two extremes, a wide range of ages were healthily represented.

Age Distribution of Newaygo County Klansmen, 1923–25

Age (at joining)	Number	Percent
20 and under*	58	7.6
21–30	197	25.7
31–40	196	25.5
41–50	152	19.8
51–60	97	12.6
61–70	53	6.9
71–80	14	1.8
81–90	1	0.1
Total	768	100

*The lower age limit for membership in the adult Klan was 18 years.

As might be expected, memberships became progressively less common toward the higher reaches of the age scale as men become less physically active or able, and very possibly less numerous. Taking this into account, it is difficult to clearly identify any particularly distinctive age pattern, other than to say that the bulk of Newaygo Klansmen belonged to a core group of men fairly evenly distributed between the ages of twenty-one and fifty, with the numerical emphasis slightly weighted to the lower end of this scale. In terms of marital status, of 768 men for whom data are available, 198 (25.8 percent) were single upon joining the Klan, while almost three quarters were married (556 or 72.4 percent) or widowed (14 or 1.8 percent). Taken together with the age figures, this would tend to suggest a movement that, while containing a sizable youthful and possibly footloose element, was populated in the main by slightly more settled, mature, and socially stable family men.

The traditional view of the 1920s Klan and the social status of the men who joined it has long held that this was an order for the resentful economic "losers" in an era of hectic modernization and urbanization. Dartmouth professor of sociology John Moffat Mecklin summed up the popular stereotype in his influential 1924 study of Klan psychology, asserting that the Invisible Empire typically drew from the ranks of the "uninformed and unthinking average man," the economic misfit, the ignorant, the easily duped, the backward, and the ill-educated. In contrast, "the high-minded and independent members of the community," Mecklin suggested, "do not identify themselves with the Klan. It is a refuge for mediocre men, if not for weaklings."[23] The following tables outline the occupations of men who joined the Klan in Newaygo County in the five principal towns in which the organization operated, namely, Newaygo, Grant, Fremont, White Cloud, and Hesperia.[24] Taken together, they begin to paint a picture that is at least considerably more nuanced than the one that Mecklin and like-minded scholars described.

Occupational Breakdown of Klansmen in the Town of Newaygo, 1923–25

Farmer	36	clerk	10
		engineer	5
Blue Collar		hotel/ resort owner	4
laborer	27	local government official	3
cement plant operative	16	salesman	3
machine operator	13	college student	3
electrician	7	high school student	2
carpenter	6	real estate agent	2
factory foreman	5	bank teller	2
mechanic	3	chemist	2
lineman	2	justice of the peace	1
railroad worker	2	clergyman	1
drayman	2	insurance agent	1
mail carrier	2	schoolteacher	1
brick mason	1	postmaster	1
printer	1	dentist	1
barber	1	physician	1
truck driver	1	high school principal	1
candy maker	1		
janitor	1	**Military**	1
tailor	1	**Retired**	1
delivery man	1		
cow tester	1	**Unknown**	1
White Collar		Total	193
merchant/ small proprietor	16		

Occupational Breakdown of Klansmen in the Village of Grant, 1923–25

Farmer	17	**White Collar**	
		local government official	2
Blue Collar		merchant/small proprietor	1
laborer	3	bookkeeper	1
carpenter	2	illustrator	1
mechanic	1	clerk	1
blacksmith	1	salesman	1
baker	1	college student	1
cow tester	1	radio work	1
		Total	35

Occupational Breakdown of Klansmen in the City of Fremont, 1923–25

Farmer	99	clerk	16
		local government official	7
Blue Collar		salesman	6
laborer	44	physician	5
carpenter	10	bookkeeper	5
mechanic	9	real estate agent	4
mail carrier	6	stock buyer	4
truck driver	5	dentist	3
barber	5	bank official	2
painter & decorator	5	bank teller	2
railroad worker	4	engineer	2
factory foreman	4	high school student	2
bus driver	4	hotel owner	2
machine operator	3	insurance agent	2
butcher	3	office manager	2
plumber	3	broker	2
teamster	2	postmaster	1
glass blower	2	chiropractor	1
electrician	2	newspaper editor	1
blacksmith	1	college student	1
taxi driver	1	schoolteacher	1
tailor	1	stenographer	1
janitor	1	accountant	1
milkman	1	clergyman	1
road contractor	1	optometrist	1
brick mason	1	piano tuner	1
tinsmith	1	performer (contortionist)	1
printer	1		
filling station attendant	1	**Unemployed**	4
cooper	1		
cabinet maker	1	**Retired**	4
		Unknown	1
White Collar			
merchant/small proprietor	45	Total	353

Occupational Breakdown of Klansmen in the Village of Hesperia (Newaygo County section), 1923–25

Farmer	25	high school student	2
		clerk	1
Blue Collar		broker	1
laborer	3	engineer	1
carpenter	1	schoolteacher	1
drayman	1		
mail carrier	1	**Unknown**	2
White Collar			
merchant/small proprietor	7	Total	46

Occupational Breakdown of Klansmen in the Town of White Cloud, 1923–25

Farmer	61	clerk	7
		schoolteacher	6
Blue Collar		local government official	4
laborer	7	salesman	4
railroad worker	4	physician	3
mechanic	4	real estate agent	3
drayman	2	clergyman	2
mail carrier	2	artist	2
carpenter	2	bank teller	1
stone mason	2	civil engineer	1
barber	1	dentist	1
decorator	1	high school student	1
elevator man	1	college student	1
fireman	1	veterinarian	1
school janitor	1	factory manager	1
teamster	1	**Unknown**	1
painter	1		
		Retired	2
White Collar			
merchant/small proprietor	19	Total	151

While farming evidently represented the largest single occupation among Klansmen in each town, this should not automatically be taken as significant evidence of some unique appeal to the uncomplicated masses. Given the overwhelmingly rural nature of Newaygo County, the number of farmers in the Klan is not wildly disproportionate to the number of farmers in the general population. Nor should rural occupations among Klansmen be taken as a sure sign of backward-looking attitudes. The county's agricultural scene was actually quite progressive, and in 1905, a group of Newaygo County dairy producers, meeting at the Fremont Grange Hall, had formed the very first "Cow-Testing Association" in the whole of the United States, by which at least two Newaygo Klansmen were later employed. Instituting the routine testing of cow herds in order to monitor milk and butter quality, weed out unproductive cows, identify good sires, and improve overall profitability, this Newaygo County innovation was soon exported to the rest of the nation. According to experts at Michigan State University in 2005, "the formation of Cow-Testing Associations (now known nationally as Dairy Herd Improvement Associations) . . . was the foundation leading to tremendous progress" in the U.S. dairy industry over the past century.[25]

The agricultural and commercial achievement of another Newaygo County Klansman, Orley A. Rhodes of Grant, would also achieve high praise. Rhodes, who served as the county drains commissioner throughout his Klan days, was later acclaimed by the *Detroit News* as "a benefactor and a man of vision," having "reached his eminence and brought prosperity to the cross roads village of Grant." He had achieved this "by sponsoring and superintending the drainage of Big Rice Lake," which had fostered the birth of a lucrative onion-growing trade on the eight thousand acres of "mucky farmland" that resulted. His ambitious scheme, which cost taxpayers $75,000 at the time, had seen him labeled a "dunderhead" and "a dreamer" back in 1918, but it was one to which he had "clung doggedly . . . and campaigned from doorstep to doorstep to win the required votes." Rhodes's singular vision was to prove decisive, and by 1938 Grant had "from a mere nothing . . . become Michigan's onion center, which ships 1,500 carloads of prime cooking onions to customers as far as the West Indies," making anything up to a million dollars per year. Rhodes, henceforth known as "Michigan's onion king," gave up the county commissioner's job in favor of operating his own farm and onion warehouse, just one of many commercial warehouses established in the thirties to take advantage of his innovations in Grant. With the once-sleepy village now attracting an influx of farmers from Ohio and Indiana "to share in the golden harvest," Rhodes insisted that "still better days are coming" for Newaygo County. "In a few years, due to Grant's contribution," Rhodes continued, "Michigan will become the nation's foremost onion-producing state. Today it is second only to New York."[26]

The tables do also show a sizable instance of unskilled labor in the Klan ranks. Again, though, it is worth noting that this is, proportionately, fairly in keeping with the makeup of society at large, occurring conspicuously only in the towns of Newaygo and Fremont, whose industry was dominated by the county's two major production plants—the Newaygo Portland Cement Company, and the Fremont Canning Company, respectively. While laborers and farmers clearly did join the Klan here, they only provide a part of the story. What is perhaps most salient, considering the dominance of rural occupations throughout the county, is that the Klan in Newaygo County managed to draw members from a remarkably wide sample of small-town vocations. With its membership running the gamut of manual and nonmanual occupations—some highly skilled, others less so; some demanding brute strength, others more cerebral; and from the loftiest of city officials to the lowliest of farmhands—the Klan seemed to have gained a foothold in the full range of economic classes and social status groups, integrating almost all sections of small-town life in town after town. On balance, the most significant membership section seems to be the merchant class, the proprietors of the small enterprises that provided the county with amenities and services. Even within this broad category, a great diversity is apparent, from providers of general conveniences (grocers, hardware stores, confectioners, undertakers, auto repair shops, fuel supply, drugstores, florists, clothing stores, jewelers, news agents) to leisure and entertainment (resorts, billiard halls, movie theaters, restaurants) to the owners of a private bus line, and local dealerships for the Ford Motor Company.

Positions of power and influence are apparent among Newaygo Klansmen, too, in local government administrations, in the clergy, in the post office, and in the local press. Highly trained professionals seemed unafraid and unashamed of affiliating with the Invisible Empire. Five dentists, a veterinarian, an optometrist, a chiropractor, and fully nine local physicians all took the oath. Less numerous but perhaps even more surprising are the members who listed their occupations in the creative arts: a performer, an illustrator, more than one artist, a newspaper editor, and a man "working in radio." For an order supposedly of the entirely unenlightened, the Klan also seemed eager to forge an uncanny number of links with the world of education. The KKK sported a membership of thirteen students (both college and high school) and nine teachers, spanning all but one Newaygo County town. Also on the books were Arthur Crawford, principal of Newaygo High School, and the Fremont Board of Education's superintendent of schools, Stephen S. Nisbet. Simply put, the Klan in this area was the exclusive preserve of neither the poorest nor necessarily the lowest occupational, educational, and social status groups, as the Mecklin thesis contends. The occupational profile of Newaygo County's Klan, above all else, appears striking for the variety, scope, and diversity of its membership. Viewed as a cross section of the wider society at large, the Klan had a foot, and sometimes much more than that, in every camp.

FROM EXCLUSIVITY TO EXPANSION:
BRIDGING THE GAPS OF SEX, AGE, AND NATIONALITY

The national Klan organization, from the outset of its rebirth in 1915, had always been abundantly clear about its criteria for eligibility—using age, nationality, gender, religious, and racial barriers to restrict membership. Outlining these conditions in its original application for incorporation as "a patriotic, secret social, benevolent order" in Fulton County, Georgia, and later repeating them formally in its official *Constitution and Laws*, the Klan stated that

The objects of this Order shall be to unite white male persons, native-born Gentile citizens of the United States of America, who owe no allegiance of any nature or degree to any foreign government, nation, institution, sect, ruler, person or people; whose morals are good; whose reputations and vocations are respectable; whose habits are exemplary; who are of sound minds and eighteen years or more of age.[27]

Including in its criteria only adult, American-born males, and applying moral conditions to the selection of even these, the 1920s Klan initially traded upon an image of exclusivity. This was to be a secret club, shrouded in intrigue, and designed for the select few supposedly capable of fully comprehending its infinite mysteries, whose possession of such secret knowledge would serve as a boundary between those inside and outside of its ranks. Above all else it was to be a difficult, and thus a desirable, club to get into, its doors open only by strict conditions of eligibility and invitation. In reality, the Invisible Empire quickly defied its stated principles in a heady pursuit of not only numerical strength, but also the financial rewards that would inevitably follow. The criteria by which an individual might be deemed eligible for Klan membership became subject to change as the order grew in popularity and began to see the possibilities of lucrative financial opportunities in new and untapped markets. Ironically, with the notion of exclusivity touted as a chief attraction, the Klan became less and less exclusive at every step as it began to diversify and open its ranks to new categories of members, pulling down the barriers to entry that it had itself erected, and bridging anew the gaps of age, sex, even nationality and race.

The Women of the Ku Klux Klan

Incorporated on 8 June 1923, with its national headquarters located in Little Rock, Arkansas, an organization known as the Women of the Ku Klux Klan (WKKK) became the sole officially recognized Klan organization for females. The idea of capitalizing upon evident female interest in the Klan had come some time before, the issue having been raised and discussed at the Klan's first Imperial Klonvocation in November 1922, and a committee put in place to investigate the possibility of founding a women's order. While a number of rival women's orders had already sprung into existence across the United States by this point (notably a white-robed group known as the *Kamelia*, a money-spinning creation of ousted Klan founder and former Imperial Wizard W. J. Simmons), the formation of the WKKK alone had received official sanction from the Klan national office in Atlanta, and would in fact entail the absorption of many of the smaller regional patriotic women's organizations. The newly created women's order was, officially at least, a legally separate entity from the men's organization, and the establishment of its headquarters away from Atlanta was a sure demonstration by the women of this supposed independence.[28]

While the male Klan officially only "sponsored" the WKKK, there is much to suggest that it exercised a much more overbearing and controlling influence. On an organizational level, the WKKK constitution, power structure, ritual, and regalia were, save for minor modifications, all but identical to those of the Klan itself. Meanwhile, the Klan hierarchy—and in particular Grand Dragon James A. Comer of Arkansas, a prominent member of the Klan's Executive Council—"supervised the affairs of the women of the Klan so closely that in practical matters it was an auxiliary of the men's organization."[29] Comer served as "Imperial Klonsel" or attorney to the women's Klan (making him a frequent and recognizable spokesperson for the group) and had himself invested $8,000 to get the WKKK up and running. He would later respond to female members' protests against his heavy-handed interference by stating that he "owned" the order. Comer's influence was heavily compounded by the fact that the woman placed at the organization's head in early 1924—Imperial Commander Robbie Gill—was singularly open to his ideas and suggestions, having already agreed to become his wife.

Although plagued throughout its lifetime by internal dissension and meddling by the men's organization, the WKKK, once on its feet, did begin to represent a successful, not to mention profit-making, Klan concern. Open to any "white female Gentile person" who was eighteen or over and "a native born citizen of the United States of America who owes no allegiance to any foreign government, nation, institution, or sect," it recruited using exactly the same patriotic "100% American" patter as its male counterpart. Just as with the male Klan, recruitment was a lucrative business. Initially, the initiation fee for a Klanswoman had stood at $5.00 (only half that of the KKK), one dollar of which went to national headquarters with the remainder staying in the state, divided between the organizing Kleagle and various subordinate officers. By the time a revised edition of the WKKK *Constitution and Laws* was printed in January 1927, the compulsory "donation" for each member had risen to $10.00, the same as the men's unit, though this did include "one robe and helmet for her free use."[30]

Despite often struggling with them for control, the women's Klan was at least able to take advantage of the earlier gains made by its like-minded menfolk. Wherever the male Klan was already well established, it provided an easily accessible source of initial memberships for the women's group, through wives, sisters, and daughters who were actively encouraged to enlist. The women's Klan in Pennsylvania, according to the account of Emerson Loucks, provides a good example. In the early days of the organization, the Major Kleagle of the Pennsylvania WKKK employed the state's male Klan network as a recruitment agency of sorts, offering both its Grand Dragon and chief recruiter $1 for every woman that could be signed up via family connections in the male unit. Requiring little more effort than for the male officials to issue an order urging state Klansmen to bring their own womenfolk into the Klan fold, the Grand Dragon declared it "some of the easiest money I ever made."[31] In return for such cooperation in the initial stages of recruitment, it was common for the wives and sisters of prominent local Klan officials to receive preferential treatment within the women's order. After taking the oath, many high-ranking wives were themselves then appointed as recruiters or Kleagles, working locally on a per-member commission basis to bring more and more women into the organization.

The WKKK made its first appearance in the state of Michigan in early September 1923, just a few months after its national inception. A front-page article in Michigan's edition of the *Fiery Cross* declared that "thousands of women" had met in some woods near Detroit on September 3, attending a "big all-day basket picnic." A succession of impressive speeches on "Americanism and the Ku Klux Klan" had been "heartily applauded" and women speakers "received with a marked degree of enthusiasm." The mammoth event, marking "the opening of the women's organization in Michigan," was concluded with the mass initiation of "a gigantic class of candidates," the very first of their kind in the whole state.[32] Building upon its initial foothold in the metropolis of Detroit, the organization would eventually extend its influence across the length and breadth of Michigan, in cities and small towns alike. The hosting of the WKKK's annual national convention, or Imperial Klonvokation, in Detroit by the summer of 1925 was a sure sign of the strength and the rapid progress of the women's Klan there in a short space of time. At the head of the organization in the Wolverine State was Major Kleagle Mary J. Bishop, the officer charged with organizing the whole of the Michigan "Realm." Bishop established her administrative headquarters in the western Michigan city of Grand Rapids, just twenty miles south of Newaygo County's southernmost border.

The first addition to the women's ranks in Newaygo County did not come until early March 1924, some six months after the organization had emerged in Detroit. Once recruitment did take hold, however, enthusiasm swept through Newaygo County every bit as rapidly as it had for the men's organization. Typically, the Women of the Ku Klux Klan flourished in areas where the corresponding men's unit already enjoyed a well-established base of support. In the towns of both Fremont and Newaygo, where the male Klan had recently built up a strong following, the women's Klan grew quickly, completing the bulk of its recruitment activities between March and September 1924. Newaygo averaged around 12 recruits per month over this period, amassing a total of 84 converts, but it was in Fremont that the WKKK really made impressive inroads. Here, fully 199 women signed up for the Invisible Empire, including 187 who took the oath in the first six months, with a bumper crop of 70 converts in the month of April 1924 alone. In the towns of White Cloud and Hesperia, where the men's Klan had not really begun to consolidate until March and April 1924, the women's Klan came slightly later. Female recruiting in these two towns only really got going in June and July 1924, the time lag between establishing the male unit and establishing its female counterpart demonstrating the direct, to some extent dependant, link between the latter and the former. White Cloud eventually produced 70 Newaygo County Klanswomen, and Hesperia (which, it should be remembered, was only half in the county) a more modest 35. A number of smaller villages scattered around the county completed the picture of female membership, with eight members in Grant, three in Woodville, two each in Stanwood (actually located in neighboring Mecosta County) and Biteley, and a solitary Klanswoman in Volney.

Organizers of the Michigan women's Klan certainly profited by coopera-tion with the existing male units in Newaygo County. The very first woman signed up was Lynda Stone of Fremont, who was brought into the organi-zation by a man from outside the county, who she referred to only as "Mr. Minton." Mrs. Stone herself was, even at this early stage, no stranger to the Fremont KKK, and was in fact the wife of prominent Fremont Klansman Elwin J. Stone, who served as the "Kligrapp" (secretary) of the Klan for the whole county. Evidently working on some sort of per-member commission payment, Mrs. Stone quickly put forward the names of a total of 30 new Klanswomen, for whom she personally vouched. This initial recruitment pattern was paralleled in Newaygo, with the first two recruits here—Ada Hendrick and Ruby Wallace—both brought into the organization on the recommendation of their own husbands, each of whom were themselves prominent Klansmen. Both Hendrick and Wallace then promptly set about boosting the WKKK rolls, with each of them personally recommending the memberships of 10 new female recruits.

In all, the names of around 410 women would eventually become asso-ciated with the Women's Klan in Newaygo County. Almost all of these were initiated into the ranks in an intensive recruitment drive taking place countywide between March and November 1924, generally meeting with success in a particular town only once the male unit had consolidated its powers there. In common with the men's unit, the members of the women's Klan spanned the entire range of age groups, with the oldest member aged seventy-nine, and the youngest a mere sixteen years old. Of 404 Newaygo Klanswomen for whom age (at joining the order) can be ascertained,[33] the breakdown reveals a wide appeal, straddling the generations.

While it is important to recognize the women's Klan's considerable success in drawing support from members of all eligible ages—from the older teenager right up to the octogenarian—the figures also reveal very clearly an even stronger pattern: that at the heart of its membership lay women in their twenties, thirties, and forties. In addition, Newaygo Klan records also list the marital status of 406 of the organization's women members. A vast majority (85 percent) were married, with a further 4 percent listed as widows. Only 11 percent of all Klanswomen joining the group were single. Statistically speaking, then, Newaygo County's membership records would seem to suggest that the WKKK in this area was an order dominated by relatively mature women who were almost always wives and, presumably, mothers.

Of the 397 Klanswomen for whom occupational data are available, 314 (an overwhelming 79 percent) listed their sole occupation as "housewife" or "homemaker." This offers up no real surprise, and says much more about the limited occupational opportunities for women, as well as the doggedly persistent nature of patriarchal social structures in rural American homes in the 1920s, than it does about the Klan itself. In this sense, the vast majority

Age Distribution of Newaygo County Klanswomen, 1924–25

Age (at joining)	Number	Percent
20 and under*	33	8.2
21–30	99	24.5
31–40	107	26.5
41–50	85	21.0
51–60	55	13.6
61–70	19	4.7
71–80	6	1.5
Total	404	100

*The lower age limit for membership in the WKKK was 18 years, according to the order's own *Constitution and Laws*. However, the Newaygo County unit appears to have modified this, adopting a lower age bracket of 16, and accepting nine members aged either 16 or 17.

of Klanswomen were absolutely ordinary and unremarkable in terms of occupational standing in a male-dominated small-town economy. There were, however, at least 83 Newaygo Klanswomen who did have regular employment outside of their own homes.

Though drawn from a relatively small number of working Klanswomen, often with only one or two women in each occupation, these data once again display the variety and range of the Klan's reach, with converts in almost every area of employment open to females at the time. Most of these jobs, though outside of the women's own personal domestic environments, still tended to focus upon traditional female roles, be they in paid housekeeping, dressmaking, millinery, beauty, caring professions such as teaching and nursing, service work in shops and restaurants, or various clerical positions. Along with the much larger group of housewives, none of these professions are particularly suggestive of anything other than being a broad cross section of the wider female employment picture. In short, the fields in which the majority of women of the time were occupied (or, more accurately, were confined to by the attitudes of the era) were the same fields, by and large, that occupied the majority of Newaygo Klanswomen.

The one area that does prove particularly striking within this picture is the concentration of schoolteachers involved in the WKKK. While on one hand this could be seen to merely reflect, proportionally, the popularity of teaching as a vocation among working women in the 1920s American small town, it could also be construed as the result of a deliberate recruitment policy, especially in the context of the Klan's constant appeals for the "protection" of the American public schools against the encroachment of foreign parochialism.

Non-Domestic Occupations of Newaygo County Klanswomen, 1923–25

schoolteacher	21	college student	2
storekeeper	7	stenographer	1
clerk	6	reporter	1
dressmaker	5	railroad company worker	1
waitress	5	postmistress	1
high school student	5	assistant postmaster	1
bookkeeper	3	office girl	1
beautician	3	milliner	1
telephone operator	3	housemaid	1
factory worker	3	chambermaid	1
nurse	3	hotel keeper	1
typesetter	2	actress	1
music teacher	2		
farmer	2	Total	83

At the very least, Klan presence among so many schoolteachers, as well as high school and, particularly, college students, indicates a movement that cast its net much more widely than in appeals to the uneducated masses. There were, in addition, a scattering of Newaygo County Klanswomen employed in less traditional, and perhaps more independent roles. Representing Fremont, for instance, were fifty-four-year-old hotel keeper Julia Purcell, who listed herself as "self-employed," and forty-four-year-old Alberta Shewell, a single woman who served as reporter for the *Times-Indicator*. The town of Newaygo, meanwhile, boasted Bessie Robbins, forty-nine-year-old professional actress, and one half of the Clint & Bessie Robbins Acting Company. In Hesperia, thirty-year-old Susie Somers was the town's assistant postmaster and would later hold the main office herself. Forty-seven-year-old Emma Moote of White Cloud, though, had already gone one better, having been appointed postmistress— the first ever woman to have held the office in the town—in January 1924, just six months before joining the WKKK.

In fact, the Klan made direct, at first glance incompatible, appeals to both the traditional and the more overtly modern aspects of American womanhood. By the summer of 1924, the *Michigan Kourier* had begun to dedicate an entire page of its weekly copy to Klanswomen, in most of which it sought both to reinforce and to validate Victorian family stereotypes of woman as virtuous, obedient wife and kind mother. Among various "tributes to womanhood," praising the "divinity, loyalty, and morality" of the American woman, were regular items clearly aimed at the traditional housewife, offering practical housekeeping, beauty, and marriage tips. Typical of such lifestyle advice was the following nugget, designed to allay the risk of marital arguments when the weather was unseasonably hot, causing tempers to fray: "One excellent way to keep the household in a good humor under such circumstances is to provide cooling things to drink. A tall glass of iced tea with a suggestive sprig of mint in it and a slice of lemon on the side of the glass has prevented many a divorce, we venture to assert." Klan pointers on beauty, meanwhile, tended to emphasize the traditional, the inexpensive, and the homemade solution, casting a scornful eye toward the modern, the faddish, and the excessively youth-centered fashion accessory. An ad in the Klan women's pages offered "complexion hints for the girl—or her grandmother—who would rather look pretty than acquire a fashionable tan," promising a "true and tried homemade lotion that cannot be excelled by the professional beauty-maker's arts. It is a lotion made from the parings of the homely cucumber, and is as efficacious as it is cheap."[34]

The Klan housewife might also be offered helpful or inspirational poems in these pages, emphasizing the vital importance of her social role as mother, protector, and moral educator, tying this idea in conveniently with the Klan's self-appointed role as America's own guardian. Take, for example, just the final two stanzas of *If All Women Were Klanswomen*, a lengthy and saccharine-sweet offering, telling the story of a poor and neglected orphan girl, ignored in the street and left close to death by hundreds of members of an uncaring non-Klan public, only to be saved by the timely intervention of a kindly Klanswoman:

> "Never mind, my little darling,
> You come right along with me.
> And I will give you every comfort,
> For I am a Klanswoman, don't you see.
> I will love you and protect you,
> Like a true American should;
> You will find out that the Ku Klux
> Stands for everything that's good."
> Now all of you can imagine
> What this world of ours would be,
> If our women were all members
> Of the Klan that's true and free.
> Let's us all be for America,
> Faithful, truthful and ever kind.
> Let us make this country purer
> For the ones we leave behind.[35]

While relentlessly aiming to sanctify and exalt the image of woman as devoted mother, homemaker, and wife, Klan literature, somewhat conversely, also seemed eager to celebrate examples of the strong, if uncommon, independent career woman. Running right alongside the homemaking advice in the *Michigan Kourier*, for instance, was a picture and laudatory note in praise of one such extraordinary individual: "The deputies say 'Yes Ma'am' to the Undersheriff at Cody, Wyoming, for the Undersheriff is Mrs. W. H. Loomis," it reads. "Her first arrest was a bootlegger with a 'mean' reputation; but he meekly said 'Yes Ma'am' when she served a warrant on him." Similarly praised were the women who could enter a man's world without compromising their femininity. "We thrill to the account of a pretty young woman in Iowa, or thereabouts who is operating a line of buses," reads the *Kourier*, adding with some wonder that she "is thoroughly normal in every way," and "yes; she rouges a little and powders her nose." Continuing in the same vein, the writer adds that "verily this is the age of woman—leaving the bragging for the men . . . business has put on petticoats—fashionable ones at that."[36]

Printed at the foot of the same page, an official WKKK recruitment ad declares that "THE FATE OF THE NATION IS IN THE HANDS OF ITS WOMEN" and that "the Women of the Ku Klux Klan offers them the one organization through which they may direct their strength" toward becoming "a power for good in the United States." Cast in the mold of protectors, educators, and moral guardians of the community, American women were urged to embrace Klan membership as a matter of duty. Providing, that is, that they were "native born, white Protestant, [and] Gentile." Centered around an explanation of core Klan ideals, the recruitment piece bound together the organization's vague and multi-tentacled appeals, offering up something for every group it had tried to canvass. To the educator, it cried that "the foundation of every state is the education of its youth," and called for "the protection and extension of the public school system . . . the complete separation of church and state." To the nurturing, devoted, and protective housewife and mother, it promised "the preservation of the sanctity of the home, and the protection of pure womanhood; the support of Protestantism and a personal acceptance of Christ and his teachings" as well as "the maintenance of those American ideals of life, society and government." Finally, of the strong, independent and newly enfranchised modern woman, it demanded an assertive political activism, calling for "the restriction of immigration; the continuance of white supremacy; the preservation of law and order."[37]

The Junior Ku Klux Klan and the Tri-K Klub

In the summer of 1923, the Grand Dragon of Oregon, in an address to the inaugural national meeting of Grand Dragons, first suggested the formation of a Klan auxiliary "exclusively for the benefit of our Protestant boys." The main object of such an order, he said, "should be the serious work of character building through right thinking, by ways and means of Klannishness." The idea was to introduce "Klannish" values to America's youth in its formative years, to instill a ready-made crop of future citizens and Klansmen with "clean and constructive thought," Protestant values, and "noble purpose." Intended as a stepping stone toward full-paying senior KKK membership, the Junior Klan was to be a site for religious, moral, and practical instruction, as well as an instrument of parental control in the face of societal concerns over the increasing independence and autonomy of youth and a perceived disintegration of traditional family life. The average boy's mind, after all, continued the Dragon, "is like a plate of putty, in which impressions are easily made. It is easy to direct and persuade him to think right, once he has assumed the right mental attitude." As a result, "the reform schools ultimately can be emptied and closed and the crop of criminals can be reduced to an unheard-of minimum." The young Klan recruits, aged twelve to eighteen, who would sport a uniform and ritual derivative of the adult order, need only be white, Protestant, native-born Americans. Children of KKK parents were obvious targets, but the lack of Klan parentage was no disadvantage, and could even work to the benefit of the adult order, as "the boy in his Klan could soon interest them" in joining the senior order themselves. While youngsters might be drawn to the Invisible Empire by little more than the prospect of horseplay and adventure to be found in outlandish regalia and strange ritual, the Grand Dragon chose to envision their attraction as a much more romantically inspired one:

> The Klan idea will appeal with resistless force to the imagination and the heart of the average Protestant boy, to whom the Klansman, let us hope, is a true hero—the incarnation of all manly virtues, a knight "without fear and without reproach." The Klan boy's auxiliary . . . speedily would become the greatest order for boys, numerically and otherwise, in all America or the world.[38]

Whatever the case, plans for a youth auxiliary were quickly realized and enthusiastically greeted, and the Junior Klan was launched before the end of the year, would spread to fifteen states by 1924, and to twenty-two states by early 1925. It was particularly strong across the Midwest, where the first units were established, with a large presence in Indiana, Ohio, and Michigan. Accompanying the new auxiliary was its own official newsletter, the *Junior Klansman*, touted as the "little brother to the *Fiery Cross*," and handled by the same editor, with "news items, sketches, drawings, [and] cartoons" contributed by the nation's Junior Klansmen.[39] At around the same time, the WKKK established a corresponding auxiliary unit for girls, known as the Tri-K Klub. Just as with the male group, this organization mimicked the style and trappings of its parent order, while declaring that it would provide young American girls with "the training which will make them capable of assuming the responsibilities of the future mothers of the race." According to a speech by New Jersey's Major Kleagle Leah H. Bell, who supervised the girl's auxiliary in the state, "It is our purpose to [teach] . . . the young women of today who will become the mothers of tomorrow . . . the vital things that they should know if the womanhood of America is to be kept clean." For the good of the nation's future, then, "moral education is the need of America today . . . and that is the reason for the Tri-K club."[40]

Very little is known about the actual membership figures for either the Junior Ku Klux Klan or the Tri-K club in any area of the United States. Membership rolls are notoriously rare, and none at all are known to survive anywhere in the state of Michigan. That is not to say, however, that there was no Junior Klan activity there. On the contrary: Michigan was one of the first strongholds of the Junior Klan auxiliaries, and all indications from the Klan press in fact point to a buoyant Klan youth scene right across the state. First indications of an interest in Michigan were apparent very early, when an August 1923 issue of the *Fiery Cross* claimed that the fledgling junior organization had received many enthusiastic written requests for chapters in this state as well as others. The Klan organ advertised the juniors' membership fee at $3 per child, with the membership qualification based around "an understanding of the meaning of the constitution."[41] Barely two months later, the *Fiery Cross* declared that interest was positively overflowing in Michigan, and that directors of the boys' junior order "are now located at Flint, Pontiac, Lansing, Saginaw, Bay City, Kalamazoo, Muskegon, and many other points . . . large organizations will be built in these cities in the near future. Other points in Michigan will be covered as fast as possible." Subsequent issues featured regular ad campaigns aimed at drumming up memberships for the junior order, urging Klan parents to "see to it that your boy or your girl joins." The Klan press would continue into the late 1920s to chart the growth and influence of the boys' and girls' orders all over Michigan. As well as noting the youngsters' frequent presence at the parades and celebrations of the senior Klan organization, there were innumerable reports of various camps, parades, band recitals, and sporting events in, among many other locations, Alma, Flint, Kalamazoo, Grand Rapids, Lansing, Detroit, and Saginaw.[42]

Wolverine Women, a Klan newsletter produced specifically by the WKKK of Michigan and sent out to all women's units in the state, particularly concerned itself with boosting the numbers of the Tri-K girls. Its first issue declared that the women's order was "anxious to charter every Tri-K organization of sufficient size in this state," and the junior order's leaders were so eager to display its numerical strength, even to other sections of the Klan movement, that they offered rewards for visible participation. In anticipation of a large outdoor July 4th celebration to be held at the Jackson County fairgrounds (to which Michigan's Klansmen had invited all Klanswomen, junior units, and interested "Protestant Americans"), the WKKK promised that "$5 in gold will be given to the largest delegation of Tri-K girls." Full membership in the

Tri-K Klub itself was offered at $5 per recruit, along with the incentive that "when they reach the age of 18 years [the girls] will graduate into the senior organization without any further donation fee." Indeed, Klan leaders were so preoccupied with the idea of securing future members for the ranks of the parent organizations that they began to look at recruiting, quite literally, from the cradle. Many Michigan Klanswomen would induct their youngest children and toddlers, aged anywhere between birth and twelve years, into the Klan "Kradle Roll," often furnishing the miniature Klansfolk with tiny versions of the Invisible Empire's robe and hood. The "presentation ceremony of the Kradle Roll" for the Saginaw Klan, for instance, as described in the pages of *Wolverine Women*, involved "eleven babies and their mothers being presented by the Excellent Commander." This officer, the highest-ranking in the local WKKK unit, then "presented each baby with a little silk American flag. The service was very beautiful and impressive, as the mothers, each in a white robe held their children in their arms or by the hand." So inspiring was the performance, apparently, that "one of the babies and its mother was presented at the national meeting in Indianapolis."[43]

Despite a lively and well-documented junior Klan presence around the state, no tangible records of junior membership exist for any Michigan Klavern, and Newaygo County Klan No. 29 is sadly no exception. The strength of both the men and women's Klan here, though, coupled with the obvious activity of the Junior Klan and Tri-K Klub in nearby vicinities, suggests that a presence in Newaygo, if not entirely a certainty, is at least highly likely. Census records show that, in all, 7,210 of the county's 17,378 residents in 1920 (or around 41.5 percent of the entire population) were under twenty-one, white, and native-born. Figures such as these would certainly suggest the presence of a sizable, eligible, and potentially receptive market—many of whom, of course, were already the offspring of known county Klansfolk. The question of why no records survive for the juniors alone remains unexplained. Perhaps the method of record-keeping for the junior units in general was a less formalized affair, or somehow administrated differently. This, at least, might begin to account for the fact that no membership rolls have ever surfaced—statewide—while adult rolls clearly have. Equally, it is possible that the junior Klan here never grew large enough to receive official recognition and a charter, its records remaining "unofficial" and falling by the wayside at some long-lost juncture. Perhaps, indeed, for Newaygo County, it never existed at all. We can but speculate—though in many respects, but for the absence of an actual list of members, it seems more difficult to conceive of a Newaygo County Klan operating without a junior unit than with one.

The American Krusaders

Ever eager to extend its financial base of paying converts, the Ku Klux Klan soon began to turn its attention towards the assimilated immigrant. Early efforts at opening the doors of the Invisible Empire to the naturalized American saw the creation of an order known as the Royal Riders of the Red Robe. Beginning sometime in 1923 in the Pacific Northwest states, it was organized by Dr. M. W. Rose, a naturalized Canadian in Portland, Oregon, with aid from Major Luther I. Powell, the powerful King Kleagle of neighboring Washington State. Sporting robes of crimson rather than white, and headed by Supreme Regents and Ragons rather than Emperors and Dragons, the Royal Riders offered "a real patriotic organization to all Canadians, Englishmen, and other white, gentile, Protestants," barring immigrants from areas such as Greece, Italy, and the Balkans. Canvassing most conspicuously in cities with large immigrant populations, notably Chicago, the Royal Riders appealed to "leaders in all walks of life . . . who, except for the accident of foreign birth, would be members of the Ku Klux Klan." While reaching out to the immigrant might have seemed a strange move for an organization that actively campaigned for immigration restriction, the potentially lucrative financial incentive, as ever, won the day. No coincidence, then, that only once it had managed to find a way to incorporate "aliens" into its vast moneymaking pyramid did the Klan suddenly begin to laud "the importance of organizing that large group of good citizens who are, and have long been, 100 percent Americans in everything except birth."[44]

With money to be made, the Royal Riders organization would very shortly be absorbed by a much larger-scale, nationwide Klan campaign with exactly the same setup and intentions. This venture saw the creation of an officially sanctioned Klan auxiliary named the American Krusaders, an organization incorporated in Little Rock, Arkansas, in August 1923 by "several leading Klansmen of the nation." Two of the four names listed as incorporators were Dr. M. W. Rose, the man behind the establishment of the Royal Riders, and Judge James A. Comer, who had a strong financial stake and substantial influence in the women's Klan. Entry requirements were all but identical to those of the regular Klan, in that applicants, even though they could not claim a native birthright, must at least be "white, Protestant, gentile, and over eighteen years of age." The only exception to this was that American citizenship, once the immovable cornerstone of Klan beliefs, was now not an absolute prerequisite. With U.S. immigration papers to be treated as degrees, and to some extent status symbols within the Krusader organization, they were aspirational rather than mandatory for those of foreign extraction seeking affiliation with the parent order. From the pages of the *Imperial Night-Hawk*:

> It is not necessary for a foreign-born resident of this country to be a citizen of the United States in order to join the Krusaders. The order seeks naturalization later, however. The first papers will be in the nature of the first degree, and the second papers establishing full citizenship will be in the nature of the second degree.[45]

The American Krusaders declared themselves to be "a Protestant Christian order of Caucasian citizens" who, alongside their Klan brethren, "would revive the spirit of chivalry" in the United States. Unfortunate nationalities of origin aside, this was a gathering of "men and women who are clean, honest, intelligent and desirable citizens," who, unlike those less desirable immigrants from Catholic sections of the globe, "are readily amalgamated, for they are amenable to the genius of our Republic." Once seemingly unworthy of the "100% American" tag, the Klan had legitimized the case of the foreign Protestant, and, though still keeping him at a slight distance because of his "alien" heritage, given him equal opportunity with any white Protestant American to part with the all-important $10 per head initiation fee.[46]

The notion of accepting foreign-born individuals into Michigan's Klan presented very few problems. In fact, one Klan insider even claimed that the idea of an auxiliary for the foreign-born, and even the name itself, was a Michigan innovation in the first place, plagiarized by the national office. The Krusader organization, wrote Edgar Allen Booth, "was conceived by two men who . . . had charge of the Klan propagation in the Wolverine state." After perfecting their plans for the unit, "they took up the matter with Imperial Wizard Evans, who turned a deaf ear to the proposition." The Krusaders did, however, appear a short time later, "but the Michigan men had no say in it," the lucrative job of building up the order instead having been given to one of Evans's closest friends and allies within the Klan.[47] Nevertheless, when it did arrive, the Klan establishment in the state of Michigan welcomed the American Krusaders auxiliary with open arms, and the "foreignness" of its recruits does not seem to have been an issue of any concern. On the contrary, one Michigan Klan paper reported with some pride on the rousing concert given by the choir of an Upper Peninsula Klavern in which "most of the singers are of Finnish extraction," and who "for the benefit of their guests sang several songs in Finnish." Their eminent guests included a number of state-level Klan officers as well as the Grand Dragon of the entire Michigan Realm himself. Other articles in the Michigan Klan press gave similar high praise to the foreign-born auxiliary and its members. "If some of the readers of the *Night-Hawk* could only meet with and talk to the members of the American Krusaders," read the Saginaw Klan organ, "you would be convinced in a very short time." These men alone were to be respected for their unique perspective, having seen "the deplorable conditions existing in the European countries today . . . [and] without hesitation robed themselves in the mantle of Christian America." Indeed, "the American Krusaders find a place in the hearts of every Klan member . . . [and] in our estimation deserve more credit than we," for the simple reason that "while we are Americans by birth, they are Americans by choice."[48]

In common with many Michigan locations in which the Klan showed a presence, Newaygo County had its very own, albeit small, unit of the American Krusaders auxiliary. This at least demonstrates that innovations within the Klan movement, even those designed to cater for the more cosmopolitan, immigrant-rich urban centers, certainly made their way to KKK units in the more provincial areas. Officially listed as Krusaders were a total of twenty-one Newaygo County residents, almost all of them (eighteen of the twenty-one) male. The first Krusader was signed up in Fremont in late October 1924, with a further thirteen recruited in the two months that followed, most of those also residing in the Fremont area. A later burst of recruitment activity more than half a year later would see seven more members added to the Krusader ranks in mid-1925, this time mostly from the White Cloud area. Entirely in keeping with recruitment patterns of the main Klan units, the Krusaders found converts first in Fremont, where the main men's Klan had very recently been doing well. Only later did they move on to success in White Cloud, which had been "kluxed" slightly later by the regular Klan. Overall recruitment in the county's other major town, Newaygo, had dropped off significantly by the time the Krusaders arrived, a fact reflected in the relative dearth of foreign-born converts there. In all, the county seat of White Cloud produced nine American Krusaders, and the business center of Fremont a comparable eight, while Newaygo managed only three, and the county border town of Hesperia just one.[49]

Nineteen of the twenty-one Krusaders listed their age at joining the order, revealing a significantly older profile than that of the rest of the county's Klan contingent. While foreign-born recruits did span a fair range of ages between the oldest member at seventy-five and the youngest at thirty-four, this was a group with an average age of fifty-three and no representation from any single individual aged below their mid-thirties.

Age Distribution of American Krusaders in Newaygo County, 1924–25

Age (at joining)	Number	Percent
31–40	2	10.5
41–50	6	31.6
51–60	6	31.6
61–70	4	21.0
71–80	1	5.3
Total	19	100

With core membership in the forties, fifties, and sixties age range, this was clearly the most mature group, age-wise, of all those associated with the Newaygo County Klan. As if to compound this air of settled middle age, not one Krusader was unmarried either, the only single man among them being not an untamed bachelor, but an aging widower. Occupations among American Krusaders (allowing for the small size of the sample) conform by and large to the patterns among other Klan groups in Newaygo County. In other words, they demonstrate that within the context of a predominantly rural, small-town economy, the Invisible Empire still managed to reach out to a wide variety of occupations and social status groups. Of three Krusader women, two, unsurprisingly, were "homemakers," while the remaining one made her living as a music teacher. The men's occupations are more demonstrably varied, split equally between blue- and white-collar jobs, with nine Krusaders in each. Of the manual workers, five were farmers, with one each working as a janitor, decorator, mechanic, and railroad section foreman. Taking the oath alongside these men were four proprietors of small businesses, a bank clerk, a cashier, and a chiropractor. At the more prestigious end of the small-town social spectrum was an elected official in the shape of longstanding county clerk G. W. Shepherd, and the Newaygo Methodist Church minister, Rev. James Leitch.

Viewed as "aliens" to the American nation, all foreign-born individuals wishing to forge an association with the KKK faced a set of questions more stringent than those put to their native-born counterparts.[50] Key to the qualifying questionnaire given to all aspiring American Krusaders was the sensitive issue of allegiance, and the implications of this upon assimilability with American values as interpreted by the Klan. First and foremost, applicants were asked to identify their nation of origin. Unsurprisingly, the individuals who successfully made their way into Newaygo County's Krusader division came, by and large, from countries with strong Protestant traditions, as well as from English-speaking nations. A third of Newaygo's

Krusaders had made the relatively short trip from Canada (seven), while Germany (three), England, Scotland, Sweden, and Finland (two each) were also represented. Meanwhile, Holland, as well as the more predominantly Catholic nations of Austria and France contributed one member each. In addition to stating birthplace, an indication of English literacy levels was required from all candidates, and the qualifying process made it clear that each one would need to "learn . . . our language and encourage others to do so." Application papers posed the question quite plainly: "Can you read and write the English language?" and implied that a negative response would be an unfavorable one. Fully satisfying the Klan's benchmark in this regard, every one of Newaygo's Krusaders answered in the affirmative.

In order to become a fully trusted member of the Klan auxiliary, prospective Krusaders would still have had to convince the KKK that they retained no ties to any foreign "political and ecclesiastical authority," which meant, in short, the Pope in Rome. As such, an identification of the applicant's church affiliation was required. Generally speaking, the Klan found favor in almost any strain of Protestantism, and certainly any kind of Protestant church was better than no church at all in the Klan view. The *Imperial Night-Hawk* insisted that "one of the foremost duties of a Klansman is to worship God. Every Klansman each Sunday should attend the church of his choice." On many occasions, notably in the pages of its various news publications, the organization urged its members simply to "Go to Church Sunday," quite happily listing a wide-ranging directory of local churches, just so long as it kept good Americans away from the clutches of the Catholic and Jewish "menace."[51] In light of this, the eighteen Newaygo Krusaders for whom a church affiliation was noted threw up no surprises at all—except, perhaps, in the variety of denominations. Aside from one member who described himself simply as a "Protestant," a total of eight different churches were represented. Baptists and Congregationalists led the way with four members apiece, followed by Methodists, Lutherans, and Swedish Mission (two members each), and finally Presbyterian, Christian Scientist, and Dutch Orthodox churches with one member each in the foreign-born auxiliary. A somewhat varied tapestry of international Protestantism, then, but all admissible to the broader church that was the Ku Klux Klan.

Further questions asked Krusaders-to-be if they were willing to renounce all civil obligations to their former governments and instead "comply with and actively support the Constitution of the United States." The ultimate indication of willingness to do so, and to thereby prove loyalty both to the Klan and the country, was to become a legal U.S. citizen. According to notes compiled on each Krusader, at least twelve of Newaygo County's eighteen male recruits had, at the time of their admittance into the foreign-born auxiliary, already been granted full U.S. citizenship by naturalization. The others, too, had begun the process of application. A significant and influential figure in this respect was George W. Shepherd, an immigrant from Ontario, Canada, who had received his own citizenship papers in 1895, having arrived in the United States some ten years earlier. Firmly establishing himself in Newaygo County, Shepherd had been elected to the office of county clerk in 1905, a position he would hold continuously until 1932. Among his many responsibilities in this professional capacity was the official administration of citizenship applications filed by all foreign-born county residents. In May 1925, Shepherd joined the tight-knit ranks of the American Krusaders, where he found himself lined up alongside three men for whom he had handled successful citizenship applications in the recent past. In 1926, he would personally hear the first sworn declarations of a further two of his foreign-born Klan brethren, both of which would ultimately result in legal citizenship status.

Each application for naturalization also required sworn affidavits from two independent witnesses who were willing to attest that the candidate was "a person of good moral character, attached to the principles of the Constitution of the United States . . . [and] in every way qualified to be admitted a citizen." Though a handful of foreign-born men had not already been U.S. citizens upon joining the American Krusaders, their subsequent applications to gain this status reveal something of the acceptance and respect that they had gained within the wider Klan community in the meantime. In all, the outstanding citizenship petitions of five Krusaders were supported by men who had also signed up with the Newaygo County Klan. Moreover, in three of these five cases, not just one, but both of the required signatures came from men who had belonged, or, to use the Klan rhetoric, could "always be depended upon."[52] Clearly, the foreign-born individuals who became Krusaders in Newaygo were able to do so because they represented, in Klan eyes, the "acceptable" face of immigration in the 1920s. Law-abiding, willing and eager to assimilate, English-speaking, and Protestant, they were the polar opposite of the demonized and dangerous Catholic and Jewish "tidal wave" of KKK propaganda.[53] Settled into family life, and well-established within their adopted neighborhoods, they were foreigners—but they were foreigners almost and very nearly "like us." As such, they were easily absorbed into a community and into a Klan whose own collective immigrant roots were anything but distant.

IN WIDER CONTEXT: INTEGRATED KLAN
SOCIABILITY AND "INVISIBLE IMPERIALISM"

Putting the obvious financial incentive aside for a moment, the motivation behind opening up the Klan movement may have been less about egalitarian inclusion and Protestant solidarity than it was about basic self-preservation, accommodation, and placation. Before the creation of a women's order, Klan periodicals regularly published letters from women protesting against their omission from the movement, and calling for ways to bring them into the KKK fold. Often claiming to be wives of Klansmen, they bemoaned the fact that the Klan oath of secrecy left them unfairly excluded from the full confidence of their husbands, with fraternal secrets remaining privileged even within the sacred confines of marriage.[54] It was a common theme in the world of all-male secret societies, a social form that had flourished in the United States for many years, and a problem that tended also to have a common solution. As Mark Carnes, in his study of secret brotherhoods in Victorian America, notes, the creation of female auxiliaries occurred initially almost entirely as a means of placation, a way of heading off a growing spousal opposition to male-only membership before it became too threatening.[55]

By reaching out and including women in the Klan movement, leaders could not only be seen to accommodate their apparent interest, but could also exercise some element of covert social control. Invariably, Klan literature projected a certain image of dutiful and pure "American womanhood," serving home and husband as well as country, and there is no doubt that women within the Klan had to put up with a tremendous amount of subservient, traditionally female roles, from food preparation to banner-sewing to general support of the male order. Klan children, too, were subject to the same manner of social molding, with the boy-scout-like Junior Klan teaching young males the basics of masculine outdoor rough-and-tumble, and the Tri-K Klub more confined to exemplifying the role of meek junior homemaker. Both were trained in the dying art of parental reverence and respect for their elders.

Whereas Mary Ann Clawson has noted in fraternal history "the development of a more couple-oriented sociability that was to emerge in full force during the 1920s,"[56] the Klan in many ways went further than this. Moving away from the male-only world of fraternal diversion toward a more family-based, gender-integrated sociability, it included even the very youngest members of the domestic unit and, beyond that, extended its notions of belonging and solidarity into the wider community. In its creation of the American Krusader auxiliary, the Klan provided a measurable space for a sanitized, Americanized version of immigration, which was perhaps the only version that it was willing or able to try and come to terms with. Having created for itself an acceptable immigration, an acceptable level of women's participation, a reinforcement of Victorian family values in regard to the place of the wife and offspring within a patriarchal structure, the Klan aimed not so much to include others, but to preserve itself. Upholding traditional values against the ravages of bewildering, fast-changing times, these were perhaps the last vestiges of white male control over women, over children, and over ethnic "others" who were all threatening as never before to burst unpredictably free.

Sometimes, the movement's relentless drive for membership led it onto uncertain ground, with the finer points of KKK recruitment policy less than strictly applied. Newaygo County's regular Klan, for instance (as opposed to its American Krusader division) contained three foreign-born men—one each from Canada, England, and Holland—as well as one German woman. Despite the Klan constitution's inflexible edict that "no foreign-born citizen can ever enter the portals of the Invisible Empire," all four were admitted to the Klan in April, May, and June of 1924, around half a year before such admissions were legitimized by the creation of a local Krusader auxiliary. Even after the Krusaders unit arrived, these four retained their status as members of the main men's and women's orders. Whether the rules were overlooked for convenience, inadequately enforced in the first place, or perhaps just poorly understood is not clear. What seems to have counted for much more is the fact that these applicants (a fifty-four-year old widow, and three married men well into their sixties, all of them Protestant) seemed harmless enough, well-integrated, eager to join, and—perhaps crucially—willing to pay for the privilege.

Having reneged at various points upon almost every facet of its original criterion of membership, the Klan was to launch its money-making formula widely and improbably at any conceivable (and sometimes quite inconceivable) market. Chief Klan publicist Edward Young Clarke, certainly, dreamed "of extending the Klan's dominion to include all Anglo-Saxon, Germanic and Scandinavian portions of the globe," and there are numerous accounts detailing real efforts to do just that.[57] Even within American borders, unlikely attempts were made to organize auxiliaries among "Protestant Negroes." The *New York Times* revealed exactly such a move by the Klan in Suffolk County, New York, and also reported the formation of a "Negro Klan" set up by KKK leaders in Youngstown, Ohio, which went by the name "the Loyal Legion of Lincoln." Kathleen Blee, similarly, noted the creation of Klan "colored divisions" in Indiana and other states. With garb consisting of red robes, white capes, and blue masks, its members were kept distinct from "real" Klansmen, as well as being "prohibited from . . . handling any membership funds."[58] More isolated (and perhaps more of a publicity stunt aimed at demonstrating the power of conversion to righteousness by the anti-Catholic Michigan Klan) was a September 1926 headline in the Klan's *Fellowship Forum*. "Romanists take stand for U.S." read the banner, telling the tale of two young Catholic men in Dearborn, Detroit, who had renounced the evils of their former faith and officially been accepted into the ranks of the KKK.[59]

Newaygo County's Klan had its own ambiguities in this direction, the unit including on its membership rolls at least two members who were of distinctly nonwhite heritage. In cousins Douglas and Lawrence Aiken, members of a family long established in the Newaygo area, the Klan had as recruits two young men who were also eighth-generation descendants of the Grand River band of Ottawa Indians.[60] Undeniably, the Aikens had a much more compelling claim to be "native-born" indigenous Americans than any white person parading in the Klan. Quite how the Newaygo KKK managed to reconcile their presence in its ranks with the internal stipulation that "the Knights of the Ku Klux Klan is . . . a white man's organization" is difficult to imagine. Indeed, national leaders of the Klan movement were very fond of self-righteously referring to their own white, Protestant constituents as being "native" to the American continent. The inconvenient truth of the existence of prior claims by Native American tribal peoples was an uncomfortable question, and one that, it seems, was never tackled in any public forum by the KKK of the 1920s.

Whether it meant tearing down the harsh restrictions of age, gender, nationality, or in extreme cases race and religion, that it had itself so carefully erected, the Klan movement evidently saw no harm in relaxing its boundaries, especially where it sensed opportunities to make money or gain influence. Adjusting its ethos to move rapidly from exclusion to inclusion, and from inclusion to expansion, the Klan had begun to take its own egotistical self-portrait of a monumental "Invisible Empire" all too seriously. The world that it had initially sought to exclude—women, children, the nonwhite, the foreign-born, even foreign territories—it now sought to colonize, to profit from, and ultimately to control. All of this, though, would be meaningless had the KKK not presented, in one way or another, an attractive prospect to the men, women, and children who joined. Not only did the 1920s Klan successfully manage to forge a broad appeal designed to draw in recruits from all ages, social classes, and occupations, but it also expanded its membership base significantly by the inclusion of nonthreatening groups outside of its initial adult, native-born, male sphere of influence. In Newaygo County, as in much of Michigan and indeed the United States, this had meant bridging the differences—between young and old, male and female, manual worker and businessman, naturalized and native-born citizen—and involving them all, side-by-side, in the Klan's patriotic campaign for "100% Americanism."

The Invisible Empire and Small-Town Sociability

Klan Recruitment Channels in Newaygo County

DURING ITS MID-TWENTIES HEYDAY, THERE WAS NO REAL ESCAPING the Klan in the rural small towns in which it had taken root. The Klan was in business, it was in politics, in church, in the fraternal lodges and social clubs, in the diners, the billiard halls, the cinemas, the post offices, in the schoolhouses, and even at home. That is not to say, of course, that it was always visible, or indeed always active, for most of the time it was not. It did not have to be seen, and it certainly did not have to be sheeted. The Klan had a presence in all of these places, and more, because these were the places in which the people who made up the Klan lived, worked, and socialized with one another. At the heart of the KKK, in this peculiar, popular phase of its development, were not the robes, the hoods, or the fiery crosses that became such trademarks of its outward expression, but the ordinary lives of the whole communities with which it became briefly, if intensely, entangled.

Fundamentally, the Klan did not alter the identities of the individuals who joined its ranks, and with or without the sheets, it did not significantly affect the ways, by and large, in which they lived their lives and spent their time. What it did do, briefly, was fit in easily, unremarkably with these lives, and perhaps provide a new and novel setting, a fresh mode of expression in which to continue doing the very same things. By acting like an exclusive lodge, it drew members from other exclusive lodges. By acting like a political party, it drew people from politics. By acting like a church, it drew people from churches—likewise with business, with charity, with entertainment, and so on. Given the initial impetus, its members, for the most part, recruited one another, and they did not—indeed could not—look too far from home. To join them in the KKK, people looked to who they knew—to their families, to their friends, to their colleagues and business associates, and to their lodge brethren. More often than not, some or all of these things intersected, and wherever people interacted socially, the KKK found new recruits, for as many reasons as there were members. That forces within the Klan itself sought members in specific spheres, particularly where that might mean some possibility of exerting influence, seems assured. That these recruits were readily forthcoming—in settings including the public schools, law enforcement, and politics—seems even more so.

ROUTES INTO THE NEWAYGO COUNTY KLAN: FAMILY, WORK, AND FRATERNITY

Among the tangled web of social connections linking individual members of the Newaygo County Klan with one another, the most typical discernable patterns saw Klansfolk acquainted through family, through the workplace, and through common membership of local fraternal associations.[1] Klan application forms required prospective members to specify the name of their spouse, where any existed. That this requirement was complied with, by and large, has made the marital links between Klan members, unlike many other family ties, relatively easy to quantify. In Newaygo County, there were at least 237 Klan couples (that is to say, marriages in which both husband and wife were card-carrying members of their respective units) present in the local KKK. Put into context, this means that a figure approaching 40 percent of all Newaygo County Klansfolk held membership alongside their spouse. In this sense, the Klan demonstrates a wider trend present in American fraternalism of the era—a movement away from the single-sex camaraderie of lodges segregated along gender lines and towards an altogether more inclusive social scene. Indeed, as Mary Ann Clawson has noted, the fraternal orders that continued to grow and find success into the early twentieth century were those that "offered a more couple-oriented sociability to their members," a development that "was to emerge in full force during the 1920s."[2] Within the confines of all-Klan marriages, it was the husband who most often joined the KKK first (195 of 237 cases, or 82 percent). There were exceptions, and in thirty of Newaygo County's Klan-affiliated couples (13 percent), the husband actually followed his wife into the organization, while on twelve occasions (5 percent), the pair signed up together (these few perhaps representing the purest example of a true fraternal, couple-oriented sociability).

To say, however, that the majority of female Klan members were led into the Invisible Empire by a male partner is to oversimplify the situation. Though clearly, as these figures show, it was usually the case within Klannish marriages, this tells only a part of the story. In addition to the 30 Klan wives who joined the order before their husbands, there were 46 single and 18 widowed WKKK members in Newaygo County, as well as another 95 who were married, but whose husbands did not share their affiliation. This gives a combined figure of 189 women in total who signed up for Klan membership either before or without a Klan husband, falling only slightly short of the 195 who followed their husbands in.[3] Despite the fact, then, that the women's Klan has often been dismissed purely and simply as a subordinate organization composed almost entirely of Klansmen's wives, it seems that in reality, female ties to the KKK were not necessarily dependent on a male partner's influence or even complicity. As a colorful illustration of this point, Robert and Helen Lynd, in their classic study of American life during the 1920s, *Middletown*, recount the tale of an Indiana man divorced by his wife for his failure to accept her Klan membership. With his wife officially filing for "non-support," the man in question "stated privately that 'she and I split up over the goddamn Klan. I couldn't stand them around any longer.'" Incidentally, the Lynds, whose book was published in 1929, characterized the Klan as a "lodge," under the subtitle of popular American "leisure activities."[4]

Even if not through the specific influence of a spouse, other intimate family ties were hugely important to Klan recruitment. Of the 189 women, for instance, who joined the WKKK without a Klan husband, at least 78 had another close relative—usually a parent or sibling—in the organization. Taking the county membership as a whole, a minimum of 515 Klansmen and women (almost half of the unit's total) are known to have had at least one other family member in the Klan.[5] Of all nonmarital links, the most frequent and evident existed between members of the nuclear family. Countless father-and-son duos, as well as sets of brothers often found themselves together in the Klan, while mother-daughter combinations and sets of sisters similarly made their way into the WKKK. Being in the Klan alongside in-laws of some description was not uncommon, and, although less frequently, cousins shared their affiliation with cousins, as did uncles and aunts with their nieces and nephews. A few large and extended Newaygo County families were particularly prominent on Klan rolls, with family members of all ages present. The Miller family of Fremont, for instance, was represented by at least 14 Klan members, while the White Cloud Branch family supplied at least 30 to the Invisible Empire (12 men and 18 women), with brothers, sisters, wives, fathers, and uncles all involved.[6] Far more typical, though, were the more modest, but not necessarily straightforward Klan links of families such as the Burkles of Fremont, whose KKK contingent was significant, but certainly not all-encompassing.

As a naturalized citizen of German origin, head of the family Charles W. Burkle was an "American Krusader" rather than a Klansman, joining the auxiliary in October 1924. Both his American-born wife, Della, and his married elder daughter, Elsie, had become affiliated with the Klan more than two months before him, mother and daughter signing up together in August 1924. Elsie's husband, Frank Penrod, had preceded all of them, joining the Invisible Empire in May 1924. Both Charles Burkle's Klan and family ties extended to the workplace, too, where he employed two Klansmen in his Fremont butcher's shop. One of these was the younger brother of Frank Penrod and had signed up for the KKK (on Frank's recommendation) on the very same day as Burkle's wife and daughter. As none of Charles Burkle's seven other children ever signed up for the Klan, it seems likely, then, that the Klan link in the Burkle family was directly attributable to their attachments, both personal and professional, to the two Penrod men.[7]

As well as through family, large numbers of Newaygo County Klansfolk were likewise connected through their jobs, and some of the area's largest employers sported significantly Klan-heavy workforces. Most notable among these was the Newaygo Portland Cement Company, which alone counted 62 Klansmen among its employees. Similarly, though on a smaller scale, the Fremont Canning Company had 28 employees on the Klan rolls by 1925. This included sales manager Daniel F. Gerber, who by 1928 would come up with the idea that would transform the company's fortunes completely, propelling it to national prominence as the enduring giant of American baby-food production, the Gerber Products Company.[8] Newaygo's Rowe Manufacturing Company, meanwhile, employed at least five Klansmen in the shape of four laborers and a foreman, while nine Newaygo Klansmen belonged to the Consumers Power Company. The Pere Marquette Railroad Company, too, employed twelve Klansmen from around the county in a variety of roles, from station foreman to section man to baggage handler.

Much more commonly, though, the KKK made its presence felt within far less grand small-town business establishments, where only a handful of people were employed fairly intimately together, and where family and work often intersected. At the Nels Christenson & Sons grocery store in

Newaygo, for instance, the Klan contingent must have included virtually every employee. Nels (a naturalized Swede and American Krusader) and his two sons Clifford and Walter Christenson (both native-born, so members of the main Klan) all belonged. Each of the three men also had Klan-affiliated wives. The grocery store's deliveryman was also in the Klan, as were its three young clerks (one male, two female). In another notable Newaygo example, the owner of the Valley Inn, Elbert Manning, was an early area Klansman, joining the order within a day of its first appearance in town. Among his Klan employees were clerk Ray Travelbee; candy maker Stacy Bouk; Bouk's bookkeeper wife, Anna; waitress Ruth Banks; and chambermaid Edith Morrison.

Even more so than Newaygo, the city of Fremont was home to a considerable number of small Klannish businesses. Most conspicuous of these were the building contractor Thomas Mullins—a prominent Klansman who recommended nine of his own employees for membership—and the Kingsford Brothers Ford Agency, whose Klan members included the co-owner, four mechanics, three salesmen, and a bookkeeper. Preston Brothers, a sizable farming business, employed eight Klansmen, five of whom were also Preston family members, while five more Klansmen worked at a small service station operating as the Fremont franchise of the Standard Oil Company. The list of small Klannish establishments in Fremont goes on and on, including Reber Brothers clothing merchants (three Klansmen, one Klanswoman); the L. G. Graff Company (four Klansmen); the L. D. Puff Hardware store (three Klansmen); C. W. Burkle Butchers (three Klansmen); the Class Mutual Insurance agency (three Klansmen); Fremont State Bank (three Klansmen); and the Grand Rapids–Fremont Bus Line (four Klansmen) among others.[9]

Often, Klan businesses operated in situations quite amenable to informal socialization, an atmosphere in which connections to the organization could conceivably have been made very easily. The White Cloud offices of Webster Auto Sales, for instance, provided the workplace of brothers Glen and Lyle Webster, as well as auto salesman Collin Decker. All three were Klansmen, and Glen in particular was notable for his twelve recommendations of White Cloud men to the order. No doubt much of this activity was helped along by his extroverted efforts at fostering sociability. As the *White Cloud Eagle* reported in 1923, "Glen Webster has installed a radio outfit in his auto salesroom, and has been holding concerts there the past ten days for the public."[10] It is not much of a stretch to imagine, either, that Fremont's M-24 Restaurant—run by WKKK mother and daughter Harriet and Lauretta Westfall, and also employing young Klansman Charles

Wilkinson—might have become a leisurely Klannish gathering place. Not only was the establishment owned by prolific local Klansman D. W. Markley (who made twenty-three recommendations for membership in Fremont), but it openly advertised its services in the press as "a 100% American café."[11] Similarly, Klansman R. R. Dawson and his WKKK wife Eregail ran a restaurant in White Cloud, also employing Dawson's nephew, W. Lloyd Trimmer. Trimmer was not only a Klansman, but also some sort of officer within the Invisible Empire. Arriving in Newaygo County from Ohio, his Klan membership card was marked "T-1," with a note that his fee had been made "complimentary." His exact role is unclear, but Trimmer certainly made himself known in KKK circles. Having worked for a period in his uncle's Klan restaurant, he left White Cloud for Newaygo in the summer of 1925, to take up employment in the even more Klannish Valley Inn.[12]

The idea of not just an individual, but also his business establishment becoming particularly closely allied with the KKK was a fairly typical one across the Midwest wherever the secret order took hold in the 1920s. In fact, the national Klan administration actively encouraged a practice that it referred to as "vocational Klanishness," calling among Klansmen "for the constant and earnest exercise of this great principle in the realm of one's business or professional life." Outlined in plain terms, with practical applications, in an official 1924 document entitled *The Practice of Klanishness*, the policy entailed, in a nutshell:

> Trading, dealing with and patronizing Klansmen in preference to all others. Employing Klansmen in preference to others whenever possible. Boosting each other's business interest or professional ability; honorably doing any and all things that will assist a Klansman to earn an honest dollar, thereby adding to his material wellbeing, lightening the burden of life for him . . . For an example: if you should come across a person interested in the purchase or sale of real estate, scan your list of known Klansmen and if there be one who is in that line of business (though you may not be so intimately acquainted with him) urge this person to see your particular real estate man . . . do your part in endeavoring to turn the profit to a Klansman. You must not tell this person why you insist on him seeing this particular real estate man, other than that he is worthy and deals honorably. He is a Klansman and you can safely recommend him. Apply this method in regard to Klansmen who are doctors, lawyers, dentists, merchants, barbers, opticians, carpenters, insurance men, taxi cab owners, automobile dealers and ANY and ALL other vocations of men.[13]

As well as favoring businesses run by members, this also meant boosting the reputations of, and thus the prospects of professional advancement for, those members a little lower down the ladder. "Deal with those firms or persons who employ Klansmen in their business," members were instructed, and "if possible let the employer know that you deal with his firm on account of this particular man being employed by him." To facilitate this practice, local Klaverns routinely compiled their own directories of Klan-owned businesses in their jurisdiction. Sometimes, particularly where the KKK was strong, the affiliation of a business was made quite plain. In parts of Indiana, for example, any shopkeepers joining the KKK received placards to display in their store windows emblazoned with the letters "T.W.K."—instantly recognizable to other affiliated parties as "Trade with a Klansman."[14] In light of this, a common charge made against the Klan of the twenties was that it used the idea of vocational Klanishness not merely as a way of boosting its members' business prospects, but rather as a thinly veiled instruction to actively impede the fortunes of competing non-Klan establishments. Kathleen Blee certainly found this to be the case in Indiana, citing the "immediate and phenomenal effect" of Klan boycotts on Jewish- and Catholic-owned stores, which apparently resulted in uncommon numbers of bankruptcies for these groups across the Hoosier state. Pointing particularly to the role played by Klan-friendly housewives in this process, Blee asserts that "a boycott brought even the act of shopping into the fight for racial and religious supremacy" and "infused the ordinary tasks of Klanswomen's lives with political content."[15]

Though there is little evidence to suggest anything approaching a boycott of non-Klan business in Newaygo County (not least because of the lack of either a sizable Catholic or Jewish population there), local merchants, by displaying their Klan affiliations, may well have been attempting to ensure that they stayed on the right side of the Invisible Empire. Coded advertisements, of varying degrees of subtlety, were very popular among Klannish merchants nationwide. Often, they alluded to the Klan's recognizable "100% American" slogan by declaring themselves to be, perhaps, an "American establishment," offering "100% service" or promising a "100% product." The Fremont hardware store of Klansman L. D. Puff, for instance, made a point of advertising the fact that it was particularly well stocked with "MONARCH 100% PURE PAINT."[16] Most frequently of all, Klan businesses tended to include some thinly concealed variation upon the familiar multiple-K theme. Given that the following examples from Newaygo County's newspapers all advertise companies known to employ, or be owned and operated by Klansmen, the signs were there for those who wished to see them. In the image of the Valley Inn candy counter, for instance, despite missing the glaring opportunity at the top of the ad to convert a triple C into a triple K, candy man and known KKK member Stacy Bouk does at least manage to depict himself as the "Kandy Kid." Also interesting, and probably not insignificant, is the otherwise bizarre assertion that "only pure, wholesome candy" is available for sale at Newaygo's very Klannish Valley Inn.

In White Cloud, meanwhile, the W. S. Bird Company employed the same popular gimmick as the Valley Inn had done, substituting K's for C's to produce a striking visual effect while leaving the acoustic message unchanged. Thus, it could knowingly, if not entirely inconspicuously, offer its customers "a most delightful breakfast" of "KREAM FRYDKAKES" along with their morning coffee.

Though much more understated than the previous two, the ad for Glen Webster's auto shop can conceivably be read in a Klannish light, too, especially given the knowledge that he was one of the most active KKK recruiters in White Cloud. Though it may be stretching the bounds a little, it could be argued as significant that the visual centerpiece of the ad forms the shape of a cross, recalling the imagery of the Klan's trademark (though not fiery on this occasion) icon, while also prominently displaying the letters K-L-A-N at its center. An ardent seeker of Klan clues might also suggest that the use of the word "Knight" holds meaning, or even point to the spelling out of the initials KKK, diagonally from top left to bottom right. One suspects, though, that this might go beyond what even Webster intended to convey.

The Valley Inn candy counter, Newaygo
Source: *Newaygo Republican*, 16 November 1923

Ads for Klan-owned businesses in White Cloud
Source: *White Cloud Eagle*, 8 October 1925

Outside of business, but connected in many ways to it, lodge associations provided another avenue of social interaction between Klansfolk. According to *Middletown*, lodges in general were just beginning to decline as "important leisure-time institutions" in the average small town by the mid-1920s, in effect killed as entertainment by "the movies and autos." While not perhaps attracting the social crowds that they had in their heyday around a decade before, the lodges still provided an important function in small-town life. "In the main," wrote the Lynds, referring to the year 1924, "business men join lodges today for business reasons—a gentile business man of any local standing can hardly afford to stay out of the Masons at least; and workers join chiefly for the sickness and death benefits."[17] In Newaygo County, certainly, numerous lodge organizations remained relatively popular, and it was from the ranks of these that many Klansmen and women were drawn. Every new Klan recruit was asked upon joining the Invisible Empire, in fact, to list all of their ties to other fraternal orders. Of 776 Klansmen and 405 Klanswomen who provided such details, a total of 445 men (57.3 percent) and 185 women (45.7 percent) admitted to being members in at least one other ritualistic order besides the Klan.[18] The following tables show the breakdown of just where these memberships were held.

Memberships in Fraternal Societies Held by Newaygo County Klansmen, 1923–25

Free and Accepted Masons	183
Independent Order of Odd Fellows	177
Mystic Workers of America*	60
Ancient Order of Gleaners	43
Grange	24
Loyal Order of the Moose	16
Woodmen of the World	15
Knights of the Maccabee	14
Order of DeMolay (Masonic youth group)	12
Knights of Pythias	10
Benevolent & Protective Order of Elks	9
Patriotic Order of the Sons of America	2
Others	4
Total	569

*The Mystic Workers was a fraternal benefit society "designed to provide financial security for the growing middle class of the Midwest and Northern states." In 1930 it became the Fidelity Life Association.

Memberships in Fraternal Societies Held by Newaygo County Klanswomen, 1924–25

Order of the Eastern Star	69
Rebekah Lodge	44
Ladies of the Maccabee	39
Royal Neighbors	25
Gleaners	16
Grange	14
Mystic Workers of America	8
Loyal Americans	5
Shrine	3
Guardians of Liberty	1
Others	14
Total	238

The KKK was clearly particularly popular among Masons and Odd Fellows, as well as their female auxiliary units, the Order of the Eastern Star and the Rebekah Lodge, respectively. According to the Klan's own careful intelligence report, though, total membership of Masonic groups in Newaygo County in 1923 stood at a comparatively large 1,350, while the figure for Odd Fellows was 585 and the Knights of Pythias 300.[19] What this would seem to indicate is that while a large portion of Klansmen were typically

Masons, Odd Fellows, or other lodge members, by no means did the Klan sign up the entire, or even a majority of the county's fraternal community. What is striking, however, is the variety of different lodges (as opposed to a wholesale overlapping with one particular lodge) whose members would also become involved in the Klan. The Invisible Empire did not simply reach out to one or two such organizations, but seemed to draw in at least some of the members of very nearly *all* of them. In short, the KKK did not appeal exclusively to any one particular fraternity: it went much farther than this, appealing to some element of the wider fraternal mentality, attracting a certain section of fraternalists across the board. Not a total eclipse, by any means, but there is no doubting that mainstream fraternal life and the Ku Klux Klan in Newaygo County overlapped to a very significant degree.

Also represented within these tables are a number of Klansmen and women who held joint, and sometimes multiple, memberships in various combinations of fraternal associations. In fact, at least 109 Klansmen and 43 Klanswomen belonged to two or more of the orders listed above. By adding the KKK to their growing list of affiliations, these individuals, at least, give credence to the idea of the Klan's particular appeal to the typical American "joiner," as articulated by John Moffat Mecklin in 1924.[20] Claiming that "the stronghold of the hundreds of secret lodges in this country is to be found in the small town," Mecklin invoked the humdrum monotony of Sinclair Lewis's *Main Street*, and offered up the lodge as rural America's characteristically inward-looking solution. Only in the clandestine workings of the secret societies could an engaging counterbalance to provincial boredom be found, the lodges providing, as they did, "an element of mystery lacking in the prosaic round of small town life."

No individual was permitted to enter the ranks of the Newaygo County Klan without first obtaining the recommendation of at least one existing member. Staking their own reputation upon the quality of recruit that they put forward, the recommending member would have to know the prospect well enough to personally vouch for his or her suitability for Klandom. In all, 440 members (just over a third) of the Newaygo County Klan made recommendations for others to join them in the Invisible Empire. Of those who did, the most common pattern by far (occurring in 234, or 53 percent of all cases) was for a recommender to put forward the name of just one other person for membership, usually a relative or other close associate. The majority of the rest also recommended only small numbers, with seventy-eight recommenders (18 percent) bringing in two new recruits each, and forty-six (10 percent) endorsing three associates for membership. A relatively small number of others, however, demonstrated a much more apparent and serious dedication to the task of bolstering the secret order's roster. Forty-seven Klan members each recommended either four, five, or six names, while seventeen enthusiasts brought in between seven and ten members apiece. At the higher extremes of recruitment activity were the thirteen energetic Klansfolk who recommended between eleven and fifteen members each, and at the very top, the county's five most zealous members put forward the names of an astonishing 122 converts between them.[21]

Perhaps the most crucial of these individuals was a Kleagle (paid recruiter) named Cyril Waters, who, beginning in August 1923, set about bringing men into the fold in the town of Newaygo, making this the first site of Klan-building in the county. Though born and raised in Newaygo, Waters had spent much of his adult life living and working in Chicago, where his introduction to the secret order had come when he joined the ranks of that city's "Thomas A. Watson Klan No. 16." Newaygo Klan records show that Waters's own KKK membership had been personally sponsored by "G-1 National," the notorious D. C. Stephenson, Grand Dragon of Indiana. Having established Indiana as the nation's premier Klan stronghold, Stephenson's power within the KKK at this time rivaled that of its Atlanta headquarters as he attempted to replicate his achievements and build up the organization across the Midwest—including in (until then largely neglected) Michigan.[22] Waters, given the Klan moniker of "W-1," was probably one of many such established Klansmen sent home by Stephenson's regime to propagate the organization in more remote and untapped areas, using the advantage that their faces were already well-known.

Back from Chicago and settled in his hometown of Newaygo, Waters held a job as a carpenter at the largest industrial plant in the area, the Newaygo Portland Cement Company (N.P.C. Co.), as well as being a member of the local Masonic lodge. His, and the Newaygo County Klan's, very first recruit was one Charles Sheridan, who was both a fellow Mason and, like Waters, maintained close family links with Chicago.[23] Either connection, or both, could have provided the association between the two men. Over the following months, Waters would recommend a total of seventeen men for the Klan in Newaygo, and one more in nearby Grant. The connections between recruiter and recruits are tangled and often difficult to reconstruct, especially where personal relationships may have been concerned, though certain patterns are nevertheless apparent. Waters's recruits, for instance, included six men who shared his Masonic affiliation, and no less than ten who worked alongside him at the N.P.C. Co. Also included were six members of another fraternal society, the Independent Order of Odd Fellows

(IOOF), and though Waters himself did not belong, almost all of them would have known him, and each other, through either work at the N.P.C. Co. or overlapping membership in the Masonic lodge. Family connections also played a part, with Waters recruiting a father and son together, another father and his two sons, and a set of brothers-in-law, all with links either to the Masons, Odd Fellows, or Newaygo Portland Cement Company. The Kleagle also operated much closer to home, with the recruitment of his very own stepson. Waters's batch of eighteen converts would themselves bring in a further twenty-nine memberships directly between them, through their own subsequent recommendations of others for citizenship in the Invisible Empire. With each new Klansman recruiting associates of their own, and these associates in turn doing the same, the pattern would continue, ripple-like throughout the county, resulting in an ever-expanding web of connected individuals that would continue to spread to the point of either saturation or indifference.

Even a glance at just some of the more prominent examples demonstrates that all of the county's top Klan recruiters, male and female, "worked" the same principal channels, exploiting some combination of business, family, and fraternal ties.[24] In Fremont, building contractor Thomas Mullins influenced more men than any other in the entire county to join the Klan. His total haul of recruits stood at twenty-eight, with fifteen of these being drawn from one or other of his three fraternal lodges, namely the Masons, the Odd Fellows, and the Knights of Pythias. One of these men was Mason James Keller, who would later become the Exalted Cyclops (the top-ranking officer) of the entire Newaygo County Klan. Fraternal links aside, Mullins was also a major Fremont employer, and recommended nine of his employees as well as two fellow contractors. Alongside a selection of the town's merchants, he signed up a local dentist, doctor, and two leading figures at the Fremont State Bank, while on the family front, he also sponsored the Klan memberships of his wife's two older brothers.

Restaurant owner D. W. Markley, meanwhile, put forward twenty-three names, including fifteen who belonged to the same fraternities that he was a member of, namely, the IOOF and the Mystic Workers of America. He brought in two father-and-son combinations through IOOF links, including the Fremont chief of police, as well as sponsoring a local Protestant minister and his own brother. Through work, he recommended two of his restaurant employees, and it was also probably in this professional capacity that he was familiar with, and able to sign up, fourteen local merchants and tradesmen. Elwin J. Stone, too, as well as being the local Klan's Kligrapp (secretary), was a prominent Fremont area farmer and Mason. He personally oversaw the entry of twenty-three members into the Klan, including seven fellow farmers and his own farmhand. Eleven Masonic colleagues were also included in the total of nineteen fraternity men he recommended. More personal connections played a part, too, with Stone promoting a pair of men often mentioned in the local papers as his hunting companions, as well as a nephew and a brother-in-law of two of his fellow Masons.

Elwin Stone's wife, Lynda, was the most industrious recruiter of them all, and the primary force driving the growth of the women's Klan in Fremont, if not the whole county. Not only was she the unit's very first Klanswoman, but she put her name to an incredible thirty recommendations of others for membership—exceeding the efforts of any man in Newaygo County, and more than doubling those of any other woman. That she was so centrally involved from the start of the WKKK, and so well connected to a high-ranking officer in the men's Klan, probably indicates that Mrs. Stone herself held office in the women's order. Whatever the case, like the majority of female recruiters, Lynda Stone's work was given a huge helping hand from the male organization simply by the fact that the men's Klan had preceded the women's by at least six months in Newaygo County, preparing the ground. Of the women Stone signed up, twenty-six of the thirty were married, and all but one of these was the wife of a Klan husband. Twenty-three of her thirty recruits worked as homemakers, and the few who did not tended to be younger women in their twenties, working as teachers, stenographers, telephone operators, and bookkeepers.

Even these seemingly more independent females, though, were still linked to the Klan either through a husband or a parent. Indeed, of the four women who remained unmarried, three were young ladies whose parents, both mother and father, were Klan members. While mothers and daughters sometimes signed up in tandem, and while certain organizational links did exist (seven of the women were members of the Order of the Eastern Star, just like Stone), the main pattern in this case is quite clear. Perhaps by virtue of the fact that they were among the very first women to join the WKKK, Mrs. Stone's group was a collection made up almost exclusively of the wives and daughters of, often quite senior, Fremont Klansmen.[25]

Other major recruiters to the women's Klan, working after Lynda Stone's initial efforts, managed to find converts in a slightly broader range of places. The county's next most prolific recruiter, Nellie Wilbur, for instance, was an active participant in Hesperia's Eastern Star and Rebekah lodges, in addition to the local Women's Literary Club, and pulled in eight of her thirteen Klanswomen from these connections. That said, the family links remained, and her list also included seven women with Klan husbands, one with a Klan brother, and one with a Klan son. White Cloud's most active female Klan recruiter, Pearl Sutherland, fared similarly. Of twelve women she recruited, at least five were fellow members of the Grange farming fraternity, while others came from family links to the Klan—five wives of Klan husbands, and her very own sister-in-law.

Often, Klansmen endeavored to recruit among the highest-flying of their respective town's citizenry. The membership contribution of Fremont physician and Mason Nick DeHaas is as good an indication as any of the drawing power of the men's organization among the respectable and prominent classes. While, numerically speaking, DeHaas delivered what seems like a relatively minor twelve members to the Klan cause, these were clearly primarily men of substance, of consequence—the leading lights of the local business elite, and some of the county's top political aspirants. His links were both fraternal and occupational: among the twelve were nine fellow Masons, and four fellow medical professionals (two physicians and two dentists). In Dr. Herman A. Stobbelaar and Dr. Louis Webber, DeHaas had captured for the Klan the president and secretary, respectively, of Fremont's prestigious chamber of commerce. Stobbelaar, having become a Klansman in late March 1924, would celebrate his election as Fremont's new mayor almost exactly twelve months later.[26] Other esteemed recruits included chamber member and long-standing president of Fremont's Old State Bank, J. Andrew Gerber, as well as a city commissioner and two candidates (one Democrat, one Republican) both running for the office of county sheriff.[27]

As if to advertise the Klan's universality, DeHaas combined his courting of such local heavyweights with a more popular appeal, bringing in also the managers of both the local movie theater and billiard parlor. Frank Robbins, too, a car salesman at Fremont's Kingsford Brothers' Ford Agency, made recommendations at work that demonstrated the Klan's ability to operate at either end of the social scale. Not only did he recruit a Kingsford Bros. mechanic to the Invisible Empire, but alongside him he brought in the co-owner of the whole company, Hugh Kingsford. This was something of a coup, if the Kingsford brothers' impressive social connections are anything to go by: in addition to operating a Ford dealership, they were also personal friends of Henry Ford himself, who had been their guest on a recent fishing excursion in the Fremont vicinity.[28]

"A HIGH CLASS ORDER OF THE HIGHEST CLASS": LOFTY IDEALS AND LOWLY LEADERS

The Klan itself was a contradiction, inclusive and exclusive in different ways. It offered an exclusive product, a world of separation from the ordinary and the uninitiated, and yet it strove to be inclusive in its offering of this product to as many residents of the "ordinary" world as possible. Once inside—however they had been brought there, and whatever their socioeconomic background in the outside world—the same inner universe of fantasy and intrigue greeted every fresh recruit, one that tangled itself in a complex and highly confusing web of ceremonies, signals, and status-exalting nomenclature. Indeed, the internal structure of the Klan was rife with opportunity for contrived grandiosity, costumed drama, and farcically overblown escapes from reality. From the national level down, a deliberately elaborate chain of command saw the so-called Invisible Empire ruled dictatorially by a single Imperial Wizard, and split into Domains headed by Grand Goblins. These Domains split similarly into Realms (effectively U.S. states), each under the jurisdiction of a Grand Dragon. Realms divided down further into Provinces, controlled by a Great Titan, which in turn were made up of the various local Klan units—often representing counties, as was the case with Newaygo, or sometimes individual cities, towns, and villages. In strict accordance with the teachings of *The Kloran*, the weekly lodge business of every local unit was conducted behind locked and guarded Klavern doors, and presided over by an Exalted Cyclops and his twelve "Terrors." These elected officers comprised, briefly, an executive and administrative branch: Klaliff (vice-president), Klokard (lecturer), Kludd (chaplain), Kligrapp (secretary), and Klabee (treasurer); a Kloranic or ritualistic branch: Kladd (conductor of members into the meeting), Klarogo (inner guard of the meeting), and Klexter (outer guard of the meeting); and an investigating and advisory branch: the three Klokann (a board of investigators, auditors, and advisors).[29]

In Newaygo County, insufficient evidence has survived to reveal a full profile of those who were elected to officers' positions within the local Klavern. There are, however, a few scattered references that allow the placement of at least a handful of individuals within the local leadership structure. Principal among those involved at the county Klan's higher echelons was Exalted Cyclops James Arthur Keller of Fremont. Married, thirty-seven years old, and working as a telegraph operator for the Pere Marquette Railroad when he joined the Klan, Keller had signed up in May 1924, within the first few days of his return from a half-year stint living in Arizona and California. Though he had missed out on witnessing the Newaygo Klan's early months of growth, he quickly made up for lost time, progressing rapidly within the organization and being elected leader before the end of the year, a position he would hold until the Klan's demise. A World War I veteran and well-connected fraternity man, Keller was particularly active in the Fremont lodge of the Free and Accepted Masons. So much so, in fact, that he also became head (Worshipful Master) of that particular lodge at almost exactly the same time as he was elevated to the office of Exalted Cyclops by his Klan brethren.[30]

The occupier of the Newaygo County Klan Kligrapp's office, too, is a known quantity. Thirty-four-year-old Fremont fruit farmer Elwin J. Stone—a member of both the Masonic and Elk lodges—first held the position, making twenty-three recommendations for membership as he did so. It is at least plausible, and seems likely, that his wife Lynda may have held an equivalent, or even higher office within the women's unit, of which very little else at all is known. Stone himself would go on to greater things, in Klan terms, and is noted in the minutes of the 1927 gathering of state-level officers (or Klolero) as holding the office of Grand Klarogo (inner guard) for the Realm.[31] Succeeding Stone as Newaygo County Kligrapp was Leonard Somers, a single, thirty-nine-year-old Fremont man. The last known occupier of this particular office, Somers was a painter and a member of the town's fire department, as well as serving the Fremont Odd Fellows lodge as treasurer. The treasurer's role in the KKK, meanwhile, went to Ledford Anderson, also of Fremont. A twenty-three-year-old single man, working as a bookkeeper at the local auto shop, the Newaygo County Klabee was also a member of the local Moose lodge. Given that all existing Newaygo County Klan records were discovered in a disused attic room in Anderson's home in 1992, it is safe to assume that he continued in his Klannish officer's role until the unit's fading.

Of most of those confirmed as, or likely to have been officers of the local Klan, certain themes are apparent. First of all, the majority came from the city of Fremont. Why this should have been the case is not clear, save for the fact that, to the extent that Newaygo County had a commercial life, Fremont was at its center. Much more significant, perhaps, is the fraternal connection. These were invariably lodge folk, who in lots of cases had served as officers in other clandestinely themed organizations prior to, or at the same time as doing so in the Klan. This was in many respects—save the minutiae of the form and outward expression—familiar ground, and in no little part a prestige-enhancing experience. And therein, perhaps, lay the key. Few of the Klan's confirmed officers, in the non-Klan world, held positions of real esteem or elevated social status. The Exalted Cyclops: a railwayman; the Kligrapps: a farmer and a painter; the Klabee: a junior bookkeeper. The other biggest players, in terms of recommendations made for membership: a building contractor and a café owner. This idea of a lack of, or a striving for, social prestige in the outside world might help to explain not simply the presence of such men in Klan office, but, more widely speaking, their presence in fraternal lodge associations in general. Many of them, after all, held membership in multiple lodges, all of which traded on secrets and codes, all of which based their notions of privilege upon possession of these secrets, and the exclusion of the "real" (less attractive and more difficult) world outside.

If nothing else, the Klan, on the inside, was a social leveler. While it did clearly contain (as the Newaygo County membership rolls attest) men of impressive social standing and undoubted local importance, the little that is known about the officers would seem to indicate that it was not these, but those of more unremarkable occupation and status who tended most often to hold leadership positions. Certainly, this was part of the image that the organization, on a national level, attempted to carve out for itself, *The Kloran* proclaiming that "the distinguishing marks of a Klansman are not found in the fiber of his garments or his social or financial standing." Rather, they were to be found in "a chivalric head, a compassionate heart," with the KKK stressing, in its literature at least, the importance of self-less community-mindedness over that of the grasping, capitalistic financial imperative. Continuing with this line, the Klan adopted the motto *Non Silba Sed Anthar* ("not for self, but for others"), insisting that only the most superior and altruistic of human qualities would qualify an applicant for membership. The esteem of being allowed to join this lodge association, then (let alone be elected as an officer), was tied up in the entirely self-con-gratulatory notion that it was a "HIGH CLASS ORDER OF THE HIGHEST CLASS." Indeed, according to one of the organization's own manuals, distributed to all members, "You are no ordinary man . . . You are a K-L-A-N-S-M-A-N!"[32]

THE MYSTERIOUS "G-MEN": OUTSIDE
IMPETUS AND SPECIFIC KLAN TARGETS

While much of the Newaygo County Klan's strength came from the involve-ment of local men and women, a number of distinctly outside influences and connections also provided vital impetus. The Klan was first brought into the county, in a sense, by the outsider's voice of Fremont minister Jay N. Booth. Arriving in Newaygo County from West Virginia, Booth had given the modern Klan its first public mention in these parts when he lectured fellow ministers on the presence and formidable growth of the organization in other regions. Exalted Cyclops James Keller, too, displayed a well-traveled experience reaching beyond the confines of the immediate local environment. In January 1924, the *Times-Indicator* reported him to be in Phoenix, Arizona, "for an indefinite period," before subsequently noting his presence in Davis, California. Reports of his return to the county in the 15 May 1924 edition of the same paper, coupled with Klan records that show Keller becoming a member on May 7, indicate that whatever the nature of his trip, Keller had grown very keen to sign up and was initiated almost immediately upon his homecoming.[33]

One destination outside of the county that most definitely had a bearing on the development of the Klan locally was the city of Chicago.[34] The Newaygo Klan's first organizer, Cyril D. Waters, had attained his own Klan membership during a stint living and working in the Illinois metropolis. Returning to his native Newaygo as an officially appointed Kleagle (and having been recommended to the order by none other than Grand Dragon D. C. Stephenson), he set about Klan-building in the provinces, putting his Chicago Klavern experience to constructive use. No accident, then, that his first recruit (barber Charles Sheridan) should also be a man with family connections to Chicago. So too was Axel Johnson (of the *Newaygo Republican*), who signed up a day later, the eldest of three Chicagoan brothers in Newaygo who would all become Klansmen. Charles Sheridan and Axel Johnson, in fact, along with their friend Allen Bowman, had actually paid a visit to the city in early August 1923.[35] It was before the end of this same month that the Klan would land in Newaygo and count all three men among its first batch of fully fledged members. Also among the very early recruits were other men from the same young and popular Newaygo social set, including Kenneth Dayton and William Vinton,[36] and it was this group, and those they recommended, who formed the first nucleus of the Klan in Newaygo.

As well as relying on members to recruit their friends, families, colleagues, and fraternity brethren, it is also very apparent that the KKK came into every community with another, much more directed recruitment strategy, with specific individuals and institutions having been identified and predetermined as desirable candidates for membership. Just as Cyril Waters had been sent back to Newaygo to recruit, apparently at the behest of D. C. Stephenson, so too were other elements of the Indiana Grand Dragon's infamous "G-2" surveillance system present in the county. Apparently, "trailing and spying on men was what the G-2 system was chiefly used for," and "under Stephenson's orders, G-2 men travelled over many states . . . on various missions."[37] The groundwork for this can clearly be seen in field regulations sent out to Klaverns across the Midwest by "G-1 National" (Stephenson). In the interests of Klan familiarization with and, ultimately, infiltration of local powers, each individual unit was, during its early days in particular, instructed to gather vital information within its immediate vicinity:

> Each organization will forthwith secure and transmit to state headquarters the name, address, rank of office, nationality, place of birth, age, political and religious affiliations of the following individuals:
> a. County Officials
> b. City Officials
> c. District Court Officials
> d. School Boards
> e. School Faculties
> f. Truant Officers
> g. Police Force
> h. Library Board
> i. Fire Department and so forth

Surveillance was customarily thorough, with the compilers of local reports also required to "state the religious affiliation of the wife and the school affiliations of the children of each of the above classified officers, as well as the attitude of each toward this organization." The attitude of the local press, too, was an important consideration for the image-conscious Klan, and units were asked to report the "name and address of every newspaper published within the bounds of your territorial jurisdiction." Not only this, but also "its political policy . . . names and addresses of controlling stockholder or owners, name, address, nationality and religious affiliation of the editors, whether 'for,' 'neutral,' or 'against' us, and whether the editor is a member of our organization, etc."[38] Bordering on the paranoid, if not the sinister, the Klan's fixation with covert and detailed information-gathering was at the very least an exercise in meticulousness. By investigating the religious and political backgrounds of these particular target individuals, the aptly named Invisible Empire, seeking influence and popular approval, could not only identify those most likely to welcome its advances, but also anticipate and prepare itself for any opposition that might conceivably arise.

Acting upon these instructions, a Klan investigative (or "G-2") team assigned to Newaygo County had begun to gather intelligence at around the same time that the KKK made its first public appearances there. The result was a document entitled "G-2 Michigan's Special Report No. 32," which provided the fledgling local Klavern with a detailed breakdown of the county's population, as well as profiling elected officials and those working in the county school administration. Compiled in November 1923, before the Klan had spread to Fremont and White Cloud, the report concentrated particularly upon the town of Newaygo, detailing city officials, the local newspaper, churches, and post office employees. As well as listing political and religious affiliations, G-2 investigators also made personal notes based on an individual's reputation and standing in the community, adding comments such as "friendly" (to the KKK), "considered a good man," "well-liked," or "a good man with old ideas."[39]

The Klan and Public Office

Clearly, the Klan had its sights set upon gaining a position of influence within the local community, and it seems to have worked toward this goal, politically at least, by actively courting local officeholders. While the nature of promises made, strings pulled, or pressures exerted remains a matter of mystery, it quickly becomes clear from the Newaygo County records that the Invisible Empire appears to have had few problems at all gaining political converts. At the county level, it certainly had enough men (and it was exclusively men) in key positions to give it access to all manner of legal, architectural, and administrative infrastructures if—and it is a big *if*—it was able to exert that degree of influence upon its members. Holding county office at the same time as their Klan membership in the mid-1920s were men who served as county clerk, sheriff (along with numerous deputies), probate judge, drain commissioner, surveyor, treasurer, truant officer, highway commissioner, coroner, agricultural agent, and register of deeds.[40]

At the municipal level, too, each of Newaygo County's town administrations was similarly populated by office-holding Klansmen. In Newaygo, the city clerk, city treasurer, fire department chief, city marshal, chief of police, and justice of the peace all became Klansmen not long after the secret order's arrival in town, along with various other municipal board members, supervisors, clerks, and township-level officeholders. Similar scenarios ensued in Grant, White Cloud, and Hesperia, but nowhere in the county was the Invisible Empire's presence so heavily apparent behind the scenes as in the city of Fremont. Here, Klan-associated names accounted for the city's mayor; three men either serving, or who had recently served, as justices of the peace; the chief of police; superintendent of the city's waterworks and filtration plant; a city supervisor; the city commissioners for finance, revenue, public properties, and utilities; the street commissioner; city health officer; a constable; two special policemen; and the city's two-man cemetery committee, among others. In the Fremont City Fire Department, which regularly employed a dozen firefighters as well as a reserve list of five, no less than twelve men were associated with the KKK.[41]

No area of public service attracted Klansmen quite so much as did the various branches of local law enforcement—which stands to reason, given the order's vociferous public commitment to "law and order." Fremont chief of police Amos F. Bacon, who would hold the position for seventeen continuous years until his death in 1935, was just one who combined police work with the secret "work" of the Invisible Empire. His counterpart in Newaygo, John A. Bullis, played a similar role as Klansman and police chief, to say nothing of the two terms he had served as sheriff of the county. In Newaygo, Fremont, and White Cloud, too, there was at least one Klannish judge each on hand to deal with law violators between Klavern meetings.

The one office above all that seemed especially attractive to men of Klannish persuasion was the county sheriff's department. Again, this is hardly surprising, given that this would have provided the highest local platform from which Klannish views on prohibition enforcement could be given practical application. All four men who held the office through the 1920s—namely, Noble McKinley (1921–24), David Moote (1925–26), Riley Tindall (1927–28), and John Rasey (1929–30)—had also, in fact, been Klansmen. Experienced campaigners Rasey (1913–15) and Moote (1909–12, and 1916–20) had both also held the job in the recent past, while Klan Kligrapp Leonard Somers would find himself donning the badge decades later.[42] During the terms of McKinley and Moote, which constituted the KKK's most active period in Newaygo County, at least five men serving the sheriff's office as deputies had also taken the Klan oath.

Sheriff McKinley certainly proved himself quite the prohibitionist, even in his pre-Klan days, with the local press regularly featuring admiring accounts of his escapades apprehending assorted liquor-law violators, confiscating makeshift stills and moonshine, and running down local drunks. More often than not, the perpetrators of such alcohol-based crimes ended up in the provincial courtrooms, standing before Klan justices who were only too happy to administer fines and even jail time.[43] Having served two successive terms as sheriff, and therefore ineligible for reelection, McKinley retired from the office at the end of 1924, having taken up Klan membership some eight months before. According to the *Times-Indicator*, he did so "with a fine record behind him . . . he has measured up to the expectations of his friends. His record in the enforcement of the dry laws is above reproach."[44]

The scramble to replace McKinley is a good indicator of the level of Klannish interest in practical law enforcement. An unusually large crop of eight candidates put their names forward for the sheriff's office, with no less than six of these—G. Ernest Rasey, David Moote, Neil E. Sharp, Robert Hartzell, Harvey Seymour, and Riley Tindall—already belonging to the Klan. The five Republican candidates (meaning all but Tindall) also made their positions very plain, each having reportedly made a declaration to the local branch of the Anti-Saloon League that they were "favorable . . . to the prohibition law and its enforcement."[45] Elected by "a substantial plurality over his nearest competitor in a large field of candidates," the victorious David Moote picked up where Sheriff McKinley had left off, and "was warmly supported by the dries as he had shown himself to be a friend of the dry cause when he held the office before." He did not disappoint on this score, immediately appointing a Klannish undersheriff and two Klannish White Cloud deputies, all of whom would ably assist him in the ongoing battle against booze and immorality.[46]

It was not only successfully elected officials who were Klansmen, but also, seemingly, almost every other candidate who put himself forward at the polls in the mid-1920s. The Fremont municipal election of April 1924 provides a good and typical illustration of this point, with every single elected office on offer being pursued by at least one Klansman, and often more. The office of mayor was a straight contest between two Klansmen—likewise the race for city commissioner—and another Klansman stood for justice of the peace unopposed. Necessarily, all three offices fell into KKK hands (albeit at the expense of fellow Klansmen). Another commissioner's post was contested between a Klansman and a non-Klansman, as was the post of city assessor. In both cases, the Klansman came through. In another contest, two men were to be chosen as constables from a pool of four (two Klansmen, two not so). In this case, one Klan candidate emerged victorious while another walked away empty-handed. Lastly, for the board of review, three men were to be chosen from a pool of six (of which three were Klansmen). Two of the KKK men were appointed, alongside a non-Klansman.[47] That the Klan experienced some degree of victory in every contest is significant, but it is not the whole point. Win or lose, and some of them did lose, many of the kind of men who typically ran for political office were also the kind of men (though not the *only* kind of men) who joined the Klan. That Klansmen ran against other Klansmen did not seem to matter, nor did they even necessarily have to belong to the same political party. Their political activism in and of itself, it appears, was enough to draw them to the Klan, or perhaps even to draw the Klan to them.

Given the dominance of their party in rural Michigan at the time, with many of Newaygo County's most politically active citizens also active in the Klan, this meant a lot of influential local Republicans donning the hood. At least thirty-six Klansmen and women, and probably more, were members of the Newaygo County Republican Party during the mid-1920s, attending meetings and standing for various offices at local elections. The level of crossover between the two organizations is difficult to ignore. In June 1920, for instance, thirteen prominent members of the county's Republican Committee were selected as delegates to attend the Republican National Convention in Chicago. Of the thirteen honored with selection, a total of ten would become members of the local Klan.[48] Four years later, with the KKK at the peak of its powers, at least eight (now fully signed-up) Klan names made the list of Newaygo County delegates to the state Republican Convention in Grand Rapids, under the direction of their Klannish committee chairman, Dr. Louis Webber of Fremont. The meeting at which these delegates were selected "was opened with a prayer" by the Reverend James Leitch of Newaygo (an American Krusader), with Dr. Webber urging "all good Americans to take a greater interest in their government and [get] to the polls at election time." A speaker then proceeded to lecture the county's gathered Republicans on the Klan's pet subject of "Prohibition and the damaging effects of liquor."[49]

Dr. Webber, who would again be a Michigan delegate to the Republican National Convention in 1928 before running as a Republican candidate for U.S. representative from Michigan in 1932, was just one of a handful of Newaygo County Klansmen who made a mark on state Republican politics. Other prominent Republican Klansmen included David H. Brake, a Krusader from Fremont who served Newaygo County in the Michigan State House of Representatives from 1923 to 1928 and again in 1931–32. Succeeding Brake in the House of Representatives was Don VanderWerp, Newaygo County Klansman and editor of the *Fremont Times-Indicator*. VanderWerp would go on to serve in the Michigan State Senate until the late 1950s. Without doubt the Newaygo Klan's highest-profile political capture, though, was Orville E. Atwood. Having previously spent four years serving Newaygo County in the Michigan State House of Representatives, Atwood at the time of his joining the Invisible Empire was actually a Michigan state senator, a position he held throughout much of the 1920s. Incidentally, two other Newaygo County Klansmen had stood as senatorial candidates during this period, with Dr. James Ubellar of White Cloud (1920) and Floyd Crandall of Newaygo (1924) failing to stop Atwood in his tracks. In 1935 Senator Atwood would be elevated to the office of secretary of state, only for his stellar political career to be cut short by his untimely death in a horrific automobile crash in 1939.[50]

Though the Republican stamp on the Newaygo County Klan was palpable, it was by no means absolute. Democrats, too, joined the secret order, and though they were in a definite minority (in the Klan as in county politics generally), it was the party's local leading lights who made their way in. Competing for county office on the Democratic ticket were Klansmen Getty L. Rosenberg (for county clerk, 1920), Duncan McCallum (for county treasurer, 1924), Fremont brothers Dr. Willis Geerlings and Dr. Lambert Geerlings (both for county coroner, 1924), and Riley Tindall (for county sheriff, 1924). All lost out, not only to Republicans, but also, ironically, to fellow Klansmen (although Tindall did actually emerge victorious in a later contest, becoming sheriff of Newaygo County in 1927–28). The biggest Democratic presence in the KKK undoubtedly came in the shape of a pair of Fremont business partners named Edwin D. L. Evans and Erwin C. Tinney. Prominent and recognizable Fremont faces, the founders of the well-established Evans-Tinney Real Estate Company had both served as Democratic mayor of the town. Evans had been the first man ever to hold the position, serving two terms before being elected justice of the peace for a total of eight years, ending in 1927. Described in the local press as "an uncompromising Democrat," he also served terms as both president and secretary of the very active Fremont Chamber of Commerce. Erwin Tinney, for his part, had been Fremont mayor until 1920, and was still very much engaged in public affairs when the Klan came to town, having successfully been elected city commissioner on the Democratic ticket in 1924.

These two men in particular, more so than any others in the county, seem to have been very specifically targeted for membership by the KKK. Their recruitment was certainly conspicuous, standing out markedly from almost all general trends. Both were signed up just two days after the Klan's first appearance in the county, during late August 1923. At this time, every other individual signed up was, without exception, a resident of the town of Newaygo, with just these two coming from Fremont. Indeed, Evans and Tinney were the only Fremont men on the rolls for at least two months, and it would be fully four months before the Klan began to look to Fremont with any conviction at all. Also distinctive was the fact that both Evans and Tinney had been recommended by an unnamed Klan officer identified only as "G-46," who recommended no one else.[51] Exactly why Evans and Tinney seem to have been so important is not entirely clear, given that the Klan in the 1920s was for the most part associated with a staunchly Republican, conservative, moralistic, dry (in terms of prohibition) political outlook. Perhaps, though, this is just the point. In Evans and Tinney, both of whom were Masons in their forties, the Klan had identified prime specimens of locally recognizable, influential men who were eminently respected and respectable. Active within their communities not only politically but also civically and commercially, they were the kind of upstanding citizens to whom others might look for example. Despite clearly being within a political minority, they held positions at the pinnacle of this political minority, and were seemingly the Klan's way in to a new constituency of potential recruits. For an organization looking to widen its appeal across the board, then, its natural base of support among Republican voters was balanced out to some degree by its more deliberate, solicited support among leading local Democrats—meaning, put crudely, a foot in both political camps.

An Invisible Presence in Church and School

Not only were local politicians active in the Klan (or, put another way, were local Klansmen active in politics), but so, too, were leading figures in almost all other small-town institutions. Perhaps most important of these were the various Protestant churches of Newaygo County, and at least twelve men who appeared on Klan rolls held influential positions with one flock or another. In the town of Newaygo, for instance, G-2 Michigan's early surveillance report had noted the presence of Rev. James Leitch, pastor of the Methodist Episcopal Church. Though at first ineligible—due to his being, as worded in the Klan report, a "Scotch man"—Leitch was an enthusiastic supporter, and joined the organization just as soon as the creation of the American Krusaders auxiliary allowed him to. In the meantime, the Klan document revealed, "meetings have been held in his church" and "he was to make 100% talk on Sunday September 30, 1923."[52] In nearby White Cloud stood the Seventh Day Baptist Church, which had grown out of a small congregation founded and still largely run by the Branch family. Church elders Dr. J. C. Branch, Mortimer Branch (an ordained minister), and Lemuel J. Branch (described as a "travelling evangelist") were all members of the KKK. Also featured on membership cards were an elder of Hesperia's Presbyterian Church, as well as Fremont Wesleyan Methodist minister Rev. N. A. Pritchard. Six other Fremont Klansmen operated as Methodist laymen, on occasion taking the pulpit in local churches, or perhaps, as one had done in late 1923, delivering a "temperance address to the W.C.T.U." or a similar moralistic public engagement.[53]

Still other churchmen were actively involved in the Newaygo County Klan without their names having appeared on any document to say that they were official members of the organization. Among these were Henry Forwood, deacon of the United Church of Christ in White Cloud, and Rev. George Van Wingerden, who served as pastor at the Methodist Episcopal

Church in the same town. Van Wingerden in particular was a well-known character around the county, having also enjoyed spells at the pulpit of Hesperia's First Presbyterian Church and Newaygo's First Baptist Church, as well as being appointed a deputy to the Klannish Sheriff Moote in 1925. Both men, though, would effectively give their endorsement to the Invisible Empire by recommending other individuals for membership. Even more closely tied in was Fremont minister Frank Robinson, whose name was absent from Klan rolls even as those of both his spouse (who proudly noted her occupation as "Minister's wife") and his daughter appeared. Perhaps most surprising of all is the absence of the name of Rev. Jay N. Booth, pastor of the Fremont Church of Christ. Booth, with the possible exception of Newaygo's Rev. Leitch, did more than anyone in the county to stir up interest in the Klan and to publicly boost the organization's image (much more of which later). The most plausible explanation, and one that has been observed of Klans in all areas of the United States during the 1920s, is that Protestant ministers were in many cases offered complimentary membership, thus doing away with the need for dues cards and financial record-keeping on the part of Klan administrators. Being particularly attractive targets of KKK recruitment, given the organization's focus upon Protestant moral values, influential ministers might even be offered a position as a Kludd (chaplain) of the new local Klavern in exchange for their spreading the Klan word among their congregations.[54]

The congregations themselves which the Klan courted were many and varied, the organization's appeal proving strong across the denominations, under the broadly defined umbrella of "Protestantism." Only one county church, St. Mark's Episcopal in Newaygo, had been reported by Klan surveillance to be "not friendly to us." Even then, its distaste for the Invisible Empire could well have been due to a local rivalry with the Newaygo Methodist Episcopal Church, located nearby, which was run by the Klan's most vociferous and enthusiastic backer, Rev. James Leitch. Members of Leitch's flock were joined in the Klan by members of at least two other town congregations: those of the Newaygo Baptist and Congregational churches. In White Cloud, Klansmen from the Branches' Seventh Day Baptist flock were joined by others from Van Wingerden's Methodist Episcopal following, as well as some from the White Cloud United Church of Christ. Hesperia's Presbyterian Church was also represented in the Klavern, as were Fremont's Baptist and Congregational churches. Two flocks with particularly large contingents of Klan members were likewise located in the Fremont area: the town's Methodist Episcopal Church was home to active recruiters Elwin and Lynda Stone, among a crop of at least twenty others, while the Fremont

Church of Christ, led by pro-Klan pastor Jay N. Booth, provided religious instruction to a similar number of Klansfolk.

Booth, in fact, was a newcomer, and arrived in Fremont from West Virginia in the summer of 1923, immediately prior to the KKK's descent upon the county. The fact that he claimed to have encountered the mysterious organization in the past endowed him with the privileged status of "local expert," a position he obviously reveled in. It seems no accident that his arrival should also coincide with the founding of a new social organization known as the "Newaygo County Ministerial Association," a group packed with men, including Rev. Leitch, who would shortly join the Invisible Empire. Formed in Fremont to "promote mutual fellowship" among selected area church leaders, reports of the association's early meetings demonstrate not just the obvious familiarity of the region's soon-to-be Klannish preachers with one another, but also their mutual fascination with the hot topic of the day:

> The Newaygo County Ministerial association met July 9, 1923, at the Congregational church of Newaygo and twelve pastors were present. This organization is only a month old but is showing a healthy growth . . . A very interesting and instructive program was given Monday morning . . . the devotions were led by Rev. Van Wingerden . . . A short business session followed . . . Dr. Branch extended an invitation to have the next meeting at the Baptist church in White Cloud and the invitation was accepted . . . Rev. Booth of Fremont spoke about the Ku Klux Klan. He spoke from personal observation as he has just come to us from the south.[55]

Also very much within Klannish reach were the county's Sunday schools, with many of the local organizers simultaneously holding Klan membership. Lynda Stone, for instance, ran a Sunday school class at the Fremont Methodist Episcopal Church, while fellow Klanswoman Helen Darling performed the same duty at Booth's Church of Christ. In Newaygo, Fred Myers—a pre-charter Klansman and deacon of the Baptist church—was also superintendent of its Sunday school, while Bitely Klanswoman Mary Zettlemoyer had given instructional speeches before a local gathering of the American Sunday Schools Union in June 1925.[56] The Newaygo County Sunday Schools Association, which sent representatives to participate in statewide gatherings and events, was also replete with Klan names, including, among others, Stephen S. Nisbet as head of the young people's division.[57]

Klansman Nisbet, aside from having "given much of his spare time to Sunday school and general religious activities," was also a key figure in the general education of much of Newaygo County's youth, being "especially active among the young people of the city (of Fremont)." Having served for three years as the principal of Fremont's high school, a twenty-eight-year-old Nisbet was elevated in June 1923 to the position of superintendent of Fremont Public Schools. A World War I naval veteran and graduate of what the *Times-Indicator* referred to as "the Government radio school at Harvard University," Nisbet was nothing if not well connected, in later years becoming a Newaygo County delegate to the Republican National Convention, as well as serving as president of Gerber Baby Foods. On the educational front, he would go on to have a distinguished career serving on the Michigan State Board of Education (1943–61), as well as on the board of trustees of both Michigan State University (1964–70) and Alma College (1944–1986). Both colleges dedicated faculty buildings, which still remain, in his honor.[58]

The Fremont school board that appointed Nisbet was itself well populated with Klansfolk, with four elected to positions in 1924. Just as in the political world, each of the four successful candidates attained their respective board positions only after overcoming strong competition from other individuals also involved with the local Klan. In the same year, six teachers employed in Fremont public schools would also feature on Klan membership rolls. They would be joined in the Klavern by at least four of the town's senior class of students for 1924, including Bernadette Markley, a member of the Klannish Markley Café family, who had also proved popular enough to have been voted "most beautiful girl in school" that year. Indeed, links forged while at school seem to have been an important factor among Fremont's young Klansfolk. The graduating senior class of the year before, 1923, contained at least six who signed up, the class of 1922 another four, and the class of 1921 five.[59]

In the town of Newaygo, too, local schools were certainly sites of Klan concentration, and the principal of the Newaygo high school, Arthur Crawford, was joined in donning the robe by a further eight of his teachers, including both busy recruiter Floyd Crandall and his fiancée Angie Wheeler. In addition, five young members of the Klan would also list their occupation at joining the order as "student at Newaygo High school." At least one Klansman was a member of the school's PTA, while two of Newaygo's five-member school board also belonged. All of this looks especially significant when taken together with the Klan's earlier surveillance work on Newaygo, which had determined that there were only a total of fourteen schoolteachers on the city payroll in late 1923.[60]

The Klan's inside information could claim a level of precision and authenticity simply because it came directly from the most reliable and knowledgeable source imaginable—the head of public schools, in fact, for the whole county. In revealing that all its knowledge had been "furnished by Miss Carrie L. Carter, County School Commissioner," the KKK was perhaps eager to see itself associated with a local figure who was, by all accounts, much loved and universally respected.[61] While Miss Carter herself never appeared on any Klan membership list, her apparent willingness to prove helpful in supplying the Klan with information, coupled with an active involvement in both church life and the Republican Party, betrays a certain level of friendly acquiescence to the Klan cause. As the KKK report put it, she had at the very least proved her credentials, as far as the Invisible Empire was concerned, as "a Baptist and a very nice lady."

Whatever the case, the Klan and the schoolhouse certainly seem to have coexisted handily in almost every instance, and White Cloud's schools were perhaps the most Klannish in the county. While just one young Klansman was actually attending school here during his membership, much of the KKK presence was instead accounted for by the very active White Cloud PTA, whose officers in 1925 included four White Cloud Klansfolk, in addition to the three who were regular members. Association business typically included public instruction, and featured community addresses based around either civic ("the need for playgrounds") or moral ("Must your child lie?") improvement.[62] Two more men would join the KKK while serving terms as trustees of the White Cloud School District (1923–1926), and county treasurer and Klansman Elbert M. Johnson was also involved, as a school director. His wife, Julia, herself belonging to the Klavern, had evidently made children's educational welfare a pet subject, and delivered a speech before the local Grange lodge asking, "What kind of teachers do we want in our public schools?" In 1924 and 1925, at least, she must have been satisfied with the standards—no less than thirteen teachers (six male and seven female) in White Cloud's public schools, including the man who would succeed Carrie Carter as county schools commissioner, became members of the Newaygo County KKK.[63]

Even the more remote and less populated villages throughout the region had Klannish teachers present. In Bitely, which supplied just twelve Klan members, one was a schoolteacher; likewise in Woodville (eight Klan members, one a teacher) and Stanwood (two members, one teacher). The border town of Hesperia, meanwhile, split between the Newaygo and Oceana Klans, was home to at least one teacher registered with the Newaygo unit, as well as two nineteen-year-old students at the public school. If any further confirmation were needed, a historical account of Hesperia's schools reveals conditions certainly in keeping with the Klannish viewpoint: by

1921, apparently, "teachers were required by the board of education to hold exercises in . . . morning Bible reading. During this period, and for a longer period after, the board had a regulation against hiring a Catholic teacher."[64]

The Klannish Face of Communications and the Media

As well as in the school system, the county Klan was also keen to limit Roman influence in another prized institution—the rural post-office network. Indeed, the vital necessity of keeping the U.S. Post Office "100% American" seems to have been a statewide Klan obsession, as evidenced by the letters home of Detroit mail carrier, Klansman, and proud "small-town product" Kenneth Blass.[65] Back in the town of Newaygo, G-2 Michigan's intelligence report had profiled all postal-service employees before declaring, with obvious satisfaction, that there were "no Roman Catholics in this Post Office." As for the resident postmaster, Norman A. McDonald (who had also been the chief organizer of the county's patriotic Labor Day celebrations that year), the Klan reported favorably that he was "Protestant, Mason, and considered a good man." No accident, then, that McDonald should subsequently find himself initiated into the secret order, alongside half of the rural mail carriers attached to the Newaygo town post office.[66] And so went the pattern throughout Newaygo County, with local postal workers, as a group, conspicuous by their relative presence on Klan membership lists. In White Cloud, two mail carriers signed up, as did postmistress (and wife of the new Klan sheriff) Emma Moote. Their Fremont colleagues were even more so inclined, with postmaster Allison I. Miller, along with two of his clerks and no less than six rural mail carriers belonging to the KKK. Likewise in Hesperia, where two mail carriers joined assistant postmaster Susie Somers in taking the oath.

The Newaygo County Klan also had representatives in the world of local media. The *Fremont Times-Indicator*, like the county's three other weekly newspapers in 1924, was staunchly Republican in outlook, a fact reflected in the person of its owner and editor, prominent Klansman and leading county Republican Don VanderWerp.[67] Also employed here were female Klan faces in reporter Alberta Shewell and typesetter Dorcas Jacokes. The *Newaygo Republican*, much like the *Times-Indicator*, was a generally pro-Klan paper under the direct influence of key Klan employees. Though its publisher, Miss Jessie Stilwell, did not appear on KKK county rolls, the Klan's newspaper survey during its late 1923 surveillance efforts noted that she was "Protestant," and indeed that her paper could be relied upon as being "100%." Of more significance, perhaps, was the presence of Axel T. Johnson, who the Klan listed as the *Republican's* reporter. A native of Chicago, and one of the very first men to sign up with the Newaygo County Klan (just one day after it arrived in town, in fact), Johnson also served as foreman of the *Republican's* printing office, and would buy a half-share in the company in 1926 before later becoming its sole publisher.[68] Also working here was typesetter Luella Wallace, another young working Klanswoman. In the town of White Cloud, such direct KKK links with the local media appear more tenuous, and while it had indeed been Klansman Louis Fuller who actually founded the *White Cloud Eagle*, he no longer held an interest, having sold the paper back in 1910.

As well as being involved behind the scenes of local newspapers, county Klansmen also seem to have been especially interested in a new and emerging form of communication—namely, the increasingly popular medium of radio. Those in the town of Fremont, in particular, took pride in what they saw as a "progressive" interest. "Fremont as a radio fan," read VanderWerp's *Times-Indicator* in early 1923, "takes a place up near the teacher's desk . . . a year back we were beginning to 'tune in' while the doubters stood around and grinned." The article went on to pay tribute to the forward-looking "loyal radio fans" of Fremont, publishing a list of twenty-two local men who now owned radio sets. Half of these, including VanderWerp himself, were men who would shortly join the Klan. One Klannish Fremont radio fan in particular, Maurice "Morrie" Odell, was well-known for his endorsement of the fledgling medium—the *Times-Indicator* exclaiming that "he was talking radio so long ago that folks thought he was a bit touched in the upper story." From Odell's fascination, however, was born innovation, and he perfected the "Odell static remover" in 1923, an invention that wowed a local reporter into claiming that "he has taken the 'bugs' out of the radio program." Odell would demonstrate his gadget before the Michigan Radio Corporation in Grand Rapids, who were "strong bidders" to purchase and install it in all of their machines, offering a "handsome" sum for the privilege.[69] In the county's other towns, too, radio was catching on among members of the secret order. Klansman Kenneth Overly of Grant, for one, was well versed, working as he did for the aforementioned Michigan Radio Corporation. In White Cloud, auto salesman Harry Branch began to advertise the fact that he had installed a radio for the entertainment of his customers—this following the success of "public concerts" in the garage of fellow KKK man and competing White Cloud car dealer Glen Webster.[70] Finally, over in Newaygo, general merchant and Klansman Arthur Dysinger by 1925 had begun to run his own home-installation service. According to his sales pitch,

"RADIO brings the world into your home." No longer a toy for the eccentric and the fanciful, then, this was the informational tool of the future. No longer to be mocked and dismissed as a passing fad, "its entertainment and its educational value has no equal."[71]

The popularity of radio among Klansmen might be partly explained by the fact that the Invisible Empire had itself made very conscious efforts to utilize the airwaves. As early as May 1923, for instance, national organ the *Imperial Night-Hawk* had boasted that the "Klan will entertain by radio" the following week, having apparently had previous trial attempts that had met with success. Granted use, for this occasion, of the "powerful broadcasting station of the *Fort Worth Star Telegram*," an on-air, all-Klan schedule was planned that "will entertain the radio fans of the nation Thursday night at 9.30." Accessible to all, "the Klan program will be heard in every section of the United States. Some novel stunts and some interesting information about Klan activities will be broadcasted at this time and every Klansman is advised to be on alert for this message." This was to prove just one of many such Klannish radio events, broadcast from various points across the United States and able to reach many more. One Kansas radio station broadcast an "entertaining Klan program" featuring "quartets, musicians and addresses," while the official "Klan Day" parade at the Central Louisiana Fair also made the airwaves. At this particular event, 2,000 Klansmen were set to be naturalized, with proceedings "broadcast by radio from station KFFY." Not only this, but "it is expected that fully 50,000 voices, and if the weather is good, 100,000 voices will participate in patriotic songs" to be transmitted to the nation.[72] If this were not enough, the anti-Catholic and Klan-affiliated periodical *Fellowship Forum* would also canvass individual Klaverns directly, seeking support for its own radio project. Writing to local units everywhere, the *Forum*'s general manager described the "erection of a powerful radio broadcasting station here in Washington, for the dissemination of Protestant Americanism over the air . . . into every community in this great country." Later communications urged that each unit "should have a good radio set in its Klavern, so that the members might listen to the fine programs that are on the air regularly from your radio station, WTFF."[73]

However, arguably the most practically useful form of local media, from the Newaygo County Klan's point of view, may have been the movie theaters. There were two large cinema houses in the area—the Park Theatre in Newaygo, and the Ideal Theatre in Fremont. That the Klan saw them as important potential propaganda outlets, through which it might reach an extended audience, is obvious from the presence of both theater proprietors on KKK membership rolls. In each town, as a result, the organization was able to screen visually attractive and crowd-drawing pro-Klan propaganda, including D. W. Griffith's infamous *The Birth of a Nation*, and the Klan's own film, *The Toll of Justice*.[74] Beyond simply the films that it showed, however, the Park Theatre became something of a Klan venue, providing ready premises for public events that might benefit the order or its members. It was at the Park, after all, that the very first authorized Klan speaker in the county had made his debut public appearance, addressing a five hundred strong audience on the virtues of "the mysterious and much discussed Ku Klux Klan." The theater, for a period, also became a de facto Klan church. Faced with disruptive expansion work on his church buildings (caused in part by the need to accommodate a fast-growing, Klannish Methodist Episcopal flock), Rev. Leitch was forced in the summer of 1924 to seek temporary premises. So it was then that with the Klan at the peak of its powers, the town's most conspicuously Klannish minister should find refuge in a comparatively large arena with proven Klan connections.[75]

There was no one way into the Newaygo County Klan; there were a multitude. Wherever people got together—at home, at work, at the lodge, in church—any of these was a potential recruiting site for the Invisible Empire. It pervaded all aspects of small-town life, drawing members from every background and social standing as it rippled across the county, growing by a potent amalgamation of organically evolving social, occupational, and fraternal networks. Holding aloft the notion of exclusivity as a lure, the Klan itself looked at its prospects inclusively, casting around all Protestant churches and every conceivable lodge to bolster its numbers. Its converts, for their part, joined for different reasons: sometimes for entertainment or adventure, sometimes for friendship or love, for belief in the cause, for curiosity, for lack of anything better to do; other times simply for acceptance, perhaps for money—even, possibly, for protection or for patronage. Almost always, though, the reason had to do with other people already being "in," and the impact that your joining them, or otherwise, would have upon the subsequent relationship. Perhaps it would mean the difference between being elected or not; between retaining customers, getting a job, being invited to the right parties, or not. Perhaps it meant nothing quite so serious at all beyond the decision to show up at the potluck dinner in a sheet or a suit.

In one way or another, the Klan in Newaygo County was everywhere, whether visible or otherwise. Its members were present in business, in politics, in church, in schools, and seemingly all aspects of public and civic life. To a certain extent this simply reflected the natural flow of recommendations from members, but in other respects, the Klan had been quite deliberate in its calculations. It seems no coincidence that where the Klan raised questions, its membership was on hand, and in just the right places, to help provide the solutions. It called for law and order, and it filled the police departments and judiciaries; it called for upright Protestantism, and it signed up the ministers and thronged the churches; it preached against "Romanist" parochial schools, and packed the public school classrooms with "100% Americans"; and it lauded prohibition and signed up all the Republicans. Whether or not this resulted in any real degree of influence over local affairs, though, is debatable. Nobody in Newaygo County politics ever came out as a "Klan" candidate, or seemed, in truth, to act much differently after the Klan had faded than before it had arrived. That the KKK filtered so thoroughly into the fabric of local life is clearly apparent: it is the reason why that may have been obscured. The people of Newaygo County did not so much adapt to the presence of the Klan, but began to join it when it adapted to suit them.

Community, Church, and Klan

The Civic Lives of Ordinary
Klansfolk and the Social Functions
of KKK Pageantry

A SEEMINGLY UNCOMPLICATED INTERSECTION WITH MANY ASPECTS
of everyday white Protestant social life lay behind the extraordinary popular
appeal of the 1920s Ku Klux Klan in Newaygo County, just as it did in
countless similar enclaves of Middle America. One aspect of this seems to
have been an emphasis upon protecting old-fashioned community spirit and
moral standards, especially as these appeared to be under threat (in the eyes
of propaganda-spinning alarmists at least) from a rapidly urbanizing, cosmopolitan, increasingly immigrant and morally ambivalent modern world.
The Klan, for its part, constantly stated its position as a force for "community betterment," aiming, it said, to protect and restore the good "old time"
Protestant moral values that had made America great. Whether its intentions were sincere or otherwise, the KKK actively sought a productive place
at the heart of any community in which it became enmeshed. "Each organization," instructed Michigan state field regulations, "will establish each
week a program in which one outstanding thing for the betterment of the
community will be accomplished." Such self-conscious, Rotary Club–style
dedication to the notion of civic service "may be rendered by aiding the public schools, ministerial associations, or any benevolent organization or civic
body in the attainment of [its] objectives." Monitored from above on its
progress in this particular direction, each local unit was required to "make a
written report each week to state Headquarters, outlining the activities and
accomplishments for the preceding week . . . of a charitable nature."[1]

In Newaygo County, the correlation between civic activism and Klan membership was a strong one. Whether Klansmen, through their membership, were particularly driven toward community-building, or whether those already active in civic life were especially drawn to the Klan, one thing is clear: whether cause or effect, the Newaygo Klan was packed with many of the county's foremost civic activists and progressive municipal improvers—the veritable pillars, in fact, of the community. The presence of such individuals as examples of the quality of Klan recruits can only have added to the organization's prestige, bringing it an aura of perceived respectability in the eyes of those around it. If the connections between such upstanding citizens and the KKK were not always immediately obvious, then those other leading local luminaries—the Protestant ministers—would certainly make up for it by aligning themselves very publicly with the hooded order. It was the churches, in fact, that did most to publicize the Klan, and indeed to facilitate its absorption of much of the local Protestant community by talking up the organization as a powerful force for good, and even conducting some of its religious ceremonies. Having become established as a public presence, in the county and indeed the whole state, the Klan became much more than a supposed vehicle for community improvement. To a large extent an accepted feature of local life, the order became a vast site of social interaction and even just plain entertainment. Through its participatory, Protestant-focused, and fiercely patriotic activities, it not only brought in eager and lucrative crowds, but also fostered (in spite of its "exclusive" image) an inclusive, protective community spirit of which the civic activists in its midst would have been proud.

BOOSTERS, CIVIC ACTIVISTS, AND LOCAL HEROES: THE "BEST CITIZENS" SIGN UP

In addition to the abundance of public figures who joined the Newaygo County Klan, many of the area's most prominent and civically active citizens also enrolled. This, it seems, was a common scenario in many places during the organization's popular phase. Basing *Middletown* on research in the town of Muncie, Indiana, Robert and Helen Lynd talked to many who were, or had been, members of the local KKK. According to a December 1924 interview, "everybody who was anything was in it . . . The KKK here was sponsored by the Masons . . . all the best citizens . . . were members. There were 1,000 of the best and near-best citizens in Muncie in the Klan."[2]

Kathleen Blee, also, when interviewing surviving Jazz Age Klanswomen in the 1980s, was met with strikingly similar responses, one informant claiming that "all the better people" were in the Klan. "Store owners," she continued, "teachers, farmers . . . the good people all belonged to the Klan . . . They were going to clean up the government, and they were going to improve the school books [that] were loaded with Catholicism. The Pope was dictating what was being taught to the children, and therefore they were being impressed with the wrong things."[3]

Aside from illustrating a certain level of public indulgence of some of the Klan's wilder anti-Catholic theories, such comments indicate the perception—at least by those who were members—of an organization with positive (if religiously skewed and one-sided) objectives. The "best citizens," then, in this interpretation, were those who took an active role in promoting the supposed best interests of the local (white Protestant) community. Commonly included in this category were individuals popularly known as "boosters," those who tirelessly pushed the idea of local civic pride, championing the cause, at every opportunity, of their own particular small-town environment over the allegedly superior or more fashionable big-city alternatives. So popular was this notion that the *White Cloud Eagle* even ran a weekly cartoon strip featuring the eponymous hero *Bill Booster*, who advised local people on the merits of pushing for municipal improvements, discouraged "knocking" and rumor-mongering, and generally promoted the cause of the small town. In a typical rhetorical exchange with readers, Bill asked, "Did you ever notice how folks who have moved away from here frequently decide there's no place like the old home town and move back?" "There may be bigger towns than this," he added with some satisfaction, "but there ain't any better ones."[4]

A considerable number of Klansmen in rural Newaygo County would certainly have counted themselves among the crowd in Bill Booster's camp. Fremont optometrist Morrie Odell, for instance, was described by the local press as "a royal booster," a man who has "done a lot of trotting about to make Fremont bigger and better" in addition to serving the town in numerous public offices. As a professional, he was lauded as a prime example of "Fremont boys who have made good," proving to be among the very best in the state "despite the fact that Fremont is not as large as Detroit nor as populated as Grand Rapids." Indeed, urged the *Times-Indicator*, "don't think because the home boys were born here, they are not leaders in their respective games, for they are quite apt to be superior to the more highly touted professionals of the city."[5] Future Klansman Adelbert Branch, too, defended the town of White Cloud in 1923 against administrative encroachments from bureaucrats in the distant metropolis, specifically concerning a proposed change in the use of time zones. "If you want to start work earlier in the day, get up and go at it. Why try and fool yourself by turning the clock ahead?" reasoned Branch in the *White Cloud Eagle*. "The demand for fast time in our state started at Detroit . . . Detroit wants to run the state anyway, and I am wondering if we are going to let them."[6]

Indeed, some of the greatest obstacles faced by Newaygo County's boosters were the negative perceptions that were aired from time to time regarding their home communities. The county's newspapers, perhaps as a means of defense, were quick to fuel local outrage by pointing out any unflattering observations from outside. In a front page article entitled "How Folks See White Cloud," for example, the *Eagle* quoted a reporter from the *Buffalo Evening Times* who had described the Newaygo County seat as "a weird, strange country of gloomy swamp lands, sparsely inhabited, and so isolated from the rest of the world that laws of God and man do not penetrate."[7] Over in Fremont, local historian Harry Spooner publicly lamented the lack of investment in the town's industrial sector, and the resultant effect that this had upon employment and population levels. "Last spring," wrote Spooner in a January 1924 letter to the *Times-Indicator*, "the city lost heavily of its laboring population because there was not enough industry here for them. The coming spring will see another exodus." Fremont's "best manhood and womanhood," he continued, was thus forced out of town, "leaving us, to enrich some outside center." Unless industry could be developed to "provide work for these people at home and conserve their energies and talents for the upbuilding of our community" then the message was bleak: "We shall have to . . . give up all hope of having anything but a 'sleepy hollow' existence."[8]

While Spooner (who, incidentally, was not a Klansman) may have had a perfectly valid and well-reasoned point, local boosters did not tend to find this type of criticism constructive. Editorials in the *Newaygo Republican*, in particular, offered an alternative and eerily Klannish-sounding point of view, claiming that "cultivating a fraternal spirit has much to do with the success of any community." Another such piece in 1925 called for citizens of Newaygo to show "the right spirit," deploring the negative standpoint of "disaffected ones" who were "pulling in the opposite direction, or even refusing to pull," and rendering ineffective "the efforts of those who are trying to do something worthwhile for the benefit of everyone." All too often, it continued, "the citizens who are the first to criticize . . . are the ones who contribute nothing," adding, ominously, that "the spirit that wins is the spirit that knows no dissension."[9] A similar editorial had appeared in the *Republican* just over a month after the Klan's first arrival in the county, a time when the organization had recruited its first sixty or so members in Newaygo, around half of whom labored at the Newaygo Portland Cement Company. If this was a Klannish broadside, it was a thinly veiled one, the column claiming to express the views of an anonymous "friend," who was "too modest to publish his views himself." While admitting that "perhaps to an extent he is a moralizer," the idea was that this well-meaning friend "in his moralizing . . . puts his finger on the spot," and had important things to say "about conditions in this town—as he sees them."

> He mentioned numerous highly respected citizens who are in the prominent class, but whose prominence seldom impels them to do anything exceptional for community betterment. In contrast to them he mentioned others who are more humble in their mode of life, yet who are energetic and determined workers for the public weal. He deplores the lack of co-operation, the petty jealousies, the religious bickerings . . . He sees in this town the good that comes to our community accomplished by the efforts of a few, working regardless of factional differences, while the many are complacent or indifferent, or willing to have others do the work for them. He sees, also, a community that should be well up toward the head of its class, yet in reality one that is just drifting along.

In short, reasoned the *Republican*'s mysterious "friend," in words barely distinct from the Klan's own well-circulated motto ("not for self, but for others"), "there are . . . not enough people who are willing to forget self for a moment and do something for others."[10]

Over the course of the next year, however, the county Klan's ranks would swell remarkably, and its members would indeed come to include many who were very conspicuous exactly for their public endeavors in the service of "community betterment." At the most fundamental of levels, this meant those who dedicated themselves in one way or another to the county's most needy or unfortunate citizens. Mortimer A. Branch, for one, was in 1925 voted superintendent of the Newaygo County Poor Commission, which oversaw projects designed to aid deprived local residents. He was joined on the commission, as well as in the Klan, by his brother, Adelbert.[11] Similarly, a number of active Klansfolk had been involved in organizing the Newaygo County Public Health Committee in mid-1923, while Carlos Kimball (a truant officer when he joined the Klan, and until recently the county's agricultural agent) had set himself up as an adoption agency of sorts. In late June 1923, the *Times-Indicator* reported that he "has a girl 14 years old for whom he would like to secure a good home." A week later, Kimball was offering "twins, a boy and a girl, 12 years of age" as well as "another girl of

12," all looking for homes, preferably in the same neighborhood.[12] Various small charitable causes overlapped with Newaygo's KKK, and at the beginning of 1925, at least six Klansmen donated money to help a family struck by serious illness in the village of Biteley. In 1928, White Cloud Klansman Riley Allers would take this notion further, starting up a string of regional organizations known as the Helping Hand societies, intended "to help our neighbors in time of bereavement." Following suit, Krusader Elmer McMullen and Klansman Ted Branch became chairman and secretary, respectively, of the Newaygo County "Goodfellows," a charitable organization that made it its business, seemingly without prejudice, "to see that no child in Muskegon, Newaygo and Oceana counties is forgotten on Christmas."[13]

When individuals involved with the county Klan talked of community "improvement," much of their talk centered around the issue of public morality. Stephen S. Nisbet, for example, had led Newaygo County's Salvation Army appeal in summer 1923, heading a committee that featured at least four other prominent (very soon-to-be) Klansfolk. Concentrating its work in prisons, children's homes, and poorhouses, the appeal pledged to go on a "quest for souls . . . those who seem down and out," adopting the motto "go for souls, and go for the worst." Proud of its ability to affect moral turnaround, the group claimed to have "taken drunkards and made respected fathers and businessmen . . . made worthy mothers from women who walked the streets . . . reformed criminals . . . [and] turned many a wavering young man and girl to the path of integrity."[14]

Without doubt the most pressing moral issue of the day, though, was prohibition—a specter looming ever-present in the philosophical background of the whole era. In Newaygo County, public support for prohibition was widespread, to the extent that the Methodist Episcopal Church had held a "Prohibition Jubilee and Ratification celebration" in Fremont when the law was passed. The Anti-Saloon League (whose common ground and significant overlaps with the KKK on the liquor issue have been noted elsewhere)[15] also held regular meetings in the county, and welcomed a succession of eminent speakers supporting prohibition. The organization's local campaign was managed by Mable Barnum, who would soon join the WKKK (as well as being an active member of the county's Republican Committee and becoming in 1924 the first woman in Fremont to serve on an election board).[16] Other prominent local Klansfolk who added their voices to this particular discussion included state senator Orville E. Atwood, through "temperance" addresses, and Don VanderWerp, editorializing upon "the prohibition situation" in his *Fremont Times-Indicator.* On violators of the dry laws, VanderWerp's judgment was typically moralistic and clear: "If a man will drink poison to satisfy his liquor appetite, he can hope for little sympathy from the public."[17]

Leading the way publicly on the anti-booze and pro-morality front were the local branches of the Women's Christian Temperance Union (WCTU). In the Fremont area, at least five Klanswomen belonged to the WCTU in the early 1920s, but it was in White Cloud that the Klannish overlap was most obvious. Of the seventy women in total who would become affiliated with the Klan in White Cloud, more than a quarter had first been involved with the WCTU in the town. In addition, the names of thirteen White Cloud Klansmen also appeared on Temperance Union rolls as "honorary members."[18] Several of the prominent figures who lent public support to the White Cloud WCTU were Klansfolk as well, including then–county sheriff Noble McKinley, and ministers George Van Wingerden and Lemuel Branch, all of whom had hosted or orated at group meetings.[19] The substance of Temperance Union speeches typically included much talk of "law enforcement" and denunciations of "the newspaper propaganda of the wets." In this sense, the organization shared not only members, but concerns with the local Klan.[20]

Indeed, membership overlaps with the Klan could be found among women's groups of all descriptions in Newaygo County. Sometimes such groups were chiefly social in function, spaces in which housewives might make the kind of acquaintances that their husbands made at work. The White Cloud sewing circle, for instance, was run by three women who were also in the WKKK.[21] Other women's groups contributing to Klan membership, however, often had an educational, empowering, or community-minded focus. At least three White Cloud Klanswomen were among the earliest members of the home extension service of Michigan State College "and were taught many interesting things . . . sharing ideas with women from all over our state."[22] The Women's Literary Club (WLC) was another local organization that dedicated itself to female education. In Hesperia it produced ten Klanswomen, as well as raising funds to secure the establishment of the village's first public library and later sponsor "improvement of the Hesperia park system."[23] Over in neighboring Fremont, a separate branch of the WLC counted at least a dozen Klanswomen among its members. As well as soliciting book donations for the Fremont public library, the content of its meetings urged active female involvement in politics ("Laws which women should change. How and Why?") and discussed modern moral issues of the day ("The influence of the movies"). While conceding the grave moral dangers of filmmaking in the wrong hands, the club was typically quick to defend its own home patch, concluding that "the pictures shown at the local theater are of a much higher class than those presented in the average town."[24] Still other local women's organizations made municipal pride their main focus. The Fremont Women's Club (with Mabel Barnum as president, and at the very least six other Klanswomen as members) dedicated an entire meeting to the subject of "civic improvement," collecting "many fine suggestions" for the practical beautification of Fremont's streets, public areas, and leisure facilities.[25]

As well as these very active female-led improvement drives, a large part of the effort to "boost" the county's fortunes typically came from among its business elite, and one organization in particular—the chamber of commerce—embodied this spirit. Having served in the early 1920s as the head of the Fremont Chamber, Morrie Odell characterized it as "an organization of the leading business men and citizens who have the welfare and interest of their community at heart and are trying by their united efforts to better the conditions of that community."[26] Overlaps between Fremont Klansmen and the Fremont Chamber of Commerce were undeniable. Joining Odell in serving terms as either president, secretary, or treasurer of the chamber during an era in which they would all also join the Klan were real estate man Hermon C. Buck, Fremont mayor Herman Stobbelaar, ex-mayors Edwin D. L. Evans and Erwin Tinney, schools superintendent Stephen S. Nisbet, leading banker Emeil Kempf, and physician Louis Webber, among others. Holding the office of president at the Klan's 1924 peak, Dr. Webber was considered "one of the live wires of Fremont," juggling these duties not just with his KKK membership, but also with his role as the county's Republican Party chairman.[27] In all, at least thirty-five Fremont Klansmen, and very likely more besides, were known to have been members of the city's chamber of commerce. This list included some of the Invisible Empire's most recognizable and dynamic local faces, such as prolific recruiters Thomas Mullins and D. W. Markley, Klannish minister Jay N. Booth, budding truck magnate Dallas Darling, newspaper editor Don VanderWerp, and baby-food entrepreneur Dan F. Gerber. Also among them was Old State Bank president J. Andrew Gerber (an older relative of Dan's), who was credited with doing "more than any other man" to promote horticulture in Fremont, even going to the length of inviting local farmers to display their best produce in the lobby of his bank. "Always alert to the advantages of his home town," he was apparently "a pioneer in the banker-farmer movement which has revolutionized country banking throughout the United States."[28]

Over in White Cloud, the chamber of commerce had been less of an influential force among Klansmen, having only been formally organized in the town in February 1926. Despite its lack of activity at the Klan's numerical peak, however, connections with the Invisible Empire were immediately apparent: its initial membership list of just over forty members featured twenty-five local men who had appeared on the Newaygo County Klan rolls just months before. One local history account also distinctly recalls the White Cloud Chamber meeting in both the restaurant owned by Art Lindquist and the café owned by Charles Ruttowski, each of which were the establishments of Klansmen.[29] Meanwhile, the less commercial town of Newaygo showed little sign of developing any such formal organization of prominent merchants. The few leading figures that the town could (and, given the chance, did) boast of, however, were invariably linked to the county Klan. Perhaps most celebrated of these was up-and-coming inventor Walter J. Pike, whose "Pike-Light" fender spotlight design proved so popular in 1924 as to necessitate the construction of larger, custom-built premises to house his company, Pike Laboratories, Ltd., the capital stock of which was valued at the time at $25,000. Not only was that year's meeting of company directors held at Newaygo's Klannish Valley Inn, but the contract for the building work was given to none other than Klansman, building contractor, and outgoing county sheriff Noble McKinley. The connection does not appear to be a difficult one to make: Pike himself was a keen KKK man, having been elevated to the second ("K-Duo") degree in July 1924, and was merely putting the well-drummed lessons of "vocational Klanishness" into practice.[30]

Though not always doing so in the explicit context of their Klan membership, there can be no doubt that individuals in Newaygo County's Klannish business community worked together in many instances to achieve communal goals. Sometimes this took the form of a Klan-dominated chamber of commerce pushing for practical improvements to its own town, such as paving county roads, improving water supplies, and installing fountains in local parks.[31] Other times, as in White Cloud during 1925 and 1926, Klansmen found themselves together on the boards of local tourist associations, attempting to sell their area to visitors from outside.[32] Occasionally, there were issues that resonated county-wide, necessitating the involvement of prominent men from more than one town. At more than one juncture, for example, White Cloud's David Brake (a state representative) and Adelbert Branch joined Fremont's Don VanderWerp, H. C. Buck, county agricultural agent Clair Taylor, and Senator Orville Atwood, among others, on an almost entirely Klan-populated mission to save a threatened local stretch of rail line from closure. Committed to the cause, the group eventually led a delegation to the state capitol at Lansing, protesting in the county's interests against the proposed abandonment of the White Cloud–Big Rapids branch of the Pere Marquette Railroad.[33]

Keen to boost the area's economy, Newaygo County Klansmen also played their part in attempting to attract or develop new industry. It seems, though, that there were limits to the ways in which this could be acceptably achieved. In mid-1923, the Department of Labor at Lansing had canvassed the county's farmers on the idea of "replenish[ing] the depleted labor supply on the farms of Michigan with negro labor . . . preferably as farm owners." The reply, worded by agricultural agent Clair Taylor (who would be a Klansman within the year), was unequivocal, speaking volumes about the fears and prejudices of a county with just thirty-one black residents from a total population of 17,378. "The farmers of this section are not desirous of any negro farmers," Taylor wrote, reasoning that "we are endeavoring to place the business of agriculture on a higher plane in order that the industry will prove attractive to the higher type of rural population."[34]

Thankfully, not all county businessmen, and not even all prospective Klansmen, thought along these lines, as Adelbert and Erastus Branch proved. It was these two White Cloud brothers, after all, who, in the years immediately preceding their joining the local KKK, had "envisioned a resort project involving blacks exclusively."[35] Acting upon these plans, the two men, along with their wives and a couple of Chicago business partners, organized the Idlewild Resort Company. Based in lush lakeland close to Baldwin, just a few miles north of the Newaygo County line, the company created the town of Idlewild, which went on to become "one of the oldest, most famous and most memorable African American resort communities in the United States." During the 1920s, land lots at Idlewild were sold to such African American notables as NAACP cofounder W. E. B. Du Bois and novelist Charles Waddell Chesnutt, while Marcus Garvey is also reported to have made a speech in the Idlewild community building in 1929. Du Bois had brought the resort to national attention in a 1921 article in his *Crisis* magazine, describing its "sheer physical beauty . . . the beautifulest stretch I have seen for twenty years" and its "fellowship—sweet, strong women and keen-witted men" from all areas of the country. Clearly not sharing the reticence of Newaygo County's farmers, then, the Branch brothers (albeit for primarily financial reasons) actually played a significant part in bringing African Americans to rural western Michigan. If nothing else, this ought to underscore the point that African Americans, at this time at least, were not perceived to carry quite the same sort of imminent threat to white Protestant society as were Catholics in Michigan. Known "throughout the United States as the Black Eden of Michigan," the resort town of Idlewild "had become one of the few places African Americans could find peace of mind, and could escape systematic practices of racism and discrimination." The influence of this seemingly sleepy backwater getaway was to prove far-reaching indeed, as Idlewild "quickly became the intellectual center for economic development and racial progress in North America during the pre–World War II era."[36]

Back in the heart of Newaygo County, other prominent Klansmen had gone about the task of community improvement simply by building things. The new county jail and sheriff's residence, for instance, had been built by none other than the sheriff himself at the time, Noble McKinley. Not only this, but he brought the project to fruition below its allotted budget, saving the county's taxpayers $6,000 in the process, a statistic that brought him much local praise.[37] Rather unusually for an active 1920s Klansman, McKinley had also happily accepted the contract to perform improvement work on White Cloud's Catholic Church in 1925, which entailed extending the church structure in order to increase its seating capacity.[38] In Fremont, it was building contractor Thomas Mullins, the county's most active male Klan recruiter, who had recently constructed the town's much-loved community building. Like McKinley, he had done so "at a cost of several thousand dollars below the estimate" and had "used better materials in parts of the building than the specifications called for," leaving the community "indebted to Mr. Mullins for the personal interest he has taken in the enterprise." Erected as a memorial to the local men who had lost their lives in the Great War, the building was a source of enormous civic pride. Amid much public fanfare and talk of Fremont's "red blooded" manhood and "intellectually and morally strong" citizenry, it was presented from one future Klansman in Mullins to another in Mayor Erwin Tinney, and dedicated to the town's local heroes.[39]

Respected local heroes, indeed, were not in short supply in the ranks of the Newaygo County Klan either. Most obviously, this meant the surviving soldiers of the recent World War, at least twenty-six of whom became Klansmen. Among these were Exalted Cyclops James Keller and Klannish minister Jay N. Booth. So too were Sergeant Dan Gerber (the future baby-foods magnate being decorated for his bravery on the front lines in France), and Dallas Darling, a man who would become a millionaire and international philanthropist through his toils in Newaygo County as "a founder of the trucking industry."[40] At least fourteen Fremont Klansmen, too, led by Erwin Tinney, had been among those who served on that city's home guard during the war. In a similar vein during peacetime, Fremont's Dr. Louis Webber in 1925 organized the "Newaygo County citizen's military training camp," assisted by two of his fellow Klan members.[41] Perhaps even more revered, though, were the Newaygo County KKK's two aging veterans of the American Civil War. Samuel Gibe and Oliver Buckingham were aged seventy-five and seventy-seven, respectively, when they joined the Klan, and both had served in the Union army. Buckingham in particular boasted impressive connections, having "served under General Sherman and General Grant," seen Lincoln "twice when he was in Washington," and even been present with Grant at Appomattox to witness the surrender of Confederate General Robert E. Lee to Union forces.[42] The local Klan also included men who carried heroic reputations on a much more provincial and everyday scale. Glen Webster, for example, had made the White Cloud front pages in summer 1923 for his "sheer nerve" as he "saved two girls from drowning." M. D. Kimball, likewise, was praised for his quick thinking when he discovered a Fremont dance pavilion being "razed by fire." Perhaps most prominently, Newaygo barber Charles Sheridan had thrust himself into the fray, battling twenty-foot flames to save a woman involved in an air balloon accident at the White Cloud homecoming picnic in August 1923. Sheridan had in fact become the county's very first Klansman just three days before, and as such provided the perfect advertisement for exactly the kind of heroic masculinity with which the Klan was so keen to be associated.[43]

"KLEAR, KLEEN KUT SERMONS": NEWAYGO COUNTY CHURCHES TAKE THE KKK PUBLIC

The preacher at Newaygo's Methodist Episcopal Church, Rev. James Leitch, made an explicit connection between patriotic masculinity and the Klan organization in a February 1924 sermon entitled "American Manhood." His speech was so well received in Klan circles that news of it even made the pages of the Michigan state edition of the *Fiery Cross*. According to this and other reports, Leitch gave a sermon "most true to the principles of the Ku Klux Klan" that concerned itself chiefly with "the developing of our American manhood." Also featuring heavily in Leitch's speech was the idea that "the Bible should be read in our public schools . . . as a scripture," and that this was a "certain requirement necessary to develop elements of our future citizens." His listeners, it seems, agreed with him enthusiastically, and "at this declaration the congregation burst into applause and it was several minutes before he could resume his talk."[44]

This was not Rev. Leitch's first public foray into Klan territory, and it was he, more than any other prominent figure in the county, who kept the organization firmly in the public eye. Buoyed by the town's response to the visit of an official Klan speaker the previous September (when a crowd reported at more than five hundred had received with "marked enthusiasm . . . a plain talk on one hundred percent Americanism"), Leitch had picked up the gauntlet and begun to cast himself as a semi-official spokesperson for the Invisible Empire. Indeed, in the two months following the first public appearance of the KKK there, he had all but dedicated his Sunday sermons to service of the Klan cause. The first of these Klannish sermons, in late September 1923, had seen Leitch tackle the subject of "The Cross, the Illuminated Cross, the Old Rugged Cross as it relates to the 100% Christian." He followed this the next week by preaching on "Americanism and Christianity," advising in his "Methodist Church Notes" column in the *Republican* that "every red-blooded American ought to be present at this service." Subsequent offerings from the pulpit of the Methodist church, at which "all interested in the general welfare are urged to be present," would include, among others, "A Clean Sword: A Real Man's Sermon"; "Religion and Politics"; and "White Supremacy: What Does It Mean?"[45]

In March 1924, with membership in the local unit rocketing, a Leitch sermon engaged the Klan issue head-on, in a very public manner. Well aware of its crowd-drawing potential, the reverend ran a large ad in the pages of the *Republican* a week prior to the event, as a tantalizing preview to his lecture:

A Question—?—?

> Sunday Night at the M.E. CHURCH
> IS THERE A PLACE IN OUR ECONOMY FOR THE
> KU KLUX KLAN?
> KOME AND HEAR
> Extra Special Music[46]

The *Fiery Cross* took an excited public response to the ad as evidence "that the people of Newaygo and vicinity are very much interested about anything concerning the Ku Klux Klan, that great Protestant movement going on throughout our land," and gleefully reported a "Church at Newaygo Thronged as Pastor Gives Klan Address." The audience that turned out for the event had apparently "filled every seat and available standing room," while "many were turned away that could not get in, though some were so determined to hear the sermon that they went into the basement of the church to listen." Although billed as a more or less impartial, informational lecture, there was never any doubt which way Rev. Leitch leaned on the issue under debate, evidenced by the fact that "an electric fiery cross illuminated the church throughout the sermon" while the pastor "went on giving the ideas and principles of the Klansman's creed." In answer, meanwhile, to the question he had himself posed, Leitch was full of praise for the secret hooded order. He pointed in particular to a positive effect upon public morality—exactly the kind of civic improvement envisioned by the organization's strong booster contingent:

> Some say there is no place for the Ku Klux Klan in the small town. It has been proven in your own town that there is. Not more than three months ago if a woman went down the street and passed by a crowd of men congregated they would pass some vile remark about her. No more do you hear such remarks, for the ruffian does not know who will call him for it. So there is a place in our economy for the Ku Klux Klan.

After the speech, a rousing rendition of "The Old Rugged Cross" by a chorus of male voices brought the evening to a close, with a triumphant Rev. Leitch basking in the spotlight of his own apparent success. According to the *Fiery Cross*, at least, his performance had been enough to change the minds of more than a few nonbelievers in the crowd, and "many who have taken a bitter stand against the Klan heretofore complimented Dr. Leitch after the service on the fine sermon he delivered." Reflecting on his speech in the following week's *Republican*, the reverend himself could afford to be a little more modest, insisting that his talk was merely an exercise in common sense. It had contained, he said, "nothing sensational, just a plain setting forth of the unvarnished facts and the needs of the present day," adding simply that "we always have something to say and we say it."[47]

Over in Fremont, Rev. Jay N. Booth, pastor of the Fremont Church of Christ, had taken on a similar role to that of Leitch in Newaygo. Having recently arrived in the county from what both the *Newaygo Republican* and *Fremont Times-Indicator* nominally referred to as "the South" (but which was actually West Virginia), Booth was seen as a natural expert on the KKK. His first speech to the Newaygo County Ministerial association, in fact, had been on this very subject, taking place just a month before the organization began recruiting members in town.[48] Before long, and at a time when the Klan was building steadily in Fremont, Booth would also take his lecture to his congregation. Advertising a sermon at the Church of Christ entitled simply "KU KLUX KLAN," Booth invited the public to attend "Patriotic Day in the church," where both his Klan talk and "a beautiful patriotic pageant in the morning immediately following the Sunday school" were to make up the program of the day "in observance of Washington's birthday." To add to the excitement, he made promises of revelations to come: "Whether the minister is for the Klan, against it, or neutral will be told in this sermon."[49]

With this announcement, according to the local press, "interest was aroused throughout the entire community," and large crowds began filing into the pews almost two hours before the sermon's scheduled start time. As a result, "it was not long until the church was filled to its utmost capacity and many were being turned away." Once underway, Booth endeavored to make it clear that he was "not a member of the organization," stating that, at the request of around fifteen members of his church, "I am merely trying to present the facts, and you can draw your own conclusions." For all his talk of impartiality, Rev. Booth went on to praise the secret order unashamedly, marveling at "the growth in membership [which] is now a thousand a day . . . there is not a state in the Union which does not now have a Klan organization." The service itself was opened with a reading of the 12th chapter of Romans and the singing of "America." To complete the lineup of well-known Klan staple performances, a quartet went on to sing "The Old Rugged Cross" (already a widely popular Christian song well before the advent of the Klan, but adopted as a favorite by the order). The speaker then proceeded to laud the benevolent qualities and practical uses of the Invisible Empire, highlighting "specific cases where the Klan has distributed clothing and food at Christmas time" as well as "law and order" benefits "where the organization's members have been instrumental in running down bootleggers and rum runners." Most of all, Booth was keen to praise KKK members as crusading Knights of Protestant Christianity. "The finest thing about the Klan to my notion," he said, in conclusion to his sermon, "is that the Bible is the basis for their constitution."[50]

That the Fremont pastor's views had proved "favorable to the ideals and principles of the Klan" delighted the Michigan *Fiery Cross*, which took particular pleasure in reporting the "disappointment of the opposition . . . who had come to hear the order flayed." According to the Klan organ, "a number of Catholics were present," and, fruitlessly as it turned out, they "had brought a stenographer along to take down the speech verbatim . . . with the expectation of hearing the Protestant Americans raked over the coals."[51] Indeed, for Booth, like all Klannish ministers, antagonism of the Roman Church and its followers was high on the agenda. Even on the occasions when he was absent from his Klan-friendly congregation on church business, he took care to arrange temporary replacements who would occupy his pulpit with suitably anti-Catholic zeal. One Sunday in May 1924, for instance, while Booth was away in Grand Rapids, services at the Fremont

Church of Christ were conducted by Charles Rice of Kalamazoo. A typical "reformed" Catholic of the kind enjoying increasing popularity with Klan audiences, Rice gave two public lectures, one in the morning entitled "My Experience in Infidelity and Return to Christ," followed in the evening by "My Experience in the Catholic and Protestant Churches." In preparation for his services, the *Times-Indicator* briefly explained Rice's personal history, in which the Protestant Church had acted as a force of redemption from a life of both immoral crime and wrong religion, with non-Protestant faiths tenuously linked to the illegal alcohol trade:

> Mr. Rice was reared a Catholic and studied for the priesthood. He left the Catholic Church and became an infidel, and was employed later by the wets against the prohibition movement in which service he was instrumental in making several counties wet. After living more than ten years as an infidel, he was converted to the Protestant faith, and was baptized and received into the Kalamazoo Church of Christ last January. He has spoken before to large audiences in several cities in Michigan.[52]

By playing to the Klan's often notoriously salacious and highly entertaining Catholic-baiting, to say nothing of its fiercely moralistic brand of patriotic Protestantism, local churches could all but guarantee to dramatically boost attendance. Indeed, the advantages to congregations of public association with the Klan quickly became apparent in Newaygo County, in terms of both finances and general popularity. In late 1924, with the Klan at the height of its powers in Fremont, the Church of Christ was reported to be "in flourishing condition financially . . . the church began the year with a deficit of $255.13 and ended with a fine balance of $207.96." The new and dynamic young minister, Rev. Booth, for his part, "has been popular with his congregation and has done splendid work during his pastorate here."[53] In Newaygo, too, the *Republican* reported that "attendance at all of the church services" of Leitch's Methodist Episcopal Church "showed a very healthy growth," and that "the church is to be congratulated on its magnificent accomplishments during the past six months." Its accounts "showed the church to be in the best financial condition in years, with all bills paid up to date, all debts paid and money in the church treasury." The paper also noted that "they are paying their present pastor the largest salary of any pastor in the past," adding that growth had been so pronounced as to require expansion to the church premises in order to accommodate such a burgeoning flock.[54] Leitch certainly made no secret of his pride at "the splendid crowds that are there each night," praising in particular the influx of new blood in recent times. "It is a rich treat," he enthused, "to be able to speak to many men who have not been in the habit of attending church anywhere"—such, it seems, was the extra draw, if only for curiosity's sake, of the KKK link. The reverend, furthermore, seems to have been in no doubt whatsoever as to the source of his church's phenomenal recent success, and on many occasions used his church notes in the pages of the local press to broadcast the point, in customarily coded fashion:

> Just come and have a good time together. Isn't it wonderful how we are growing? Some can't understand it, but we do and that is all that is necessary, so we just
> **K**eep smiling, and we just
> **K**eep happy, and we just
> **K**eep growing bigger all the time.

Clearly pandering to the whims of an audience very much captivated by the trappings of a Klannish mystique, he had found a winning formula, and longed only for its continuance: "Keep on coming," he wrote, "you will always get a very Kordial welcome and you will hear Klear, Kleen Kut Sermons."[55]

Perhaps sensing a mutually beneficial opportunity, the Klan and the local Protestant churches would extend their association well beyond the confines of the regular Sunday service. On a purely practical level, for instance, the county Klan's weekly Tuesday night meetings, according to the *White Cloud Eagle*, were hosted by that town's Baptist church. Founded by the largely Klannish Branch family, and led by Klansman-minister Lemuel J. Branch, this was certainly the chosen venue for celebrations when the provisional organization proudly graduated to "official" status in 1925. On that occasion, the little church was honored with a rare visit by a representative of national Klan headquarters in Atlanta, a Mr. Davis. To mark the event, "a lecture was given and the county charter was delivered to the organization," following which "the large gathering enjoyed a social evening and a supper."[56]

Much more fundamentally than this, though, the KKK, with the aid of Klan-friendly ministers, sought to affect and to appropriate the everyday rituals that commemorated the very lives of its members. Not content with the creation of a convoluted world of secret ritual inside the Klavern, the order also introduced its own distinctive variations upon existing traditional religious rites of passage in the outside world, marking birth, marriage, and death. As the popularity of the order grew, Klan newspapers across

Michigan, as elsewhere, abounded with stories of elaborate Klan weddings, with brides, grooms, ministers, attendants, and guests fully robed in the regalia of the Invisible Empire. Among countless examples, the Michigan edition of the *Klan Kourier* reported "a large gathering of Ku Klux Klan members" as a "Pair Weds in Glow of Fiery Cross," while the *Fellowship Forum* told of Klannish nuptials taking place in the Michigan cities of Royal Oak and Kalamazoo, the latter of which was to feature a one-hundred-piece Klan band from Detroit, and a speech from Michigan's Grand Dragon.[57] The *Bay City Night-Hawk*, too, regaled readers with the story of two young Klan lovers "married in [the] Muskegon Klavern," united by a white-robed preacher before "a full house" of their friends and fellow Klansfolk. The *Michigan Kourier*, meanwhile, reported from one small town that a "Klan wedding is planned . . . causing considerable curiosity in this community." Intended to be "an all-Protestant American affair, including playing of the wedding march," the plans called for "a ceremony to be performed in the local Klavern," with all members of the local organization invited, and ceremonial roles for "at least three hundred uniformed Klansmen and Klanswomen."[58] Still another report of a 1925 marriage in Lapeer, Michigan, conveys something of the prevailing Klannish notions of matrimony, by which two people are united not merely in love, but also in cooperative and constructive patriotic purpose:

> Klansman No. 947 took unto himself a wife to have and to hold indefinitely . . . she readily agreed . . . because everyone loves a Klansman . . . and now Mr. Ku Klux boastingly declares, and with every right, that he has a perfect Klan family, even his employer being a member of the American organization . . . No. 947 has always been one of the "wheel horses" of this county, and if his good wife pulls as hard in this new Ku Klux team in the future as her mate has in the past they will sure be a great little pair of boosters for Americanism.[59]

From the time the KKK first appeared in Newaygo County in August 1923 until its dwindling by the end of 1926, there were at least thirty-six registered marriages involving Klan members.[60] In the vast majority of these unions (twenty-eight of the thirty-six), a Klan member took a partner who was seemingly unconnected to the Invisible Empire and indeed never came to join. In a further two cases, connections via the order were indirect, with single young Klansmen marrying the daughters of older male members. In these two instances, neither daughter belonged to the WKKK, either before or after marriage (even so, the common affiliation between father and son-in-law would at least have gone a long way toward securing parental approval). There were, though, six marriages that took place between single men and women who were both members of the Klan at the time of their marriage. Not only do these cases present by far the most likely setting for a fully fledged "Klan wedding," they also give legitimacy to the idea of the KKK as a site of sociable interaction, a place where unattached men and women might reasonably expect to be able to meet and enjoy the company of a suitable prospective partner. Though detail is thin on the ground, it is clear that Klannish ministers were indeed in charge of the ceremonies for at least three of these six weddings, with Rev. James Leitch presiding over one in Newaygo, and Lemuel J. Branch another in White Cloud. Most conspicuous of all, however, was the only one to have been officially reported as an all-Klan affair, albeit under a protective mask of anonymity. "Klan attends wedding," read the headline, describing "a very pretty wedding . . . in the Grant Community hall" in which "a very prominent couple of Newaygo County were united in marriage." Very apparent by their presence were "hundreds of Klansmen and Klanswomen [who had] journeyed there to witness the beautiful event." As entertainment for the spectacularly garbed crowd, "many musical numbers were rendered," before the bride and bridegroom finally departed on their honeymoon "to parts unknown."[61]

It was from the consummation of such Klannish unions that another opportunity for the organization presented itself. Just as the Klan had appropriated the traditional wedding ceremony, so now it looked to a different religious rite of passage—baptism. Just as with marriages, Michigan's Klan papers reported far and wide on instances of Klannish christenings, with both ceremonies regularly taking place en masse and in public at large regional KKK outdoor events. During the month of July 1924 alone, the *Saginaw Star* told of "a mammoth Ku Klux picnic which will include the christening of 12 babies and a Klan wedding," while the Michigan edition of the *Klan Kourier* reported "public weddings at the Klan Klolero" followed by a band concert and addresses from visiting Klan ministers. The week before, the same organ had described "a huge open air celebration staged by the Klan [with] fully 4000 persons present and everybody in the borough turned out for the affair." This "thrilling spectacle . . . which will long be remembered by all who witnessed it," featured mass open-air initiations as well as a ceremony where "five babies and one young man of 20 . . . were baptized with Klan rites."[62] Throughout the life of the Newaygo County Klan, at least nine children were born to parents who were both active members at the time. Though the county Klan itself never hosted a public KKK baptism ceremony, it is likely that if these children were brought into the organization at all, it would have been at a regional or cross-county event, where they might feature impressively as part of a larger group of youngsters baptized publicly together. The following account of a Klannish baptism ceremony in Stamford, Connecticut, picked up by the *Michigan Kourier*, describes in detail the pomp and circumstance with which the Klan typically conducted such events:

> Ten children ranging in ages from one to six years were christened while some 400 persons, including Klansmen, their families and friends, looked on with absorbing interest. The ceremony, in which 50 robed Klansmen took part . . . [attracted] Klansmen from all parts of the state and from New York . . . [who] came with their families and made a day of it. While the ceremonies were being conducted by a clergyman member of the Invisible Empire, the Klansmen formed a hollow square, with one side open around the children who were being baptized. Previous to this, half of the group formed themselves into a living cross while the others stood below them so as to form three K's . . . When the conducting Klansman called for them the children who were to be baptized came forward with their parents, some in arms and others toddling at their sides. The regular Klan baptismal ceremony was used, the distinctive feature of which was the securing of promises from the parents of the children that they would try to bring them up according to the principles and ideals of Americanism.[63]

In the hands of the KKK, then, what might ordinarily have been modest and private religious ceremonies became outlandish, spectacular set pieces of showy public theater, often performed en masse before a crowd—the staging of which took the organization out of the Klaverns, out of the churches even, and very much into the public domain.

Perhaps owing to the sheer natural solemnity of the event—which lent itself very well to the organization's earnest and sober exterior image—there was no more dramatic demonstration of the Klan's penchant for theatricality than the final rite-of-passage ceremony—the funeral. To an even greater extent than the more obviously celebratory rites of birth and marriage, Klan funerals were common, spectacular, and, perhaps most importantly, very much directed toward public performance. Seemingly everywhere that the Klan built up a presence, public funeral parades became a fixture of organizational life. In Michigan, the *Fellowship Forum* alone described such scenes in Bay City, Cadillac, Muskegon, Jackson, Detroit, Tecumseh, Charlevoix, Saginaw, and Flint, among others.[64] Indeed, the practice had proved popular in Klaverns nationwide, so much so that the ceremony was formalized by national headquarters in 1925 with the publication of *Funeral Services:*

Knights of the Ku Klux Klan. This document, prepared for the consumption of all local units, made the minutiae of the ceremony very clear: the specific hymns and Bible selections to be offered; speeches to be made by the Exalted Cyclops and Klan minister; the visual effect and formation of the funeral march; the order in which officers and Klansmen should march; and even the manner ("walk erect and slowly") and mood ("perfect silence and a sympathetic demeanor") in which all this was to take place. Appearances and popular impressions, of course, were of the highest priority. The Klan document insisted that "Klansmen attending the funeral in regalia should have their costumes neat and clean," while the mandatory floral offering should "have the letters KKK on it, either in ribbon or worked in, in flowers." As for the stricken family, "a sealed communication should be sent [to] the grieved ones—resolutions of sympathy by the Klan, or otherwise, as ordered by the Exalted Cyclops."[65]

Any single issue of the weekly *Fiery Cross* for the mid-1920s could amply illustrate the Klan's tendency toward striking visuals during funeral parades. One late March 1924 edition, for instance, features around half a dozen separate funerals spanning the Midwestern states of Illinois, Ohio, and Michigan. Almost every report featured uniformed Klansmen mingling, typically, among "a much larger crowd of curious onlookers" and grieving relatives. At one such funeral, a large fiery cross was "kept burning in front of the home during the ceremony," alongside a lavish floral tribute that "bore the emblem and inscription of the organization." In another instance, "Klansmen formed a human cross while marching to the cemetery," and during yet another, a legion of robed knights "marched to the cemetery and conducted services at the grave," with local authorities being "forced to detour traffic on account of the congestion caused by the long cortege."[66] Such stock descriptions could just as easily have referred to many of the Klan funerals involving deceased members of the organization in the Newaygo County area, as illustrated in the photographs of the funeral procession and graveside ceremony for Max E. Tyler.

Max E. Tyler, the expired subject of this particular example, was aged just thirty-two when he died—the victim of a horrific accident, crushed by the telegraph pole upon which he had been working, replacing transmission cables. Tyler had been a founding member of the Newaygo County provisional Klan, his name appearing among those upon its very earliest membership lists. Actually a resident of the small town of Hart, around fifteen miles west of Newaygo County's western border, he later helped to establish a separate unit closer to his home. Indeed, it is Hart that features in these photographs, and the regard in which he was held by Hart

Funeral procession for Max E. Tyler (Hart, Michigan)
Source: Labadie Special Collections Library, University of Michigan

Klansmen is reflected in the fact that, as a mark of respect, the local Klan opted thereafter to dedicate itself to his memory, changing the unit's name officially to the "Max E. Tyler Klan, No. 50." If the heavily clichéd local press accounts are any indication, then Klansman Tyler had been a popular and much-loved figure in Hart, his death (perhaps because of its shocking and unexpected manner) warranting three separate mournful and dedicatory memorial pieces in the *Hart Journal*. Lauded as "a rare spirit," who apparently "numbered every acquaintance a friend," his passing was a real jolt to the small community. "The whole village mourns his death," continued the *Journal*, "and probably no individual will be missed more than Max, with his ready smile and willing hands." In describing the Klannish ceremony itself, the local paper was brief and matter-of-fact, noting only that "the business places closed during the funeral," and that it was "held from the M.E. church . . . under the auspices of the Ku Klux Klan, of which Mr. Tyler was a member." A much more poetic, and quite possibly Klannish piece in the same issue, meanwhile, cast him as a latter-day hero, and

"IN HONOR OF ONE OF OUR 100 % AMERICANS," MAX. E. TYLER.
Oct. 30. 1924.
Photo By R.M. Bedell.

Graveside ceremony for Max E. Tyler (Hart, Michigan)
Source: Labadie Special Collections Library, University of Michigan

perhaps an officer of the organization. "And so lashed to the cross of duty's call," it opined, "he died a martyr . . . a man whose mere greeting honored men . . . there is a multitude come to do honor to his memory."[67]

Among the "multitude," clearly, were around seventy Klansmen and women in full regalia, marching cross-armed while leading a solemn funeral procession in the shape of a giant white cross. Behind these were a trail of at least twenty automobiles (and perhaps more, out of shot), including the hearse itself, flanked on either side by three more Klansmen, presumably pallbearers. Watching on from both pavements were the customary crowds of curious and intensely interested onlookers, though there were, too, almost as many civilians who appear entirely indifferent—looking in other directions or merely walking on by, as if what is occurring is perhaps not altogether an unusual sight. Arriving at the graveside, the crowd is a mixed one, made up of close family and friends in the foreground, a protective half-circle of robed (but, just as in the procession, not masked) Klansfolk, and a mass of civilian mourners in the background. As fitting tribute to a

"100% American," each Klan member carries a miniature U.S. flag, matching the larger one that takes pride of place, alongside a floral red fiery cross, upon the coffin of the deceased.

If Tyler's was the classic Klan funeral, the death of another Newaygo Klansman, Thomas Mullins in 1925, showed a more flexible aspect of the Invisible Empire's policy on ceremonials. As well as making much of Mullins's status as a leading citizen and long-time civic booster, the *Fremont Times-Indicator* notably listed the Invisible Empire simply and unashamedly alongside his other fraternal affiliations, implying a sense of respectability and public acceptance by doing so. "Mr. Mullins," read his obituary, "was a member of the Independent Order of Odd Fellows, Knights of Pythias, the Masonic lodge and the Knights of the Ku Klux Klan." It was in this aspect— his more enduring fraternal commitments elsewhere—that the Klan was willing to compromise. Although the funeral services were conducted by Klansman Rev. N. A. Pritchard, officially the KKK took a back seat, retaining only the visual aspect of their normal proceedings: "The services were in charge of the Odd Fellows, with an escort of robed members of the Ku Klux Klan."[68] Apparently, interfraternal cooperation, rather than competition, was quite common in this situation. Among various instances noted by the *Michigan Kourier*, for example, was one in which a Masonic funeral party, having conducted its own rites, "very kindly withdrew and stood in reverence while the Klan ceremonies were performed. The courtesy exhibited between the two organizations has been remarked about extensively here."[69]

Just as with Mullins, it was with utter nonchalance that the local press announced that the funeral proceedings for Fremont's Elsie Penrod had been held "from the Church of Christ and were under the auspices of the woman's division of the Ku Klux Klan." Being a member of the order herself, and indeed survived by a Klan husband and two Klan parents, this was always likely to have been the case. It was no surprise, then, that in the event, "the sermon was preached by the pastor of the church, the Rev. Jay N. Booth," presumably conducted in full, brash patriotic style with all the lavish Klan trimmings.[70] Despite the (Klansman-edited) *Times-Indicator's* frankness in the cases of both Mullins and Penrod, though, such transparency appears to have been rather curiously selective. Take the example of Charles Rice of Hesperia, a Klansman who died in May 1925. Details in the *Times-Indicator's* report just a few days after the event were terribly scant, mentioning only that Rice was "brought to Hesperia for burial," and that "the funeral was held Sunday afternoon at the Methodist church, Rev. Van Wingerden officiating. Besides the widow he leaves one daughter . . . and three grandchildren."[71] Aside from the name of a Klan-friendly minister, there is nothing to betray this, to someone who had not been present, as a KKK affair. In reality, however, even the slightest glance at a photograph of the graveside ceremony for Charles Rice (one of several photographs taken to commemorate Rice's passing, and kept locked away with Klavern records) could leave nobody in any conceivable doubt as to the true nature of the proceedings.

Marked "In honor of a 100% American," the photograph was taken by Robert Bedell, the same Hart-based photographer who captured Max Tyler's funeral more than six months earlier. Never a member of the Newaygo County Klan, Bedell may have been a member in Hart or, more intriguingly, may simply have been happy to take the Klan's business, operating in the role of official photographer for such events in western Michigan.

Whereas other funerals could not have been more open, the lack of publicity for this particular ceremony may merely have been an example of Klannish respect for the personal wishes of surviving relatives. Certainly there is evidence that the KKK took such things seriously, being able to influence but also ultimately bound by the final decision-making power of the grieving family. A Klan organ's report of a funeral in Indiana, for instance, heaped praise upon the "beautiful cross of red roses placed at the head of the grave," but noted that this had only taken place after "the wife of the deceased requested that the Klan have full charge of the funeral." Similarly, the organization's official *Funeral Services* suggested that "the Robe and Helmet of the deceased Klansman may be interred with the remains," adding to that suggestion "if desired by the family." The obvious fear for family members, especially non-Klan ones, was the perceived reaction, real or imagined, of their neighbors. At a 1924 funeral in Adrian, Michigan, for example, it was only when "Klansmen in full regalia held the last rites

Graveside ceremony for Charles Rice (Hesperia, Michigan)
Source: Clarke Historical Library, Central Michigan University

over his grave" that "many persons were surprised to learn for the first time that Mr. Kiersey had been a member of the Ku Klux Klan." With this kind of scenario in mind, during a service in Metamora, Michigan, "Klansmen did not attend funeral in regalia owing to request of the family." Not to be defeated, "the organization was represented in civilian attire scattered among the relatives and friends of whom there were a large gathering." The floral offerings, meanwhile, "were many and beautiful and spoke silently of the affection and esteem in which the Klansman was held in the county."[72] With reputations at stake, then, it is at least possible too that the converse situation may have occurred from time to time, with the Klan attempting to distance itself from departed members who might bring an aura of dishonor to the organization. Bedford W. Stevens, for instance, had been a Klansman in Newaygo for around a year at the time of his 1924 suicide. Having reportedly been "acting strangely for some time" and doing "other things that were so unlike him to do," he was found hanging by the neck in his own barn. Whether or not his "mental condition" (as the *Newaygo Republican* described it) and subsequent death constituted a badge of social shame for those associated with him, there was certainly no lavish Klan funeral forthcoming, as there had been for others. His family's memorial service, instead, had been held quietly, "from the home."[73]

FROM SECRECY TO SPECTACLE:
THE KLAN AS MAINSTREAM MASS ENTERTAINMENT

Despite sourcing its prestige in a reputation as a mysterious and exclusive secret society, the Ku Klux Klan in Michigan was, in truth, nothing of the sort. Throughout the organization's life, it continued to be popularly portrayed in such terms (with its own organs working hard to perpetuate the myth), but the practical mechanics of membership at the local level created a very different reality. In many areas of Michigan, as elsewhere during this era, branches of the Klan were so far from secret as to advertise their presence publicly in much the same way as any organization or company might. Appearing, for instance, in one Michigan town's business directory—apparently unremarkably, and alongside merchants, service providers, and clubhouses—was an entry for the local unit of the KKK. Not only did the listing identify the unit specifically as "Knights of the Ku Klux Klan, Michigan Realm, No. 16," it also made plain exactly when and where it regularly convened ("meets every Monday evening at 132 N. Winter"), as well as naming a local man, "F. H. Lewes, E.C. (Exalted Cyclops)" as the point of contact for further information.[74]

One inescapable reality, very strikingly apparent from all of the Michigan Klan's appearances in public (and amply demonstrated by the funeral pictures), is the fact that its members did not make any efforts to conceal their faces. The reason behind this, at base, was a legal one. During the summer of 1923, amid growing rumors of Klan appearances in rural Michigan, state legislators (working on what they had heard about the Klan from the South) had acted swiftly to nip any prospective trouble in the bud. Act No. 276 of the Public Acts of the State of Michigan, 1923, better known as the "Burns anti-mask law," came into effect on 29 August 1923, during the very same week in which KKK organizers had first begun taking names in Newaygo County. The act stated that "hereafter it shall be unlawful to assemble, march or parade on any street, highway or public place in this State while wearing a mask or covering which conceals in whole or in part the face of the wearer." Clearly aimed specifically at gatherings of the Ku Klux Klan, the act went on to allow mask-wearing of almost any other kind, notably not applying to "children at Halloween . . . those going to and from Masquerade parties . . . those participating in any public parade of educational, religious or historical character," circuses, stage shows, and even "those participating in the parades of minstrel troupes." Punishment for violation of the anti-mask law was fairly hefty, with any individual transgressor liable for a fine of anything between $25 and $100, and up to thirty days in the county jail. Despite conceding that "Michigan has had no particular Klan troubles to date," the local press was full of praise for the precautionary stance and commendable foresight of state legislators. "With Klan organizers at work in Grand Rapids and throughout western Michigan," wrote the *Alma Record*, "it is well to point out that the statutes of Michigan have anticipated the chief source of difficulty . . . namely the irresponsibility that goes with a mask," and outlawed it. The reasonable assumption, and the challenge for the Klan in Michigan, was clear—that "any organization dedicated to the defense of Americanism can verify its creed only by rigid adherence to the Law."[75]

By all accounts, this would indeed turn out to be the case, as almost any photograph of any Klan public event in Michigan during the twenties will attest. One way of reading this is to say that members of the Klan unmasked themselves in Michigan, perhaps reluctantly, because they were forced to do so—a situation that, in other states, under other laws, might very well never have happened. More fundamentally, though, it seems the anti-mask law actually legitimized the Klan in Michigan, helping it to maintain an air of respectability and acceptance. Signing up with the Klan, after all, was at least in theory a matter of choice, and anybody joining the "Invisible" Empire there could surely have been under no illusions about the fact that they would be required to show their faces, along with their Klan-garbed bodies, in public. And yet the reality of regularly parading the streets, "visors up," particularly in small towns where every face was sure to be known, seems not to have acted as any serious deterrent to enrolling. Coupled with fairly casual mentions of individuals' Klan affiliations in the regional press, such unselfconscious public appearances, in which maskless members often mixed with civilian crowds, point toward rather accommodating local attitudes toward the organization. There seems to be both a lack of any real stigma attached to Klan membership, and an absence of concern, on the part of members, about the consequences of their Klan membership being public knowledge. It is possible, indeed, that the anti-mask law even swung things the other way, by routinely putting on display the exact caliber of Klan members (who included, in Newaygo County at least, the foremost boosters, civic activists, and "best" citizens), and by doing so actually convinced and reassured wavering doubters and encouraged prospective members to sign up.

If nothing else, widespread adherence to the Burns law proved that the Klan was willing and capable of doing exactly that one thing—obeying the laws of the land. At its own dogged and much-repeated insistence, in fact, the Invisible Empire had always taken great pride in proclaiming itself "a law and order organization." The act of unmasking, in public and without fuss, could only add credibility to this notion. Such an attitude of compliance is further demonstrated by internal Michigan Klan operational instructions governing the conduct of units on public outings, with each county organization being required to "regulate with entire conformity . . . the conduct of its members wearing regalia when on parade." The parades themselves, for all their visual drama and seeming spontaneity, were heavily stage-managed and entirely legal affairs, with Klan regulations demanding that they "shall be held only with knowledge of proper city or county officials."[76] The same was true of that most distinctive, and seemingly lawless, signature symbol of the Klan—the giant fiery cross. During the Klan's active period in 1920s Newaygo County, there were at least nine separate incidences of fiery cross burnings. All of these were striking, dramatic affairs, with flaming structures thirty feet and more in height suddenly illuminating the night sky from one hilltop or another, often accompanied by noisy, attention-grabbing fireworks. Invariably such incidents were excitedly reported as if they were mysterious bolts from the blue ("Newaygo Surprised at Burning of Cross"), prompting much local fascination and befuddlement. One White Cloud doctor (and later Klansman) claimed to have "found a burned cross in his cabbage patch" and was left "not sure whether the incident is an honor extended to him by the Klan or whether it is a threat."[77] Of course, the heavily pro-Klan local media had every interest in maintaining this aura of spellbinding intrigue around the organization, especially during its most fertile recruitment phase, but this does not quite represent the facts. Closer to the truth, if far less awe-inspiring, are the contents of this internal KKK memo, found in the files of a local Klavern in neighboring Ohio:

> No person or persons shall burn a cross or crosses without first securing permission of the Exalted Cyclops, and then only will permission be granted by the Exalted Cyclops when he is satisfied that the burning of a cross or crosses is not in violation of any city ordinance. After a city permit is obtained for the burning of the same, where required, and the cross is to be burned on private property, the permission of the owner must first be secured in writing . . . care should be taken to remain until after the fire dies out, and every precaution taken to prevent any fires.[78]

Clearly anxious—to the point of bureaucratic banality—to keep the organization's activities within the bounds of the law, Klan leaders at least exhibited a desire to put into practice the good citizenship that they preached. While such everyday practicalities might run counter to the more thrilling popular perceptions of life inside the mysterious KKK, their law-abiding sensibilities must also have greatly resonated with its growing army of more civically active recruits.

Essentially law-abiding and carefully regulated as it may have been, the Klan's public pageantry was nonetheless legendary in its visual and ceremonial extravagance, producing elaborate participatory spectacles that absorbed, modified, and rebranded under the Klannish banner almost every form of mainstream popular entertainment. It was on this level that the Ku Klux Klan became real and vital for many people in 1920s Michigan: no longer was it a mysterious order lurking behind the bolted doors of some murky and unknown Klavern, but a colorful and energetic street presence, intent upon overblown gestures and unabashed shows of white Protestant American strength. Among the Klan's armory of public attractions were highly choreographed processions, celebrations, and banquets; vivid costumes and banners; lavishly decorated parades and floats; marching band, drill, and bugle corps; Klan vocal, drama, and verse recitals; inter-Klan games and athletic contests; local screenings of Klan-themed movies;

sophisticated pyrotechnics and public visual displays—all of these things and more characterized the Klan's theatricality and appeal to the public appetite for flamboyant entertainment and spectacle.

Usually incorporated in all of the pomp and ceremony were inspirational open-air political speeches of one sort or another, invariably on the broad, often vague themes of "100% Americanism," "pure American womanhood," or, least clearly of all, "Klankraft." Most commonly, the speakers sought to align the order in the public mind with such traditional American symbols and institutions as the flag, the public schools, and the Protestant church. At a large and pre-advertised Klan meeting in Fremont, for example, a visiting Klan minister assured the crowd (which, at eight hundred, was around half as big as the town itself) of the basic decency and patriotism of the KKK. Not only was the order "built on the principles of the Christian religion . . . and no one can become a member who doesn't believe in the religion of Jesus Christ," it would also work for the improvement of their community, being "active in law enforcement and . . . bound by oath to give every assistance to the constituted authorities." At around the same time in nearby Hart, Klanswomen conducted a lively sing-song and informational meeting. Amid much patriotic merrymaking and a vocal rendition of "America," the female members preached to the general public on "the principles of the order, the protection of the public school and the bringing up of children with the American idea of life."[79]

While Klan speakers made all the right noises in service of "Americanism," it was often not the speeches but the spectacle that surrounded them which provided the most compelling initial draw. In May 1924, for instance, reports from Fremont told of a remarkable public show of "Klan pyrotechnics," during which "hundreds of citizens witnessed a beautiful display of fireworks set off by the Americans." Fashioned around the theme of patriotism, the impressive display included "a parachute flare which floated an American flag more than three feet long. The illuminated flag made a beautiful appearance as it floated serenely in the evening breeze." At the center of the show, and helping in this context to merge the ideas of Klan and country, was "a fiery cross, thirty feet in height [which] attracted a great deal of attention." The gathering crowd, apparently, was a receptive one, and "the principles and ideals of the Klan were warmly received by citizens here." Evidently the imaginations of the Fremont-area public had been fired up by the order. "Meetings are being held each week at which Klankraft in all its different phases are being enthusiastically discussed," the report continued. "There is a constant flow of applications for membership into the headquarters of the great American order, which is proof conclusive that the organization is working for the best interests of the county."[80]

Also held outdoors, very much before the eyes of the community, were Klan initiation ceremonies, where new members were formally taken in by the hundreds in front of mass gatherings of curious onlookers. According to the local press, one such nocturnal event near Hart saw "5,000 persons watch open air ceremonies" in a field a few miles south of town, "where the organized Klans of Oceana, Newaygo, Muskegon and Mason counties gathered for initiation and meeting." Against a moonlit backdrop, three huge fiery crosses were burned, and three hundred new Klan members were initiated that night alone, while "a great many non-members, attracted by the banners of the visitors, followed the string of cars and witnessed the demonstration." Despite all eerie appearances, law and order was clearly upheld, and "hundreds of the visitors wore the white flowing robes and peaked hats of the order, but none were masked." Even road safety had been considered, and "the system and order with which the 5,000 people gathered and disbanded was marvelous. 'Klan Kops' directed all traffic and parking."[81]

Similar nighttime mass initiations were held at other nearby points—at Big Rapids "in the lurid glow of a huge fire," and at Holton, just a couple of miles over the Newaygo County border. The Holton meeting in the summer of 1924 saw local Klan units assemble at the crowded baseball grounds, where "a large class of candidates was initiated into the order." In a particularly visually effective ceremony, the Klan made use of not just its members, but also their vehicles. Klansmen in automobiles "came in a steady stream from all directions for about two hours before the ceremonies took place, and inside the grounds about seven hundred of them formed a circle, throwing their lights to the center and making a picturesque diffusion of rays." Adding to the dazzle of white sheets and car headlights, within the circle stood "a forty-foot fiery cross which loomed in the darkness high in the air and could be seen for miles around." The hundreds of candidates, waiting to "take their obligation," were themselves arranged in the formation of a human cross "and were surrounded by a line of Klansmen in full regalia which brought the whole formation into relief." Proceedings were also enlivened by "a woman's quartette," the patriotic songs of which "entertained the crowd for some time and received many encores on songs rendered in a most pleasing fashion." A Klan speaker, too, outlining the principles of the order, was met by an enthusiastic crowd, and "was interrupted several times with long and loud applause." Meanwhile, a huge gathering of non-Klan bystanders, drawn by the carnival of sights and sounds, had assembled on the road outside the baseball park, taking in what they could from that vantage point. Apparently anxious to avoid exclusion, "some of them asked the Klan guards if it was possible for them to go in and join before the ceremonies were over."[82]

At least part of the Klan's appeal, then, lay in its capacity to entertain—both in terms of the street theater provided by its public rites, ceremonies, and initiations, and also in the more conventional (if Klan-themed) activities and diversions it offered up to its members. Klan movies, for example, which acted as both entertainment and recruitment propaganda, were always popular, and both *The Birth of a Nation* and *The Toll of Justice* enjoyed periodic repeat runs in Klannish Newaygo and Fremont theaters during the mid-1920s. Even more theatrically, members of some local Klaverns turned their own hands to the performing arts. The *Imperial Night-Hawk* reported on a collaboration between one Klan and a local theater company that had adapted Thomas Dixon's novel *The Clansman* for the stage. During the final act of the play, which would have featured fictional Klansmen anyway, bona fide members of the KKK instead took over proceedings for real, incorporating one of their ceremonies as "a class of aliens was naturalized upon the stage before a huge audience." The play was received very well and proved "a very good drawing card . . . the Klan made a few thousand new friends in one night." Other similarly themed and often Klan-penned plays, such as the well-traveled *The Awakening*, became Klavern favorites across the country.[83] In Michigan, bulletins from state headquarters offered local units the chance to purchase copies of popular scripts so that they could put on their own shows. One of these, entitled *The Crucible*, was offered as "one of the best plays on the market for the proper education of the general public as [to] the meaning of Klankraft . . . its purpose is to entertain while it educates." Designed for a cast of eighteen characters with a running time of one and a half hours, Michigan Klans would be able to perform the play "either indoors or out," with "the flaming cross called for in the third act" ensuring that "the effect will be striking to say the least."[84]

In Newaygo County, many of the names that regularly appeared in the weekly newspapers in connection with small town stage and dramatic productions of one kind or another had also become members of the Klan. Among many similar examples were Klansfolk (or future Klansfolk) who were involved in putting on a play in Fremont, a vaudeville show in the same town, and a musical blackface minstrel performance in Newaygo.[85] Given the hooded organization's penchant for drama, it seems likely that "local talent" may have been given every opportunity, too, to stretch their theatrical muscles within the ranks. Much of ordinary Michigan Klan fraternal life, in fact, seems to have revolved around a heady mix of entertainment and socialization, with the organization holding, among other amusements, regular dances, variety stage shows, and the occasional masquerade ball or open-air picnic, all of which—undoubtedly aided by public curiosity—tended to attract great interest. Newaygo County was typical of much of the rest of Michigan in this respect, with the *White Cloud Eagle* reporting heavy attendance at the public "Klan picnic held at the grove" in July 1925, while "the evening meeting was also attended by a large crowd."[86]

The personal observations of Detroit Klansman and former Baldwin resident Kenneth Blass provide a rare glimpse inside the remarkably mainstream Klan social scene in Michigan. Even before entering the Klavern doors, he had clearly been influenced by the organization's self-projected image of an elite membership club peopled by the "best citizens," and already anticipated a crowd of "for the most part, men of trades and small business men." Whether or not that turned out to be the case, he certainly saw his own attendance at Klan events as an opportunity to better himself socially and make useful contacts of a certain standing, looking forward somewhat anxiously, in his own words, to "tripping the light fantastic and hob-nobbing with the Ku-Kluxers." Once inside, Blass may have been pleasantly surprised by just how familiar and easily accessible the activities on offer proved to be. Though presented under the overt novelty of the Klan banner, the forms of entertainment furnished within the Invisible Empire were barely distinct from already popular and mainstream entertainment forms in the non-Klan world. Describing a typical Klan dance, Blass writes that he "danced . . . quadrilles, a one-step, a Charleston and one fox-trot, from 9 'till 12.30 . . . [the] orchestra was good and [there was] a nice appearing and well behaving crowd. The kids were there in force. Most kids I've seen at a public gathering in a long while. Just a family party." On another occasion, immediately following the screening of a movie depicting Klan parades in Lansing and Pontiac, the Klavern was treated to "a short comedy, songs by a quartet and a good one-man vaudeville act," the entire show costing just 25 cents and proving extremely popular. "They did not advertise," comments Blass, and yet "the house was jammed . . . and was very well patronized all week." Months later, describing yet another "Klan vaudeville show," Blass pays tribute to the organization's propensity to provide high-quality entertainment at affordable prices. "They are putting on a ten act show for 50 cents and with nationally known artists," he writes. "[I] don't know of any other place one might get the same thing for that price."[87]

One character likely to have figured in Michigan Klan vaudeville performances was Newaygo County's very own variety superstar, Harlan Sanford Mankin. A remarkable and unique performer, it is no exaggeration to say that Mankin was a world-class entertainer, boasting a glittering career with various national circus and vaudeville companies that had seen him tour not only the United States but also much of the rest of the globe, including

Canada, Australia, Samoa, the South Sea Islands, New Zealand, South Africa, and Argentina. Despite being the owner of a simple farm near Fremont, then, it was with anything but an isolated small-town mentality that Mankin joined the Newaygo County Klan in the summer of 1924, alongside his mother, Ida (who was also his wardrobe mistress and constant travel companion), as well as his sister and brother-in-law. Aged thirty-five when he joined the Klan, he continued to make a living as a contortionist, "as a human frog, juggler, escape artist, animal trainer and trapeze performer in circuses, travelling stage shows and vaudeville." Counting such high-profile showbiz names as Buster Keaton, Harry Houdini, and Al Jolson among his personal acquaintances, it was Mankin's limb-wrenching signature act—in which he dressed up as, and impersonated the movements of, a frog—that had brought him widespread fame, seeing him top many a bill as "the Frog Man" or "Man-kin, the man who can do what no other man kin."

Neither did his reputation and love of the limelight end there. According to a tribute in the *Vaudeville Times*, "at one point during the 1925–1926 season," while in New York City, "he clambered up the sheer face of a 28 story building in Times Square as a publicity stunt to promote his vaudeville appearance at the old Orpheum theater." Filmed by news cameras as he reached the roof of the building, the intrepid Mankin "performed a fake fall on the narrow ledge . . . and concluded the stunt with a few trapeze tricks on the flagpole braces over the street."[88] In Newaygo County, too, Mankin had made public performances, appearing at least twice during the mid-1920s as the main attraction at the annual Farmers and Merchants picnic in Fremont. "Famed all over the world," this local boy made good had, according to the *Times-Indicator*, "entertained with a contortion act early in the afternoon at the 1923 event. This made a big hit and he had the crowds

Harley Mankin: Contortionist, "Frog-man," and Fremont Klansman
Source: Fremont Area District Library

gasping as he went through his various 'dare-devil' stunts in mid-air." The picnic at which he appeared had been organized by Fremont's Klannish chamber of commerce, under the direction of leading Klansmen Erwin C. Tinney, Clair Taylor, and Dr. Louis Webber. Even without their robes and hoods, the chamber's entertainment committee exuded the Klan's moralistic style, vowing "to close the grounds to all fakirs and grafters," the aim of the organization being "to make it a clean, wholesome affair which would leave no regrets or bad after effects."[89]

Also popular with Klans across the Midwest were musical recitals featuring dedicated KKK bands, some of which became quite well known and even sold recordings of their work. Local Klan units often sported their own bands, and sometimes played in conjunction with visiting KKK musicians. In January 1927, for instance, Blass describes how a seventy-piece Detroit Klan band was joined by "four coaches of Toledoens [who] drove up with a small band and drum corps." The organization's musical groups even, on occasion, made appearances at religious events involving nonwhite Protestant flocks. As an example, Blass describes the "Darktown celebration,"

Promotional ad for a popular Klan quartet
Source: *Fiery Cross (Michigan State Edition)*, 28 September 1923

which turned out to be "a highly successful affair," apparently involving a peaceful cooperation among a mixed group of participants that included both African Americans and Klansmen. "The white folks came in some 60-odd cars and were around 200 in number, including about 30 members of the Klan band," writes Blass. "Prayers and addresses were offered by one white minister and four colored ones. Klansmen were not in robes, but their identity wasn't much of a secret." Perhaps a promotional stunt, or even an effort at cross-racial Protestant solidarity (in the face of an apparently much more threatening Catholic foe), the event ended amicably, with the Klan making a publicity-friendly token gesture of cash to the "colored" church fund. As Blass observed, "the donation was gratefully accepted and I'm sure as heartily given."[90]

Newaygo County's own various band organizations do appear to have had strong links to the local Klan. The White Cloud fife-and-drum corps was led by Klansman John H. Collier, and included at least four other Klansmen in its ranks. In the same town, the White Cloud City Band, sponsored by the chamber of commerce, contained at least two Klan members, and even appears photographed in a local history compilation assembled before what appears to be a ten-foot electric fiery cross mounted on the back wall of the practice hall. In Newaygo, meanwhile, the Newaygo Portland Cement Company Band, described as "the pride of the village," had no less than six Klansmen as members, including their leader, that most Klannish of local Klan ministers, Rev. James Leitch.[91] With all of these musical Klansmen in evidence, it is not much of a leap to imagine them combining to form a lively county Klan band. Perhaps the most conspicuous sign of this actually happening was the appearance in 1925 of a five-piece orchestra calling themselves the "Newaygo Nite-Hawks," who then regularly provided the music at Friday- and Saturday-night dance halls around the county.[92]

Another area of mainstream leisure into which the Klan was eager to diversify was the traditional vacation resort experience. By the summer of 1924, Michigan's *Klan Kourier* had begun to carry ads for the so-called "Kool Koast Kamp," the "recreation center of Klandom," a coastal vacation spot in Texas billed as "a real Christian resort for Christian people." Offering a range of amusements as well as opportunities for fishing, swimming, and sports, the Kamp provided an idyllic setting and "an opportunity for Klansmen, regardless of their means, to enjoy a real family recreation under high class moral conditions."[93] If Texas seemed a stretch too far for many of Michigan's Klan families, then help was at hand. Within a couple of months of first advertising the Kool Koast Kamp, the Michigan Klan press was promoting much more local alternatives, including a "100 percent lake resort . . . just thirty miles from Detroit." On offer here were "camping sites for rent by day, week or season . . . at one of Oakland County's beautiful lakes." Lots were also made available for permanent sale, with the reassurance that this was "a strictly 100 percent proposition" with "lots sold to Klansmen only." Those doing the selling in this instance were also Klansmen, though exercising business options here as private individuals rather than in any official capacity for the Michigan Klan.[94]

Indeed, against the backdrop of immoral foreign influences that the Klan had conjured up in much of its propaganda, the organization put great emphasis upon the idea of providing what it saw as wholesome, American, family-oriented activities for its members. Of particular importance were activities for the children of Klan parents, used as a medium to steer the youngsters in the "right" moral and educational direction, and ultimately to bring them into the Klan fold alongside their parents. Both the men's and women's divisions of the Newaygo County Klan, along with every other in Michigan, received regular bulletins from the office of the state's Grand Dragon, George E. Carr. On countless occasions, the main subject of these was the progress of the Realm's own "Klan Kamp" at Woodward Lake in Ionia County, a venture funded collectively by donations from the coffers of KKK units across Michigan. Created chiefly for the use of the male Junior Klan order, although sometimes turned over to the Tri-K Klub for the girls' use, this was "a camp where members . . . may spend their vacations" and enjoy "basket dinner, bathing, boating, and fishing." A "fine Klan resort" by the lake, the camp hosted an annual swimming tournament, where Klan juniors represented their local units against one another in competitive state championships. Every August, similarly, it provided the venue for the championship game of Michigan's Junior Klan baseball league. The camp's guiding philosophy was that "clean and healthy bodies are a requisite to clean, active minds," and it provided a variety of activities "to challenge the boys to an all-round life of mental, physical, devotional and patriotic achievement." Klan parents sending their children here for the summer could be assured, then, that "every part of the program has been made up with a view in mind of impressing . . . the value of American citizenship."[95] The Klan clearly envisioned its activities with the junior order as an alternative to the national Boy Scout movement. The fact that the KKK was to make very real attempts to smear its rival only illustrates the extent to which the two were in serious competition. "The Roman Catholic hierarchy has taken over the Boy Scouts of America, lock, stock and barrel," claimed one 1925 headline, adding for good measure that the Junior Klan is the "only remaining boy's organization free of papal influence."[96]

Dedicated "junior pages" in the *Michigan Kourier* even attempted to interest youngsters in the order, using Klan-styled variations upon popular forms of amusement. Thus the nationwide craze for crossword puzzles became, in Klan hands, "the Fiery Cross-word puzzle," with the missing words to be arranged around the shape of the familiar Klan symbol. A note of encouragement added that "everyone cross-words now! So, while you're cross-wording, you can Kluck a bit too!" Other junior-centric features included a regular column dedicated to the adventures of "Klan Ket," a feline member, no less, of the KKK.[97] Women and Tri-K Klub girls, meanwhile, were encouraged to take part in activities commonly associated with traditional female or "homemaker" roles, often involving food preparation, craftwork, and charitable fundraising. Newaygo's Klanswomen, for instance, were asked by the state office for their "co-operation in arranging a meeting for mothers and daughters" of a Klannish persuasion, "with a good, appropriate program . . . either a banquet or a pot-luck dinner."[98] Klanswomen in the Michigan town of Chicora, on the other hand, put their considerable sewing skills to use in order to raise funds for their local unit, producing a very distinctive "KKK Quilt." Alongside the boldly embroidered name and number of their Klan, the ladies stitched the figure of a horse-riding Klansman, holding aloft a cross. In the blank squares surrounding these designs, the names of individual members of the Klavern, male and female, were added. More than two hundred names featured in all, with each (clearly unashamed) member paying 10 cents for the privilege, before the completed quilt was raffled off at a Klan meeting.[99]

If Klan women were required to act out their stereotypical gender roles, then Klan men were certainly expected to do the same. Almost every KKK speech associated its own brand of patriotism with rugged masculine virtues, the organization constantly describing itself as a place for "big manly men," "real red blooded American manhood," and even "He-men." Tied in with this association was a reverence for outdoorsmanship, athleticism, and healthy physical competition, all of which the Klan considered virile, wholesome, and somehow American. In rural Newaygo County, this particular association certainly seems to have struck a chord among local men. Not only did many members of the county's various football and baseball teams come to join the local KKK, but so too did at least half of the members of the Newaygo County Rod and Gun Club, a sporting association dedicated to the manly pursuits of hunting and fishing.[100] The Klannish Fremont Chamber of Commerce, in fact, sponsored its own baseball game in summer 1924, picking two teams of nine men from among its members. One team, "Fry's Kickers," included top Klan recruiter Dan Markley along

Quilt stitched by the Chicora, Michigan, Ku Klux Klan, No. 77
Source: Michigan State University Museum Collections

with three other Klansmen, while their opponents, "Tinney's Beefers," contained six men who were also in the Klan at the time, including ex-mayor Tinney and Rev. Jay N. Booth. Though perhaps providing little more than spirited recreation, the game proves at least that Newaygo Klansmen not only worked together but played together, and the games that they played were wholesome, American, "man's" games.[101]

Nowhere, though, was the mainstream appeal of the Klan's social activity in Michigan more apparent than in its huge regional gatherings or "Klonvocations." These vast, openly advertised carnivals brought the Klan directly to the streets and fairgrounds of many Michigan towns via an ostentatious mix of public parades, picnics and barbecues, live music, patriotic speeches, initiations and cross-burnings, religious services, spectacular fireworks shows, and all manner of related pageantry. Taking place typically in commemoration of distinctly American or patriotic holidays, most notably Labor Day, Memorial Day, and Independence Day, Newaygo Klan correspondence mentions numerous such gatherings during the 1920s, at locations including Grand Rapids, Ionia, Royal Oak, Bay City, Pontiac, Detroit, Imlay City, Owosso, Jackson, and Lansing.[102] Among the very grandest of these was an event held on Memorial Day 1924 in Saginaw. The *Newaygo Republican* called it "the largest meeting ever held in the state of Michigan by the Ku Klux Klan," attended by "over one hundred thousand Klansmen and Klanswomen." The day's main attraction featured "ten thousand robed men and women who took part in the parade through the main streets of Saginaw," the *Republican* noting with some pride that "the Newaygo County Klan was well represented in the parade."[103]

While agreeing with the *Republican's* figure on total Klan attendance, which apparently saw the city's population "doubled before nightfall" on the day of the Klonvocation, Saginaw's own newspapers claimed an even larger number of marchers, with "approximately 35,000 Klansmen in the big evening parade." Klansmen had arrived in droves throughout the day on special trains from other cities, with rumors even circulating, according to the *Saginaw Star*, "that every special train bringing Klan members over the Pere Marquette was to be operated by a train crew made up entirely of Protestants." The street parade itself, made up of (robed but not masked) male, female, and junior Klan members; mounted officers; Klan bands; automobiles; and lavishly decorated floats "presented an inspiring sight," and "the marching thousands . . . were greeted with cheers and the tooting of horns along the entire route." An eighty-acre field site, hired by the Klan for use as a base throughout the day, was the setting for "six huge crosses [which] blazed forth to herald the beginning of the evening's ceremony . . . to make more than a thousand men Knights." In addition to a huge Klan crowd, "several thousand spectators lined all four sides of the field during the entire ceremonial," which saw initiates kneel before the crosses to take the Klan oath and "renew their allegiance to their God and their country." After the ceremony, "one of the most picturesque events in Saginaw's history" came to a close with a large display of patriotically themed fireworks, visible for miles around. Describing how the Saginaw population had handled the bumper Klan crowds, the *Star* reported little in the way of trouble. "Exceptional courtesy," it observed, was "a marked feature . . . nowhere was there a show of roughness or impatience . . . no untoward incident occurred throughout the entire day and evening to mar any part of the ceremonies, which ended about midnight." Indeed, taking stock a day after the event, it was the booming trade done in supplying the ravenous crowds of reveling Klansfolk and onlookers that seems to have been most worthy of remark:

> Some idea of the immensity of the celebration can be gleaned from the amount of food consumed at the field. Hundreds of cooks were busy all day long preparing and serving the hungry visitors. Over a ton and a half of wieners were used to make approximately 100,000 "red hots." In addition, 2,800 pounds of roast meats found its way into hungry mouths, combined with over 4,000 loaves of bread. A whole barrel of pickles vanished. Fifteen thousand cakes, and between 5,000 and 6,000 pies, as well as several hundred gallons of ice cream were used to furnish everyone with dessert. An estimate of the thousands of cups of coffee served would be impossible. Gross after gross of quart bottles of milk found their way into the grounds as the day wore on . . . Restaurants never did such business before, one of the more prominent ones stating this morning that they were entirely sold out before the day was over . . . never in the history of the city was so much food consumed in a single day.[104]

Attendance at such colossal gatherings was a routine part of the social life of the Newaygo County Klan, and one that would see it take part in some of the most spectacular pageants that Michigan had ever seen. Encouraged by the huge success of its Memorial Day event, the Michigan Klan undertook a still more ambitious affair—a similar, but even larger Klonvocation held in the city of Jackson over the long Independence Day weekend in 1924. A brash and highly visible public display of Klan strength in Michigan, this was to be a huge celebration of Protestant culture. "The three days," promised the organizers, "will be full of every conceivable sort of amusement and entertainment for all," the main attraction of the weekend seeing the Imperial Wizard himself journey up from Atlanta to speak to the Wolverine State masses.

The Wizard's address, by Klan estimates at least, attracted a crowd of 100,000 from all parts of the state and beyond, while "there were at least 200,000 persons on the grounds when the grand finale came in the way of a giant fireworks display," making this "a decided success from start to finish . . . the biggest event Jackson has ever witnessed." The number of automobiles parked at the 112-acre field site (rented by the Klan for the purpose) was recorded "by actual count" at 47,281.[105] Though these figures are likely to have been exaggerated somewhat for maximum effect,

Advance publicity for the 4th of July Klonvocation at Jackson, Michigan
Source: *Klan Kourier (Michigan State Edition)*, 27 June 1924

photographic evidence leaves little doubt that this was indeed a significantly sizable affair, and one in which crowds in civilian attire mixed quite freely with their robed counterparts.

The political message of the event revolved around the broad issue of Americanism—both in patriotic celebration on this most American of days, and in calls for the defense of traditional American values from the encroachment of supposed foreign threats. Speaking before an assembled crowd, the head of the Michigan Women's Klan, Mary J. Bishop, announced that "it is up to us to protect this nation, our constitution and institutions" from "imported evils which threaten the moral life of our nation." In their respective speeches, both Bishop and Imperial Wizard Evans were sure to voice their support for the patently anti-Catholic "parochial schools amendment,"

Crowd scene at one part of the Klan camp during 4th of July celebrations, Jackson, Michigan, 1924
Source: Michigan State University Special Collections

due to be voted on by the public at the upcoming election, and in doing so were met with "the loudest and longest applause of the afternoon."[106]

The plethora of floats, banners, and displays brought to the campgrounds by visiting Klan units very much reflected this sentiment, as did the warm reception given them by the crowd. As described by the *Jackson Citizen Patriot*, "three 'little red school houses' were included in the array of floats," each bearing a legend with slight variations upon the theme that "the public school, open to all, for all, should be attended by all." Other displays included "Faith, Hope and Charity," "Protection of Womanhood," "Uncle Sam," "The Fiery Cross," "Spirit of 1924," "KKK," and "The Public School Is My Child. Protect It!" Many of the motorized displays bore a mix of traditional patriotic imagery and Klan symbolism, attempting to ally the two. The following image, for example, of a car decorated by the women of the Kalamazoo Klan, features a sign at the rear calling for "Protection of Womanhood," a stock Klan slogan. As well as a mounted fiery cross of red carnations, the vehicle also carries Uncle Sam on one fender and Lady Liberty on the other. Note also the huge, as yet unlit, fiery cross in the background skyline.

Maskless Klansfolk and civilian onlookers mix at Jackson
Source: Michigan State University Special Collections

Other floats made their pro-American and anti-foreign points much more directly, including one that "depicted a number of low class immigrants with the caption 'we are opposed to undesirable immigration,'" the *Citizen Patriot* adding that "the immigration pageant and several others drew applause from the many thousands which lined the streets."[107] Xenophobic as it may have sounded, with the National Origins Act on immigration restriction making its way into federal law at around this time (and displaying exactly the same basic sentiments), this was by no means an

"Protection of Womanhood" float, Kalamazoo WKKK at Jackson, 4th of July 1924
Source: Michigan State University Special Collections

unpopular or even an uncommon stance among white Protestant Americans. Music, meanwhile, was furnished throughout by the many Klan bands present at the scene, which played a mix of special Klan numbers, patriotic American classics, and religious anthems, notably accompanying marchers with "Onward Christian Soldiers." At one point, a huge American flag was carried horizontally by Klansmen for people to throw money into as they passed, an activity in which they duly obliged.[108]

In all, the general reception seems to have been a hospitable one, and apparently "men and women all along the line carried pitchers of water" to Klansfolk marching in the summer heat. According to reports in the Klan press, at least, "cheering and handclapping kept up all the way and the Klansmen were received by the people of Jackson in a way that brought joy to the hearts of all Americans."[109] Even if this description seems, perhaps, a little too gushing, it is at least true to say that the Klan received an immense amount of help and cooperation from local residents and officials in the staging of such a huge and successful pageant. In terms of transport alone, the Michigan Electric Railway company laid on at least seventeen special trains and twelve buses into Jackson from other cities specifically for the event, while the Michigan

Central Railroad added extra coaches to its regular trains to accommodate the crowds. To cater for those traveling by car, too, "the roads of Jackson County [were] placarded with arrows which will carry motorists from any part of the county direct to the grounds." With many hotels prebooked well before the event, local residents even helped with accommodation by renting out their spare rooms to visiting Klansmen.[110]

The Klan's spacious base for the three-day gathering was described as "a city of tents," with one large tent to serve as headquarters for each visiting unit. The Newaygo County Klan occupied such a spot in the makeshift Klan city, amid a network of "streets . . . named and tents numbered as in a permanent city . . . to help visitors find various places that would otherwise be lost in the vast tented area." Indeed, the planning had been exemplary, and in cooperation with local authorities, it had been previously agreed that "special water pipes will carry the water supply to the grounds." Other amenities included a Klan nursery, with the forty-six women on duty caring for around two hundred babies over the course of the event. Also provided on site was a Klan hospital, which treated hundreds of people for exhaustion during the long summer days of energy-draining showboating. The gathering, according to the local press, "resembled a large fair." The area swarmed with automobiles, many draped in the Stars and Stripes and others "carrying fiery crosses on the radiators." In and around the tents, "men sat and smoked . . . men, women and children gathered and talked." Meanwhile, the commercial aspect thrived, and "conveniences of every class and description were available . . . soft drinks, food, confections, fruit, tobacco, and souvenirs were all in abundance." Very conspicuously, "a large sign announced that a Michigan concern had supplied the Jackson Klan with five thousand cases of carbonated beverages."[111]

One glance at that sign (and more specifically at the highly familiar corporate logo emblazoned on the side of the soda crates) reveals a very prominent, if perhaps surprising, commercial sponsor for the Michigan Klan. In its own eyes, at least, the Invisible Empire's association with the iconic brand—a cultural emblem both utterly mainstream and very distinctly American—was one entirely fitting for the times.

To this and the many similar events taking place around the state, Klansmen were commonly urged to "bring your Protestant friends," or "bring your eligible friends and their families" because "we want them to see our work."[112] Far from shying away in the Klavern, then, the Klan was eager to provide a spectacle to members and nonmembers alike, and seems to have been supremely confident in its own ability to deliver a program of successful, family-oriented, patriotic, and most importantly, accessible—and

Mainstream commercial sponsorship for the Klan at Jackson, 1924
Source: Michigan State University Special Collections

to some extent participatory—entertainment that would be of interest to any right-thinking "good, Protestant American." The organization's basic method of drawing a crowd was, for the most part, flat-out gimmickry. In Jackson, certainly, "during the morning hours thousands witnessed the daring feats of a Knight of the Klan as he performed on the wings of an aeroplane." After further stunts in the afternoon, the same plane was deployed to serve up another Klannish trick. "With the black sky as a background, a flaming red cross streaked across the heavens and over the grounds when the aviator turned on a red electrically lighted cross showing from the bottom of the plane." This "brought a round of applause and shouts of approval from the surging mass," warming them up nicely for the initiation ceremony, cross-burning, and "fabulous fireworks" display to follow. In the midst of all this, the *Citizen Patriot* was on hand to praise "the orderly manner of those present," which "prevailed throughout the day and evening."

To an extent, this route was tried and tested territory as far as fraternal orders were concerned. Referring primarily to her work on nineteenth-century fraternal movements, Mary Ann Clawson could easily have been describing the 1920s Klan when she noted the social and diversionary roles played by a typically spectacular line in public ritual and rhetoric. "It functioned," she writes, "as a form of entertainment that enlivened and gave purpose to the sociability it justified."[113] The Newaygo County Klan, in its participation in large-scale regional KKK events such as the Klonvocation at Jackson, was playing a full part, alongside a multitude of comparable units across the state, in creating a wider Klan community or culture. At the same time, these gatherings served as both an outward demonstration of the apparent strength of the Klan as a force in national life, and a cohesive source of solidarity and common ground between the related but disparate local branches that collectively made up the "Invisible Empire." Providing opportunities for socialization and networking between otherwise unrelated Michigan units, the great gatherings brought demonstrably similar-minded Klannish communities together in celebration of their shared "Americanism." Projecting a sense of camaraderie and wider relevance, of real connection with a nationwide Klan movement, such events may have been particularly exciting for units in more remote areas (very much like rural Newaygo County), whose social connections beyond a small constellation of local towns and villages would normally have been fairly limited. With the ready-made sociability provided by a statewide, and even nationwide, Klan network, any member could, in theory at least, travel to any town as an unknown, and yet, by virtue of their shared association and common rituals, find a welcoming and hospitable Klan community among strangers.

Aiding in the articulation of a Klan group identity, and helping bring about a strong sense of belonging, KKK public ceremonies and social activities dramatically demonstrated what Kathleen Blee has referred to as "the totality of Klan culture."[114] Many aspects of everyday life—entertainment, leisure, commercial life, church life, politics, even birth, marriage, and death—could now be conducted, quite legally and acceptably, entirely under the Klan banner in the white Protestant communities in which the organization gained a foothold, helping to "normalize" the Invisible Empire. Social life within such Klannish communities became almost indistinguishable from white Protestant life without the hood. And in the end, it *was* merely a matter of a simple hood—the fact that Michigan Klansmen were unable to cover their faces with a mask serving only to further demonstrate their lack of separation from the non-Klan.

The KKK's association—or perceived association—with wholesome and respectable ideas like patriotism, community spirit, law and order, and traditional family values was, for a fleeting historical moment in the early 1920s, the organization's greatest public-relations asset and the strongest basis of its brief but spectacular popularity. It was enough, at least, to attract the membership of some of the "best" and most active citizens, who would have stood as respectable examples to others, spurred on by talk of the protection of (a religiously and ethnically homogeneous) community, country, and home. In their culturally isolated, almost all-white context, these were overwhelmingly ordinary and representative Americans, which is not to say that their views were not bigoted or xenophobic. What is clear, though, is that they intended to champion the idea of a wholesome Protestant Americanism as they saw it, in the face of all opposition. The *Klan Kourier* summed up a pleasing situation for the order at its statewide peak in summer 1924, declaring with satisfaction that "Michigan is turning to the Klan in a way that is warming the hearts of all true Americans, and the Klan is held in high esteem by leading citizens in all parts of the state."[115] Despite enjoying the glories of its undeniable successes, KKK promoters only ever managed to maintain a tentative grip upon the favor of the watching community. Should the Klan's positive associations begin publicly to break down and falter, as the hooded order would in time find out to its great detriment, then membership figures and popular sympathy would quickly follow them in disappearing into the ether.

Epilogue

THE 1920s KU KLUX KLAN IN RURAL NEWAYGO COUNTY, AND IN THE state of Michigan more widely, certainly appears to fit in with the "new historical appraisal" of the organization as championed in more recent regional studies by writers such as Shawn Lay and Leonard J. Moore. In his introduction to a particularly notable edited volume of case studies featuring six western Klaverns (drawn from Colorado, Texas, California, Utah, and Oregon), Lay pointed out that the organization "demonstrated a great appeal among mainstream elements across the nation," and labeled it "simultaneously a vast social, political and folk movement."[1] Moore, meanwhile, in assessing the findings of what he called "populist" Klan studies (including his own in Indiana), concluded that "Klansmen were too much a part of America's social mainstream to be dismissed as an extremist aberration."[2] It is statements such as these that, above anything else used to describe members of the order, seem most genuinely fitting to describe the Klansmen and Klanswomen of Michigan.

In order to help either confirm or deny their interpretation of the 1920s Klan movement, and in the process build up a national picture of the organization, Lay and his associates stated the need for a wave of future Klan researchers to provide "a sufficient number of case studies from a variety of regions."[3] It is hoped that this effort, the first to concentrate entirely upon the state of Michigan, can in some way contribute to this wider national picture. Certainly its findings agree by and large with those of the "Populist-Civic" school of thought on the Klan, revealing an organization that, at the peak of its popularity, was chiefly social and civic in nature, was essentially law-abiding, and drew members from across the white Protestant religious spectrum as opposed to simply the fundamentalist fringes. The mass of its members, here as elsewhere, came from all strata of local Protestant life and, just as Lay noted of his own Klan subjects, "whatever their social or economic standing, a commitment to civic activism united members of the order."[4] Naturally for the average upstanding white Protestant Midwesterner of the time, the word "activism" in this description could just have easily have been replaced by "moralism," and it was the moral arena in which the Klan mounted its greatest public campaigns. At the national level this meant an obsession with prohibition enforcement and the prevention of "undesirable" immigration, while more local manifestations included worries about the supposedly corrupting effects of "Romanist" influence in local government and public schools. Either way, in its Northern, homogeneously white surroundings, the Klan's primary concerns turned out to be far more religious than racial, and its ungodly enemies, as depicted in crowd-drawing caricatures of foreign moral depravity, far more imagined than real.

Even so, engaging self-portrayals by the KKK were nothing if not accessible, making their way to the public through a prism of pop-culture distractions and deviations that included romance novels, drama, song, and—most impressively of all—the movies. Using impossibly clichéd imagery depicting a thoroughly American self and a deeply un-American adversary, the Invisible Empire succeeded almost as much, it seems, in entertaining the crowds as persuading them. That the Klan's arrival in towns and cities across the nation during the 1920s was accompanied by a faddish Klan-themed merchandizing craze is a sure sign of its entry into popular culture. Trading on attractive notions of a prestigious, patriotic, and exclusive member's club, commission-hungry Kleagles "sold" the Klan, or at least the idea of the Klan, to expectant communities everywhere, while sales of robes, assorted regalia, and all manner of novelty items boomed accordingly. Despite the banal outer material trappings of the Klan phenomenon, the meat of its recruitment activity took place at the very heart of the community, as the Newaygo County membership records clearly show. As well as winning recruits from every social class via informal mechanisms of family, work, and fraternity, the KKK took particular pains to make members of the influential and the reputable. Protestant ministers, local government officials, newspapermen, school boards, the civically active, the socially and financially prominent, and the "best" citizens—all provided, in their robes, a respectable, and public, example. As the Klan banner began to fly over all manner of entertainments—whether they be picnics, potlucks, parades, celebrations, 4th of July fireworks, even christenings, weddings, and funerals—the culture of the Ku Klux Klan and the culture of white Protestant America for this brief moment in time became one. With its members' leisure time and social lives organized in much the same way, with or without their regulation robes, their Klannish activities, such as they were, did little but reaffirm the seamless connections between the order and the ordinary.

Much more accurately described as a popular social movement than an extremist terror group, the KKK in 1920s Michigan essentially lacked any of the destructive edge of the kind that would come to characterize modern-day incarnations of the Ku Klux Klan. In a study penned in the mid-1950s looking at the Jazz Age Klan across four Midwestern states, Norman Frederick Weaver had in fact specifically noted that "none of the meetings or parades produced anything violent in Michigan; there was no violence at all connected with the wolverine Klan." On this point, indeed, there seems very little evidence of any kind from across the state, and certainly Newaygo County, to contradict Weaver's assertion.[5] As a partial explanation, it is possible that the Klan's image in Michigan was in fact aided and not hindered by the state's specific anti-mask law—the overt secrecy and public distrust generated by the mask (which had become an Achilles heel to the organization in other areas) having a much-reduced effect there.

In other respects, however, Weaver seems to have underestimated the Klan in Michigan and, along with the few others who have touched upon the Wolverine State at all, concentrated his analysis upon the larger metropolitan areas where the Klan was perhaps more vocal or well-reported. He even went so far as to assert that the organization "must have been relatively small and unimportant in the state outside of Detroit, for records of Klan activity are extremely thin."[6] Clearly, the latter-day emergence of exactly the kinds of records that Weaver lacked, and especially those from rural, small-town locations such as Newaygo County, provide a strong counter-argument, making the case for a buoyant and populous Klan movement involving Michiganians of all types everywhere, and most certainly outside of the state's major urban centers.[7]

Rural Michigan in particular then, though evidently a relative hotbed of Klan activity, is one area that has been heretofore little studied in this context. Though the major focus here has been upon one specific rural county Klan unit (the records of which allow us to see the organization at work close up), an occasional switch to the metropolitan equivalent (through the eyes of Detroit Klansman Kenneth Blass) allows some sense of a uniformity of experience that defies any kind of simplistic urban-rural split as an explanation for Klan activity. Whereas John Moffatt Mecklin in 1924 characterized the stereotypical Klansman as emerging from "the dreariness of small-town life,"[8] Kenneth T. Jackson challenged this longstanding traditionalist assumption head-on in his groundbreaking 1967 book *The Ku Klux Klan in the City*. But as far as Michigan in the 1920s is concerned, both viewpoints hold a degree of accuracy. The Klan there was not simply an expression of isolated rural "backwardness," nor was it an urban response to the close proximity and growing encroachment of cosmopolitan strangeness. The Klan in Michigan was everywhere.

If the Klan of the twenties was, as Lay attests, "a vast social, political and folk movement," then it is largely the social and the cultural elements, rather than the overtly political, that have been prioritized here. Many interpretations of the interwar Klan, particularly before the advent of the "Populist-Civic" approach, have tended to focus almost wholly upon the ideology of the organization at a national level, analyzing its often acrid political rhetoric to the general neglect of any kind of examination of how the Klan worked socially. By aiming the spotlight at a Klan social and cultural scene certainly touched by, but by no means confined to or defined by, the political, this study has attempted to provide clues to the wider, multifaceted, popular appeal of the organization. Viewing the Klan at a local level—the state of Michigan, the county of Newaygo, and even the towns and villages making up the county of Newaygo—its focus is upon the rank-and-file membership and the often stunningly ordinary ways in which everyday aspects of their lives found relevance and expression, albeit for a short-lived period, through the KKK.

Scholars of the 1920s KKK everywhere have noted that, numerically speaking, the pace of its dramatic rise to prominence was matched, if not surpassed, by a corresponding sharp and sudden decline in fortunes in the second half of the decade. The Klan in Newaygo County was certainly no exception. Organizational records indicate that the unit, in its early days, was charged by Michigan state headquarters with a membership quota of 1,075—the minimum number of recruits it would need to attract in order to be awarded an official charter by the national Klan administration. Having met, and indeed exceeded, these requirements, the Newaygo County KKK was visited by a representative from Atlanta and awarded its official charter in a ceremony at the White Cloud Baptist Church on 29 September 1925.[9] Within the short space of six months, however, the local Klan had entered terminal decline. By the end of March 1926, according to quarterly membership and dues reports completed by Newaygo County Kligrapp (Secretary) Elwin J. Stone, the unit had dwindled to a tenth of its chartered size, with just 109 fully paid-up members and a nonexistent women's order. The report for the next quarter would prove even more disheartening. Between March and June 1926, although the Klan had managed to reinstate 12 memberships, its efforts were negated by the loss of another 52 recruits, most of whom it had been forced to suspend for failure to pay dues, leaving its total strength at a paltry 69 members "in good standing." Of these, fully 55 were situated in Fremont. Everywhere else in Newaygo County, the Klan's death knell had been well and truly sounded: just three members remained in White Cloud, three in Newaygo, four in Hesperia, and a further four scattered among the county's rural hamlets and villages. Though later records show that the Newaygo County Klan remained—technically at least—in existence, it was but a pathetic shadow of its former self. By 1928, only 12 members remained in total—not enough men to even provide a full set of officers. In 1929, the once-mighty local Klan stood seven strong, after which point all official trace of the unit disappears.[10]

Many of the keys to understanding the Klan's spectacular demise are tied up in the very nature of its phenomenal popular success, and in a number of ways the two things are inherently and inextricably linked. At the most basic and superficial of levels, the popular Klan was a marketable fad, the gimmicky merchandizing that surrounded it carrying a novelty value that was inevitably destined to wear thin once it reached saturation point. Beyond its outer theatrical trappings and visually spectacular lodge culture, for many members there was little of substance to keep them interested in the order—or little, at least, that was so unique to the Klan that it could not be experienced elsewhere in small-town life. Certainly, there seems to have been no central program of activity—the local unit, once established, was left largely to its own devices by the national office. Seldom involved beyond the collection of membership dues, national Klan headquarters provided very little in the way of positive, applicable impetus from above, leaving local units without any real direction or purpose. In Newaygo County, the local unit burned crosses, staged a few public meetings, and attended regional Klan gatherings, but in truth the prospects of genuine action beyond these few activities were very limited. Even the national Klan's colorful propaganda held a short-lived appeal. Casting images of a demonic and monolithic enemy in dire need of defeat, its gruesomely entertaining tales ultimately failed to ring true, with no authentic trace of this "enemy" ever actually materializing in Newaygo, or in any typically white Protestant locality that resembled it.

The closest that the local Klan came to any sense of driving purpose was in its support of the "parochial schools" bill, a proposed amendment to the Michigan constitution that, if successful, would have seen the abolition of all private and religious schools in the state. Aimed squarely at reducing the influence of Catholicism in education, this was a long-running campaign in Michigan, predating the Klan by a number of years, but which, with the enthusiastic backing of a large number of KKK signatures, "became the hottest issue of the election campaign in 1924."[11] When the time came to put the amendment to the ballot, the almost homogeneously white Protestant rural population of Newaygo County did indeed find in favor of outlawing parochial schools, by 3,161 votes to 2,351. Their efforts, though, were to prove absolutely in vain, the more cosmopolitan makeup of other areas of the state reflected in a decisive vote against the school amendment by a margin of 760,571 votes to 421,472. The cause was a lost one, and politically speaking, the Michigan Klan's brief moment had passed. Adding to the sense of local political redundancy was the feeling that nationally, too, the order's endeavors had begun to descend into pointlessness. With immigration restriction a much-cited Klan objective, the passing of the National Origins Act of 1924 essentially took the impetus out of Klan hands and placed it into those of the federal government. In this sense, the Klan's quest for conventional appeal had worked only too well, confirming the mainstream validity of its pro-American ideals, while at the same time depriving the order of one of its key reasons for existence.

Such a drift toward impotence and irrelevance would also characterize the Klan's electoral efforts at the state level in Michigan, which, despite a number of near misses—particularly in Detroit's mayoral elections—failed ultimately to leave any lasting impression at all.[12] Members of the Newaygo County unit, in fact, were left with little to do but bicker among themselves regarding the one remaining issue of any concern, mourning the disappointing state election showings of "dry," prohibition-friendly candidates, who represented a cause supposedly close to Klan hearts. After the 1924 Republican primary, prominent Klansman and newspaper editor Don VanderWerp in fact used the pages of his *Fremont Times-Indicator* to rip into his lodge brothers statewide, declaring that "Michigan Klansmen have doubtless learned something from the recent election." He went on to accuse members of the order of handing the Republican nomination for Michigan's lieutenant governorship to "wet" candidate George Welsh, having disastrously split the "dry" vote by their stubborn support for an improbable and unsuccessful Klan candidate. "The Klan apparently was more interested in voting for its own candidate and lose the issue than support a non-Klansman and win the principle," he wrote, adding that "if Welsh ever opposed the organization he owes it an apology now." Furthermore, VanderWerp branded senatorial nominee James Couzens "the enemy of prohibition" and "a Republican in name only." A week later, the members of Newaygo County's Klan-packed Republican convention held heated discussions on this very issue before finally deciding to deny Couzens their official endorsement, on the grounds that "as a wet he does not reflect the true sentiment of Michigan voters on the prohibition question."[13]

All talk of politics aside, while public parading and fraternal ritualism clearly held a certain appeal, from a mass entertainment point of view the kind of diversions offered by the Klan were also very much on the way out. Newer, more varied, and innovative forms of entertainment continued to be ushered in, with such technologically sophisticated mediums as records and, in particular, an emergent radio, continuing to grow in popularity alongside the now well-established movie theaters. Relatively archaic and rudimentary by comparison, the mass parades and dramatic pageantry reveled in by the KKK, and lodge organizations in general, would quickly wane in popular appeal.[14] In a sense, the Klan had anticipated something of this mood, and to a certain extent had sought to prolong its own life by bridging the gap between the newer and the more traditional forms of mass entertainment, incorporating elements of the fashionable where it saw an advantage in doing so. Indeed, as well as producing its own musical recordings, the Klan had made a number of conscious efforts to utilize the airwaves throughout its lifetime, to say nothing of its almost clichéd overuse of the ever-popular movie version of *The Birth of a Nation* as a recruitment tool. In its partial embrace of modern media, though, the Invisible Empire was merely staving off the advances of the inevitable, and these innovations, ultimately, would come not to aid the order, but to replace it.

Another factor in the Klan's meteoric rise—the fact that in its pomp it had been a lucrative source of income for its streetwise organizers—would likewise come to haunt the organization and contribute to its decline. With the spoils of membership fees and merchandising money to wrangle over, internal dissension and quarreling became an all-too-common feature within the higher echelons of the Klan ranks, and pointed, perhaps, to a lack of strong and decisive leadership. In Detroit, two high-profile court cases even saw ex-Klan employees sue the organization and its head officers, alleging nonpayment and seeking compensation for services rendered (one had worked as an attorney, the other a propagandist). Descending into very public financial scandal, the image of the order in Michigan took a battering, with the testimony of various witnesses revealing much evidence of unscrupulous dealing behind the scenes, as well as opportunistic, greed-driven, and highly suspect business ventures set up by individuals trading on the strength of the Klan "brand."[15]

The murky, unsavory light that this threw upon the Klan reputation was echoed, too, at a more local level. Tales of money-grabbing Kleagles absconding with KKK funds were fairly common all over, and this was exactly the fate that befell Mecosta County, which bordered the Newaygo unit immediately to the east. In separate interviews conducted with two ex-members of the Mecosta County Klan in the 1980s, Calvin Enders found that the recruiter's betrayal, more than many other details of their former membership, had stuck firm in the minds of both men. One distinctly remembered Kleagle Ward S. Powers "making off with the money," while the other likewise recalled how the "Kleagle from Big Rapids just suddenly disappeared . . . got all the money he could and left."[16] Powers had apparently taken many orders from the area's Klansmen for robes, helmets, and regalia, collecting their money in full before failing spectacularly to deliver the goods and subsequently disappearing entirely with the takings in the summer of 1925. It was a blow from which both the finances and, much more crucially, the reputation of the order in western Michigan would never recover. Lewis Capen, Exalted Cyclops of the Mecosta unit, in a string of despondent letters to Michigan Grand Dragon George E. Carr, would continually return to the subject, citing the longstanding negative effects upon both morale and funds. The basic business of keeping the unit up to date with quarterly dues to the state and national offices, Capen wrote, "leaves us practically penniless" after "the indebtedness caused by the Kleagle trouble here." As for the members themselves, "many of them fail any more to respond to written notices about special meetings or to dues notices." Indeed, outraged Klan members had voted with their feet and would not be returning, a situation that left Capen quite genuinely lamenting the immoral behavior of his former Kleagle colleague, and longing wistfully for the glory days of popularity that his Klan had only recently enjoyed, but had now lost forever:

> It seems that many of the old timers can not get over the old Kleagle days and especially the way the county was left when Mr. Powers left. It is to be regretted that after building up a fine body of men in each of these counties that he should so completely wreck it all by his own lack of that which he was preaching—Klankraft. My big regret is that I am not eloquent speaker enough that I can again bring these men to see the need of this great American body.[17]

Worse still, these local financial scandals had taken place against the backdrop of a much more worrying moral malaise surrounding the Klan. In March 1925, D. C. Stephenson—who as Indiana's Grand Dragon had been arguably the most powerful man in the KKK outside of the South, and certainly its most recognizable leader—was spectacularly charged with kidnapping, rape, and second-degree murder. Madge Oberholtzer, a young Indiana woman, having been invited to "Steve's" mansion, had been drugged and forced to accompany him on a train to Chicago, during which journey he was alleged to have sexually assaulted, brutalized, and maimed her, violently biting and chewing upon her tongue, breasts, legs, and back. Shortly afterwards, Oberholtzer attempted suicide by swallowing poison and, while not immediately successful, died as a result of her injuries a few weeks later. In the meantime, her testimony was enough to see Stephenson charged in a trial that would ultimately result in a sentence of life imprisonment. During the course of the legal proceedings, newspapers local and national abounded with shameful stories from Stephenson's past, including charges of desertion of a former wife and child. Much was made by Stephenson opponents, too, of the gruesome, titillating, and highly sexual details of his moral atrocity, in entirely the same manner, in fact, that the Klan had used anti-Catholic pornographic tales against its own "enemies." Despite the fact that Stephenson had broken his official ties with the Klan a year or so before, his association with the order in the public mind was so strong that his shocking and much-publicized downfall proved devastating for the Invisible Empire. With a popular support self-righteously based upon morality, respectability, and enforcement of law, members fell away rapidly in Indiana, just as they did everywhere else that Stephenson had exerted an influence, which certainly included Michigan.[18]

As if all of this were not enough to forever sully the KKK's respectable image, Michigan managed to produce its very own Klan-related scandal. In late May 1926, at a lake resort located just ten miles to the west of Newaygo County, a bomb delivered by mail exploded, killing three people. Within less than a week of the explosion, Asa Bartlett, a local political rival of one of the dead, was on his way to Marquette state penitentiary, having confessed to the murderous act and been rapidly sentenced to life imprisonment.[19] It was widely believed at the time (though not definitively proven) that Bartlett, as well as being the "Blue Lake Bomber," was in fact also the Exalted Cyclops of the Muskegon County Klan, Newaygo's close neighbor. Responding to rabid press speculation upon the subject, Michigan Grand Dragon George E. Carr came out publicly to deny any association between Bartlett and the Invisible Empire.[20] The damage, however, had already been done, the public linking of the Klan name with yet another moral scandal dealing an almost overwhelming hammer blow to the organization in Michigan. Indeed, Bartlett's arrest and conviction, and the outrage that surrounded it, produced mass resignations in the state as the throng of largely respectable and community-minded recruits, no longer able to square the image of the organization with the one that they had joined, began to ditch the Klan in droves.[21]

Such a strong negative reaction from the mass of Michigan Klansfolk suggests a majority membership ordinarily unaccustomed to, and seemingly repelled by, such violence. It mattered little that Bartlett's atrocities—or Stephenson's, come to that—were not even conducted under official Klan auspices. Faced with the disturbingly real possibility of brutal acts from within their own ranks, even if those acts were carried out by rogue individuals, local KKK members voted with their feet. For the overwhelming bulk of former advocates and everyday Klansfolk of Michigan—the well-meaning and the upstanding, the masses caught up in the fascination with the order and attracted by its moralism or its civic activism—the picture had become abundantly clear with the arrest of the Blue Lake Bomber: If this was the caliber of man attracted by the Klan, then affiliation with the order was henceforth worthless, if not morally repugnant.

Nancy MacLean, in her stunningly effective deconstruction of KKK organizational ideology, has asserted that "Klan culture generated a propensity to vigilantism like an acorn does an oak," and that, quite naturally, "vigilante violence was the concentrated expression of that culture."[22] During the Invisible Empire's cultural peak in 1920s Michigan, however (despite the local hooded order having enthusiastically adopted the national Klan's caustic rhetoric and destructive ideology), this simply does not seem to have been the case. While every issue of the *Michigan Kourier* overflowed with, in particular, anti-Catholic wrath, the local KKK did not routinely translate these sentiments into violence. There is no evidence to suggest that anything more than a tiny minority of the membership ever actually responded in any real way to such provocation from its leaders and propagandists. Indeed, as we have seen, the rare prospect of actual violence, or any association with it, sent the large, apparently moralistic majority element of popular Michigan Klan support running for the hills and disowning the order. Only after this had happened, leaving behind the ardent few ideological devotees and true believers, did hate politics become the Klan's sole reason for being.

Though the Klan in Michigan had been dramatically reduced by mid-1926 and would continue to fall away, previous reports of its complete ruination have nevertheless overstated the case somewhat, or at least accelerated the rate of decline. Norman Weaver insisted, for example, that by 1928 "the Klan organization in Michigan was reduced to a pair of units in Detroit and Flint, and they were barely clinging to life."[23] There is much to suggest, however, that the Michigan Klan's greatly shrunken remains actually continued to grasp, however desperately, for the last vestiges of existence for at least the remainder of the decade, and in some places even beyond this. KKK units in the cities of Saginaw, Alma, and Bay City, for instance, were still strong enough to each be publishing a monthly newspaper through 1928. Indeed, the 1928 nomination of New Yorker Al Smith as Democratic candidate for president had effected a mini-revival of Klan enthusiasm nationally.

As a Catholic, a product of Tammany Hall, and a staunch critic of prohibition, Smith represented the archetypal Klan nemesis, and a perfect target for its particular brand of anti-immigrant, anti-corruption, anti-Romanist vitriol.[24] While the effect was short-lived, and the basis of real support had long since evaporated, the ailing Klan in Michigan had not yet been snuffed out to the point where it could be declared officially dead.

The pages of the state's Klan organs, furthermore, featured stories from active Klans in other Michigan towns, such as Muskegon, St. Johns, and even the remote Upper Peninsula setting of Bruce's Crossing. Similarly, the Grand Rapids–based WKKK magazine *Wolverine Women* only put out its first edition in 1928, and ran continuously until at least June 1931, mentioning during this period the names of no less than thirty active WKKK units operating throughout the state. Claiming proudly in the June 1931 edition that "the Ku Klux Klan [is] still an active agency," its editors were still perhaps somewhat overoptimistic in their suggestion that while "for a time it appeared that the Klan was being rapidly eliminated . . . Klankraft is as virile and effective today as it ever was in the early days of the past decade."[25] The internal correspondence of the Mecosta County Klan, too, runs continuously until at least September 1932, and includes bulletins received from a clearly still active Realm headquarters, again mentioning the active work of many Michigan units over the same period. Only the Grand Dragon's letterhead, indicating a shrunken administration now responsible for Ohio and Indiana as well as Michigan, gives any obvious concession to the Klan's much reduced circumstances.[26]

In Newaygo County, although the KKK continued to operate even in the wake of scandals national and local, its activities, such as they were, disappeared from public view entirely, and it never again warranted even the slightest of mentions in an apparently now uninterested local press. Despite this, organizational correspondence indicates that there were at least slight signs of life, with the unit's Fremont Klavern playing host in January 1927 to a regional officers' meeting, as well as a "K-Trio" degree presentation ceremony almost exactly a year later. The county Klan was also represented at the annual state meeting in Flint during August 1927, and again at a similar province-level event in Bay City the following June.[27] To all intents and purposes, though, the Klan's term as a palpable presence in Newaygo County was without question at an end, its skeleton crew of twelve members by 1928 and seven by 1929 rendering it completely unrecognizable from the loud and sociable prospect it had once presented. With the popular phase of Klan membership firmly a thing of the past, it was now only the truly dedicated, whatever their reasons, who remained. And, with the respectable social, civic, and entertainment aspects of the organization disappearing with the crowds, their reasons, increasingly, were based in the territory of the marginal and the politically extreme.

In May 1928, Michigan Grand Dragon George Carr, with the creation of an organization known as the Michigan Bible Study League, essentially took his floundering Klan on an undercover mission. Pursuing an aggressive variation upon the failed "parochial schools amendment," his extensive petition campaign vowed to clean up the education of America's youth, defy the corrupting influence of an unnamed "invisible un-American agency," and "PUT THE HOLY BIBLE IN EVERY PUBLIC SCHOOL BY LEGISLATIVE ENACTMENT." Appointing himself president of the new organization, Carr produced a 150-strong list of names of his "Directors and District Chairmen," which, needless to say, read like a proverbial "who's who" of KKK leadership in Michigan at that time. Convinced that his thinly veiled plan would rebrand the Klan, Carr "maintained that people not 'in the know' would believe that the chosen men had no particular significance." Two of the men in question were Elwin J. Stone and James Keller, Newaygo County's Kligrapp and Exalted Cyclops respectively, whose loyalty to the order quite obviously extended far beyond the casual, straying well into the realms of the politically, or at the very least fraternally, committed. Stone, in fact, had in August 1927 been elected to a state-level Klan officer's post (Grand Klarogo), having been personally nominated for the honor by Grand Dragon Carr.[28]

As one of the very few left standing at the bitter end of the Newaygo County Klan's existence, Stone also provides a good example of the more dedicated and enduring breed of Klansman, who was perhaps much more devoted to the order's politics than had been the mass of uncommitted thrill-seekers who had found it so easy to cut their ties and leave. For sure, he had displayed a certain purity of political line through the years, and during World War I had made moves to set up a branch of the pro-American and anti-foreign "American Protective Society" in Fremont.[29] Interestingly, his two partners in this 1918 venture, Hermon Buck and J. Andrew Gerber, had also gone on to feature heavily in the Newaygo County Klan, with Gerber, just like Stone, among the few remaining "in good standing" after June 1926. Another Newaygo County Klansman still very much involved right into the 1930s was Noble D. Moon. Having been one of the forty-odd names on Newaygo's very first provisional Klan list back in 1923, Moon had been elected to a state-level office (Grand Kladd) in 1928, a position he would continue to hold until at least 1932. Again, it is possible that his enthusiasm and uncommon longevity can be explained at least in part by his politics: according to interviews in neighboring Mecosta, Moon was certainly well known in his hometown of Big Rapids, notorious especially for the fact that he "hated the Catholics."[30]

For a short-lived period, respectable, moralistic white Protestant culture at large chose to express its very mainstream self, for good or ill, through the outwardly bizarre medium of the Ku Klux Klan. Despite the striking effect of countless "bed sheets" cast here and there, the Klan's presence fundamentally altered very little else in this social world, at least while the organization retained a state of public favor. People still socialized at work, did business with their lodge brothers, attended movies, fairs, picnics, dances, parades, and church, much as they would have done had the Klan not been a factor. They voted, they vacationed, they mourned, they celebrated, with the Klan as without. In short, they went about their normal business, and the Klan's presence posed no barrier whatsoever. For a moment, it was utterly compatible with white Protestant culture. It *was* white Protestant culture. When the Klan bubble burst, however—its illusory veneer of respectability shattered suddenly by harsh and ugly reality—white Protestant culture simply discarded its sullied sheets and marched on as it always had, leaving the Klan to find itself a new form.

With the once popular KKK stripped down to its basics, and shorn of all of the assets that formerly rendered it so attractive to so many—its novelty, entertainment value, sociability, and perhaps most vitally, respectability and good name—there was little to see beyond a maligned, withered, and marginalized fringe group, populated by the undeterred and enduring few whose continued and unwavering dedication had begun increasingly to look like fanaticism. Having lost forever the ear of the masses, the Klan now veered more towards attracting, and holding, the attentions of the alienated white-supremacist minority, who would in time find ever more politicized and extreme directions in which to vent their disaffected rage. Only at this point, after the popular hooded organization had receded into nothing—to be replaced by a ragged and splintered succession of quite different and palpably extremist Klan descendants and imitators—did violence begin to enter the picture as a matter of course.

These were the primordial roots of a familiar modern hate movement, and as early as the mid-1930s, Michigan looked on as the wreckage of its once vast and mainstream Invisible Empire began the steep descent into the realms of racial terrorism. Emerging around this time was "a radical branch of the Michigan Ku Klux Klan" calling itself the Black Legion (which had also been known alternately as the United Brotherhood of America and the Wolverine

Republican League). Whether its small constituency of rabid followers was actually drawn from the residual dregs of the popular 1920s organization is unclear, though there is no doubt that this was "a secret, masked organization, operating in former Klan territory and with the Klan's heritage about them." Reportedly "more sinister and violent" than the 1920s Klan had ever been in its day, the Black Legion developed a spirit of vigilantism far in excess of that of its predecessor, and became notorious in and around Detroit, its membership having "tried their hand at flogging, bombing, and finally murder." Its ranks provided a haven for "the firebrands, the unstable [and] the neurotics who found violence and persecution a tonic," and, in its operations, organized brutality "replaced ordered activity as the main action pattern." The group comprised "pro-white, native-born Protestants," and its politics set it firmly "against Jews, Blacks, Communists, Anarchists, and Catholics."[31] Rather than vociferously celebrating white Protestant culture, as its popular Jazz Age forebear had done, the Black Legion—in its dedication, utterly, and forcibly if necessary, to the complete religious, racial, and political separation of white Protestants from all other elements of society—was entirely typical of the countless new incarnations of the Klan that would follow. Resembling already the monster that it would eventually become in the Civil Rights era and beyond,[32] it was this new and dangerous radical core, ultimately born of the remnants of a failed popular movement, that would usher in the modern, malignant age of the Ku Klux Klan.

Notes

INTRODUCTION

1. Stanley Frost, *The Challenge of the Klan* (Indianapolis: Bobbs-Merrill Company, 1924), 1.
2. John Moffat Mecklin, *The Ku Klux Klan: A Study of the American Mind* (New York: Harcourt, Brace and Co., 1924), 103. Other examples include Frank Bohn, "The Ku Klux Klan Interpreted," *American Journal of Sociology* 30 (January 1925): 385–407; and Guy B. Johnson, "A Sociological Interpretation of the New Ku Klux Movement," *Journal of Social Forces* 1, no. 4 (May 1923): 440–45.
3. Leonard J. Moore, "Historical Interpretations of the 1920s Klan: The Traditional View and the Populist Revision," *Journal of Social History* 24 (Winter 1990): 342.
4. Frost, *The Challenge of the Klan*. Robert L. Duffus wrote various influential articles on the Klan for *World's Work* magazine, including "How the Ku Klux Klan Sells Hate," *World's Work* 46 (1923): 174–83; and "The Ku Klux Klan in the Middle West," *World's Work* 46 (1923): 363–72.
5. Moore, "Historical Interpretations of the 1920s Klan," 343.
6. Richard Hofstadter, *The Age of Reform* (New York: Knopf, 1955); William Peirce Randel, *The Ku Klux Klan: A Century of Infamy* (London: Hamish Hamilton, 1965); Arnold S. Rice, *The Ku Klux Klan in American Politics* (Washington, DC: Public Affairs Press, 1962).
7. David M. Chalmers, *Hooded Americanism: The History of the Ku Klux Klan* (2nd ed., New York: Franklin Watts, 1976).
8. Charles C. Alexander, *The Ku Klux Klan in the Southwest* (Lexington: University of Kentucky Press, 1966); Kenneth T. Jackson, *The Ku Klux Klan in the City, 1915–1930* (2nd ed., Chicago: Ivan R. Dee, 1992).
9. Robert Moats Miller, "The Ku Klux Klan," in *Change and Continuity in Twentieth-Century America: The 1920s*, ed. John Braeman, Robert H. Bremner, and David Brody (Columbus: Ohio State University Press, 1968); Seymour Martin Lipset and Earl Raab, *The Politics of Unreason: Right Wing*

Extremism in America, 1790–1977 (2nd ed., Chicago: University of Chicago Press, 1978).

10. Glenn Feldman, *Politics, Society, and the Klan in Alabama, 1915–1949* (Tuscaloosa: University of Alabama Press, 1999), 5.

11. The best compilation of such case studies is Shawn Lay, ed., *The Invisible Empire in the West: Toward a New Historical Appraisal of the Ku Klux Klan of the 1920s* (Urbana: University of Illinois Press, 1992). Individual studies on particular regions include Christopher N. Cocoltchos, *The Invisible Government and the Viable Community: The Ku Klux Klan in Orange County, California during the 1920s* (Ph.D. dissertation, University of California, Los Angeles, 1979); Robert Alan Goldberg, *Hooded Empire: The Ku Klux Klan in Colorado* (Urbana: University of Illinois Press, 1981); Larry R. Gerlach, *Blazing Crosses in Zion: The Ku Klux Klan in Utah* (Logan: Utah State University Press, 1982); Shawn Lay, *War, Revolution, and the Ku Klux Klan: A Study of Intolerance in a Border City* (El Paso: Texas Western Press, University of Texas at El Paso, 1985); William D. Jenkins, *Steel Valley Klan: The Ku Klux Klan in Ohio's Mahoning Valley* (Kent, OH: Kent State University, 1990); Leonard J. Moore, *Citizen Klansmen: The Ku Klux Klan in Indiana, 1921–28* (Chapel Hill: University of North Carolina Press, 1991); Shawn Lay, *Hooded Knights on the Niagara: The Ku Klux Klan in Buffalo, New York* (New York: New York University Press, 1995).

12. Moore, "Historical Interpretations of the 1920s Klan," 353.

13. Nancy MacLean, *Behind the Mask of Chivalry: The Making of the Second Ku Klux Klan* (New York: Oxford University Press, 1994).

14. Kathleen M. Blee, *Women of the Klan: Racism and Gender in the 1920s* (Berkeley: University of California Press, 1991).

15. Lay, *The Invisible Empire in the West*, 219; Norman Frederic Weaver, *The Knights of the Ku Klux Klan in Wisconsin, Indiana, Ohio and Michigan* (Ph.D. dissertation, University of Wisconsin, 1954), 299–306.

16. Allen Safianow, "'You Can't Burn History': Getting Right with the Klan in Noblesville, Indiana," *Indiana Magazine of History* 100 (June 2004): 109–54.

17. See *Muskegon Chronicle*, 25 October 1992, 3A; and 1 November 1992, 2A; *Detroit Free Press*, 29 October 1992, 1A.

18. *Ku Klux Klan (Newaygo County, Mich.) Membership Cards, 1923–1926*, Clarke Historical Library, Central Michigan University, Mount Pleasant.

19. Weaver, *Knights of the Ku Klux Klan*, 267–92; Jackson, *Klan in the City*, ch. 9. Also see Chalmers, *Hooded Americanism*, 194–97. Seemingly, there is only one scholar who has published an analysis of a Michigan Klan unit outside of Detroit, by way of two short articles. See Calvin W. Enders, "White Sheets in Mecosta: The Anatomy of a Michigan Klan," *Michigan Historical Review* 14,

no. 2 (Fall 1988): 59–84; and "Under Grand Haven's White Sheets," *Michigan Historical Review* 19, no. 1 (Spring 1993): 47–61.

20. Weaver, *Knights of the Ku Klux Klan*, 275.
21. Jackson, *Klan in the City*, 129.
22. Scattered Realm office bulletins can be found in folders marked "Organizational Correspondence," boxes 1 and 2, *Ku Klux Klan (Mecosta County, Michigan) Collection, 1916–1974*, Clarke Historical Library, Central Michigan University. Also see *Owosso Argus Press*, 1 October 1926, 1; and 2 October 1926, 1.
23. Weaver, *Knights of the Ku Klux Klan*, 276–77; Jackson, *Klan in the City*, 127–43; Chalmers, *Hooded Americanism*, 194–97.
24. *Niles Daily Star-Sun*, 16 July 1923, 1; *Hartford Day Spring*, 25 July 1923, 1.
25. Weaver, *Knights of the Ku Klux Klan*, 276.
26. *Washington Post*, 2 November 1930, 1; Jackson, *Klan in the City*, 273.
27. Earl Michener to Harry V. Michener, 23 February 1924, box 9, Earl C. Michener Papers, 1898–1954, Bentley Historical Library, University of Michigan, Ann Arbor.
28. Weaver, *Knights of the Ku Klux Klan*, 277–78; Enders, "Under Grand Haven's White Sheets."

CHAPTER 1. MARKETING, MEMBERSHIP, AND MERCHANDISE

1. *Newaygo Republican*, 6 September 1923, 5.
2. *Fiery Cross (Michigan State Edition)*, 21 September 1923, 8. Also see the Indiana State edition, 28 September 1923, 10.
3. *Newaygo Republican*, 13 September 1923, 5.
4. *Newaygo Republican*, 27 September 1923, 1.
5. *Newaygo Republican*, 27 September 1923, 1; *White Cloud Eagle*, 4 October 1923, 7.
6. *White Cloud Eagle*, 18 October 1923, 1.
7. *White Cloud Eagle*, 6 December 1923, 2; *Newaygo Republican*, 12 June 1924, 5; and 19 June 1924, 1.
8. *Fremont Times-Indicator*, 24 January 1924, 6; 31 January 1924, 1, 8.
9. *Fremont Times-Indicator*, 8 May 1924, 1.
10. Rev. Ross was a well-known and active advocate for the Klan cause during this period, and traveled widely in the state of Michigan to this end. His presence has been particularly heavily noted in the towns of Battle Creek, Midland, Adrian, and Sault Ste. Marie, and by 1926 he held the position of "Grand

Klexter," a high officer of the state Klan administration. See, for example, *Fellowship Forum*, 31 May 1924, 2; 7 February 1925, 3; 15 January 1927, 5; and *Adrian Daily Telegram*, 26 January 1924, 3; 19 January 1925, 5; 20 January, 1925, 2. Rev. Ross apparently also championed the organization in the extreme north of the state's Upper Peninsula, traveling at least as far as Iron County. See Ramon E. Bisque, *Iron: A River, a Town, a County, a Mine, a Family* (Golden, CO: West by Southwest, 2000), 236.

11. *Fremont Times-Indicator*, 31 July 1924, 6.

12. *Fiery Cross (Indiana State Edition)*, 17 August 1923, 1.

13. "Michigan KKK 1923, 1924," in box 2, *Calvin W. Enders Collection, 1917–1997*, Clarke Historical Library, Central Michigan University. This collection contains a large clippings file, gathered from more than forty regional Michigan publications and documenting the arrival of the KKK in various localities from the summer of 1923. Though some way from providing comprehensive coverage, these reports do span a wide geographical range and reveal uniform patterns of operation wherever the organization appeared.

14. Scattered bulletins can be found in folders marked "Organizational Correspondence," boxes 1 and 2, *Ku Klux Klan (Mecosta County, Mich.) Collection, 1916–1974*, Clarke Historical Library, Central Michigan University.

15. *Owosso Argus Press*, 1 October 1926, 1; and 2 October 1926, 1.

16. While there is a dearth of organizational information on junior units, their existence was often explicitly noted in the Klan press. See, for example, *Wolverine Women*, April 1928, 2, which talks specifically about a drive to charter existing "Tri-K club" units (the girls' organization) in Michigan.

17. Examples of this are myriad. See, for instance, *Detroit Free Press*, 14 June 1923, 1; *Kalamazoo Gazette*, 16 July 1923, 3, and 18 July 1923, 1; *Mancelona Herald*, 19 July 1923, 1; *Adrian Daily Telegram*, 21 July 1923, 1; *St. Joseph Herald Press*, 26 July 1923, 1; *Dowagiac Daily News*, 3 August 1923, 1; *Hartford Day Spring*, 8 August 1923, 1, and 3 October 1923, 1; *Cheboygan Daily Tribune*, 24 August 1923, 1; *Owosso Argus Press*, 28 August 1923, 1; *Fiery Cross (Indiana State Edition)*, 14 September 1923, 1; *Berrien County Journal*, 27 September 1923, 4; *Jackson Citizen Patriot*, 30 September 1923, 1; *Isabella County Enterprise*, 5 October 1923, 1; *Fiery Cross (Michigan State Edition)*, 30 November 1923, 1, 10.

18. *Grand Haven Daily Tribune*, 25 August 1923, 1; and 18 September 1923, 1; *Lansing Capital News*, 22 September 1923, 1; *Flint Journal*, 28 August 1923, 8. Also see the clippings file marked "Michigan KKK 1923, 1924," in box 2, *Calvin Enders Collection*, for countless similar reports.

19. *Clare Sentinel*, 26 October 1923, 1; *Midland Republican*, 30 August 1923, 1. Again, the clippings file marked "Michigan KKK 1923, 1924" in Central

Michigan's *Calvin Enders Collection* documents many other instances of Klan organizers and organizational growth in various Michigan towns during this period.

20. *Clinton County Republican*, 23 August 1923, 1, 3.

21. *Isabella County Enterprise*, 21 September 1923, 1; *Saginaw Star*, 18 September 1923, 2.

22. See, among many other examples, *Clinton County Republican*, 23 August 1923, 1; *Manistee News-Advocate*, 19 September 1923, 1; *Saugatuck Commercial Record*, 28 September 1923, 1; *Holland News*, 4 October 1923, 3; *Niles Daily Star Sun*, 6 October 1923, 1; *Muskegon Chronicle*, 26 October 1923, 17.

23. *Isabella County Enterprise*, 21 and 28 September 1923, 1; *Mount Pleasant Times*, 27 September 1923, 1.

24. *Saugatuck Commercial Record*, 28 September 1923, 1.

25. *Royal Oak Tribune*, 3 August 1923, 1.

26. *Hartford Day Spring*, 25 July 1923, 1; 1 August 1923, 1; *Fiery Cross (Michigan State Edition)*, 19 October 1923, 1.

27. *Dawn*, 22 September 1923, and 22 December 1923; *Fiery Cross (Michigan State Edition)*, 19 October 1923, 1; *Imperial Night-Hawk*, 2 July 1924, 5.

28. *Adrian Daily Telegram*, 14 July 1923, 1; *Dowagiac Daily News*, 8 August 1923, 1; *Barryton Press*, 3 July 1924, 1.

29. *Dawn*, 20 January 1923, 11; 21 July 1923, 16; 27 October 1923; Jackson, *Klan in the City*, 170. The Klan made its presence felt on many a university campus during the 1920s. Official Klan chapters at Illinois Wesleyan University, Bloomington and the University of Wisconsin, as well as a "Fiery Cross Club" at Kansas University are just a few examples. See *Dawn*, 15 December 1923, 19; Timothy Messer-Kruse, "Memories of the Ku Klux Klan Honorary Society at the University of Wisconsin," *The Journal of Blacks in Higher Education*, no. 23 (Spring 1999): 83–93; *Imperial Night-Hawk*, 1 October 1924, 8. Serious attempts, both ultimately unsuccessful, were also made by national Klan leaders to purchase Valparaiso and Lanier universities, with the intention of operating them as training grounds in complete accordance with Klan principles. See *Dawn*, 2 June 1923, 4; 29 September 1923, 9; 11 November 1923, 3; Jackson, *Klan in the City*, 36; Henry Peck Fry, *The Modern Ku Klux Klan* (Boston: Small, Maynard, 1922), 21, 31.

30. Mary Ann Clawson, *Constructing Brotherhood: Class, Gender, and Fraternalism* (Princeton, NJ: Princeton University Press, 1989), 4, 17, 216–17.

31. See, for example, Chalmers, *Hooded Americanism*, 31; Emerson H. Loucks, *The Ku Klux Klan in Pennsylvania: A Study in Nativism* (Harrisburg, PA: Telegraph Press, 1936), 17; Charles O. Jackson, "William J. Simmons: A Career in Ku Kluxism," *Georgia Historical Quarterly* 50 (December 1966): 351–65.

32. Mark C. Carnes, *Secret Ritual and Manhood in Victorian America* (New Haven, CT: Yale University Press, 1989), 145–46.

33. William G. Shepard, "How I Put Over the Klan," *Collier's National Weekly*, 14 July 1928.

34. William G. Shepard, "Ku Klux Koin," *Collier's National Weekly*, 21 July 1928, 39.

35. Estimates of membership vary widely, though few would place the Klan's strength during its brief peak in the mid-1920s at below three million members. Commenting on the Klan's utter decline by 1930, the *Washington Post* (2 November 1930, 1) produced possibly the largest estimate by a non-Klan source, quoting a figure for peak membership in 1925 of 8,904,871.

36. Rice, *The Ku Klux Klan in American Politics*, 14; Jackson, *Klan in the City*, 10; Chalmers, *Hooded Americanism*, 34.

37. United States Congress, House of Representatives, Committee on Rules, *Hearings on the Ku Klux Klan* (67th Congress, 1st session, Washington, DC, 1921), 17; Fry, *The Modern Ku Klux Klan*, 47.

38. Rice, *The Ku Klux Klan in American Politics*, 15. Also see Fry, *The Modern Ku Klux Klan*; and William M. Likins, *Patriotism Capitalized or Religion Turned into Gold* (Uniontown, PA: The Watchman, 1925). Both Fry and Likins served in the Klan, but had become hugely disillusioned by the conduct of crooked Kleagles, and dropped out in favor of writing exposés on the excesses of the order.

39. William G. Shepard, "The Fiery Double-Cross," *Collier's National Weekly*, 28 July 1928, 8; Charles C. Alexander, "Kleagles and Cash: The Ku Klux Klan as a Business Organization, 1919–1930," *Business History Review* 39 (Autumn 1965): 358.

40. Duffus, "How the Ku Klux Klan Sells Hate," 174–83.

41. The commercialization of fraternal membership for financial gain, particularly for individuals in leadership roles, and often in direct opposition to noncommercial ideals espoused by such organizations, had become commonplace by the late nineteenth Century. See Clawson, *Constructing Brotherhood*, 212–14.

42. Alexander, "Kleagles and Cash," 355; Fry, *The Modern Ku Klux Klan*, 31; Shepard, "Ku Klux Koin."

43. Alexander, "Kleagles and Cash," 359–60.

44. Alexander, "Kleagles and Cash," 350, 361; Loucks, *The Ku Klux Klan in Pennsylvania*, 95.

45. Alexander, "Kleagles and Cash," 355; Fry, *The Modern Ku Klux Klan*, 8; *Dawn*, 31 March 1923, 11.

46. *Imperial Night-Hawk*, 28 March 1923, 4.

47. The progress and growth of the Klan in various Michigan locations received ample mention in the pages of national KKK organs. Examples are numerous, but a selection includes: *Imperial Night-Hawk*, 25 April 1923, 4; 17 October 1923, 8; 13 February 1924, 5; 2 July 1924, 5; 17 September 1924, 7–8; *Kourier* magazine, October 1925, 14–15; *Dawn*, 17 March 1923, 7; 2 June 1923, 19; 22 September 1923, 18; 22 December 1923, 9; *Fellowship Forum*, 23 June 1923, 9; 19 January 1924, 8; 17 May 1924, 5; 13 September 1924, 6.

48. Shepard, "Ku Klux Koin," 38; Fry, *The Modern Ku Klux Klan*, 7; Alexander, "Kleagles and Cash," 354–5.

49. *Imperial Night-Hawk*, 12 September 1923, 8; 2 April 1924, 8; 9 April 1924, 7; 28 May 1924, 8.

50. *Imperial Night-Hawk*, 15 August 1923, 5; 2 April 1924, 8; *Dawn*, 28 July 1923, 9.

51. *Kourier* magazine, September 1925, 4; Knights of the Ku Klux Klan, *Catalogue of Official Robes and Banners* (Atlanta: Knights of the Ku Klux Klan, 1925).

52. Weaver, *Knights of the Ku Klux Klan*, 272–75.

53. *Fiery Cross (Michigan State Edition)*, 28 September 1923, 1, 8, 13; 21 December 1923, 1; 21 March 1924, 7.

54. "Supply Catalogues, 1920s," in box 2, *Ku Klux Klan (Mecosta County, Mich.) Collection*.

55. *Dawn*, 9 December 1922; 6 January 1923, 4.

56. *Fiery Cross (Michigan State Edition)*, 14 December 1923, 1; 21 March 1924, 3; *Fremont Times-Indicator*, 31 January 1924, 1; 16 October 1924, 1; *Newaygo Republican*, 19 June; and 2 October 1924, 1.

57. Lutz Music Printing Company (York, Pennsylvania), *Catalogue of Sheet Music, Records, Player Rolls and Buddy*, in "KKK Merchandise," vertical file, Michigan State University Special Collections. Also see *Campaign Songs, Ku Klux Klan*, Performing Arts Reading Room, Library of Congress, Washington, DC.

58. Klan Manufacturing Company (Dayton, Ohio), *The Latest Additions to Our Exclusive Line of KKK Jewellery*, in "KKK Merchandise," vertical file, Michigan State University Special Collections.

59. National Emblem Company (Omaha, Nebraska), *Wholesale Price List*, in "KKK Merchandise," vertical file, Michigan State University Special Collections. Also see "Supply Catalogs, 1920s," in box 2, *Ku Klux Klan (Mecosta County, Mich.) Collection*.

60. *Michigan Kourier*, 1 August 1924; 5 September 1924; 24 October 1924.

61. The "Klean Kut Kid" was frequently advertised in Klan organs. See, for example, *Dawn*, 15 December 1923; also "Supply Catalogs, 1920s," in box 2, *Ku Klux Klan (Mecosta County, Mich.) Collection*.

62. *Fiery Cross (Michigan State Edition)*, 19 October 1923; *Dawn*, 19 May 1923; 8 December 1923; 2 February 1924.

63. William E. Leuchtenburg, *The Perils of Prosperity, 1914–32* (Chicago: University of Chicago Press, 1958), 200; Michael E. Parrish, *Anxious Decades: America in Prosperity and Depression, 1920–1941* (New York: W. W. Norton, 1992), 76.

64. Quoted in Leuchtenburg, *The Perils of Prosperity*, 242. Also see Robert S. and Helen Merrell Lynd, *Middletown: A Study in Contemporary American Culture* (London: Constable, 1929), 81–82, 158, 161; Donald R. McCoy, *Coming of Age: The United States during the 1920s and 1930s* (Baltimore, MD: Penguin, 1973), 117–18.

65. McCoy, *Coming of Age*, 117.

66. Clarence Darrow, "Salesmanship," in *The American Mercury*, August 1925; Frederick Lewis Allen, *Only Yesterday: An Informal History of the 1920s* (New York: Harper and Brothers, 1931), 140; Sinclair Lewis, *Babbitt* (New York: Harcourt, Brace & Co., 1922), 183.

67. *Fiery Cross (Michigan State Edition)*, 9 November 1923; and 21 March 1924, 7; *Dawn*, 22 December 1923, 21; *Klan Kourier*, 27 June 1924, 6; *Michigan Kourier*, 8 August 1924, 3.

68. *Fiery Cross (Michigan State Edition)*, 7 September 1923, 9; *Michigan Kourier*, 8 August 1924, 3.

69. Philip Dray, *At the Hands of Persons Unknown: The Lynching of Black America* (New York: Random House, 2002), 44.

70. Aldrich Blake, *The Ku Klux Kraze* (Oklahoma City: Aldrich Blake, 1924), 17.

CHAPTER 2. THE KNIGHTS IN IMAGE AND IDEA

1. Michael Rogin, *Ronald Reagan, the Movie, and Other Episodes in Political Demonology* (Berkeley: University of California Press, 1987), 236.

2. *Fremont Times-Indicator*, 31 January 1924, 1, 8.

3. *Fremont Times-Indicator*, 16 October 1924, 1, 6.

4. *Newaygo Republican*, 19 June 1924.

5. *Newaygo Republican*, 27 September 1923, 1; 24 July 1924; 18 June 1925, 5.

6. Thomas Dixon, *The Clansman: An Historical Romance of the Ku Klux Klan* (New York: A. Wessels Co., 1907). On Dixon's credentials as a "mob novelist," white supremacist, and glorifier of the Reconstruction-era Klan, see F. Garvin Davenport, "Thomas Dixon's Mythology of Southern History," *Journal of Southern History* 36, no. 3 (August 1970): 350–67; Maxwell Bloomfield, "Dixon's 'The Leopard's Spots': A Study in Popular Racism," *American Quarterly* 16, no. 3 (Autumn 1964): 387–401.

7. Dray, *At the Hands of Persons Unknown*, 200–201.
8. Quoted in MacLean, *Behind the Mask of Chivalry*, 13.
9. Rogin, *Ronald Reagan, the Movie*, 192.
10. "Remarkable Scenes from a Remarkable Film," *Vanity Fair*, May 1915, 48; Rogin, *Ronald Reagan, the Movie*, 217.
11. Dray, *At the Hands of Persons Unknown*, 196–98, 205; William Loren Katz, *The Invisible Empire: The Ku Klux Klan Impact on History* (Seattle: Open Hand, 1987), 74; Rogin, *Ronald Reagan, the Movie*, 190.
12. Dray, *At the Hands of Persons Unknown*, 196–97.
13. *White Cloud Eagle*, 13 December 1923, 1.
14. *New York Evening Post*, 13 March 1915.
15. Dray, *At the Hands of Persons Unknown*, 204–5.
16. Chalmers, *Hooded Americanism*, 430.
17. Randel, *The Ku Klux Klan*, 164.
18. Bishop Alma White, *Klansmen: Guardians of Liberty* (Zarephath, NJ: The Good Citizen, 1926); *Heroes of the Fiery Cross* (Zarephath, NJ: The Good Citizen, 1928).
19. Bishop Alma White, *The Ku Klux Klan in Prophecy* (Zarephath, NJ: The Good Citizen, 1925).
20. Hiram Wesley Evans, *The Attitude of the Knights of the Ku Klux Klan toward the Jew* (Atlanta: Knights of the Ku Klux Klan, 1923), 7–8.
21. E. F. Stanton, *Christ and Other Klansmen, or Lives of Love: The Cream of the Bible Spread upon Klanism* (Kansas City, MO: Stanton & Harper, 1924).
22. Evans quoted in MacLean, *Behind the Mask of Chivalry*, 161.
23. Knights of the Ku Klux Klan, *Papers Read at the Meeting of Grand Dragons, Knights of the Ku Klux Klan at Their First Annual Meeting Held at Asheville, North Carolina, July 1923; Together with Other Articles of Interest to Klansmen* (Atlanta: Knights of the Ku Klux Klan, 1923), 5–6.
24. Hiram Wesley Evans, "The Klan: Defender of Americanism," *Forum* 74 (December 1925): 6–7; and "The Spirit of the Fathers," *Kourier* magazine, February 1927, 12–13; Knights of the Ku Klux Klan, *America for Americans* (Atlanta: Knights of the Ku Klux Klan, 1922).
25. A. Saxon, *Knight Vale of the KKK: A Fiction Story of Love, Patriotism, Intrigue and Adventure* (Columbus, OH: Patriot, 1924).
26. Egbert Brown, *The Final Awakening: A Story of The Ku Klux Klan* (Brunswick, GA: Overstreet & Co, 1923); "A Klansman's Loyalty," serialized in *Kourier* magazine, June 1929, 6–11; September 1929, 39–43; December 1929, 26–29; June 1930, 30–33; George Alfred Brown, *Harold the Klansman* (Kansas City, MO: Western Baptist, 1923).
27. See ad and review comments in *Dawn*, 19 January 1924, 20.
28. *Dawn*, 9 December 1922; 6 January 1923; 20 January 1923, 5.

29. *Imperial Night-Hawk*, 22 August 1923, 6.

30. *Newaygo Republican*, 2 October 1924, 1.

31. *Fremont Times-Indicator*, 2 October 1924, 1, 8.

32. Sean McCann, *Gumshoe America: Hard-Boiled Crime Fiction and the Rise and Fall of New Deal Liberalism* (Durham, NC: Duke University Press, 2000), 39–86.

33. United States Congress, *Hearings on the Ku Klux Klan*, 67th Cong., 1st session, 1921.

34. The term "melting pot" was popularized by Zangwill's 1908 stage play of the same name, a paean to the virtues of ethnic assimilation.

35. Hiram Wesley Evans, "The Catholic Question As Viewed by the Ku Klux Klan," *Current History*, July 1927, 563–68; "For and Against the Ku Klux Klan," *Literary Digest*, 24 September 1921, 34–40; William R. Pattangall, "Is the Ku Klux Klan Un-American?" *Forum*, September 1925, 321–32; George S. Clason, ed., *Catholic, Jew, Ku Klux Klan: What They Believe, Where They Conflict* (Chicago: Nutshell, 1924); Fred Bair, *Does the U.S.A. Need the K.K.K.?* (Girard, KS: Haldeman-Julius, 1928); Edward P. Bell, *Is the Ku Klux Klan Constructive or Destructive? A Debate between Imperial Wizard Evans, Israel Zangwill and Others* (Girard, KS: Haldeman-Julius, 1924). These few titles represent a mere sample of a much larger body of debate in the local and national press during the 1920s.

36. For an account of the mystery, curiosity, and excitement generated by the first signs of KKK arrival in a typical Michigan setting, see Enders, "Under Grand Haven's White Sheets," 49–52.

37. *Lake County Star*, 4 January 1918, 1; and 20 April 1934. The full correspondence covering the courtship of Kenneth Blass and Marie Kleiner over several years can be found in its entirety as an archival collection entitled *Blass Family Papers, 1922–2002*, held at the Clarke Historical Library, Central Michigan University. All citations of correspondence between the two from this point onward refer to letters found within this single collection.

38. Letters from Blass to Kleiner dated 5 September 1924; 29 September 1924; and 24 October 1924, *Blass Family Papers*.

39. Blass to Kleiner, 16 January 1925, *Blass Family Papers*. The street vending of another Klan publication, the *Fiery Cross (Michigan State Edition)*, apparently encountered early opposition in Detroit, with police confiscating the newspaper and arresting and detaining newsboys. In 1923, however, the local Klan attained an injunction from the circuit court preventing any further interference with sales. Jackson, *Klan in the City*, 132–33.

40. Blass to Kleiner, 14 and 15 September 1924, *Blass Family Papers*. Dr. William L. Stidger, according to the title of a biography by his grandson, was "evangelism's

first modern media star" as well as an official spokesman for Detroit industrialist Henry Ford. At this time, he was pastor of St. Mark's Methodist Church on Jefferson Avenue. Discussing his address on the KKK, the *Detroit Free Press*, 15 September 1924, claimed that Stidger had referred to the organization as "one of the great moral movements of the world," as well as insinuating that the Catholic Church in Rome practices "cruelty, intimidation or murder." In the *Detroit Evening Times* of the same day, Stidger denounced this claim as "a lie from beginning to end," insisting that his sermon was intended to tell "the truth about the Klan . . . good, bad, or indifferent."

41. To the dismay of Blass, O'Brien's speech was canceled at short notice, leaving an expectant crowd waiting out in the cold. Blass to Kleiner, 21 October 1924, *Blass Family Papers*; Blake, *The Ku Klux Kraze*. Also see clippings file on Blake's lectures in *Evangelical Lutheran Synod of Missouri, Ohio, and Other States, Michigan District, Lutheran Schools Committee Papers, 1921–1926*, Bentley Historical Library, University of Michigan.

42. "Anti-Klan Rally Mobbed; Police Clash with 6,000," *Detroit Free Press*, 22 October 1924.

43. Blass to Kleiner, 19 September 1924; and 22 October 1924, *Blass Family Papers*. There is nothing to suggest that the owners of either the *Free Press* (theater mogul Edward D. Stair) or the *Times* (media magnate William Randolph Hearst) were involved in any sort of religious conspiracy against the Klan. Hearst, however, was especially noted for his tendency toward scandal-mongering, sensationalist "yellow journalism."

44. Jackson, *Klan in the City*, 128, details Michigan's past struggles with "Romanism." Also Weaver, *Knights of the Ku Klux Klan*, 280.

45. Knights of the Ku Klux Klan, *Thirty-Three Questions Answered* (Atlanta: Knights of the Ku Klux Klan, n.d.), 9; Weaver, *Knights of the Ku Klux Klan*, 23–24.

46. Hiram Wesley Evans, "The Klan's Fight for Americanism," in *The North American Review* 223 (Spring 1926): 33–63; "The Klan: Defender of Americanism," 3–16. Also see MacLean, *Behind the Mask of Chivalry*, 133–34. MacLean's book offers the most thorough and insightful analysis to date of the modern Klan's full range of adversarial literature and varied list of enemies.

47. Perhaps the most prominent example of Klan thinking on immigration restriction was penned by the order's Imperial Wizard Hiram Wesley Evans. Originally an address delivered on "Klan Day" at the state fair of Texas at Dallas in October 1923, it was later published in full and copyrighted by the official Klan press as *The Menace of Modern Immigration* (Atlanta: Knights of the Ku Klux Klan, 1924).

48. Jackson, *Klan in the City*, 127–29.

49. Blass to Kleiner, 10 November 1925, *Blass Family Papers*. Blass was probably referring here to Henry Ford's *Dearborn Independent*, a magazine that he published and distributed through his thousands of car dealerships. During the early 1920s, the magazine notoriously featured many anti-Semitic articles, later compiled and published in their own right, warning against the dangers of the profit-hungry "international Jew." Though in Michigan the Jew was very much a secondary Klan target behind the Roman Catholic, numerous KKK pamphlets circulated nationally warning of the "libertine Jew," an immoral and predatory "moral leper" who was implicated in all manner of organized crime, sexual degeneracy, and corruption of wholesome American youth. See Evans, *The Attitude of the Knights of the Ku Klux Klan toward the Jew*; Sam H. Campbell, *The Jewish Problem in the United States* (Atlanta: Knights of the Ku Klux Klan, 1923); Leroy Amos Curry, *The Ku Klux Klan under the Searchlight* (Kansas City, MO: Western Baptist, 1924); Blaine Mast, *KKK Friend or Foe: Which?* (Kittanning, PA: Herbrick & Held, 1924), 18–20.

50. Blass to Kleiner, 10 November 1925, *Blass Family Papers*; Knights of the Ku Klux Klan, *America for Americans*, 5–6; Herbert Kaufman, *Scum O' The Melting Pot* (Atlanta: Knights of the Ku Klux Klan, 1920); Hiram Wesley Evans, *Attitude of the Knights of the Ku Klux Klan toward Immigration* (Atlanta: Knights of the Ku Klux Klan, 1923).

51. *Fremont Times-Indicator*, 4 November 1920, 4; 16 December 1920, 4; 26 July 1923, 3; 15 November 1923, 1; 17 April 1924, 8. *Newaygo Republican*, 16 August 1923, 4; 1 November 1923, 4.

52. Woodrow Wilson quoted in Rogin, *Ronald Reagan, the Movie*, 238, 97.

53. Madison Grant, *The Passing of the Great Race; or the Racial Basis of European History* (New York: C. Scribner's Sons, 1921).

54. Blass to Kleiner, 27 October 1924; 5 November 1924; 16 October 1925, *Blass Family Papers*.

55. *Fremont Times-Indicator*, 8 May 1924, 1; 31 July 1924, 6.

56. *White Cloud Eagle*, 13 July 1922, 8; 27 July 1922, 1; 13 September 1923, 1; 23 July 1925, 1; *Fremont Times-Indicator*, 10 January 1924, 1; 11 December 1924, 4; *Newaygo Republican*, 17 April 1924, 1.

57. *Fremont Times-Indicator*, 8 June 1922, 4; 22 June 1922, 4; 3 January 1924, 4; *Newaygo Republican*, 9 August 1923, 4.

58. *Fremont Times-Indicator*, 29 June 1922, 4; 7 February 1924, 8; 21 February 1924, 3; *Newaygo Republican*, 26 July 1923, 4; *White Cloud Eagle*, 5 January 1922, 5.

59. For a wide-ranging history and analysis of anti-Catholic propaganda into the early twentieth century, see Michael Williams, *The Shadow of the Pope: The Story of the Anti-Catholic Movement in America* (New York: Whittlesey House, McGraw-Hill, 1932). Also MacLean, *Behind the Mask of Chivalry*, 119–20.

60. J. F. Mathews, *The Red Plague* (Portland, OR: J. F. Mathews, 1925), 18.

61. John S. Fleming, *What Is Ku Kluxism? Let Americans Answer—Aliens Only Muddy the Waters* (Birmingham, AL: Masonic Weekly Recorder, 1923), 39, 49.

62. Tom Watson, quoted in MacLean, *Behind the Mask of Chivalry*, 120; William Lloyd Clark, *The Devil's Prayer Book, or an Exposure of Auricular Confession as Practiced by the Roman Catholic Church: An Eye-Opener for Husbands, Fathers and Brothers* (Milan, IL: Rail Splitter Press, 1922).

63. *Dawn*, 13 January 1923, 16; and 2 February 1924, 19.

64. L. J. King, ed., *The Converted Catholic and Protestant Missionary Annual* (Toledo, OH: L. J. King, 1924); Helen Jackson, *Convent Cruelties: or My Life in the Convent: Awful Revelations* (Toledo, OH: Helen Jackson, 1919).

65. Blee, *Women of the Klan*, 86–91.

66. Blass to Kleiner, 19 November 1926, *Blass Family Papers*.

67. See *Lutheran Schools Committee Papers, 1921–1926*.

68. Blee, *Women of the Klan*, 88.

69. "The Public Schools Worry Dr. Forsyth," *Michigan Catholic*, 19 June 1924.

70. Blass to Kleiner, labeled "April sequence . . . 1927," *Blass Family Papers*. There are other instances, too, where Blass becomes infuriated at what he sees as anti-Klan bias in the workplace, including a case in March 1927 when the 75-year old "Mr. Sipes" is denied a job he had previously been promised by the Department of Public Works. "We don't want fellows like you anyway," he is apparently told; ". . . the people you are affiliated with will take care of you."

71. Blass to Kleiner, 25 and 27 October 1924; 17 October 1925; 5 and 16 April 1927, *Blass Family Papers*.

72. "Vote for Mayor," *Detroit Times*, 11 September 1924, 1; Blass to Kleiner, 11, 24, and 25 September 1924; 5 November 1924, *Blass Family Papers*. For full details of Bowles's 1924 campaign, see Jackson, *Klan in the City*, 133–39.

73. Quoted in the *Fremont Times-Indicator*, 2 October 1924, 1.

74. *Lutheran Schools Committee Papers, 1921–1926*; Weaver, *Knights of the Ku Klux Klan*, 280–82; Jackson, *Klan in the City*, 133.

75. Oregon's 1922 Compulsory Education Act, though passed in the state, proved short-lived, and was struck down as unconstitutional in 1925 by the U.S. Supreme Court.

76. Various sources specifically cite the public schools issue as the major source of conflict, or perceived conflict, between members of the Klan and local Catholics. See, for example, Enders, "White Sheets in Mecosta," 67–68; Letter marked "to friends, 18 May 1924," in *Fenno E. Densmore Papers, 1917–1957*, Bentley Historical Library, University of Michigan.

77. *Fremont Times-Indicator*, 8 May 1924, 1.

78. *Fremont Times-Indicator*, 11 September 1924, 5; 2 October 1924, 2.

79. *Fremont Times-Indicator*, 21 August 1924, 7; 18 September 1924, 2; 23 October 1924, 5.

80. *Fremont Times-Indicator*, 28 August 1924, 5; 30 October 1924, 4.

81. Having failed to eliminate the teaching of Catholic doctrines to youngsters with the defeat of the parochial schools amendment, the Michigan KKK would later attempt to ensure that the public schools, at least, would remain as Protestant as possible. One Klan-backed campaign, "The Flag I Love," intended to "Keep Old Glory over every public school" in the state, while by 1928 the "Michigan Bible Study League," which promoted the compulsory reading of the Bible in public schools, had become a front organization for the Michigan Klan.

82. *Fremont Times-Indicator*, 13 November 1924, 1, 3; *Lutheran Schools Committee Papers, 1921–1926*.

83. Humphrey J. Desmond, *The Know-Nothing Party* (reprint; New York: Arno Press, 1969); Williams, *The Shadow of the Pope*.

84. *Dawn*, 21 October 1922, 3; *Kourier* magazine, August 1926, 13–20; April 1927, 20; March 1925, 14–17; Hiram Wesley Evans, *The Attitude of the Ku Klux Klan toward the Roman Catholic Hierarchy* (Atlanta: Knights of the Ku Klux Klan, 1927), 5.

85. See, for example, Robert Coughlan, "Konklave in Kokomo," in *The Aspirin Age: 1919–1941*, ed. Isabel Leighton (New York: Simon and Schuster, 1949); Lynd, *Middletown*, 482; Blee, *Women of the Klan*, 92–93.

86. Don Bollman, *Run for the Roses: A 50 Year Memoir* (Mecosta, MI: Canadian Lakes, 1975), 18.

87. George Estes, *The Roman Katholic Kingdom and the Ku Klux Klan* (Portland, OR: Empire, 1923), 7–12. Also see Fleming, *What Is Ku Kluxism?*

88. "Newaygo KKK Correspondence, 1923," in box 1, *Calvin Enders Collection*.

89. This passage is taken from a version of the "Alleged Bloody Oath of the Knights of Columbus" as printed in *Congressional Record*, 15 February 1913 (3rd session), vol. 49, part 4, pp. 3216–17.

90. Fry, *The Modern Ku Klux Klan*, 113–14.

91. The Bath School Disaster, in which 45 people—mostly children—were killed and another 58 injured, received extensive press coverage locally and nationally, and to this day still constitutes the deadliest act of mass murder in a school in U.S. history. The perpetrator was roundly attacked as "a madman," who, having first slaughtered his wife and destroyed his own farm and home, then went on to attack the school, having been driven to rage over his financial hardship, for which he blamed a property tax that had been levied to fund the construction of the school building. See Monty J. Ellsworth, *The Bath School Disaster* (N.p., 1927).

92. May 1927 flyer entitled *Roman Catholic Dynamites Bath Public Schools*, American Radicalism Collection, Michigan State University Special Collections.

93. Blass to Kleiner, 31 May 1927, *Blass Family Papers*.

94. See David Brion Davis, "Some Themes of Counter-Subversion: An Analysis of Anti-Masonic, Anti-Catholic, and Anti-Mormon Literature," *Mississippi Valley Historical Review* 47 (1960): 205–24.

95. Rogin, *Ronald Reagan, the Movie*, 50, 284.

96. Weaver, *Knights of the Ku Klux Klan*, 280.

97. Coughlan, "Konklave in Kokomo," 111, 114.

98. Rogin, *Ronald Reagan, the Movie*, xiii, 237; Davis, "Some Themes of Counter-Subversion." See also David Brion Davis, "Some Ideological Functions of Prejudice in Ante-Bellum America," *American Quarterly* 15 (Summer 1963): 115–25, and *The Fear of Conspiracy: Images of Un-American Subversion from the Revolution to the Present* (Ithaca, NY: Cornell University Press, 1971); also Richard Hofstadter, *The Paranoid Style in American Politics and Other Essays* (New York: Knopf, 1965).

99. Davis, *The Fear of Conspiracy*, and "Some Themes of Counter-Subversion"; Hofstadter, *The Paranoid Style*, 21.

100. Davis, *The Fear of Conspiracy*, xiii–xxiv.

101. Hofstadter, *The Paranoid Style*, 4.

CHAPTER 3. AN EVERYMAN'S KLAN

1. *Fremont Times-Indicator*, 17 January 1924, 4.

2. All statistics from United States Bureau of the Census, *Fourteenth Census of the United States: 1920: Population* (Washington, DC, 1922); and *Fifteenth Census of the United States: 1930: Population* (Washington, DC, 1931–1933).

3. United States Bureau of the Census, *Census of Religious Bodies: 1926* (Washington, DC, 1929).

4. Michigan Department of State, *Michigan Official Directory and Legislative Manual, 1923–4* (Lansing, 1923), 289.

5. "Newaygo (Provisional)," in box 2, *Ku Klux Klan (Mecosta County, Mich.) Collection, 1916–1974*.

6. Earl Gibson, of Baldwin, Michigan, appeared on both the Newaygo County provisional list, and in Blass's letters, invited to his 1927 wedding as "[one] of those who have been near to us both or especially close to me." See letter of 11 March 1926, *Blass Family Papers, 1922–2002*.

7. *Grand Rapids Press*, 25 October 1992, 1A.

8. *White Cloud Eagle*, 1 October 1925, 4.

9. Jackson, *Klan in the City*, 133; Enders, "White Sheets in Mecosta," 74.

10. *Ku Klux Klan (Newaygo County, Mich.) Membership Cards, 1923–1926*.

11. Figures as printed in the *Fremont Times-Indicator*, 26 August 1920, 1.

12. Each of the following, loosely defined "Southern" states was the birthplace of either one or two Newaygo County Klan members: Kentucky, Missouri, Virginia, Florida, Arkansas, and Tennessee.

13. *Ku Klux Klan (Newaygo County, Mich.) Membership Cards, 1923–1926*.

14. The photographs of Charles Rice's 3 May 1925 funeral were one of the more sensational items to be sold off at auction following the discovery of the Newaygo County Klan records. See reprint in *Detroit Free Press*, 29 October 1992.

15. *Ku Klux Klan (Newaygo County, Mich.) Membership Cards, 1923–1926*.

16. "God Give Us Men" made frequent appearances in official Klan literature of all kinds. This particular version featured in the *Gratiot County Night-Hawk*, August 1928, 4.

17. Untitled KKK speech in *Ku Klux Klan (Miscellaneous) Collection, 1924–1929*, Clarke Historical Library, Central Michigan University.

18. David Horowitz, "Order, Solidarity, and Vigilance: The Ku Klux Klan in La Grande, Oregon," in Lay, ed., *The Invisible Empire in the West*. Also David Horowitz, ed., *Inside the Klavern: The Secret History of a Ku Klux Klan of the 1920s* (Carbondale: Southern Illinois University Press, 1999).

19. The following statistics on geographical recruitment patterns are all apparent from an in-depth study of membership details in Newaygo County. See *Ku Klux Klan (Newaygo County, Mich.) Membership Cards, 1923–1926*.

20. "Newaygo KKK Correspondence, 1923," in box 1, *Calvin Enders Collection*.

21. Edgar Allen Booth, *The Mad Mullah of America* (Columbus, OH: Boyd Ellison, 1927), 28, 17, 37.

22. *Ku Klux Klan (Newaygo County, Mich.) Membership Cards, 1923–1926*.

23. Mecklin, *The Ku Klux Klan: A Study of the American Mind*, 103, 189. Further examples of this point of view can be seen in Allen, *Only Yesterday*, 54–57; Bohn, "The Ku Klux Klan Interpreted," Johnson, "A Sociological Interpretation of the New Ku Klux Movement"; Duffus, "How the Ku Klux Klan Sells Hate," and "The Ku Klux Klan in the Middle West"; Rice, *The Ku Klux Klan in American Politics*.

24. *Ku Klux Klan (Newaygo County, Mich.) Membership Cards, 1923–1926*.

25. Ted Ferris, *DHIA in America: A Foundation for Progress* (East Lansing, MI: Michigan State University Department of Animal Science, 2005).

26. "He Knew His Onions!" *Detroit News* pictorial for 9 October 1938, 4.

27. Knights of the Ku Klux Klan, *Constitution and Laws of the Knights of the Ku Klux Klan, Incorporated* (Atlanta: Knights of the Ku Klux Klan, 1921), 10. Also see Knights of the Ku Klux Klan, *Petition for Articles of Incorporation*

Made to the Superior Court of Fulton County, Georgia, dated 26 April 1916, copy in Clarke Historical Library, Central Michigan University.

28. *Michigan Kourier*, 26 September 1924, 3. Also see Loucks, *The Ku Klux Klan in Pennsylvania*, ch. 10; Alexander, *The Ku Klux Klan in the Southwest*, 100–105. Perhaps the most comprehensive account of the women's order to date, particularly in its consideration of female autonomy within the Klan movement, can be found in Blee, *Women of the Klan.*

29. Alexander, "Kleagles and Cash," 364–65.

30. Loucks, *The Ku Klux Klan in Pennsylvania*, ch. 10; Women of the Ku Klux Klan, *Constitution and Laws of the Women of the Ku Klux Klan* (Little Rock: Women of the Ku Klux Klan, 1927), 10.

31. Loucks, *The Ku Klux Klan in Pennsylvania*, 151.

32. *Fiery Cross (Michigan State Edition)*, 7 September 1923, 1.

33. *Ku Klux Klan (Newaygo County, Mich.) Membership Cards, 1923–1926.*

34. *Michigan Kourier*, 8 August 1924, 5.

35. *Michigan Kourier*, 5 September 1924, 5.

36. *Michigan Kourier*, 8 August 1924, 5.

37. *Michigan Kourier*, 8 August 1924, 5. Also see 5 September 1924, 5.

38. Knights of the Ku Klux Klan, *Papers Read at the Meeting of Grand Dragons*, 81–89.

39. *Imperial Night-Hawk*, 23 April 1924, 7; *Kourier* magazine 1, no. 3 (February 1925): 23; *Fiery Cross (Michigan State Edition)*, 28 September 1923, 16; Blee, *Women of the Klan*, 157–62.

40. *Fellowship Forum*, 25 July 1925, 5–6; New Jersey Kleagle Leah H. Bell, quoted in Blee, *Women of the Klan*, 160.

41. *Fiery Cross (Indiana State Edition)*, 17 August 1923, 1.

42. *Fiery Cross (Michigan State Edition)*, 19 October 1923, 1. For multiple reports of Junior Klan and Tri-K activity around Michigan, see *Fiery Cross (Michigan State Edition)*, 7 September 1923, 7; 28 September 1923, 5; 9 November 1923, 1; 23 November 1923, 1; 26 September 1924, 6; 24 October 1924, 6; *Saginaw Night-Hawk*, 1 April 1927. The national pro-Klan magazine *Fellowship Forum* also reported on juniors all around Michigan. See, for example, 17 May 1924, 5; 13 September 1924, 3; 18 April 1925, 2; 27 June 1925, 3; 25 July 1925, 5–6.

43. *Wolverine Women*, April 1928, 2; June 1928, 4; July 1928, 4.

44. *Dawn*, 29 December 1923, 7; Chalmers, *Hooded Americanism*, 217. For examples of public appearances by the Royal Riders alongside their Klan counterparts, see *Imperial Night-Hawk*, 19 March 1924, 4; and 18 June 1924, 7.

45. *Imperial Night-Hawk*, 19 September 1923, 8.

46. American Krusaders, *The Sprit of the Crusades As Interpreted and Revived by the American Krusaders Incorporated* (Little Rock: American Krusaders, n.d.); *Kourier* magazine, October 1925, 11–13.

47. Booth, *The Mad Mullah*, 18.

48. *Saginaw Night-Hawk*, January 1928, 3–4. For other references to the Krusaders in Michigan's Klan press, see *Michigan Kourier*, 10 October 1924, 1; *Wolverine Women*, July 1928, 4.

49. All statistical information derived from *Ku Klux Klan (Newaygo County, Mich.) Membership Cards, 1923–1926.*

50. "Form 100-PH: Questionnaire—American Krusaders," in *Ku Klux Klan Membership Materials, 1920s,* Special Collections library, vertical file, Michigan State University.

51. *Imperial Night-Hawk*, 18 April 1923, 5; *Dawn*, 21 October 1922, 13; and 28 October 1922, 13.

52. *Ku Klux Klan (Newaygo County, Mich.) Membership Cards, 1923–1926*; *Newaygo County Naturalization Records, 1855–1966*, RG 99–82, State Archives of Michigan, Lansing.

53. See, for example, Evans, *The Menace of Modern Immigration*, and "The Klan's Fight for Americanism," 33–63.

54. Blee, *Women of the Klan*, 24–25.

55. Carnes, *Secret Ritual and Manhood in Victorian America*, 81–83.

56. Clawson, *Constructing Brotherhood*, 210.

57. As well as a Klan established aboard a U.S. Navy vessel, the order operated with considerable success north of the border in the form of the "Kanadian Knights of the Ku Klux Klan." Reports filtered back from abroad, too, detailing scattered Klan activity in Germany and England, as well as more unlikely outposts including Shanghai, Lithuania, Czechoslovakia, Cuba, Mexico, and New Zealand. It seems likely, though, that many of these were unofficial, unsuccessful, and ultimately abortive short-term ventures. See Chalmers, *Hooded Americanism*, 217, 279–80; Julian Sher, *White Hoods: Canada's Ku Klux Klan* (Vancouver: New Star Books, 1983); Booth, *The Mad Mullah*, 255–58.

58. *New York Times*, 19 October 1924, 31; and 22 March 1924, 12; Blee, *Women of the Klan*, 169.

59. *Fellowship Forum*, 25 September 1926, 1.

60. *Aiken Family History*, Fremont Area District Library (Local History Collection), Fremont, Michigan.

CHAPTER 4. THE INVISIBLE EMPIRE AND SMALL-TOWN SOCIABILITY

1. *Ku Klux Klan (Newaygo County, Mich.) Membership Cards, 1923–1926.*

2. Clawson, *Constructing Brotherhood*, 209–10, 262.

3. These figures are taken from the total of 396 Newaygo County Klanswomen for whom full details of a partner (or lack of one) were available. See *Ku Klux Klan (Newaygo County, Mich.) Membership Cards, 1923–1926.*
4. Lynd, *Middletown*, 122n, 308.
5. This figure represents only the individuals most readily traceable via local history and census sources. With scant biographical detail available on many other Klan members, the true figure is likely to have been significantly higher. Especially problematic in this regard are the many married female members who, in terms of public references and particularly in newspapers, tended to lose not only their maiden names but also their given names to their husbands (all references to "Miss Angie Wheeler," for example, immediately becoming references to "Mrs. Floyd Crandall" after the young Klan couple's 1925 marriage). While this does make husband-wife links explicitly clear, it also serves to obscure (if only for the historian) the married woman's links to both her siblings and parents.

   Such factors, along with the somewhat piecemeal nature of available source materials, complicate the already substantial task of reconstructing the many and varied connections between Newaygo County Klan members. Beyond the naming of a spouse, KKK records themselves required no declaration from members of their personal or business links with other individuals within the organization. The only means, therefore, of ascertaining such ties comes by a painstaking cross-referencing of more than 1,200 names appearing on Klan rolls with local history and genealogy sources. Drawing upon scattered surviving editions of area newspapers, scrapbooks of news, wedding and obituary announcements, vintage area directories, and census listings, the level of detail on individual members varies widely in scope and quality. Meanwhile, the more itinerant local Klan members—those moving into and out of the area in the years before and after their membership—are often absent altogether, untraceably so, from local histories and county census records. Despite such occupational constraints, it has still been possible to gain a partial, if imperfect and far from exhaustive, insight into the connections and acquaintances existing between Klan members.
6. *Ku Klux Klan (Newaygo County, Mich.) Membership Cards, 1923–1926*; *Fremont Times-Indicator* and *White Cloud Eagle*, 1922–26.
7. *Ku Klux Klan (Newaygo County, Mich.) Membership Cards, 1923–1926*; *Fremont Times-Indicator*, 9 July 1925.
8. As the story goes, Dan Gerber and his wife Dorothy, having struggled with a sieve and spoon to manually strain the peas required for their infant daughter Sally's special diet, came up with the plan of using the canning company's specialized food processing equipment for the purpose. Meeting with success,

Dan extended the idea to appeal to a gap in the market, and with this, the Gerber baby foods industry was born. A wholesome family tale well fitted to the company's corporate image, it can be found in the pages of many a piece of Gerber commemorative literature. See, for example, Gerber Products Company, *The Story of an Idea and Its Role in the Growth of the Baby Foods Industry* (Fremont, MI: Gerber Products Company, 1953); and *Fifty Years of Caring: Our Golden Anniversary Year, 1928–1978* (Fremont, MI: Gerber Products Company, 1978).

9. *Ku Klux Klan (Newaygo County, Mich.) Membership Cards, 1923–1926.*
10. *White Cloud Eagle*, 15 March 1923.
11. *Fremont Times-Indicator*, 24 August and 7 September 1922.
12. *White Cloud Eagle*, 2 July 1925, 4.
13. Knights of the Ku Klux Klan, *The Practice of Klanishness* (Atlanta: Knights of the Ku Klux Klan, 1924), 2–4.
14. Blee, *Women of the Klan*, 151–53.
15. Blee, *Women of the Klan*, 147–51.
16. *Fremont Times-Indicator*, 5 June 1924, 6.
17. Lynd, *Middletown*, 306–7.
18. *Ku Klux Klan (Newaygo County, Mich.) Membership Cards, 1923–1926.*
19. "Newaygo KKK Correspondence, 1923," in box 1, *Calvin Enders Collection.*
20. Mecklin, *The Ku Klux Klan: A Study of the American Mind*, 221–24.
21. *Ku Klux Klan (Newaygo County, Mich.) Membership Cards, 1923–1926.*
22. On Stephenson's remarkable demagogic career and subsequent scandalous downfall, see, for example, Booth, *The Mad Mullah*; Alva W. Taylor, "What the Klan Did in Indiana," *New Republic* 52 (16 November 1927): 330–32; William G. Shepard, "Indiana's Mystery Man," *Collier's National Weekly*, 8 January 1927, 8–9; M. William Lutholtz, *Grand Dragon: D. C. Stephenson and the Ku Klux Klan in Indiana* (Lafayette, IN: Purdue University Press, 1991).
23. In the same month that he would become Newaygo Klansman No. 001, the local press reported that Sheridan had also paid visits to Chicago to see his brother, Ed. *Newaygo Republican*, 2 August 1923, 5.
24. All statistical data derived from *Ku Klux Klan (Newaygo County, Mich.) Membership Cards, 1923–1926.*
25. *Ku Klux Klan (Newaygo County, Mich.) Membership Cards, 1923–1926.*
26. *Fremont Times-Indicator*, 10 April 1924, 1; and 26 March 1925, 1.
27. George Ernest Rasey (Republican) and Riley Tindall (Democrat) both ran for county sheriff in 1924. See *Fremont Times-Indicator*, 14 August 1924, 1. Neither man won the contest, both losing out to White Cloud's David Moote, a Republican and also a Klansman. The outgoing sheriff, Noble McKinley of White Cloud, was yet another member of the Klan.

28. *Fremont Times-Indicator*, 2 June 1921, 1.

29. Knights of the Ku Klux Klan, *Constitution and Laws*, 65–72. Also see Knights of the Ku Klux Klan, Department of Realms, *Klan Building* (Atlanta: Knights of the Ku Klux Klan, n.d.).

30. *Fremont Times-Indicator*, 10 January 1924, 2; 15 May 1924, 4; 22 November 1917, 1; 24 December 1924, 1.

31. "Proceedings of Second Annual Realm Klolero," in box 2, *Ku Klux Klan (Mecosta County, Mich.) Collection, 1916–1974*.

32. Knights of the Ku Klux Klan, *Kloran: Knights of the Ku Klux Klan: First Degree Character* (Atlanta: Knights of the Ku Klux Klan, 1917); and *The Practice of Klanishness*, 8.

33. *Fremont Times-Indicator*, 10 January 1924, 4; 15 May 1924, 2.

34. For analysis of the Klan in Chicago, see Jackson, *Klan in the City*, ch. 8; Chalmers, *Hooded Americanism*, ch. 25.

35. *Newaygo Republican*, 2 August 1923, 5; and 11 October 1923, 3.

36. The *Republican* from time to time reported on the high-spirited exploits of this well-known local bunch. Just two nights after the first few of them had become Klansmen, apparently, "a number of young people from town spent a most enjoyable evening . . . at the A. W. Gleason cottage." (Gleason, who was Kenneth Dayton's employer, would also shortly be a Klansman.) Among those present were Klansmen Kenneth Dayton, Einar and Axel Johnson, William Vinton, and Allen Bowman. After a bonfire and "old fashioned 'weenie' roast . . . Messrs. Vinton and Bowman obliged with a little comedy sketch to the entertainment of all," with all of the boisterous action caught on camera by "Kenneth Dayton, photographer extraordinaire." *Newaygo Republican*, 6 September 1923, 5.

37. On the infamous D. C. Stephenson and his "G-2" spy system, see in particular Booth, *The Mad Mullah*, 78–81.

38. "Field Regulations No. 3" in *Ku Klux Klan (Miscellaneous) Collection, 1924–1929*.

39. "Newaygo KKK Correspondence, 1923," in box 1, *Calvin Enders Collection*.

40. Newaygo County Clerk's Office, *Newaygo County 2005 Official Directory: Federal, State, County, Township, City and Village Officers* (White Cloud, MI: Newaygo County Clerk, 2005), 59–62; *White Cloud Eagle*, 5 January 1922, 1; *Fremont Times-Indicator*, 18 October 1923, 1. Much of the information on individual members that follows is derived directly from the data contained in *Ku Klux Klan (Newaygo County, Mich.) Membership Cards, 1923–1926*.

41. Most of these political appointments are confirmed in the *Fremont Times-Indicator*, 17 April 1924, 1; and 14 February 1924, 1. Also see Newaygo County Historical Society, *Profile of Yesteryear* (White Cloud, MI: Newaygo County Historical Society, 1976), 25.

42. Newaygo County Clerk's Office, *Newaygo County 2005 Official Directory.*

43. For scattered examples, see *Fremont Times-Indicator*, 3 November 1921, 4; 31 October 1923, 1; 28 August 1924, 1; 24 December 1924, 1; and *White Cloud Eagle*, 13 April 1922, 1; 8 November 1923, 1; 13 December 1923, 1.

44. *Fremont Times-Indicator*, 31 December 1924, 1.

45. *Fremont Times-Indicator*, 3 July 1924, 1; and 4 September 1924, 1; *Newaygo Republican*, 10 July 1924, 1.

46. *Fremont Times-Indicator*, 31 December 1924, 1; *White Cloud Eagle*, 8 January 1925, 1; 19 March 1925, 4; and 25 November 1926, 1.

47. *Fremont Times-Indicator*, 3 April 1924, 1; and 10 April 1924, 1, 6.

48. *Fremont Times-Indicator*, 10 and 17 June 1920.

49. *Fremont Tines-Indicator*, 1 May 1924, 1, 4.

50. *Fremont Times-Indicator*, 14 August 1924, 1; 11 September 1924, 1; and 1 July 1926, 2; *White Cloud Eagle*, 8 July 1926, 8; *Harry Spooner Scrapbooks*, White Cloud Public Library local history room, White Cloud, Michigan.

51. *Fremont Times-Indicator*, 5 August 1920, 1; 14 August and 11 September 1924, 1; *Harry Spooner Scrapbooks*; *Ku Klux Klan (Newaygo County, Mich.) Membership Cards, 1923–1926.*

52. "Newaygo KKK Correspondence, 1923," in box 1, *Calvin Enders Collection.*

53. *Ku Klux Klan (Newaygo County, Mich.) Membership Cards, 1923–1926*; White Cloud Centennial Committee, *The First Hundred Years, 1873–1973: White Cloud Area* (White Cloud, MI: Industrial Printing, 1973), 111; *Fremont Times-Indicator*, 16 August, 25 October, and 27 December 1923, 1.

54. Katz, *The Invisible Empire*, 79.

55. *Newaygo Republican*, 21 June 1923, 1; and 12 July 1923, 4.

56. *Fremont Times-Indicator*, 21 June 1923; *White Cloud Eagle*, 4 June 1925, 1.

57. *Fremont Times-Indicator*, 4 October 1923, 1; *White Cloud Eagle*, 24 September 1925, 1.

58. *Fremont Times-Indicator*, 21 June 1923, 1; *Harry Spooner Scrapbooks*. The two structures in question are Alma College's Nisbet Hall and Michigan State University's Stephen S. Nisbet Building.

59. *Fremont Times-Indicator*, 17 April 1924, 4; 17 July 1924, 1; 14 June 1923, 1; 15 June 1922, 1; 19 May 1921, 1.

60. "Newaygo KKK Correspondence, 1923," in box 1, *Calvin Enders Collection*; *Ku Klux Klan (Newaygo County, Mich.) Membership Cards*; *Newaygo Republican*, 27 September 1923, 1.

61. *Harry Spooner Scrapbooks* for 1937; Howard Douglass, "Memories of the One Room School," *Newaygo County Historical Society Quarterly* 2, no. 2 (Summer 1978): 1.

62. *White Cloud Eagle*, 18 May 1922; 15 November 1923; 22 October 1925.

63. *White Cloud Eagle*, 2 August 1923, 1. White Cloud Klansman and schoolteacher Lloyd Fry followed Carter into the commissioner's job, a position she had held continuously for 22 years, after her retirement due to ill health in 1936.

64. Hesperia Centennial Book Committee, *Hesperia Centennial, 1866–1966* (Greenville, MI: Greenville Printing Co., 1966), 65.

65. *Blass Family Papers, 1922–2002*.

66. "Newaygo KKK Correspondence, 1923," in box 1, *Calvin Enders Collection*; *Fremont Times-Indicator*, 23 August 1923, 1.

67. Michigan Department of State, *Michigan Official Directory, 1923–4*, p. 289.

68. *Newaygo Republican*, 11 October 1923.

69. *Fremont Times-Indicator*, 18 January 1923, 4; and 8 February 1923, 4.

70. *White Cloud Eagle*, 15 March and 22 November, 1923.

71. *Newaygo Republican*, 5 March 1925, 1.

72. *Imperial Night-Hawk*, 16 May 1923, 8; and 30 July 1924, 2; *Kourier* magazine, April 1925, 19; and August 1926, 3.

73. "Organizational Correspondence, Jan–June, 1927," in *Ku Klux Klan (Mecosta County, Mich.) Collection, 1916–1974*.

74. *Newaygo Republican*, 18 June 1925, 5; and 2 October 1924, 1; *Fremont Times-Indicator*, 2 October 1924, 1.

75. *Newaygo Republican*, 27 September 1923, 1; 6 March 1924, 1; 24 July 1924, 1.

CHAPTER 5. COMMUNITY, CHURCH, AND KLAN

1. "Field Regulations No. 3," in *Ku Klux Klan (Miscellaneous) Collection, 1924–1929*. On the similar service activities of the Rotary Club movement in the mid-1920s, see Lynd, *Middletown*, 301–6.

2. Notes on Klansman Harold Hobbs, Jr., 12 December 1924, who "stayed in 6 months and got out," claiming that the quality of recruits had eventually tailed off. *Papers of Robert Staughton and Helen Merrell Lynd, 1895–1968*, microfilm 18297–8p (container 9, reels 5–6), Library of Congress Microfilms.

3. Blee, *Women of the Klan*, 2.

4. *White Cloud Eagle*, 24 May 1923, 1. Also see, for example, 3 May 1923, 1; and 7 June 1923, 1.

5. *Fremont Times-Indicator*, 16 February 1922, 2.

6. *White Cloud Eagle*, 3 May 1923, 1–2.

7. *White Cloud Eagle*, 28 December 1922, 1–2.

8. *Fremont Times-Indicator*, 17 January 1924, 4.

9. *Newaygo Republican*, 26 February 1925, 3.

10. *Newaygo Republican*, 4 October 1923, 4.

11. *Fremont Times-Indicator*, 16 October 1924; and 19 April 1923, 1; *White Cloud Eagle*, 30 April 1925, 2.

12. *White Cloud Eagle*, 22 March 1923, 4; *Fremont Times-Indicator*, 28 June 1923, 2; and 5 July 1923, 8.

13. *White Cloud Eagle*, 15 January 1925, 1; *Harry Spooner Scrapbooks*; White Cloud Centennial Committee, *The First Hundred Years, 1873–1973*, 103.

14. *Fremont Times-Indicator*, 30 May 1923, 8; and 7 June 1923, 1.

15. Thomas R. Pegram, "Hoodwinked: The Anti-Saloon League and the Ku Klux Klan in 1920s Prohibition Enforcement," *Journal of the Gilded Age and Progressive Era* 7, no. 1 (January 2008): 89–120.

16. *Fremont Times-Indicator*, 13 March 1919, 1; and 23 January 1919, 6; *Newaygo Republican*, 8 November 1923, 2.

17. *Fremont Times-Indicator*, 14 August 1924; 28 August 1924, 1; 26 January 1922, 4.

18. *Martha Mudget Evans Papers, 19uu*, Clarke Historical Library, Central Michigan University.

19. *White Cloud Eagle*, 8 October 1925, 1; also see 15 January 1925; and 12 April 1923, 2; *Fremont Times-Indicator*, 20 March 1924, 8.

20. *Fremont Times-Indicator*, 2 February 1922, 4.

21. *White Cloud Eagle*, 29 October 1925, 2.

22. White Cloud Centennial Committee, *The First Hundred Years*, 108.

23. Hesperia Centennial Book Committee, *Hesperia Centennial, 1866–1966*, 87.

24. *Fremont Times-Indicator*, 5 July 1923, 1; 2 October 1924, 1; 6 November 1924, 6; 15 December 1921, 9.

25. *Fremont Times-Indicator*, 23 March 1922, 8.

26. *Fremont Times-Indicator*, 18 December 1919.

27. *Fremont Times-Indicator*, 31 January 1924, 1; 17 July 1924, 1; 31 July 1924, 1.

28. Martha Evans, *History of Fremont Bank and Trust Co., 1904–1979* (Fremont, MI: Clarke Historical Library, 1979), 1; *Harry Spooner Scrapbooks*.

29. *White Cloud Eagle*, 25 February 1926, 1; and 22 April 1926, 7; White Cloud Centennial Committee, *The First Hundred Years*, 108.

30. *White Cloud Eagle*, 12 November 1925, 7; and 19 November 1925, 1; Knights of the Ku Klux Klan, *The Practice of Klanishness*, 2–4.

31. *White Cloud Eagle*, 3 June 1926, 1; and 16 December 1926, 1.

32. *White Cloud Eagle*, 19 February 1925, 1; and 22 April 1926, 1.

33. *White Cloud Eagle*, 12 January 1922, 1; and 9 March 1922, 1; *Fremont Times-Indicator*, 24 April 1924, 1; and 15 May 1924, 1.

34. *Fremont Times-Indicator*, 26 April 1923, 1.

35. Lewis Walker and Ben C. Wilson, *Black Eden: The Idlewild Community* (East Lansing: Michigan State University Press, 2002), 6–7.

36. Ronald J. Stephens, *Idlewild: The Black Eden of Michigan* (Chicago: Arcadia Publishing, 2001).

37. *Fremont Times-Indicator*, 17 January 1924, 1; and 7 August 1924, 4.

38. St. Joseph Church, White Cloud, *Our First 100 Years, 1891–1992* (White Cloud, MI: St. Joseph Church, 1992), 3.

39. *Fremont Times-Indicator*, 24 February 1921, 1; *Community City Hall Dedication Program, 1920*, copy in Fremont Area District Library, local history section, Fremont, Michigan.

40. *Fremont Times-Indicator*, 3 October 1918, 1; and 18 December 1924, 1; *Dallas L. Darling: Pioneer in Trucking*, in Fremont Area District Library, local history section.

41. *Fremont Times-Indicator*, 4 April 1918, 1; *Newaygo Republican*, 26 March 1925, 2.

42. *Newaygo Republican*, 29 July 1926; *Fremont Times-Indicator*, 28 May 1936.

43. *White Cloud Eagle*, 5 July 1923, 2; and 6 September 1923, 1; *Fremont Times-Indicator*, 23 October 1924, 2.

44. *Newaygo Republican*, 31 January 1924, 7; and 7 February 1924, 2; *Fiery Cross (Michigan State Edition)*, 15 February 1924, 5.

45. *Newaygo Republican*, 13 September 1923, 5; 27 September 1923, 1; 4 October 1923, 1; 18 October 1923, 1; 3 July 1924, 4; 13 August 1925, 4.

46. *Newaygo Republican*, 6 March 1924, 1.

47. *Fiery Cross (Michigan State Edition)*, 21 March 1924, 1; *Newaygo Republican*, 13 March 1924, 5.

48. *Fremont Times-Indicator*, 21 June 1923, 1; and 12 July 1923, 1; *Newaygo Republican*, 12 July 1923, 4.

49. *Fremont Times-Indicator*, 21 February 1924, 1.

50. *Fremont Times-Indicator*, 28 February 1924, 1.

51. *Fiery Cross (Michigan State Edition)*, 7 March 1924, 5.

52. *Fremont Times-Indicator*, 22 May 1924, 1.

53. *Fremont Times-Indicator*, 16 October 1924, 1.

54. *Newaygo Republican*, 6 March 1924, 1.

55. *Newaygo Republican*, 21 February 1924, 2; 28 February 1924, 2.

56. *White Cloud Eagle*, 1 October 1925, 4.

57. *Klan Kourier (Michigan State Edition)*, 27 June 1924, 6; *Fellowship Forum*, 2 January 1926, 6; and 25 June 1927, 2. Also mentioned are weddings in other states—see, for example, 21 July 1923, 5 (New Jersey); and 27 December 1924, 6 (North Carolina).

58. *Michigan Kourier*, 28 November 1924, 1; *Bay City Night-Hawk*, March 1928, 2.

59. *National Kourier*, 20 August 1925, 6.

60. *Newaygo Republican, White Cloud Eagle*, and *Fremont Times-Indicator*, 1923–26; *Ku Klux Klan (Newaygo County, Mich.) Membership Cards, 1923–1926*.

The flipside to all of this, of course, is the number of divorces involving Klansfolk over the same period, which stands at a minimum of four confirmed cases. Two of these involved a split between a Klansman and a non-Klan wife; the other two were splits between partners who were both in the Klan.

61. *Michigan Kourier*, 10 October 1924, 1.

62. *Saginaw Star*, 4 July 1924, 1; *Klan Kourier (Michigan State Edition)*, 11 July 1924, 2; and 4 July 1924, 6. Among many other references to Klan christenings and baby dedications, see *Fellowship Forum*, 23 August 1924, 6; and 2 May 1925, 6.

63. *Michigan Kourier*, 8 August 1924, 6.

64. *Fellowship Forum*, 29 November 1924, 3; 28 March 1925, 2; 4 April 1925, 7; 12 December 1925, 6; 27 February 1926, 3; 27 March 1926, 5; 10 July 1926, 6; 25 August 1928, 6.

65. Knights of the Ku Klux Klan, *Funeral Services: Knights of the Ku Klux Klan* (Atlanta: Knights of the Ku Klux Klan, 1925).

66. *Fiery Cross (Michigan State Edition)*, 21 March 1924, 4, 6, 8.

67. *Hart Journal*, 30 October 1924, 1, 2; also see "Realm of Michigan: Lists of Members, 1920s," in box 2, *Ku Klux Klan (Mecosta County, Mich.) Collection, 1916–1974*.

68. *Fremont Times-Indicator*, 3 December 1925, 1.

69. *Michigan Kourier*, 2 May 1924, 3. Also see 24 October 1924, 7.

70. *Fremont Times-Indicator*, 9 July 1925, 1.

71. *Fremont Times-Indicator*, 7 May 1925, 8.

72. *Fiery Cross (Michigan State Edition)*, 25 January 1924, 5; and 1 February 1924, 4; Knights of the Ku Klux Klan, *Funeral Services*, 1; *Klan Kourier (Michigan State Edition)*, 27 June 1924, 8.

73. *Newaygo Republican*, 25 September 1924, 1.

74. "Directory, Adrian, Michigan, 1926," in box 10, *Calvin Enders Collection*.

75. *Mancelona Herald*, 30 August 1923, 1; *Alma Record*, 18 October 1923, 4.

76. "Field Regulations No. 3," in *Ku Klux Klan (Miscellaneous) Collection, 1924–1929*.

77. Reports of fiery crosses in Newaygo County can be found in *Newaygo Republican*, 6 September 1923, 5; 27 September 1923, 1; 12 June 1924, 5; and 19 June 1924, 6; *White Cloud Eagle*, 4 October 1923, 7; 18 October 1923, 1; and 6 December 1923, 2; *Fiery Cross (Michigan State Edition)*, 21 September 1923, 8; and 2 May 1924, 1.

78. Stanley L. Swart, "A Memo on Cross-Burning—and Its Implications," *Northwest Ohio Quarterly* 43 (1971): 70–73.

79. *Fremont Times-Indicator*, 29 July 1924, 6; *Michigan Kourier*, 8 August 1924, 1.

80. *Fiery Cross (Michigan State Edition)*, 2 May 1924, 1.

81. *Hart Courier*, 22 June 1924, 1.

82. *White Cloud Eagle*, 18 October 1923, 1; *Klan Kourier*, 4 July 1924, 4; *Fremont Times-Indicator*, 26 June 1924, 1.

83. *Imperial Night-Hawk*, 6 August 1924; and 4 July 1923, 8; *Dawn*, 3 November 1923, 26.

84. "The Crucible," in box 2, *Ku Klux Klan (Mecosta County, Mich.) Collection, 1916–1974*.

85. *Fremont Times-Indicator*, 30 March 1922, 1; and 15 February 1923, 1; *Newaygo Republican*, 26 February 1925, 1.

86. *White Cloud Eagle*, 2 July 1925, 8.

87. Letters from Kenneth Blass to Marie Kleiner dated 18 February 1926; 25 February 1926; 1 March 1926; 7 December 1925; and 22 May 1926, in *Blass Family Papers, 1922–2002*.

88. Linda Weisner Maranis, "Harley Mankin: The Frog Man," *Vaudeville Times* 6, no. 1 (2003): 10–14. Also see clippings file on both Harlan and Ida Mankin in the local history section of the Fremont Area District library.

89. *Fremont Times-Indicator*, 9 August 1923, 1; 23 August 1923, 4; 12 June 1924, 5. Also see 18 October 1923, 1; 13 December 1923, 3; 2 October 1924, 5.

90. Letters from Blass to Kleiner dated 26 January 1927 and 30 January 1927, *Blass Family Papers*. The Klan press was always very keen to report charitable donations to churches and schools. Among mentions of Klan charity specifically to black institutions are *Dawn*, 19 January 1924, 7; *Imperial Night-Hawk*, 24 October 1923, 5; 28 May 1924, 6; 4 June 1924, 6; *Kourier* magazine, February 1925, 8.

91. *Newaygo County Historical Society Quarterly* 2, nos. 3 and 4 (Summer and Fall 1978), 5–6; *White Cloud Eagle*, 7 October 1926, 1; White Cloud Centennial Committee, *The First Hundred Years*, 104; *Newaygo Republican*, 4 October 1923, 1.

92. *Newaygo Republican*, 26 February 1925, 4; 5 March 1925, 3; 28 March 1925, 3; 9 April 1925.

93. *Klan Kourier (Michigan State Edition)*, 27 June 1924, 4.

94. *Michigan Kourier*, 1 August 1924, 2; and 8 August 1924, 1. One such exclusive resort project, due to be located at Schwartz Lake in Oakland County, never actually materialized. Despite being heavily touted in the Klan press, and collecting substantial funds, the venture was crippled by the destruction of resort company records in a mysterious fire, leaving out of pocket the many Michigan Klansmen who had invested. See Weaver, *Knights of the Ku Klux Klan*, 273–74.

95. Bulletins from the Office of the Grand Dragon, Realm of Michigan, numbered 97, 108, and 121, in "Organizational Correspondence," box 1, *Ku Klux*

Klan (Mecosta County, Mich.) Collection, 1916–1974. Also see *National Kourier*, 3 July 1925, 6; *Gratiot County Night-Hawk*, August 1928, 33.

96. *National Kourier*, 3 July 1925, 1.

97. See, for example, *Michigan Kourier*, 28 November 1924, 6. On the 1920s crossword-puzzle craze in general, see George E. Mowry, ed., *The Twenties: Fords, Flappers, and Fanatics* (Gloucester, MA: Peter Smith, 1988), 71.

98. Bulletin No. 90 in *Newaygo County WKKK Correspondence* (uncataloged), local history section, White Cloud Public Library, White Cloud, Michigan.

99. *Ku Klux Klan Quilt (Shoo-Fly Variation) 1926, Chicora, Michigan*, Michigan Traditional Arts Program Research Collections, Michigan State University Museum.

100. *White Cloud Eagle*, 12 October 1922, 1; *Fremont Times-Indicator*, 15 September 1921, 1; and 26 January 1922, 6.

101. *Fremont Times-Indicator*, 19 June 1924, 1.

102. Large regional Klan gatherings attracted much local press attention. For a small but representative sample of articles, see *Adrian Daily Telegram*, 19 May 1924, 1; *Saginaw News Courier*, 30 May 1924, 1; *Lansing Capital News*, 30 May 1924, 1; *Saginaw Star*, 31 May 1924, 1; *Jackson Citizen Patriot*, 5 July 1924, 1; *Lansing State Journal*, 7 December 1980, B8; *Ionia Sentinel Standard*, 1 June 1925, 1; *Ionia County News*, 4 June 1925, 1; *Grand Rapids Press*, 3 July 1925, 2; 4 July 1925, 1; 6 July 1925, 2.

103. *Newaygo Republican*, 5 June 1924, 1.

104. *Saginaw News Courier*, 30 May 1924, 1; *Saginaw Star*, 30 May 1924, 1; 31 May 1924, 1.

105. *Klan Kourier (Michigan State Edition)*, 11 July 1924, 1–2.

106. *Klan Kourier (Michigan State Edition)*, 11 July 1924, 1–2.

107. *Jackson Citizen Patriot*, 5 July 1924, 1.

108. *Lansing State Journal*, 7 December 1980, B8.

109. *Klan Kourier (Michigan State Edition)*, 11 July 1924, 3.

110. *Jackson Citizen Patriot*, 3 July 1924, 1; *Klan Kourier (Michigan State Edition)*, 4 July 1924, 1.

111. *Jackson Citizen Patriot*, 4 July 1924, 1; 5 July 1924, 1; *Klan Kourier (Michigan State Edition)*, 4 July 1924, 1.

112. See, for example, *Dawn*, 1 September 1923, 5; 13 October 1923, 12–13.

113. Clawson, *Constructing Brotherhood*, 228–29.

114. Blee, *Women of the Klan*, 165.

115. *Jackson Citizen Patriot*, 5 July 1924, 1; *Klan Kourier (Michigan State Edition)*, 4 July 1924, 1.

EPILOGUE

1. Lay, *Empire in the West*, 3.
2. Moore, "Historical Interpretations of the 1920s Klan," 354.
3. Lay, *Empire in the West*, 219.
4. Lay, *Empire in the West*, 220.
5. Weaver, *Knights of the Ku Klux Klan*, 280n, 298–99. The single violent confrontation of any real note came in 1925 and featured the Klan only indirectly. The incident involved Detroit physician Dr. Ossian Sweet, an upwardly mobile African American professional who, in common with a growing number of his peers, sought to purchase property outside of the restrictive confines of the traditional urban ghetto areas of that city. With residential competition accelerating in the fast-growing and increasingly diverse metropolis, Sweet's purchase of a house "in a white workingman's neighborhood on Detroit's East Side" aggravated already bubbling racial and ethnic tensions, and was met by physical opposition from segregationist mobs. While defending the family home from a barrage of bricks, bottles, and stones, Sweet's brother Henry shot and killed a white neighbor who was demonstrating in the street, resulting in both he and Ossian being tried for murder. According to Kenneth Jackson, "the Ku Klux Klan was not officially involved in the incident," and the mob of angry white neighbors had actually included "many foreign-born Catholics." Nevertheless, the Klan clearly supported neighborhood segregation, and the failure of Detroit police to protect the Sweet home during the melee led to claims by the NAACP of heavy and insidious Klan influence in city law enforcement. Detroit's Catholic mayor, John W. Smith, also publicly declared the KKK guilty of capitalizing on the hostility of such disturbances. See Jackson, *Klan in the City*, 139–41; and Chalmers, *Hooded Americanism*, 196.
6. Weaver, *Knights of the Ku Klux Klan*, 275. Other scholarly treatments of the Klan in Michigan, albeit centered entirely upon the city of Detroit, can be found in Jackson, *Klan in the City*, ch. 9; and Chalmers, *Hooded Americanism*, 194–97. Each features the Motor City as part of a broader national analysis of Klan activity, spanning prominent locations right across the United States, and is therefore understandably restricted in the depth of its coverage of Michigan. Nevertheless, both are hugely revealing on KKK involvement in Detroit politics in particular, and much of what is uncovered about the hooded order's origins, workings, political leanings, and, ultimately, financial and moral failings here holds relevance also for the rest of the state.
7. My own study, based upon the discovery of unique Michigan Klan records in Newaygo County, follows in the wake of Calvin Enders's work on small KKK

collections found in other less-populated Michigan locations. See Enders, "White Sheets in Mecosta"; and "Under Grand Haven's White Sheets."

8. Mecklin, *The Ku Klux Klan: A Study of the American Mind*, 104.

9. *White Cloud Eagle*, 1 October 1925, 4.

10. "Newaygo KKK Correspondence, 1923," in box 1, *Calvin Enders Collection*; *Muskegon Chronicle*, 27 October 1992, 2A; *Detroit Free Press*, 29 October 1992, 11A.

11. Weaver, *Knights of the Ku Klux Klan*, 280–82.

12. The Michigan Klan, it seems, never successfully entered politics on anything like the scale that it had done in neighboring Indiana, though it did make significant efforts in the cities of Flint, Lansing, and Detroit, as well as at the state level. Operating against a backdrop of unified GOP dominance, the Klan failed to sufficiently ally itself with the political establishment, and its encroachments were repelled by a powerful and experienced state Republican Party. Even before defeat of the parochial schools amendment (the hooded order's only issue of any real local significance), a splintered Klan front typified by cliques and rivalries was already evident. See Michael G. Hodges, *The Ku Klux Klan as a Political Influence in Michigan in the 1920s* (M.A. thesis, Central Michigan University, 1998).

13. *Fremont Times-Indicator*, 18 September 1924, 4; 25 September 1924, 1.

14. See Clawson, *Constructing Brotherhood*, 263.

15. Weaver, *Knights of the Ku Klux Klan*, 269–75.

16. Notes from interviews with Klansman 136 (21 May 1981) and Willard Schultz (17 August 1982), in "Michigan KKK Interviews and Notes, 1980–1982," box 1, *Calvin Enders Collection*.

17. Letters from Lewis Capen to Grand Dragon George E. Carr marked 31 July 1926, August 1926, and 24 March 1927, "Organizational Correspondence," boxes 1 and 2 in *Ku Klux Klan (Mecosta County, Mich.) Collection, 1916–1974*.

18. Blee, *Women of the Klan*, 95–96. Edgar Allen Booth describes the Michigan Klan's (pre-scandal) loyalty to Grand Dragon Stephenson over national Klan leader Hiram W. Evans: "When the break finally came between Stephenson and Evans, the Lansing Klan was more a 'Steve' organization than it was an Evans Klanton." See Booth, *The Mad Mullah*, 99.

19. *Muskegon Chronicle*, 6 June 1982, B1.

20. *Lansing State Journal*, 9 June 1926, 9; *Muskegon Chronicle*, 9 June 1926, 1; *Owosso Argus Press*, 9 June 1926, 1; *Fellowship Forum*, 12 June 1926, 1.

21. Chalmers, *Hooded Americanism*, 197; Michael and Judy Ann Newton, *The Ku Klux Klan: An Encyclopedia* (New York: Garland, 1991).

22. MacLean, *Behind the Mask of Chivalry*, 173. Besides her work on violence and race, also particularly impressive is MacLean's analysis of sexual themes

apparent in Klan literature, with the organization's conservative moral stance linked to much deeper anxieties over masculinity, traditional family roles, and a losing battle for control of female sexuality. All of these ideas are evident in the case of the Michigan Klan, and bear further investigation.

23. Weaver, *Knights of the Ku Klux Klan*, 289.

24. Chalmers, *Hooded Americanism*, 300–303.

25. The *Saginaw Night-Hawk*, *Bay City Night-Hawk*, *Gratiot County Night-Hawk*, and *Wolverine Women* for this period are all available in the archives of the Clarke Historical Library, Central Michigan University.

26. "Organizational Correspondence," boxes 1 and 2 in *Ku Klux Klan (Mecosta County, Mich.) Collection, 1916–1974.*

27. Letters dated 29 December 1926, and 1 February 1927, "Organizational Correspondence," boxes 1 and 2 in *Ku Klux Klan (Mecosta County, Mich.) Collection*; *Wolverine Women*, June 1928.

28. "Klan Publications, Advertisements, 1920s," and "Organizational Correspondence" dated 8 May 1928, in *Ku Klux Klan (Mecosta County, Mich.) Collection, 1916–1974*; "Michigan Bible Study League (MBSL) Papers," in box 1, *Calvin Enders Collection.*

29. *Fremont Times-Indicator*, 24 January 1918, 8.

30. Letters dated 7 May 1928, and 1 February 1932, in "Organizational Correspondence," *Ku Klux Klan (Mecosta County, Mich.) Collection, 1916–1974*; Interview with William and Verne Totten, 10 October 1981, in "Michigan KKK, Interviews, Notes, 1980–1982," box 1, *Calvin Enders Collection*; Enders, "White Sheets in Mecosta," 67–68.

31. *Black Legion Collection, 1936–1945*, Clarke Historical Library, Central Michigan University; Jackson, *Klan in the City*, 143; Chalmers, *Hooded Americanism*, 308; Weaver, *Knights of the Ku Klux Klan*, 289–91.

32. While the scope of this study has been deliberately and necessarily limited to discussion of the historical Klan organization of the 1920s, there are a number of excellent sources available that examine the influence of the KKK right up to the present day. Perhaps most comprehensive and contemporary is the Southern Poverty Law Center's *Intelligence Project* (formerly known as *Klanwatch*), and its related quarterly publication, *Intelligence Report*. Originally conceived in order to gather information on the Klan, the project has now widened its scope to monitor a vast range of related hate groups in the United States, including, in addition to the KKK, the full array of neo-Nazi, Skinhead, White Nationalist, Christian Identity, and extremist militia organizations. Though now a hugely fragmented movement (if indeed it can even be called a movement at all), according to SPLC data there still remains in 2010 a Klan presence in Michigan, with at least five different known organizations in the state bearing some variation upon the Ku Klux Klan name.

Bibliography

MANUSCRIPT COLLECTIONS, BY REPOSITORY

Central Michigan University (Mount Pleasant), Clarke Historical Library:

Ancient Order of Gleaners Collection, 1915–1927
Beardslee, Clarence B., Family Papers, 1884–1951
Black Legion Collection, 1936–1945
Blass Family Papers, 1922–2002
Enders, Calvin W., Collection, 1917–1997
Evans, Martha Mudget, Papers, 19uu
Ku Klux Klan (Mecosta County, Mich.) Collection, 1916–1974
Ku Klux Klan (Miscellaneous) Collection, 1924–1929
Ku Klux Klan (Newaygo County, Mich.) Membership Cards, 1923–1926
Ku Klux Klan (Owosso, Mich.) Collection, 1926–19uu
Noble Studio (Fremont, Mich.) Photographic Collection, 1920–2006
Wantz, Terry, *Over 4,000 Old Photos of Newaygo County, Michigan*

Fremont Area District Library (Fremont, Michigan):

Local History Collection

Library of Congress (Washington, DC):

Ku Klux Klan, Anaheim, Records, 1924–25
Ku Klux Klan, Campaign Songs, Performing Arts Reading Room
Ku Klux Klan Pamphlets, 1912–1946
Lynd, Robert Staughton and Helen Merrell, Papers, 1895–1968

Library of Michigan (Lansing):

Newaygo County History and Genealogy Index Cards
Newaygo County, Michigan, Tombstone Inscriptions

Michigan State University (East Lansing) Museum:

Michigan Quilt Project, *Ku Klux Klan Quilt (Shoo-Fly Variation), 1926*

Michigan State University (East Lansing), Special Collections Division:

American Radicalism Collection
Hardin, Myrtle Mary King, Photographs (uncataloged)
Ku Klux Klan (Clipping File)
Ku Klux Klan in Michigan
Ku Klux Klan Membership Material, 1920s, 1930s
Ku Klux Klan Merchandise, 1920s–30s
Wade, Wyn Craig, Ku Klux Klan Collection

Public Records Office (Kew):

BT 31/28323/195388—Klu Klux Klan, Ltd.
FO 115/2916—K. K. Klan—Legal. Nos. 1–4
FO 115/3289—Introductions. Nos. 21–33

State Archives of Michigan (Lansing):

Green, Fred W. (Governor), Correspondence—Ku Klux Klan, 1927
Groesbeck, Alex (Governor), Official Correspondence, 1924
Idlewild Summer Resort Security Application, 1913–53
Materials Relating to Women of the Ku Klux Klan, c1926
Michigan Official Directory and Legislative Manual, 1923–4
Newaygo County Naturalization Records, 1855–1966

University of Michigan (Ann Arbor), Special Collections:

Labadie Pamphlet Collection

University of Michigan (Ann Arbor), Bentley Historical Library:

Densmore, Fenno E., Papers, 1917–57
Evangelical Lutheran Synod of Missouri, Ohio, and Other States, Michigan District,
    Lutheran Schools Committee Papers, 1921–1926
Michener, Earl C., Papers, 1898–1954

White Cloud Public Library (White Cloud, Michigan):

Harry Spooner Scrapbooks
Local History Collection
*Newaygo County WKKK Correspondence (un*cataloged)

NEWSPAPERS AND PERIODICALS

Adrian Daily Telegram (Adrian, Michigan)
Alma Record (Alma, Michigan)
American Mercury (New York)
American Standard (Washington, DC)
Barryton Press (Barryton, Michigan)
Bay City Night-Hawk (Bay City, Michigan)
Berrien County Journal (Berrien Springs, Michigan)
Cheboygan Daily Tribune (Cheboygan, Michigan)
Clare Sentinel (Clare, Michigan)
Clinton County Republican (St. Johns, Michigan)
Congressional Record (Washington, DC)
Dawn (Chicago, Illinois)
Detroit Evening Times (Detroit, Michigan)
Detroit Free Press (Detroit, Michigan)
Detroit News (Detroit, Michigan)
Dowagiac Daily News (Dowagiac, Michigan)
Fellowship Forum (Washington, DC)

Fiery Cross (Indiana State Edition)
Fiery Cross (Michigan State Edition)
Flint Journal (Flint, Michigan)
Fremont Times-Indicator (Fremont, Michigan)
Gerber News (Fremont, Michigan)
Grand Haven Daily Tribune (Grand Haven, Michigan)
Grand Rapids Press (Grand Rapids, Michigan)
Gratiot County Night-Hawk (Alma, Michigan)
Hart Courier (Hart, Michigan)
Hart Journal (Hart, Michigan)
Hartford Day Spring (Hartford, Michigan)
Holland News (Holland, Michigan)
Ionia County News (Ionia, Michigan)
Ionia Sentinel Standard (Ionia, Michigan)
Isabella County Enterprise (Mount Pleasant, Michigan)
Jackson Citizen Patriot (Jackson, Michigan)
Kalamazoo Gazette (Kalamazoo, Michigan)
Klan Kourier (Michigan State Edition)
Kluxer: The Ku Klux Klan Magazine (Dayton, Ohio)
Knights of the Ku Klux Klan, Inc., *Imperial Night-Hawk* (Atlanta, Georgia)
————, *Kourier* magazine (Atlanta, Georgia)
————, Realm of Michigan. Office of the Grand Dragon, *Bulletin* (Owosso, Michigan)
Lake County Star (Chase, Michigan)
Lansing Capital News (Lansing, Michigan)
Lansing State Journal (Lansing, Michigan)
Mancelona Herald (Mancelona, Michigan)
Manistee News-Advocate (Manistee, Michigan)
Michigan Kourier (Washington, DC)
Midland Republican (Midland, Michigan)
Mount Pleasant Times (Mount Pleasant, Michigan)
Muskegon Chronicle (Muskegon, Michigan)
National Kourier (Washington, DC)
New York Evening Post (New York)
New York Klanswoman (Buffalo, New York)
New York Times (New York)
Newaygo County Historical Society Quarterly (White Cloud, Michigan)
Newaygo Republican (Newaygo, Michigan)
Niles Daily Star-Sun (Niles, Michigan)
Owosso Argus Press (Owosso, Michigan)
Protestant, The (Washington, DC)

Royal Oak Tribune (Royal Oak, Michigan)
Saginaw News Courier (Saginaw, Michigan)
Saginaw Night-Hawk (Saginaw, Michigan)
Saginaw Star (Saginaw, Michigan)
Saugatuck Commercial Record (Saugatuck, Michigan)
St. Joseph Herald Press (St. Joseph, Michigan)
Traverse City Record-Eagle (Traverse City, Michigan)
Washington Post (Washington, DC)
Watcher on the Tower (Seattle, Washington)
White Cloud Eagle (White Cloud, Michigan)
Wolverine Women (Grand Rapids, Michigan)

ALL OTHER SOURCES

Alexander, Charles C. "Kleagles and Cash: The Ku Klux Klan as a Business Organization, 1919–1930." *Business History Review* 39 (Autumn 1965): 348–67.
———. *The Ku Klux Klan in the Southwest.* Lexington: University of Kentucky Press, 1966.
Allen, Frederick Lewis. *Only Yesterday: An Informal History of the 1920s.* New York: Harper and Brothers, 1931.
Amann, Peter H. "Vigilante Fascism: The Black Legion as an American Hybrid." *Comparative Studies in Society and History* 25, no. 3 (July 1983): 490–524.
American Krusaders. *The Spirit of the Crusades As Interpreted and Revived by the American Krusaders, Incorporated.* Little Rock: American Krusaders, n.d.
"Anti-Klan Rally Mobbed; Police Clash with 6,000." *Detroit Free Press*, 22 October 1924.
Bair, Fred. *Does the U.S.A. Need the K.K.K.?* Girard, KS: Haldeman-Julius, 1928.
Ball, Frank P. *Faults and Virtues of the Ku Klux Klan.* Brooklyn, NY: F. P. Ball, 1927.
Bell, Edward P. *Is the Ku Klux Klan Constructive or Destructive? A Debate between Imperial Wizard Evans, Israel Zangwill and Others.* Girard, KS: Haldeman-Julius, 1924.
Bentley, Max. "The Ku Klux Klan in Indiana." *McClure's Magazine* 57 (May 1924): 23–33.
———. "The Ku Klux Klan in Texas." *McClure's Magazine* 57 (May 1924): 11–21.
Berlet, Chip, and Matthew Lyons. *Right-Wing Populism in America: Too Close for Comfort.* New York: The Guilford Press, 2000.
Bisque, Ramon E. "The K.K.K.: A Sinister Element Moves North." In *Iron: A River, a Town, a County, a Mine, a Family.* Golden, CO: West by Southwest, 2000.

Blake, Aldrich. *The Ku Klux Kraze.* Oklahoma City: Aldrich Blake, 1924.

Blee, Kathleen M. "Evidence, Empathy, and Ethics: Lessons from Oral Histories of the Klan." *Journal of American History* 80, no. 2 (September 1993): 596–606.

———. "The Gendered Organization of Hate: Women in the U.S. Ku Klux Klan." In *Right-Wing Women: From Conservatives to Extremists around the World*, edited by Paola Baccetta and Margaret Power. New York: Routledge, 2002.

———. *Women of the Klan: Racism and Gender in the 1920s.* Berkeley: University of California Press, 1991.

Bloomfield, Maxwell. "Dixon's 'The Leopard's Spots': A Study in Popular Racism." *American Quarterly* 16, no. 3 (Autumn 1964): 387–401.

Bohn, Frank. "The Ku Klux Klan Interpreted." *American Journal of Sociology* 30 (January 1925): 385–407.

Bollman, Don. *Run for the Roses: A 50 Year Memoir.* Mecosta, MI: Canadian Lakes, 1975.

Booth, Edgar Allen. *The Mad Mullah of America.* Columbus, OH: Boyd Ellison, 1927.

Braeman, John, Robert H. Bremer, and David Brody, eds. *Change and Continuity in Twentieth-Century America: The 1920s.* Columbus: Ohio State University Press, 1968.

Brown, Egbert. *The Final Awakening: A Story of the Ku Klux Klan.* Brunswick, GA: Overstreet & Co, 1923.

Brown, George Alfred. *Harold the Klansman.* Kansas City, MO: Western Baptist, 1923.

Butler, Robert A. *So They Framed Stephenson.* Huntingdon, IN: R. A. Butler, 1940.

Campbell, Sam H. *The Jewish Problem in the United States.* Atlanta: Knights of the Ku Klux Klan, 1923.

Carnes, Mark C. "Middle-Class Men and the Solace of Fraternal Ritual." In *Meanings for Manhood: Constructions of Masculinity in Victorian America*, edited by Mark C. Carnes and Clyde Griffin. Chicago: University of Chicago Press, 1990.

———. *Secret Ritual and Manhood in Victorian America.* New Haven, CT: Yale University Press, 1989.

Carter, Everett. "Cultural History Written with Lightning: The Significance of 'The Birth of a Nation.'" *American Quarterly* 12, no. 3 (Autumn 1960): 347–57.

Carter, Paul A. *The Twenties in America.* London: Routledge and Kegan Paul, 1969.

Cashman, Sean Dennis. *America in the Twenties and Thirties: The Olympian Age of Franklin Delano Roosevelt.* New York: New York University Press, 1989.

"Catholic Babies' Rifles." *Literary Digest*, 8 December 1923, 31.

Chalmers, David M. *Hooded Americanism: The History of the Ku Klux Klan.* 2nd ed. New York: Franklin Watts, 1976.

Citizens League of Dallas, Texas. *The Ku Klux Klan.* Denver: American Publishing Society 1922.

Clark, William Lloyd. *The Devil's Prayer Book or an Exposure of Auricular Confession as Practiced by the Roman Catholic Church: An Eye-Opener for Husbands, Fathers and Brothers.* Milan, IL: Rail Splitter Press, 1922.

Clason, George S., ed. *Catholic, Jew, Ku Klux Klan: What They Believe, Where They Conflict.* Chicago: Nutshell, 1924.

Clawson, Mary Ann. *Constructing Brotherhood: Class, Gender, and Fraternalism.* Princeton, NJ: Princeton University Press, 1989.

Coben, Stanley. "The Assault on Victorianism in the Twentieth Century." *American Quarterly* 27, no. 5 (December 1975): 604–25.

———. "Ordinary White Protestants: The K.K.K. of the 1920s." *Journal of Social History* 28 (1994): 155–65.

Cocoltchos, Christopher N. *The Invisible Government and the Viable Community: The Ku Klux Klan in Orange County, California during the 1920s.* Ph.D. dissertation, University of California, Los Angeles, 1979.

Conroy, Thomas M. "The Ku Klux Klan and the American Clergy." *Ecclesiastical Review* 70 (1924): 45–57.

Cook, Ezra A. *Ku Klux Klan: The Strange Society of Blood and Death! Exposed!* Chicago: Ezra A. Cook, 1923.

Cooper, John T. *"Komments" on the Ku Klux Klan: The Etymology and Deeper Significance of Those Titles Used to Designate the Officials of That Organization.* Checotah, OK: J. T. Cooper, 1924.

Coughlan, Robert. "Konklave in Kokomo." In *The Aspirin Age: 1919–1941*, edited by Isabel Leighton. New York: Simon and Schuster, 1949.

Crew, Danny O. *Ku Klux Klan Sheet Music: An Illustrated Catalogue of Published Music, 1867–2002.* Jefferson, NC: McFarland, 2003.

Cross, Gilton Gregory. "Fought for It and Paid Taxes Too: Four Interviews with Cyrus Colter." *Callaloo* 14, no. 4 (Autumn 1991): 855–97.

Curran, Thomas J. *Xenophobia and Immigration, 1820–1930.* Boston: Twayne Publishers, 1975.

Curry, Leroy Amos. *The Ku Klux Klan under the Searchlight.* Kansas City, MO: Western Baptist, 1924.

Darrow, Clarence. "Salesmanship." *American Mercury* 5 (August 1925): 385–92.

Davenport, F. Garvin. "Thomas Dixon's Mythology of Southern History." *Journal of Southern History* 36, no. 3 (August 1970): 350–67.

Davis, David Brion. "Constructing Race: A Reflection." *William and Mary Quarterly* 54, no. 1 (January 1997): 7–18.

———, ed. *The Fear of Conspiracy: Images of Un-American Subversion from the Revolution to the Present.* Ithaca, NY: Cornell University Press, 1971.

———. "Some Ideological Functions of Prejudice in Ante-Bellum America." *American Quarterly* 15 (Summer 1963): 115–25.

———. "Some Themes of Counter-Subversion: An Analysis of Anti-Masonic, Anti-Catholic and Anti-Mormon Literature." *Mississippi Valley Historical Review*47 (1960): 205–24.

Desmond, Humphrey J. *The A.P.A. Movement.* Reprint; New York: Arno Press, 1969.

———. *The Know-Nothing Party.* Washington, DC: New Century Press, 1904.

Dever, Lem A. *Masks Off! Confessions of an Imperial Klansman.* Portland, OR: Dever, 1925.

Dixon, Thomas. *The Clansman: An Historical Romance of the Ku Klux Klan.* New York: A. Wessels Co., 1907.

Douglass, Howard. "Memories of the One Room School." *Newaygo County Historical Society Quarterly* 2, no. 2 (Summer 1978): 1–2.

Dray, Philip. *At the Hands of Persons Unknown: The Lynching of Black America.* New York: Random House, 2002).

Duffus, Robert L. "Ancestry and End of the Ku Klux Klan." *World's Work* 46 (1923): 527–36.

———. "Counter-Mining the Ku Klux Klan." *World's Work* 46 (1923): 275–84.

———. "How the Ku Klux Klan Sells Hate." *World's Work* 46 (1923): 174–83.

———. "The Ku Klux Klan in the Middle West." *World's Work* 46 (1923): 363–72.

Ellsworth, Monty J. *The Bath School Disaster.* N.p., 1927.

Enders, Calvin. "Under Grand Haven's White Sheets." *Michigan Historical Review* 19, no. 1 (Spring 1993): 47–61.

———. "White Sheets in Mecosta: The Anatomy of a Michigan Klan." *Michigan Historical Review* 14, no. 2 (Autumn 1988): 59–84.

Erickson, Christine K. "'Kluxer Blues': The Klan Confronts Catholics in Butte, Montana, 1923–1929." *Montana: The Magazine of Western History* (Spring 2003): 44–57.

Esrov, Inu. *The End of the Ku Klux Klan.* Des Moines, IA: Human Services Association, n.d.

Estes, George. *The Roman Katholic Kingdom and the Ku Klux Klan.* Portland, OR: Empire, 1923.

Evans, Hiram Wesley. *Attitude of the Knights of the Ku Klux Klan toward Immigration.* Atlanta: Knights of the Ku Klux Klan, 1923.

———. *Attitude of the Knights of the Ku Klux Klan toward the Jew.* Atlanta: Knights of the Ku Klux Klan, 1923.

———. *Attitude of the Knights of the Ku Klux Klan toward the Roman Catholic Hierarchy.* Atlanta: Knights of the Ku Klux Klan, 1927.

———. "The Ballots behind the Ku Klux Klan." *World's Work* 55 (1927): 243–52.

———. "The Catholic Question As Viewed by the Ku Klux Klan." *Current History* (July 1927): 563–68.

———. "For and Against the Ku Klux Klan." *Literary Digest*, 24 September 1921, 34–40.

———. "The Klan: Defender of Americanism." *Forum* 74 (December 1925): 801–14.

———. "The Klan's Fight for Americanism." *North American Review* 223 (Spring 1926): 33–63.

———. *The Menace of Modern Immigration*. Atlanta: Knights of the Ku Klux Klan, 1924.

———. *The Public School Problem in America*. Atlanta: Knights of the Ku Klux Klan, 1924.

Evans, Martha. *History of Fremont Bank and Trust Co., 1904–1979*. Fremont, MI: Clarke Historical Library, 1979.

"Faithful Trek to Zarephath Zion." *Literary Digest*, 5 September 1936, 30–31.

Feldman, Glenn. *Politics, Society, and the Klan in Alabama, 1915–1949*. Tuscaloosa: University of Alabama Press, 1999.

Fellowship Forum. *Quiz Book: About Pope, Bishop and Rabbi*. Washington, DC: The Fellowship Forum, 1928.

Ferris, Ted. *DHIA in America: A Foundation for Progress*. East Lansing, MI: Michigan State University Department of Animal Science, 2005.

Fine, Lisa. "Reo Joe's New Deal, 1924–1939." In *The Story of Reo Joe: Work, Kin, and Community in Autotown, U.S.A.* Philadelphia: Temple University Press, 2004.

Fisher, Paul A. *Behind the Lodge Door: Church, State, and Freemasonry in America*. Rockford, IL: TAN Books, 1994.

Fisher, William H. *The Invisible Empire: A Bibliography of the Ku Klux Klan*. Metuchen, N.J.: Scarecrow Press, 1980.

Fleming, John S. *What Is Ku Kluxism? Let Americans Answer—Aliens Only Muddy the Waters*. Birmingham, AL: Masonic Weekly Recorder, 1923.

Fowler, C. Lewis. *The Ku Klux Klan: Its Origin, Meaning and Scope of Operation*. Atlanta: C. Lewis Fowler, 1922.

Frost, Stanley. *The Challenge of the Klan*. Indianapolis: Bobbs-Merrill Company, 1924.

———. "The Klan Restates Its Case: Special Correspondence from Kansas City." *Outlook* 138 (15 October 1924): 244–45.

———. "When the Klan Rules: The Crusade of the Fiery Cross." *Outlook* 136 (2 January 1924): 20–24.

Fry, Henry Peck. *The Modern Ku Klux Klan*. Boston: Small, Maynard, 1922.

Fuller, Edgar I. *The Visible of the Invisible Empire*. Denver: Maelstrom, 1925.

Gallagher, Brian. "Racist Ideology and Black Abnormality in 'The Birth of a Nation,'" *Phylon* 43, no. 1 (Winter 1982): 68–76.

Gerber Products Company. *Fifty Years of Caring: Our Golden Anniversary Year, 1928–1978.* Fremont, MI: Gerber Products Company, 1978.

——. *The Story of an Idea and Its Role in the Growth of the Baby Foods Industry.* Fremont, MI: Gerber Products Company, 1953.

Gerlach, Larry R. *Blazing Crosses in Zion: The Ku Klux Klan in Utah.* Logan: Utah State University Press, 1982.

Gillette, George A. *Dr. Ku Klux Questioned: A Consideration of Crime Contagion and Klan Cure.* Springfield, MO: Geo. A. Gillette, 1925.

Gillis, James M. *The Ku-Klux Klan.* New York: Paulist Press, 1922.

Gist, Noel P. "Structure and Process in Secret Societies." *Social Forces* 16, no. 3 (March 1938): 349–57.

Goldberg, David J. *Discontented America: The United States in the 1920s.* Baltimore: Johns Hopkins University Press, 1999.

Goldberg, Robert Alan. *Hooded Empire: The Ku Klux Klan in Colorado.* Urbana: University of Illinois Press, 1981.

Goodin, H. H. *Scriptural Points on Romanism: Romanism and Protestantism Contrasted.* N.p., n.d.

Gordon, Glenn. *The Ku Klux Ball: A Satire on the Younger Set.* Macon, GA: N.p., 1926.

Gordon, John J. *Unmasked.* New York: John J. Gordon, 1924.

Grant, Madison. *The Passing of the Great Race; or the Racial Basis of European History.* New York: C. Scribner's Sons, 1921.

Greene, Ward. "Notes for a History of the Klan." *American Mercury* 5 (June 1925): 240–43.

"Guarding the Gates against Undesirables." *Current Opinion* (April 1924): 400–401.

Haldeman-Julius, Emanuel, et al. *K.K.K.; The Kreed of the Klansmen: A Symposium by Haldeman-Julius and Others.* Girard, KS: Haldeman-Julius, 1924.

Hesperia Centennial Book Committee. *Hesperia Centennial, 1866–1966.* Greenville, MI: Greenville Printing Co., 1966.

Hicks, John D. *Republican Ascendancy, 1921–1933.* London: Harper Torchbooks, 1960.

Higham, John. *Strangers in the Land: Patterns of American Nativism, 1860–1925.* New York: Atheneum, 1967.

Hobsbawm, E. J. *Primitive Rebels: Studies in Archaic Forms of Social Movement in the 19th and 20th Centuries.* Manchester, UK: Manchester University Press, 1959.

Hodges, Michael G. *The Ku Klux Klan as a Political Influence in Michigan in the 1920s.* M.A. thesis, Central Michigan University, 1998.

Hofstadter, Richard. *The Age of Reform.* New York: Knopf, 1955.

——. *The Paranoid Style in American Politics and Other Essays.* New York: Knopf, 1965.

Horowitz, David A., ed. *Inside the Klavern: The Secret History of a Ku Klux Klan of the 1920s.* Carbondale: Southern Illinois University Press, 1999.

Ingalls, Robert P. *Hoods: The Story of the Ku Klux Klan.* New York: Putnam, 1979.

Jackson, Charles O. "William J. Simmons: A Career in Ku Kluxism." *Georgia Historical Quarterly* 50 (December 1966): 351–65.

Jackson, Helen. *Convent Cruelties or My Life in the Convent: Awful Revelations.* Toledo, OH: Helen Jackson, 1919.

Jackson, Kenneth T. *The Ku Klux Klan in the City, 1915–1930.* 2nd ed. Chicago: Ivan R. Dee, 1992.

Jacobs, Joanne R. *Ku Klux Klan Treatment of Roman Catholics as Expressed in Two Michigan Klan Publications during the 1920s.* M.A. thesis, Central Michigan University, 1980.

Jenkins, William D. *Steel Valley Klan: The Ku Klux Klan in Ohio's Mahoning Valley.* Kent, OH: Kent State University, 1990.

Jessop, Michael. *The Decline of the 1920s Ku Klux Klan: A Sociological Analysis.* Ph.D. dissertation, Southern Illinois University, 1992.

Johnsen, Julia E. (comp.). *Ku Klux Klan.* New York: Wilson, 1924.

Johnson, Guy B. "A Sociological Interpretation of the New Ku Klux Movement." *Journal of Social Forces* 1, no. 4 (May 1923): 440–45.

Judge magazine (New York), Ku Klux Number, 16 August 1924.

"K.K.K. and the People." *Journal of Social Forces* 1, no. 3 (March 1923): 318–19.

"K.K.K. Washington Parade Thrills America." *American Standard* 2, no. 16 (15 August 1925): 366–72.

Kanadian Knights of the Ku Klux Klan. *Why You Should Become a Klansman.* N.p., n.d.

Katz, William Loren. *The Invisible Empire: The Ku Klux Klan Impact on History.* Seattle: Open Hand, 1987.

Kaufman, Herbert. *Scum O' The Melting Pot.* Atlanta: Knights of the Ku Klux Klan, 1920.

"Keep on Guarding the Gates." *Current Opinion* (June 1923): 652–54.

Kelly, Robert J. "The Ku Klux Klan: Recurring Hate in America." In *Hate Crime: The Global Politics of Polarization*, edited by Robert J. Kelly and Jess Maghan. Carbondale: Southern Illinois University Press, 1998.

King, L. J., ed. *The Converted Catholic and Protestant Missionary Annual.* Vol. 13. Toledo, OH: L. J. King, 1924.

Kirschner, Don S. *City and Country: Rural Responses to Urbanization in the 1920s.* Westport, CT: Greenwood, 1970.

Klanwatch: A Project of the Southern Poverty Law Center. *The Ku Klux Klan: A History of Racism and Violence.* 3rd ed. Montgomery, AL: Southern Poverty Law Center, 1988.

Knights of the Ku Klux Klan. *America for Americans.* Atlanta: Knights of the Ku Klux Klan, 1922.

———. *Catalogue of Official Robes and Banners.* Atlanta: Knights of the Ku Klux Klan, 1925.

———. *Constitution and Laws of the Knights of the Ku Klux Klan, Incorporated.* Atlanta: Knights of the Ku Klux Klan, 1921.

———. *Delivery of Charter: Issued by Imperial Palace, Invisible Empire, Knights of the Ku Klux Klan, H. W. Evans, Imperial Wizard.* Atlanta: Knights of the Ku Klux Klan, 1923.

———. *A Fundamental Klan Doctrine.* Atlanta: Knights of the Ku Klux Klan, 1924.

———. *Funeral Services: Knights of the Ku Klux Klan.* Atlanta: Knights of the Ku Klux Klan, 1925.

———. *Ideals of the Ku Klux Klan.* Atlanta: Knights of the Ku Klux Klan, 1923.

———. *In Memoriam: Klorero of Sorrow: Invisible Empire.* Atlanta: Knights of the Ku Klux Klan, 1925.

———. *Installation Ceremonies.* Atlanta: Knights of the Ku Klux Klan, 1924.

———. *K.K.K. Katechism and Song Book.* Columbus, OH: Patriot, 1924.

———. *Klansman's Manual.* Atlanta: Buckhead, 1924.

———. *Kloran: Knights of the Ku Klux Klan: First Degree Character.* Atlanta: Knights of the Ku Klux Klan, 1917.

———. *Kloran.* Atlanta: Knights of the Ku Klux Klan, 1928.

———. *The Ku Klux Klan Presents Its View of the Public Free School.* N.p., n.d.

———. *The Obligation of American Citizens to Free Public Schools.* Atlanta: Knights of the Ku Klux Klan, n.d.

———. *Papers Read at the Meeting of Grand Dragons, Knights of the Ku Klux Klan at Their First Annual Meeting Held at Asheville, North Carolina, July 1923; Together with Other Articles of Interest to Klansmen.* Atlanta: Knights of the Ku Klux Klan, 1923.

———. *The Practice of Klanishness.* Atlanta: Knights of the Ku Klux Klan, 1924.

———. *Principles and Purposes of the Knights of the Ku Klux Klan, Outlined by an Exalted Cyclops of the Order.* Atlanta: Knights of the Ku Klux Klan, n.d.

———. *Proceedings of the Second Imperial Klonvokation: Held in Kansas City, Missouri, September 23, 24, 25, and 26, 1924.* Atlanta: Knights of the Ku Klux Klan, 1924.

———. *Some Accomplishments of the Knights of the Ku Klux Klan.* N.p., n.d.

———. *Thirty-Three Questions Answered.* Atlanta: Knights of the Ku Klux Klan, n.d.

———. *The Whole Truth about the Effort to Destroy the Klan.* Atlanta: Knights of the Ku Klux Klan, 1923.

———. *Why the Ku Klux Klan Opposed the World Court.* N.p., n.d.

———, Department of Realms. *Klan Building.* Atlanta: Knights of the Ku Klux Klan, n.d.

———, Realm of Michigan. *America for Americans: The Why and Wherefore of the Ku Klux Klan.* N.p., n.d.

———, Realm of Michigan. *The Ku Klux Klan Makes an Observation on the Presidency.* N.p., n.d.

Larralde, Carlos M., and Richard Griswold Del Castillo. "San Diego's Ku Klux Klan, 1920–1980." *Journal of San Diego History* 46, no. 2–3 (Summer 2000).

Lay, Shawn. *Hooded Knights on the Niagara: The Ku Klux Klan in Buffalo, New York.* New York: New York University Press, 1995.

———. "Hooded Populism: New Assessments of the Ku Klux Klan of the 1920s." *Reviews in American History* 22, no. 4 (December 1994): 668–73.

———ed. *The Invisible Empire in the West: Toward a New Historical Appraisal of the Ku Klux Klan of the 1920s.* Urbana: University of Illinois Press, 1992.

———. *War, Revolution, and the Ku Klux Klan: A Study of Intolerance in a Border City.* El Paso: Texas Western Press, University of Texas at El Paso, 1985.

Leighton, Isabel, ed. *The Aspirin Age, 1919–1941.* New York: Simon and Schuster, 1949.

Leuchtenburg, William, E. *The Perils of Prosperity, 1914–1932.* Chicago: University of Chicago Press, 1958.

Lewis, Sinclair. *Babbitt.* New York: Harcourt, Brace & Co., 1922.

Likins, William M. *Patriotism Capitalized or Religion Turned into Gold.* Uniontown, PA: The Watchman, 1925.

Lipset, Seymour Martin, and Earl Raab. *The Politics of Unreason: Right Wing Extremism in America, 1790–1977.* 2nd ed. Chicago: University of Chicago Press, 1978.

Loucks, Emerson H. *The Ku Klux Klan in Pennsylvania: A Study in Nativism.* Harrisburg, PA: Telegraph Press, 1936.

Lutholtz, M. William. *Grand Dragon: D. C. Stephenson and the Ku Klux Klan in Indiana.* Lafayette, IN: Purdue University Press, 1991.

Lynd, Robert S., and Helen Merrell. *Middletown: A Study in Contemporary American Culture.* London: Constable, 1929.

MacLean, Nancy. *Behind the Mask of Chivalry: The Making of the Second Ku Klux Klan.* New York: Oxford University Press, 1994.

Many Are the Virtues of the Ku Klux Klan. Flint, MI: Flint Weekly Review, 1925.

Maranis, Linda Weisner. "Harley Mankin, the Frog Man." *Vaudeville Times* 6, no. 1 (2003): 10–14.

The Martyred Klansman in Which Events Leading Up to the Shooting Death of Klansman Thomas Rankin Abbott on August 25, 1923, Are Related, Together with a

Record of the Court Proceedings That Followed. Pittsburgh, PA: Patriotic American, 1923.

Mast, Blaine. *K.K.K. Friend or Foe: Which?* Kittanning, PA: Herbrick & Held, 1924.

Mathews, J. F. *The Red Plague.* Portland, OR: J. F. Mathews, 1925.

McCann, Sean. *Gumshoe America: Hard-Boiled Crime Fiction and the Rise and Fall of New Deal Liberalism.* Durham, NC: Duke University Press, 2000.

McCoy, Donald R. *Coming of Age: The United States during the 1920s and 1930s.* Baltimore, MD: Penguin, 1973.

McVeigh, Rory. "Structural Incentives for Conservative Mobilization: Power Devaluation and the Rise of the Ku Klux Klan, 1915–1925." *Social Forces* 77, no. 4 (June 1999): 1461–96.

Mecklin, John Moffatt. *The Ku Klux Klan: A Study of the American Mind.* New York: Harcourt, Brace and Co., 1924.

Meltzer, Milton. *The Truth about the Ku Klux Klan.* New York: Franklin Watts, 1982.

Mencken, H. L., ed. *Americana 1925.* London: Hopkinson, 1925.

Merritt, Russell. "Dixon, Griffith, and the Southern Legend." *Cinema Journal* 12 (1972): 26–44.

Messer-Kruse, Timothy. "Memories of the Ku Klux Klan Honorary Society at the University of Wisconsin." *Journal of Blacks in Higher Education*, no. 23 (Spring 1999): 83–93.

Miller, Robert Moats. "The Ku Klux Klan." In *Change and Continuity in Twentieth-Century America: The 1920s*, edited by John Braeman, Robert H. Bremner, and David Brody. Columbus: Ohio State University Press, 1968.

———. "A Note on the Relationship between the Protestant Churches and the Revived Ku Klux Klan." *Journal of Southern History* 22, no. 3 (August 1956): 355–68.

Monteval, Marion. *The Klan Inside Out.* Claremore, OK: Monarch, 1924.

Moore, Leonard J. *Citizen Klansmen: The Ku Klux Klan in Indiana, 1921–1928.* Chapel Hill: University of North Carolina Press, 1991.

———. "Historical Interpretations of the 1920s Klan: The Traditional View and the Populist Revision." *Journal of Social History* 24 (Winter 1990): 341–57.

Moore, William V. *A Sheet and a Cross: A Symbolic Analysis of the Ku Klux Klan.* Ph.D. dissertation, Tulane University, 1975.

Mowry, George E., ed. *The Twenties: Fords, Flappers, and Fanatics.* Gloucester, MA: Peter Smith, 1988.

Murphy, Paul L. "Sources and Nature of Intolerance in the 1920s." *Journal of American History* 51, no. 1 (June 1964): 60–76.

Neill, Maudean. *Fiery Crosses in the Green Mountains: The Story of the Ku Klux Klan in Vermont.* Randolph Center, VT: Greenhills Books, 1989.

New York World. *The Facts about the Ku Klux Klan.* New York: The World, 1921.

Newaygo County Clerk's Office. *Newaygo County 2005 Official Directory: Federal, State, County, Township, City and Village Officers.* White Cloud, MI: Newaygo County Clerk, 2005.

Newaygo County Historical Society. *Profile of Yesteryear.* White Cloud, MI: Newaygo County Historical Society, 1976.

Newaygo County Society of History and Genealogy. *Images of America: Newaygo County, 1850–1920.* Charleston, SC: Arcadia Publishing, 2006.

Newton, Michael. *The Invisible Empire: The Ku Klux Klan in Florida.* Gainesville: University Press of Florida, 2001.

———and Judy Ann. *The Ku Klux Klan: An Encyclopedia.* New York: Garland, 1991.

Oliver, Lawrence J. "Writing from the Right during the 'Red Decade': Thomas Dixon's Attack on W. E. B. DuBois and James Weldon Johnson in 'The Flaming Sword.'" *American Literature* 70, no. 1 (March 1998): 131–52.

"Our New Nordic Immigration Policy." *Literary Digest,* 10 May 1924, 12–13.

Parrish, Michael E. *Anxious Decades: America in Prosperity and Depression, 1920–1941.* New York: W. W. Norton, 1992.

Pattangall, William R. "Is the Ku Klux Klan Un-American?" *Forum* 74 (September 1925): 321–32.

Pegram, Thomas R. "Hoodwinked: The Anti-Saloon League and the Ku Klux Klan in 1920s Prohibition Enforcement." *Journal of the Gilded Age and Progressive Era* 7, no. 1 (January 2008): 89–120.

"Public Schools Worry Dr. Forsyth." *Michigan Catholic,* 19 June 1924.

Quarles, Chester L. *The Ku Klux Klan and Related American Racialist and Antisemitic Organizations: A History and Analysis.* Jefferson, NC: McFarland, 1999.

Rambow, Charles. "The Ku Klux Klan in the 1920s: A Concentration on the Black Hills." *South Dakota State Historical Society and Board of Cultural Preservation Quarterly* (Winter 1973).

Randel, William Peirce. *The Ku Klux Klan: A Century of Infamy.* London: Hamish Hamilton, 1965.

"Remarkable Scenes from a Remarkable Film." *Vanity Fair,* May 1915, 48.

Rice, Arnold S. *The Ku Klux Klan in American Politics.* Washington, DC: Public Affairs Press, 1962.

"Rise and Fall of the Ku Klux Klan." *Outlook* 138 (15 October 1924): 237–38.

Rivers, Clovis D. *Pope of America and Wizard of Ku Klux.* Summerville, GA: Clovis D. Rivers, 1925.

Rogers, J. A. *The Ku Klux Spirit.* New York: Messenger, 1923.

Rogin, Michael. *Ronald Reagan, the Movie and Other Episodes in Political Demonology.* Berkeley: University of California Press, 1987.

Safianow, Allen. "'You Can't Burn History': Getting Right with the Klan in Noblesville, Indiana." *Indiana Magazine of History* 100 (June 2004): 109–54.

Sawyer, Reuben H. *The Truth about the Invisible Empire Knights of the Ku Klux Klan.* Portland, OR: Pacific Northwest Domain, 1922.

Saxon, A. *Knight Vale of the K.K.K.: A Fiction Story of Love, Patriotism, Intrigue and Adventure.* Columbus, OH: Patriot, 1924.

Schaefer, Richard T. "The Ku Klux Klan: Continuity and Change." *Phylon* 32, no. 2 (Spring 1971): 143–57.

Shepard, William G. "The Fiery Double-Cross." *Collier's National Weekly*, 28 July 1928, 8–9.

———. "How I Put Over the Klan." *Collier's National Weekly*, 14 July 1928, 5–7.

———. "Indiana's Mystery Man." *Collier's National Weekly*, 8 January 1927, 8–9.

———. "Ku Klux Koin." *Collier's National Weekly*, 21 July 1928, 38–39.

Sher, Julian. *White Hoods: Canada's Ku Klux Klan.* Vancouver: New Star Books, 1983.

Shultz, Terry. "Klan's 1924 March in City a 'Monster' Event." *Lansing State Journal*, 7 December 1980.

Simcovitch, Maxim. "The Impact of Griffith's 'Birth of a Nation' on the Modern Ku Klux Klan." *Journal of Popular Film* 1 (1972): 45–51.

Simmons, William J. *The A.B.C. of the Ku Klux Klan.* Atlanta: W. J. Simmons, 1917.

———. *America's Menace or the Enemy Within.* Atlanta: Bureau of Patriotic Books, 1926.

———. *Americans, Take Heed!* Atlanta: Knights of the Ku Klux Klan, 1920.

———. *The Klan Unmasked.* Atlanta: Wm. E. Thompson, 1923.

Sinclair, Andrew. *An Anatomy of Terror: A History of Terrorism.* London: Macmillan, 2003.

Snell, William R. "Fiery Crosses in the Roaring Twenties: Activities of the Revised Klan in Alabama, 1915–1930." *Alabama Review* 23 (October 1970): 256–76.

St. Joseph Church, White Cloud. *Our First 100 Years, 1891–1992.* White Cloud, MI: St. Joseph Church, 1992.

Standard Atlas of Newaygo County. Chicago: G. A. Ogle, 1922.

Stanton, E. F. *Christ and Other Klansmen, or Lives of Love: The Cream of the Bible Spread upon Klanism.* Kansas City, MO: Stanton & Harper, 1924.

Stephens, Ronald J. *Idlewild: The Black Eden of Michigan.* Chicago: Arcadia Publishing, 2001.

Stroud, Malden. *Poems and Other Matter on the Ku Klux Klan.* Hammond, IN: Protestant Non-Klan Society, 1925.

Swart, Stanley L. "A Memo on Cross-Burning—and Its Implications." *Northwest Ohio Quarterly* 43 (1971): 70–73.

Taylor, Alva W. "What the Klan Did in Indiana." *New Republic* 52 (16 November 1927): 330–32.

Thornbrough, Emma Lou. "Segregation in Indiana during the Klan Era of the 1920s." *Mississippi Valley Historical Review* 47, no. 4 (March 1961): 594–618.

Toll, William. "Progress and Piety: The Ku Klux Klan and Social Change in Tillamook, Oregon." *Pacific Northwest Quarterly* 69 (April 1978): 75–85.

Toy, Eckard V. "The Ku Klux Klan in Tillamook, Oregon." *Pacific Northwest Quarterly* 53 (April 1962): 60–64.

Tucker, Richard K. *The Dragon and the Cross: The Rise and Fall of the Ku Klux Klan in Middle America*. Hamden, CT: Archon Books, 1991.

United States Bureau of the Census. *Census of Religious Bodies: 1926*. Washington, DC: G.P.O., 1929.

———. *Fifteenth Census of the United States: 1930: Population*. Washington, DC: G.P.O., 1931–1933.

———. *Fourteenth Census of the United States: 1920: Population*. Washington, DC: G.P.O., 1922.

United States Congress. House of Representatives. Committee on Rules. *Hearings on the Ku Klux Klan*. 67th Cong., 1st session. Washington, DC, 1921.

"Vote for Mayor." *Detroit Times*, 11 September 1924, 1.

Wade, Wyn Craig. *The Fiery Cross: The Ku Klux Klan in America*. New York: Simon and Schuster, 1987.

Waithman, Robert. "Those Dreaded Letters: K.K.K." *Everybody's Weekly*, 7 June 1952, 9.

Wakefield, Larry. "The Night the Klan Rode into Traverse City." *Traverse City Record-Eagle*, 17 January 1986.

Wald, Kenneth D. "The Visible Empire: The Ku Klux Klan as an Electoral Movement." *Journal of Interdisciplinary History* 11, no. 2 (Autumn 1980): 217–34.

Walker, Lewis, and Ben C. Wilson. *Black Eden: The Idlewild Community*. East Lansing: Michigan State University Press, 2002.

Weaver, Norman Frederic. *The Knights of the Ku Klux Klan in Wisconsin, Indiana, Ohio and Michigan*. Ph.D. dissertation, University of Wisconsin, 1954.

Wen, Pehyun. *Idlewild: A Negro Village in Lake County, Michigan*. M.A. thesis, University of Chicago, 1972.

White, Bishop Alma. *Heroes of the Fiery Cross*. Zarephath, NJ: The Good Citizen, 1928.

———. *Klansmen: Guardians of Liberty*. Zarephath, NJ: The Good Citizen, 1926.

———. *The Ku Klux Klan in Prophecy*. Zarephath, NJ: The Good Citizen, 1925.

White Cloud Centennial Committee. *The First Hundred Years, 1873–1973: White Cloud Area*. White Cloud, MI: Industrial Printing, 1973.

Williams, Michael. *The Shadow of the Pope: The Story of the Anti-Catholic Movement in America*. New York: Whittlesey House, McGraw-Hill, 1932.

Witcher, Walter C. *The Unveiling of the Ku Klux Klan.* Fort Worth, TX: American Constitutional League, 1922.

Women of the Ku Klux Klan. *America for Americans.* Little Rock: Women of the Ku Klux Klan, n.d.

———. *Constitution and Laws of the Women of the Ku Klux Klan.* Little Rock: Women of the Ku Klux Klan, 1927.

———. *Ideals of the Women of the Ku Klux Klan.* Little Rock: Women of the Ku Klux Klan, n.d.

———. *Installation Ceremonies.* Little Rock: Women of the Ku Klux Klan, n.d.

———. *Ritual in the Second Degree of the Women of the Ku Klux Klan.* Little Rock: Women of the Ku Klux Klan, n.d.

———. *The Truth about the Women of the Ku Klux Klan.* Little Rock: Women of the Ku Klux Klan, n.d.

———. *Women of America! The Past! The Present! The Future!* Little Rock: Women of the Ku Klux Klan, n.d.

Wood, J. O. *Are You a Citizen?* Atlanta: Searchlight, 1923.

Wright, Walter C. *The Ku Klux Klan Unmasked.* Dallas: Dallas Press, 1924.

———. *Religious and Patriotic Ideals of the Ku Klux Klan.* Waco, TX: Grove Printing, 1926.

Zunz, Olivier. *The Changing Face of Inequality: Urbanization, Industrial Development, and Immigrants in Detroit, 1880–1920.* Chicago: University of Chicago Press, 1982.

Index